Jealousy or Furnace Remelting? A Response to Nissim Amzallag

MATTHEW RICHARD SCHLIMM
mschlimm@dbq.edu
The University of Dubuque Theological Seminary, Dubuque, IA 52001

Nissim Amzallag recently argued that words from the Biblical Hebrew root קנא have very different meanings depending on whether they are used in the human or divine context. While "jealousy" is an acceptable translation in the human sphere, Amzallag claims that in the divine sphere these words refer to furnace remelting, signaling that Israel's God was viewed as a smelting deity. There are several problems with Amzallag's argument. By paying closer attention to linguistic evidence and methodological considerations, one finds that in both human and divine contexts words from the root קנא are best understood with the traditional translation "jealousy," an emotion closely related to anger, rather than the elaborate metallurgical imagery that Amzallag proposes.

In a recent issue of this journal, Nissim Amzallag examined the Hebrew root קנא to argue that "the God of Israel was acknowledged as the smelting god."[1] Amzallag claims that words related to קנא mean very different things depending on whether they are used in human or divine contexts. Whereas human קנאה can be translated as "jealousy," he asserts that divine קנאה instead evokes metallurgic connotations to suggest that YHWH, like a smelter, is one who purifies and revitalizes.[2]

Amzallag's argument is built on the list of claims below:

1. Divine קנאה and human קנאה should be viewed differently because the verb קנא is followed by the preposition ב only when it describes human jealousy.

I would like to thank Jeremy M. Hutton, Christopher B. Hays, and the anonymous *JBL* reviewers for their insightful comments, which greatly enhanced this article.

[1] Nissim Amzallag, "Furnace Remelting as the Expression of YHWH's Holiness: Evidence from the Meaning of *qannāʾ* (קנא) in the Divine Context," *JBL* 134 (2015): 233–52, here 250.

[2] For reasons that are not entirely clear to me, Amzallag prefers speaking about *qannāʾ* as a noun. This word, however, is typically understood as an adjective. Therefore, I have chosen to speak instead about קנאה. In doing so, I seek to evoke not only appearances of the lexeme *qinʾâ* but also words derived from the root קנא.

2. Another reason for differentiating divine קנאה and human קנאה is that the adjectives *qannāʾ* and *qannôʾ* are used only to describe divine קנאה.
3. Human קנאה is primarily a psychological state, unlike divine קנאה, which refers to a specific mode of action and an essential quality of Israel's God.
4. Jealousy is a negative sentiment, at odds with how one would expect the exalted deity YHWH to be described.
5. Texts of the Hebrew Bible often link divine קנאה with fiery imagery, suggesting that it carries metallurgic and volcanic overtones.
6. In Arabic, a cognate term for קנא means "rust." In Sir 12:10–11, קנא also means "rust."
7. Given the preceding points, "*Qannāʾ* ... designates both the rust metal to be recycled and the process of its regeneration by furnace remelting."[3]
8. Furnace remelting provided a valuable image for ancient peoples when they thought of rejuvenation.
9. Exodus 4:1–9 illustrates the close relationship between furnace remelting and rejuvenation.
10. Divine קנאה in the Hebrew Bible can be seen as a process by which YHWH performs "rejuvenation by melting." Thus, many biblical texts describe YHWH's קנאה while speaking about not only destruction (cf. melting) but also revitalization (cf. rejuvenation).
11. Divine קנאה in the Hebrew Bible has parallels in divine holiness.

At times these claims could be more precise; at other times they are less significant than Amzallag suggests; and at still other times they fail to reflect the complexities of all available evidence. It is possible to arrive at more nuanced conclusions. Below I will show that divine קנאה can best be understood with the typical translation "jealousy," rather than the elaborate metallurgical imagery that Amzallag proposes.

•

I. Divine and Human קנאה

The Particle ב

How human emotion compares and contrasts with divine emotion is a fascinating research topic, one that has been explored in several recent publications.[4] This sort of research is challenging, however, since emotions tend to evoke highly complex associations specific to one's culture and linguistic system.

---

[3] Amzallag, "Furnace Remelting," 241.

[4] Deena E. Grant, *Divine Anger in the Hebrew Bible*, CBQMS 52 (Washington, DC: Catholic Biblical Association of America, 2014); Matthew R. Schlimm, review of *Divine Anger in the Hebrew Bible*, by Deena E. Grant, *JHebS* 15 (2015), http://www.jhsonline.org/reviews/reviews_new/review743.htm; Schlimm, "Different Perspectives on Divine Pathos: An Examination of Hermeneutics in Biblical Theology," *CBQ* 69 (2007): 673–94.

These associations include taxonomy (what types of emotions exist and the boundaries between them), ecology (which situations cause which emotions), semantics (what is implied by an emotion, e.g., action tendencies such as fear implying a fight-or-flight response), communication (how emotions can and should be expressed), social regulation (which emotions can be expressed in which situations), and management (how to deal with inexpressible emotions).[5] Interpreters face ample difficulties discerning how their own conceptions of emotions compare and contrast with the cultural associations reflected in biblical texts. The additional task of sorting out which associations a particular text highlights to describe the divine (and which ones are not primarily in view) is particularly complicated.

Despite these challenges, Amzallag seeks to differentiate divine קנאה and human קנאה. According to him, one reason for doing so is that "the verbal construction קנא + the preposition ב, which in the human context explicitly expresses the negative sentiment of jealousy, is never encountered in the divine context."[6] There are times, however, when one finds precisely this construction in the divine context. Deuteronomy 32:16 reads, יקנאהו בזרים ("he [i.e., Jeshurun] made him [i.e., God] jealous *because of* strange things"). Five verses later, the deity speaks saying, הם קנאוני בלא־אל ("They themselves made me jealous *because of* what is not god"). Psalm 78:58 similarly states, ובפסיליהם יקניאוהו ("And *because of* their idols they made him [i.e., God] jealous").[7] Clearly, there are cases where the ב-particle is used in conjunction with the verb קנא to describe divine jealousy.

Adjectives

Amzallag also suggests that readers differentiate divine and human קנאה because "the adjective form (*qannāʾ* or *qannôʾ*) is attested only in the divine

---

[5] Matthew R. Schlimm, *From Fratricide to Forgiveness: The Language and Ethics of Anger in Genesis*, Siphrut 7 (Winona Lake, IN: Eisenbrauns, 2011), 24–25. See also Richard A. Shweder, *Thinking through Cultures: Expeditions in Cultural Psychology* (Cambridge: Harvard University Press, 1991), 242–52.

[6] Amzallag, "Furnace Remelting," 237. See, e.g., Gen 37:11: ויקנאו־בו אחיו ("his brothers were jealous of him").

[7] Granted, these verses feature *hiphil* and *piel* forms of קנא with the particle ב, rather than the *qal* forms typically used to describe human jealousy. Nevertheless, it is obvious that the deity becomes jealous because of whatever follows the particle ב, as is the case with humans. One could argue that ב works differently in human and divine contexts, designating the object of jealousy in human cases and designating cause (as translated above) in divine cases; but this is a false distinction. With both human and divine examples, the object of jealousy *is* its cause. Thus, Ps 78:58 could be translated either "[God] became jealous *because of* their idols" or "[God] became jealous *of* their idols" (ובפסיליהם יקניאוהו). Likewise, Gen 37:11 could be translated either "[Joseph's] brothers became jealous *because of* him" or "[Joseph's] brothers became jealous *of* him" (ויקנאו־בו אחיו).

context."⁸ This observation may be insignificant. When one looks at all words from the root קנא in the Hebrew Bible, one finds an even distribution: forty-two appearances in divine contexts and forty-two appearances in human contexts.⁹ Furthermore, there are only eight times in the Hebrew Bible where adjective forms of קנא appear at all. It is fair to ask whether six appearances of *qannāʾ* and two appearances of *qannôʾ* provide a sufficient sample size from which to draw firm conclusions.¹⁰ To put things in perspective: there are 22,946 verses in the Hebrew Bible (excluding the Aramaic verses). So, 0.00 percent of those 22,946 verses use an adjective derived from קנא in the human context, while approximately 0.03 percent use such an adjective in the divine context. Is that difference significant? Not without other evidence.

Decades ago, Edward Ullendorff provocatively asked the question, *Is Biblical Hebrew a Language?*¹¹ One of his basic points was that Classical Hebrew is only a fragment of a much broader linguistic system. Because biblical interpreters are dealing with fragmentary evidence, they should exercise caution rather than draw sweeping conclusions based on the limited extant remains of this language. Ullendorff notes, for example, that some *hapax legomena* are very important words, and it is merely accidental that they show up only once in the Hebrew Bible. Similarly, it may be insignificant that the adjective forms of קנא are found in divine contexts in their eight appearances.

Psychology and Action

Amzallag asserts: "In the *human* context … *qannāʾ* is restricted to a psychological dimension."¹² In this regard, human קנאה contrasts with divine קנאה, which he argues is "a specific mode of action."¹³ This assignment of psychology to humanity and action to divinity, however, is problematic.

Studying a wide range of languages and cultures, cognitive linguists have shown that emotions tend to follow prototypical scripts.¹⁴ Frequently, these scripts entail the following:

---

⁸ Amzallag, "Furnace Remelting," 237.
⁹ This count includes the words קנא, קנוא, and קנאה. There is one additional appearance where the trees of Eden are described as jealous (Ezek 31:9).
¹⁰ Each adjective appears in only two books: *qannāʾ* in Exod 20:5, 34:14 (2x), Deut 4:24, 5:9, 6:15; *qannôʾ* in Josh 24:19, Nah 1:2.
¹¹ Edward Ullendorff, *Is Biblical Hebrew a Language? Studies in Semitic Languages and Civilizations* (Wiesbaden: Harrassowitz, 1977), 3–18, esp. 14, 16–17.
¹² Amzallag, "Furnace Remelting," 237 (italics added).
¹³ Ibid.
¹⁴ Phillip Shaver et al., "Emotion Knowledge: Further Exploration of a Prototype Approach," *Journal of Personality and Social Psychology* 52 (1987): 1061–86, https://doi.org/10.1037/0022-3514.52.6.1061; Catherine A. Lutz, *Unnatural Emotions: Everyday Sentiments on a Micronesian Atoll and Their Challenge to Western Theory* (Chicago: University of Chicago Press, 1998), 10;

1. The person experiences an inward feeling while perceiving that something of consequence has taken place.[15]
2. This inward feeling leads to an outward action.[16]

Naturally, the specifics of this script vary depending on the emotion, the culture, and even the individuals in view. Amzallag, however, primarily associates number 1 with human קנאה and number 2 with divine קנאה.[17] A better approach entails recognizing that both humanity and divinity experience both elements of this script when קנאה is in view.

Regarding psychology, those experiencing קנאה (whether they are human or divine) tend to perceive that someone has possessed or experienced something they should not. The following list explains:[18]

1. Verses where YHWH is *jealous because* other gods have *wrongly received* worship and allegiance: Exod 20:5; 34:14; Num 25:11; Deut 4:24; 5:9; 6:15; 29:19[20]; 32:16, 21; Josh 24:19; 1 Kgs 14:22; Ezek 5:13; 8:3, 5; 16:38, 42; 23:25; Zeph 1:18; Ps 78:58. See also Zeph 3:8; Ps 79:5.
2. Verses where humans, on YHWH's behalf, are *jealous because* other gods have *wrongly received* worship and allegiance: Num 25:11, 13; 1 Kgs 19:10, 14; 2 Kgs 10:16. See also Pss 69:10[9]; 119:139.
3. Verses where YHWH, on Israel or Judah's behalf, is *jealous because* God's people have *wrongly received* unmerited or disproportionate harm: Ezek 36:5–6; 38:19; 39:25; Joel 2:18; Nah 1:2; Zech 1:14; 8:2. See also Isa 59:17.

James A. Russell, "Culture and the Categorization of Emotions," *Psychological Bulletin* 110 (1991): 426–50, esp. 442–44; Zoltán Kövecses, "Introduction: Language and Emotion Concepts," in *Everyday Conceptions of Emotion: An Introduction to the Psychology, Anthropology and Linguistics of Emotion*, ed. James A. Russell et al. (Dordrecht: Kluwer Academic, 1995), 3–15, esp. 10, https://doi.org/10.1007/978-94-015-8484-5_1; Schlimm, *From Fratricide*, 48–64.

[15] Martha C. Nussbaum, *Upheavals of Thought: The Intelligence of Emotions* (Cambridge: Cambridge University Press, 2001), 43, 71, 78, 181.

[16] See Shweder, *Thinking through Cultures*, 242–52. The idea that emotions have various movements is an ancient one (see, e.g., Seneca, *Ira* 2.4.1, as well as the discussion in Richard Sorabji, *Emotion and Peace of Mind: From Stoic Agitation to Christian Temptation; The Gifford Lectures* [Oxford: Oxford University Press, 2000], passim).

[17] The word *primarily* in this sentence is important. Amzallag concedes that human קנאה can result in action, even while he attempts also to "restrict" it to the psychological dimension ("Furnace Remelting," 237).

[18] This list is adapted from Schlimm, *From Fratricide*, 66. In addition to the verses here, some verses containing a word from the root קנא do not specify why a party is jealous (Prov 14:30, 27:4, Job 5:2, Song 8:6, Qoh 9:6). With a small number of verses, the word from the root קנא may refer to zeal rather than jealousy (2 Kgs 19:31, Isa 9:6[7], 26:11, 37:32, 42:13, 63:15; see Dominik Markl, "Ein 'leidenschaftlicher Gott': Zu einem zentralen Motiv biblischer Theologie," *ZKT* 137 [2015]: 193–205, which may overstate the connections between zeal and קנאה [e.g., regarding Exod 20:5] but nevertheless makes many valid points).

4. Verses where a party is *jealous because* another party has *wrongly received* goods or property: Gen 26:14; 2 Sam 21:2;[19] Isa 11:13; Ezek 31:9; 35:11. See also Qoh 4:4.
5. Verses where a party is *jealous because* another party has *wrongly received* power, honor, or status: Gen 37:11; Num 11:29; Ps 106:16.
6. Verses where a party is *jealous because* another party has *wrongly received* sexual encounters: Num 5:12–31; Prov 6:34. See also Gen 30:1; Ezek 16:38.
7. Verses where godly individuals are *jealous because* sinners have *wrongly received* more than the godly: Pss 37:1; 73:3; Prov 3:31; 23:17; 24:1, 19.

Rather than assuming that human קנאה and divine קנאה are radically different, interpreters should recognize that קנאה consistently results from a perceived wrongdoing, namely, that another party possesses or experiences something they should not.

Amzallag contends that, in contrast to human קנאה, divine קנאה is not a psychological state. The Hebrew Bible, however, frequently describes divine קנאה using psychological terms. Of the thirty-five verses mentioning divine קנאה, seventeen also mention a term for anger.[20] In the Hebrew Bible, anger prototypically results from a perceived wrong.[21] As we have just seen, jealousy usually results from a particular type of perceived wrong, namely, that parties possess or experience what they should not. Divine קנאה, therefore, is frequently associated with other emotional terms, particularly those for anger. Interpreters should avoid supposing that קנאה belongs to a different semantic field.

Regarding action, the second part of the prototypical script, Amzallag emphasizes that divine קנאה issues in a specific mode of action—unlike human קנאה. To support this point, he essentially makes an argument from silence. He points to verses where divine קנאה is presumed to issue in a course of action but that course of action is not explicitly described. As an example, Amzallag mentions Ezek 23:25, where YHWH says, ונתתי קנאתי בך ("I will send my קנאה against you"). Amzallag writes, "The fact that the prophet does not detail its nature [i.e., the nature of YHWH's קנאה] suggests that this specific mode of action was well known by his audience."[22] This conclusion is problematic.

---

[19] Like some other verses in this list, 2 Sam 21:2 is open to more than one interpretation. Here I assume that Saul experiences jealousy because he believes the Gibeonites wrongly received land. While this interpretation is reasonable (given Josh 9), 2 Sam 21:2 does not give many details about Saul's motives or actions.

[20] Num 25:11; Deut 6:15; 29:19[20]; 32:16, 21; Ezek 5:13; 16:38, 42; 23:25; 36:6; 38:19; Nah 1:2; Zeph 1:18; 3:8; 8:2; Pss 78:58; 79:5. Earlier, I mentioned forty-two appearances of divine קנאה, which is different from the thirty-five mentioned in the sentence above. The reason for the difference is that forty-two refers to appearances of words from the root קנא, whereas thirty-five refers to the number of verses in which the words appear.

[21] Schlimm, *From Fratricide*, 53–56.

[22] Amzallag, "Furnace Remelting," 237.

The rest of Ezek 23:25 actually details a very specific course of action: the Babylonians and others will mete out wrath, slicing off noses and ears, taking life with the sword, capturing sons and daughters, and burning others with fire. There is little ambiguity about the course divine קנאה takes here. Additionally, Amzallag's argument that the biblical text uses divine קנאה to evoke a specific course of action without describing it in detail applies just as much to human קנאה as divine קנאה. For example, Prov 27:4 reads, "Fury is fierce and anger is a flood, but who can stand before jealousy?" In this verse, human jealousy will obviously result in an undesirable course of action, even though this course of action goes unnamed.

In fact, both divine קנאה and human קנאה tend to result in destructive consequences. When people worship other gods and YHWH's jealousy is aroused, punishment prototypically follows.[23] Similarly, when humans become jealous, they often engage in violence or put others through ordeals to alleviate their jealousy.[24]

To summarize, then, there are problems with distinguishing divine and human spheres along the lines that Amzallag proposes. Both divine קנאה and human קנאה tend to arise when a party perceives that someone experiences or possesses something they should not. Both divine קנאה and human קנאה have psychological elements closely related to anger. Both divine קנאה and human קנאה have the potential to issue in a course of action, especially a destructive one.

While there are more similarities between divine jealousy and human jealousy than Amzallag's article admits, one can agree with his point that differences do exist. For example, YHWH experiences jealousy primarily when other gods are worshiped or when Israel or Judah suffers disproportionate harm. YHWH is less likely to be described with a word from קנא when goods and property end up in the wrong hands.[25] Humans, in contrast, often grow jealous over the misappropriation of goods and property. While differences between divine and human קנאה exist, they are not as significant as Amzallag suggests.

II. Jealousy: Unworthy of YHWH?

One of Amzallag's concerns is to explain why jealousy, which is "far from a positive sentiment," would be named as "an essential attribute of a god acknowledged as the supreme creator."[26] In voicing this concern, he seems to be importing

---

[23] Cases where YHWH's jealousy leads to punishment include Exod 20:5; Deut 4:24; 5:9; 6:15; 29:19[20]; 32:16, 21; Josh 24:19; Isa 26:11; 42:13; 59:17; Ezek 5:13; 8:3, 5; 16:38–42; 23:25; 36:5; 38:19; Nah 1:2; Zeph 1:18; 3:8; Zech 8:2.

[24] On violence, see Num 25:7–13, 2 Sam 21:2, 1 Kgs 19:10–14, 2 Kgs 10:16, Prov 6:34, 27:4; cf. Isa 11:13. On other ways of alleviating the cause of jealousy (which can have violent undertones), see Gen 37:11–28, Num 5:11–31.

[25] On the other hand, worshiping other gods would involve bringing them gifts or sacrifices. YHWH's jealousy over misdirected worship would thus involve some property.

[26] Amzallag, "Furnace Remelting," 234.

modern assumptions about the negativity of jealousy into ancient texts. Emotions are viewed differently in different cultures. For example, many people in the modern Western world see fear as a negative and even shameful emotion. Yet cultural anthropologists have shown that people of the South Pacific frequently consider fear a positive emotion that can be celebrated.[27] Mutatis mutandis, it is worth asking whether jealousy in the Hebrew Bible is really the negative emotion modern people often assume it is.

Within the Hebrew Bible's framework, there is nothing inherently wrong with YHWH judging humanity's behavior. To the contrary, many texts extol the deity for assessing and counteracting human wrongdoing (e.g., Exod 34:7, 2 Sam 12, 1 Kgs 21, Ps 96:13). Given that jealousy in the Hebrew Bible arises when there is a perception of wrongdoing (as shown above), such an emotion seems wholly appropriate for Israel's divine judge.[28] There is no reason to presuppose that jealousy would be a negative, unfitting, or unworthy descriptor of YHWH.

Certainly, some texts warn that human jealousy can lead to negative results (e.g., Prov 14:30). The Hebrew Bible's primary deity, however, does not possess all the shortcomings that humans do. Moreover, some texts see human jealousy as a normal part of human existence (e.g., Num 5:12–31) or an emotion that can please YHWH (e.g., Num 25:10–13). What strikes modern readers as a problematic association (i.e., jealousy with the divine) may have posed no problem to ancient readers. Interpreters should avoid importing their own assumptions about emotions into the biblical text.[29]

III. Divine קנאה and Fiery Imagery

On the road to linking divine קנאה with furnace remelting, Amzallag notes several cases where the Hebrew Bible connects divine קנאה with fiery imagery.[30] Unfortunately, Amzallag could have better emphasized the essential role that anger plays in all of the documented cases. There are nine verses that link divine קנאה

---

[27] Lutz, *Unnatural Emotions*, 184–85; Robert I. Levy, *Tahitians: Mind and Experience in the Society Islands* (Chicago: University of Chicago Press, 1973), 307–8.

[28] Bernd Janowski correctly connects divine קנאה with justice and holiness (albeit while seeking to downplay divine connections with human selfishness and feeling offended) ("Eigenschaften Gottes [AT]," in *Handbuch theologischer Grundbegriffe zum Alten und Neuen Testament (HGANT)*, ed. Angelika Berlejung and Christian Frevel, 4th ed. [Darmstadt: Wissenschaftliche Buchgesellschaft, 2015], 147–49, esp. 148).

[29] Schlimm, *From Fratricide*, 19–34. One could go so far as to ask whether the English word jealousy is the best way to translate the Hebrew word קנאה. Some translators prefer "zeal," "passion," or something similar (see Markl, "Ein 'leidenschaftlicher Gott,'" passim; Janowski, "Eigenschaften Gottes," 148). These alternatives, however, suggest a wider semantic range than קנאה prototypically has in view. In translation, perfect equivalents are often elusive, as is the case here.

[30] Amzallag, "Furnace Remelting," 238–39.

with fire, and each one also mentions divine anger in the same or the following verse.³¹ It is worth asking, therefore, whether the fiery imagery found in these verses relates more to the קנאה described or to the anger described. Verses containing קנאה mention fire only when anger is also in view. Verses talking about anger, however, often describe fire when קנאה is not mentioned. In fact, of the 519 verses referring to anger in the Hebrew Bible, over 10 percent contain a reference to fire (אש), burn[ing] (בער, בערה), extinguish[ing] (דעך, כבה), or smoke of some sort (עשן, קטר, קטרת, קיטור, מקטר, מקטרת).³² Therefore, it is more appropriate to connect fiery imagery with the emotion of anger than to assume that something about קנאה is innately fiery.

As is well known, many Hebrew words for anger speak of this emotion in terms of heat or burning, most likely because people often perceive themselves as feeling hot while angry:³³

ANGER IS A BURNING NOSE (חרה אף).

ANGER IS HEAT (חמה, חרה).

These terms are used so frequently for anger that they often function as dead metaphors (or more precisely, dead metonyms).³⁴ Thus, a verse like Gen 27:45 talks about Esau's אף turning away, and it clearly refers to his anger subsiding, not the literal direction of his nose.³⁵

At the same time, Paul Ricoeur points out that sometimes writers revive dead metaphors, employing them in fresh ways that allow readers to see metaphorical

---

³¹ See Deut 4:24–25, 29:19[20], Isa 26:11, Ezek 23:25, 36:5–6, 38:19, Zeph 1:18, 3:8, Ps 79:5; cf. Num 25:11, Deut 32:21–22, Nah 1:2–5. Most of these nine verses speak of fire (אש), though Deut 29:19[20] mentions "smoke" (עשן). I here assume that אף in Isa 26:11 functions as a noun meaning "anger," rather than as a particle meaning "also" (cf. CEB).

³² Schlimm, *From Fratricide*, 69–70.

³³ Several scholars have asserted that biblical writers operated with the cognitive metaphor ANGER IS THE HEAT OF FLUID IN A CONTAINER (Paul A. Krüger, "A Cognitive Interpretation of the Emotion of Anger in the Hebrew Bible," *JNSL* 26 [2000]: 181–93; Zacharias Kotzé, "A Cognitive Linguistic Methodology for the Study of Metaphor in the Hebrew Bible," *JNSL* 31 [2005]: 107–17; Ellen van Wolde, "Sentiments as Culturally Constructed Emotions: Anger and Love in the Hebrew Bible," *BibInt* 16 [2008]: 1–24, esp. 9–10; cf. van Wolde, *Reframing Biblical Studies: When Language and Text Meet Culture, Cognition, and Context* [Winona Lake, IN: Eisenbrauns, 2009], 72). On problems with this approach, see Schlimm, *From Fratricide*, 79–81.

³⁴ A dead metaphor is one used so frequently that its metaphorical qualities are no longer noticed. One could ask whether this language for anger functions as dead metaphors or simply conventionalized metaphors. It is difficult to say with certainty, given our distance from the original speakers of Classical Hebrew. Nevertheless, when a word like חרה always refers to anger in the *qal* stem, it probably is closer to being a dead metaphor than a commonly used one (see Schlimm, *From Fratricide*, 82–83, 197–98).

³⁵ Ibid., 75–88, esp. 82–83.

qualities once again.³⁶ On several occasions, the Hebrew Bible reanimates the dead metaphor ANGER IS HEAT. Thus, Jer 4:4 reads, "Lest my wrath [חמתי] go forth like fire [כאש] and burn [ובערה] with no one to extinguish it [מכבה]." In this case, literal fire is not in view, given the particle כ. Yet the worn-out idea of anger functioning like something hot comes to life in a fresh way. At other times, the text portrays YHWH's anger as resulting in actual fire, as in Num 11:1–3, part of which reads, "[YHWH] grew angry [ויחר אפו], lit., 'his nose burned'], and the fire [אש] of YHWH burned [ותבער] against them. It consumed [ותאכל] the edges of the camp." Here, language that is normally figurative becomes actualized as divine anger results in literal fire and burning. Given that jealousy functions much like anger, arising in response to a particular type of perceived wrongdoing, it sometimes is mentioned in these cases where God's anger is described as burning, smoking, or fiery. One need not assume, however, that קנאה entails any sort of furnace remelting in order to see why it appears in these fire-filled contexts.³⁷

Furthermore, the more literal idea of fire found in Num 11:1–3 is missing in a number of the cases Amzallag cites. Shortly after citing Zeph 1:18's reference to the fire of YHWH's קנאה "consuming the whole earth," Amzallag claims, "in contrast to the human context of meaning, the fiery expression of the *qannāʾ* should be considered to be not a metaphor but rather a genuine mode of divine action."³⁸ This remark about the nonmetaphorical nature of קנאה is puzzling. In a text that talks about the entire earth (or at least the entire land, ארץ) being consumed, is there not some level of metaphor at work? Or, when Amzallag later claims that divine קנאה refers to furnace remelting, does he not imply the following metaphor: YHWH IS A SMELTER WHO DESTROYS AND REJUVENATES? How could YHWH be seen as consuming people with literal fire when, as Amzallag himself notes, "No volcanic activity is known in Canaan during biblical times"?³⁹ Amzallag's article would have been more persuasive if it better answered such questions.

IV. קנא AND METALLURGY

קנא as Rust: Arabic and Sirach 12:10–11

To support his argument that divine קנאה relates to metallurgy, Amzallag claims that in Arabic a cognate term for קנא means "rust."⁴⁰ Edward William Lane,

---

³⁶ Paul Ricoeur, *The Rule of Metaphor: Multi-disciplinary Studies of the Creation of Meaning in Language*, trans. Robert Czerny, Kathleen McLaughlin, and John Costello (Toronto: University of Toronto Press, 1981), 291–95.

³⁷ Moreover, fire is used in many contexts besides metallurgy.

³⁸ Amzallag, "Furnace Remelting," 238.

³⁹ Ibid., 239.

⁴⁰ Ibid., 240. As support, he cites "קנאה II," *DCH* 7:266, 602. Both *DCH* and Amzallag go on to cite G. R. Driver, "Hebrew Notes on the 'Wisdom of Jesus Ben Sirach,'" *JBL* 53 (1934):

however, defines the word in terms of redness and blackness, not mentioning rust at all.⁴¹ *HALOT*, *TDOT*, and BDB similarly give this Arabic cognate a broader meaning, namely, "to become red, or alternatively black."⁴² Obviously, things that rust do develop a reddish hue. Yet, if there is a connection between the Hebrew קנא and the Arabic *qnʾ*, it could just as easily relate to people becoming red in the face while growing jealous. In any event, James Barr's famous exposé of the etymological fallacy gives interpreters reason to pause before assuming too much on the basis of cognates in other languages.⁴³

Amzallag asserts that the words קנא and קנאה refer to "rust" also in Sir 12:10–11. He quotes the Good News Bible translation of these verses, adding Hebrew words in brackets: "[v. 10] Never trust an enemy; his wickedness is as destructive as rust [קנאה]. [v. 11] Watch out, and be on guard against him, even if he acts ever so humble. He is like a metal mirror that rusts away [קנא] if you don't keep it polished."⁴⁴ Unfortunately, the matter is not as clear as the brackets provided by Amzallag imply. Manuscript A is the only extant Hebrew manuscript of Sirach that includes these verses. There, the Hebrew lacks any reference to קנא or קנאה in verse 10. Instead, it uses the verb יחליא to speak of rust. Meanwhile, verse 11 lacks the verb קנא that Amzallag inserts, though it does include the noun קנאה. The end of that verse in the Hebrew (cf. Syriac), however, differs considerably from the Greek on which the Good News Bible appears to rely. In the extant Hebrew, to translate קנאה as "jealousy" makes sense, as Benjamin H. Parker and Martin G. Abegg have shown: "And even if he shows regard for you and walks peacefully commit your heart to being in fear of him. Treat him as one who will betray your confidence and he will not discover a means to destroy you. For know that in the end there will be

---

273–90, esp. 276. Driver attempts to reconcile the Hebrew and Greek of Sir 12:11. He refers to the Arabic *qnʾ* but goes beyond the basic sense of the Arabic ("red") to talk about a rare and questionable meaning ("red rust"). Driver's tendency to focus on rare secondary meanings in the Arabic has been thoroughly criticized by John Kaltner, *The Use of Arabic in Biblical Hebrew Lexicography*, CBQMS 28 (Washington, DC: Catholic Biblical Association of America, 1996), e.g., 24–27.

⁴¹ E. W. Lane, *An Arabic-English Lexicon*, 8 vols. (London: Williams & Norgate, 1863; repr., Beirut: Libr. du Liban, 1968), 7:2565, http://www.tyndalearchive.com/tabs/lane/. Volumes 7 and 8 of Lane's work should be used judiciously, and biblical scholars should focus on well-attested meanings rather than meanings that are rare or secondary (Kaltner, *Use of Arabic*, 98–100). Classical Arabic's well-attested meaning relates to redness and blackness, not to rust.

⁴² *HALOT*, s.v. "קנא"; cf. E. Reuter, "קנא," *TDOT* 13:47–58, here 48; BDB, s.v. "קנא." Similarly, when Wolf Leslau lists the cognates of קנא in various Semitic languages, none refers to rust; only Arabic refers to anything reddish, and all of the rest relate to jealousy, envy, or zealousness ("*qanʾa*," *Comparative Dictionary of Geʿez [Classical Ethiopic]: Geʿez-English / English-Geʿez with an Index of the Semitic Roots* [Wiesbaden: Harrassowitz, 1987], 433).

⁴³ James Barr, *The Semantics of Biblical Language* (London: SCM, 1983), ch. 6, esp. 107–10, 158–60.

⁴⁴ Amzallag, "Furnace Remelting," 240. The Hebrew words are found in Amzallag's text. I added the verse numbers.

jealousy [קנאה]."⁴⁵ While this verse has its share of textual-critical issues (more than can be explored here), the extant Hebrew manuscript fails to point unambiguously in the direction of Amzallag's argument.⁴⁶

From Fire and Rust to Furnace Remelting

Given the supposed connections between קנאה, fiery imagery, and rust, Amzallag claims additionally that we can "identify the meaning of *qannāʾ* in a metallurgical context: the process of *furnace remelting*, by which the copper of corroded metallic artifacts becomes recycled."⁴⁷ Even if Amzallag were correct that something innate to קנאה evokes fiery imagery, and even if he were correct that קנאה means "rust" in Sir 12:11, it is nevertheless quite a leap in logic to assume that, for biblical writers, the word קנאה would mean "furnace remelting." More evidence would be needed to support this conclusion.

Furnace Remelting as Rejuvenation

Amzallag also claims that furnace remelting had symbolic significance in the ancient world. He observes, "Furnace remelting produces a complete regeneration of the metal, *without any loss of matter*."⁴⁸ He then argues that in antiquity this process of furnace remelting provided a valuable symbol for destruction and rejuvenation. At one point, he goes so far as to talk about furnace remelting as "the *only* process of rejuvenation known in antiquity."⁴⁹

Amzallag overstates the case here. Furnace remelting may have been one of the few means of rejuvenation without the loss of matter, but one wonders whether the loss of matter was particularly significant prior to modernity and the scientific enterprise. More to the point, the Hebrew Bible does not confine itself to talking about rejuvenation in terms of furnace remelting. The dominant theme of Jer 18:1–11 is rejuvenation, and it uses the image of a potter reworking clay rather than of a smith remelting metal. Elsewhere, the conclusion of Isaiah describes all of creation being rejuvenated, again without reference to metallic refinement (Isa 65:17–25). The psalmist speaks of rejuvenation by employing metaphors of washing and

---

⁴⁵ Benjamin H. Parker and Martin G. Abegg, trans., "The Book of Ben Sira ספר בן סירא: A V Recto," http://www.bensira.org/navigator.php?Manuscript=A&PageNum=9. The word קנאה is similarly translated as "envy" in Patrick W. Skehan and Alexander A. Di Lella, *The Wisdom of Ben Sira: A New Introduction with Notes*, AB 39 (New York: Doubleday, 1987), 243.

⁴⁶ Amzallag cites Driver, "Hebrew Notes," 276, to support his case; however, in his article Driver deals only with verse 11, not verse 10. Furthermore, Driver's claim that the Hebrew קנאה means "rust" is problematic, as described in n. 40 above.

⁴⁷ Amzallag, "Furnace Remelting," 241 (italics Amzallag's).

⁴⁸ Ibid. (italics Amzallag's).

⁴⁹ Ibid., 251 (italics mine).

cleaning (e.g., Ps 51:9[7]). In legal texts, both atonement and purification rites entail some level of rejuvenation, again without metallic reshaping in view. Renewal is obviously evoked when prophets speak of the dead coming to life (Ezek 37:1–14), streams gushing forth in the desert (Isa 35:6), light shining in darkness (Isa 9:1[2]), and rubble being rebuilt (Isa 58:12). Furnace remelting is not the only or even the primary means of speaking about rejuvenation in the Hebrew Bible.

When Amzallag gives examples of how people in antiquity viewed furnace remelting as rejuvenation, he describes evidence from ancient Egypt, Mesopotamia, Vedic India, ancient Africa, and prehistoric Europe, including Bronze Age Scandinavia. The examples outside of the ancient Near East shed only dim light on the Hebrew text, given their geographic distance from it.[50] Regarding ancient Near Eastern evidence, Amzallag observes how Ptah, the patron god of metalworkers, "was considered the main healing god in Egypt, exactly like Ea/Enki, his Mesopotamia counterpart."[51] Amzallag's argument suggests that the metaphor FURNACE REMELTING IS REJUVENATION was so important that deities associated with metalworkers were naturally chosen as the ones responsible for healing. It seems equally likely, however, that the role of these deities as creators allowed people to associate them with both metalworking and healing.[52] The metaphor FURNACE REMELTING IS REJUVENATION may have played only an ancillary role in some people's thinking, if it played any role at all.

Obviously, some Hebrew texts do refer to YHWH as one who, like a smelter, refines metal,[53] but words from the root קנא never appear in verses that mention metallic refinement (צרף ["smelt"] and זקק ["purify"]).[54] By contrast, of the seventy verses where words related to the root קנא appear, twenty-three mention a word for anger (33 percent).[55] The semantic field of קנא is emotional, not metallurgic.

---

[50] See Shemaryahu Talmon, "The 'Comparative Method' in Biblical Interpretation—Principles and Problems," in *Congress Volume: Göttingen 1977*, VTSup 29 (Leiden: Brill, 1978), 320–56.

[51] Amzallag, "Furnace Remelting," 242 n. 33.

[52] See M. Heerma van Voss, "Ptah," *DDD*, 668–69; H. D. Galter, "Aya," *DDD*, 125–27.

[53] E.g., Judg 7:4, Isa 48:10, Jer 9:6[7], Zech 13:9, Mal 3:2–3, Pss 17:3, 26:2, 66:10, 105:19, Prov 17:3.

[54] Similarly, words from the root קנא never appear in the same verse as metallic terms like זהב ("gold"), כסף ("silver"), נחשת ("copper"), and ברזל ("iron"). In fact, words from the root קנא do not appear in the same verse as any of the other words mentioned in *NIDOTTE* as belonging to the same semantic field as צרף and זקק: ברר ("purge out"), זכה ("be pure"), חף ("clean"), טהר ("be clean"), אופיר ("gold of Ophir"), בצר ("gold ore"), חרוץ ("gold"), כתם ("gold"), סגור ("pure gold"), פז ("refined gold"), פזז ("set with fine gold"), דונג ("wax [metaphor for melting]"), מוג ("melt"), מסס ("melt"), מסה ("melt"), שיח ("melt away"), בחן ("test"), נסה ("test"), and תוה ("provoke") (Gerald A. Klingbeil, "2423 זקק," *NIDOTTE* 1:1140–42, here 1141; Robin Wakely, "7671 צרף," *NIDOTTE* 3:847–53, here 852). The only exception is Zeph 1:8, which mentions gold (זהב) and silver (כסף). This verse, however, does not talk about the melting of gold and silver. Rather, it says that neither of these precious metals will be able to deliver people from God's jealousy (קנאה).

[55] As a point of comparison, many publications mention that words from the root צדק ("be

Exodus 4:1–9 as Related to Furnace Remelting

Another argument Amzallag makes is that Exod 4:1–9 illustrates the close relationship between furnace remelting and rejuvenation. The text recounts three wonders (אות): the transformation of Moses's מטה into a נחש, the healing of Moses's hand, and the transformation of water into blood. With the first, Amzallag interprets מטה as a "scepter" rather than as a "shepherd's staff," and he sees נחש as "copper" rather than as a "serpent." He writes, "This wonder is therefore nothing other than furnace remelting, a process by which the copper scepter of Moses is renewed through transitory loss of shape, at the serpentine/liquid phase. This metallurgical interpretation clarifies how Egyptian specialists were able to perform the same wonder without difficulties."[56] This interpretation, while creative, also raises questions: Why would Moses use a copper scepter when shepherding Jethro's flock, rather than a wooden shepherd's staff (cf. Exod 3:1)? Why is it that when this sign is performed before Pharaoh, Aaron casts down his מטה, which presumably is wooden, given that it later blossoms and grows almonds (Exod 7:10, Num 17)? Why does Exod 7:10 speak of the מטה becoming תנין ("a serpent"), rather than something metallic? Or, if נחש is a reference to copper rather than a snake, why does the text avoid the expected נחשת?[57] Why does Exod 7:15 use נחש as a synonym of תנין? The simplest answer to these questions is that Exod 4 and 7 relate not to metallic remelting but rather to a wooden rod becoming a snake.

Furthermore, while the second sign (involving Moses's hand) obviously involves rejuvenation, interpreters should be reluctant to agree with Amzallag that the third sign (involving the transformation of water into blood) also entails rejuvenation. Amzallag correctly observes that parts of the Hebrew Bible relate blood to life.[58] Yet Exod 7:18, 24 relate blood to death, saying that, once the Nile's waters became blood, the fish therein died, a foul stench arose, and Egyptians could drink from it no longer.

Thus, Amzallag claims to find a pattern of metallic remelting in Exod 4 that points to the symbolic import of smelting as rejuvenation. We find instead,

---

righteous") have a tendency to appear in conjunction with the word משפט ("justice"), e.g., B. Johnson, "צדק," *TDOT* 12:239–64, here 247. This observation can be statistically verified using a computer search engine: of the 406 verses containing a word from the root צדק, 24 percent also contain the word משפט (ninety-nine verses). To the subject at hand: of the seventy verses containing a word from the root קנא, 33 percent also contain a word for anger (twenty-three verses). The connection between קנאה and anger is thus quite strong, more so than well-known collocations (צדק and משפט), and far more so than any supposed connection between קנאה and metallic refinement.

[56] Amzallag, "Furnace Remelting," 244.

[57] Granted, this question does make something of an argument from silence. Furthermore, perhaps a *tav* was lost in transmission. Or, perhaps the text spells the adjective נחוש in its defective form. There are many other questions, however, that also arise from Amzallag's interpretation.

[58] Amzallag, "Furnace Remelting," 245. See Lev 17:11, 14.

however, that metallic remelting probably has nothing to do with Exod 4 and 7. Even if it did, the end result is not renewed life but rotting fish and undrinkable water.

V. Divine קנאה

Destruction and Renewal

In fairness to Amzallag's argument, there are texts that describe divine קנאה when talking about destruction followed by renewal.[59] Yet there is no reason why such texts need to be linked to furnace remelting, especially when verbs for smelting are noticeably absent. A central motif of the Hebrew Bible is that devastation is followed by a time of rejuvenation.[60] How else could the God of the exile and return be understood?[61] Words from the root קנא naturally appear amid such a motif. Instead of evoking metalworking, however, they explain why YHWH is angry: the people have given to other gods their worship, which rightfully belongs to YHWH. Frequently, YHWH's anger is described as real, dangerous, and even deadly. At the same time, it does not endure (e.g., Isa 54:8, Ps 30:6[5]). YHWH's jealousy functions much as does YHWH's anger. Not surprisingly, it is connected with destruction followed by renewal.

Holiness

Near the conclusion of his article, Amzallag observes that קנאה can function in parallel with terms for YHWH's holiness.[62] Certainly, texts like Josh 24:19 do link God's קנאה and God's holiness. Yet there are problems with assuming with Amzallag that "exactly as with *qannāʾ*, YHWH's holiness was closely related to the experience of rejuvenation by destruction through furnace remelting."[63] Words from the root קדש never appear in the same verse as verbs for furnace remelting (צרף and זקק). Furthermore, one can understand קנאה as a reference to jealousy and still understand its relationship to holiness.

---

[59] Ibid., 246–47.

[60] One finds such a message not only throughout the Latter Prophets (with judgment being a dominant note that finds a counterpoint in texts like Isa 40–55, Jer 30–33, Ezek 40–48) but also in books like Exodus (where slavery gives way to freedom), Judges (with its cycle that involves oppression followed by deliverance), Psalms (which often move from cries of despair to notes of hope), and Chronicles (which ends optimistically with Cyrus proclaiming that captives may return to Jerusalem).

[61] See Donald E. Gowan, *Theology of the Prophetic Books: The Death and Resurrection of Israel* (Louisville: Westminster John Knox, 1998).

[62] Amzallag, "Furnace Remelting," 248–50.

[63] Ibid., 250.

As described above, jealousy results from one party perceiving that another party wrongly possesses something. Holiness, meanwhile, pertains to giving to YHWH what is set apart for YHWH. A violation of holiness, therefore, means that YHWH has not received what YHWH should—a situation that would naturally make YHWH jealous. In Josh 24, the issue is whether the people will give their service to YHWH or to other deities (v. 15). The people insist they will serve YHWH, while Joshua is skeptical (vv. 16–18). Joshua reminds the people that YHWH is a "holy God," deserving what has not been profaned elsewhere (v. 19). In the same verse, Joshua adds that YHWH is a "jealous God," that is, perceiving when others (in this case, other gods) receive what they should not (in this case, the people's promised service). Here jealousy is an especially useful image because it tends, like anger, to issue in something harsh for those causing the jealousy. Thus, Joshua next says that, should the people fail to give this holy God what this God deserves, then harm and death will come to them (v. 20). The entire passage makes perfect sense without bringing metallurgic imagery into one's interpretation.

VI. Conclusion

Words can evoke complicated associations over time, associations not always apparent even to everyday users of a language.[64] Perhaps among the complicated associations evoked by קנאה, furnace remelting played some role with some users of the word at some points in time. It is unlikely, however, that the root קנא as it appears in the Hebrew Bible relates more to metallurgy than to emotions. While differences exist between divine and human קנאה, the Hebrew Bible conceptualizes both divine and human קנאה as an emotion sharing much in common with anger. It arises in response to a particular type of wrongdoing: an entity has received what rightfully should have gone to another party. Interpreting קנאה as an emotional term related to anger best explains a wide variety of textual dynamics, including the presence of fiery imagery, the prevalence of anger vocabulary alongside קנאה, the absence of smelting verbs alongside קנאה, and the relationship between holiness and קנאה. Imagining YHWH as jealous may cause problems for modern readers, but for biblical writers it provided a choice medium for expressing YHWH's justice, holiness, dangerousness, and interrelatedness with humanity.

[64] See Barr, *Semantics of Biblical Language*, ch. 6; Schlimm, *From Fratricide*, 80.

Who Is Doing What to Whom Revisited: Another Look at Leviticus 18:22 and 20:13

GEORGE M. HOLLENBACK
gmh616@yahoo.com
5401 Rampart St., Apt. 413, Houston, TX 77081

According to the overwhelming majority of modern English Bible translations, the proscriptions of male-on-male sexual intercourse in Lev 18:22 and 20:13 appear to be directed to the activity of the insertive party, the few remaining versions simply proscribing male-on-male sex in such a general way that there is no indication one way or the other as to whose activity is being addressed. Jerome T. Walsh has challenged the status quo, however, persuasively arguing that, when correctly interpreted, the Hebrew text indicates that it is instead the activity of the receptive party that is being addressed ("Leviticus 18:22 and 20:13: Who Is Doing What to Whom?," *JBL* 120 [2001]: 201–9). Building on the foundation laid by Walsh, the present work analyzes the two verses in their immediate Hebrew context and applies the same analysis to the earliest translations, the result being a validation of Walsh's contention that the proscriptions were indeed directed to the activity of the receptive rather than the insertive party.

Leviticus 18:22 and 20:13 proscribe male-on-male sexual intercourse, the latter verse even going so far as to mandate the death penalty for both parties involved. Modern translations tend to render the passages in such a way as to suggest that it is the activity of the insertive, rather than the receptive, participant in the transgression that is being addressed, for example:

> You shall not lie with a man as with a woman; it is an abomination. (Lev 18:22 RSV)

> If a man lies with a male as with a woman, both of them have committed an abomination; they shall be put to death, their blood is upon them. (Lev 20:13 RSV)

A groundbreaking work by Saul M. Olyan convincingly demonstrated that the proscribed sexual act was anal intercourse between males. Olyan also pressed the case that it was the activity of the insertive participant that was being addressed.[1]

---

[1] Saul M. Olyan, "'And with a Male You Shall Not Lie the Lying Down of a Woman': On the

When I had occasion to translate from the Hebrew myself, however, the gist of the passages seemed to indicate that it was the activity of the receptive, rather than the insertive, participant that was being addressed. I rendered 18:22a—ואת־זכר לא תשכב משכבי אשה—as "and with a male you shall not lie down lyings down of a woman," and 20:13a—ואיש אשר ישכב את־זכר משכבי אשה—as "and a man who lies down with a male lyings down of a woman." That a man would "lie down lyings down of a woman" intuitively suggests that the man was lying down the way a woman would lie down to play the receptive role in sexual intercourse. Olyan's take on the Hebrew was that the prohibitions were not directed against "lying the lying down of a woman," which he understood to be a man's experiencing of a woman's receptive role in sex, but that the prohibitions were rather directed against the experiencing of said act *with a male* instead of with a female.[2] My follow-up research, however, indicates that I am not the only one who had doubts about whether the verses in fact dealt with the activity of the insertive party.

Jerome T. Walsh challenged Olyan's supposition about the insertive participant, correctly noting that "lie a lying down" was a cognate direct object construction like "dream a dream" or "sin a sin," describing an action performed by the subject himself, not an action performed by someone else and experienced by the subject as suggested by Olyan. For example, in 2 Sam 4:5b, Ish-bosheth is said to be "lying the lying down of noontime" (שכב את משכב הצהרים); that is, Ish-bosheth himself is doing the lying down to take a nap as opposed to experiencing someone else's act of lying down for a nap. Therefore, a man "lying a lying down of a woman" would be a man actually lying down as a woman would in a sexually receptive capacity; he would not be the insertive party who experiences the receptive party's act of lying down as a woman would.[3]

Walsh also correctly noted that the description of someone's experiencing someone else's act would involve the use of "know" (ידע) in the sense of "experience." Thus, in Num 31:18 a virgin is a female who does not "know a lying down of a male" (ידע משכב זכר), the "lying down of a male" being the way a male would lie down in a sexually insertive capacity.[4] If the Levitical proscriptions were meant to address the activity of the insertive party, we should expect wording along the lines of "and with a male you shall not *know* the lyings down of a woman." The curious use of the construct plural "lying*s* down" is explained by Walsh as indicating that, whereas a man must necessarily be facing toward the woman during coitus, the woman may be facing toward the man or facing away from the man.[5]

Meaning and Significance of Leviticus 18:22 and 20:13," *Journal of the History of Sexuality* 5 (1994): 179–206.

[2] Ibid., 186, 188.

[3] Jerome T. Walsh, "Leviticus 18:22 and 20:13: Who Is Doing What to Whom?," *JBL* 120 (2001): 201–9, here 205, https://doi.org/10.2307/3268292.

[4] Ibid., 205.

[5] Ibid., 204 n. 9.

Olyan has since responded to Walsh:

> Though Walsh believes that it is the receptive partner who is the center of the law's concern, I find this difficult to accept given the way in which Lev 18:22 is phrased in Hebrew: "*And with a male* you shall not lie...." By implication, the addressee ("you" masculine singular) may lie "the lying down of a woman" with a woman, suggesting that it is the penetrator who is addressed, and not the receptive partner. If it were the receptive partner, why state that he should not perform the act in question with a *male*? With whom other than a male could he possibly perform it?[6]

In other words, if the receptive partner is being addressed, the qualifier *with a male* is superfluous because no one other than a male could perform the insertive role; so it has to be the insertive partner who is being addressed, enjoined from performing an act with a male that appropriately should be performed only with a female. That the qualifier *with a male* is in fact superfluous when used in addressing the receptive partner does not, however, mean that the receptive partner is not being addressed. The Hebrew Bible is rich in pleonasm as a literary device; Olyan himself even cites examples of such in his own work. It is therefore inconsistent on his part to insist on absolute conciseness and to find fault with a superfluous qualifier in this particular passage.[7] Moreover, the contexts in which both passages are found contain multiple prohibitions of sex acts with named entities such as "the wife of your neighbor" or "an animal"; the specific mention of "a male" is in keeping with the parallelism of this listing of named entities.

In this article, I examine the disputed passages in the light of the preceding and following passages, which indisputably refer to the insertive agency of a man. Next I compare the disputed passages with these neighboring passages for consistency of expression. Since the treatment of the disputed passages by early translators also sheds light on whether they were perceived as referring to the receptive or insertive party, I also examine several early translations.

Lev 18:20a, 22a, and 23a (HB):

ואל־אשת עמיתך לא־תתן שכבתך לזרע

and unto the wife of your neighbor you shall not give your lying down of semen (v. 20a)

ואת־זכר לא תשכב משכבי אשה

and with a male you shall not lie down lyings down of a woman (v. 22a)

---

[6] Saul M. Olyan, *Social Inequality in the World of the Text: The Significance of Ritual and Social Distinctions in the Hebrew Bible*, JAJSup 4 (Göttingen: Vandenhoeck & Ruprecht, 2011), 54.

[7] Olyan cites the following examples of pleonasm: "texts such as Judg. 21:12 and Num. 31:17 use two equivalent expressions to make the same point, where either alone would be sufficient"; and "Compare Gen. 24:16, where 'virgin' (bĕtûlâ) is further defined by the comment 'no man had known her'" ("And with a Male," 184 and n. 13).

ובכל־בהמה לא־תתן שכבתך
and with any animal you shall not give your lying down (v. 23a)

In verse 20a and verse 23a, the insertive agency of a man is represented by the idiom "give your lying down of semen" or simply "give your lying down." If he is enjoined from "giving his lying down (of semen)" to a woman or to an animal, there is no reason why he should not similarly be enjoined from "giving his lying down (of semen)" to a male, especially if he is understood to be the insertive party in a male-on-male sexual union. Instead, he is enjoined from "lying down lyings down of a woman" with a male, decidedly curious phraseology representing a semantic shift from what is going on in the neighboring verses.

Lev 20:11a, 12a, 13a, and 15a (HB):

ואיש אשר ישכב את־אשת אבי
and a man who lies down with his father's wife (v. 11a)

ואיש אשר ישכב את־כלתו
and a man who lies down with his daughter-in-law (v. 12a)

ואיש אשר ישכב את־זכר משכבי אשה
and a man who lies down with a male lyings down of a woman (v. 13a)

ואיש אשר יתן שכבתו בבהמה
and a man who gives his lying down with an animal (v. 15a)

In this group of verses, 15a retains the same idiom as in Lev 18:20a and 23a, "give a lying down"; verses 11a and 12a, however, employ the idiom "lie down with" to express the insertive agency of a man in connection with female relatives. If he is enjoined from "lying down with" certain females—and this is understood to mean sexually penetrating them—there should be no reason why that simple and unqualified idiom in and of itself should not suffice to indicate the sexual penetration of a male as well. The exact phraseology ואיש אשר ישכב את־ ("and a man who lies down with"), followed by the appellation of the party he is enjoined from lying down with appears in perfect parallel in verses 11a, 12a, and 13a—except that in verse 13a the curious qualifier משכבי אשה ("lyings down of a woman") was appended after the party he was enjoined from lying down with was identified as a fellow male. Again, this represents a semantic shift from what was going on in the neighboring verses.

Lev 18:20a, 22a, and 23a (LXX):

καὶ πρὸς τὴν γυναῖκα τοῦ πλησίον σου οὐ δώσεις κοίτην σπέρματός σου
and to the wife of your neighbor you shall not give a lying down of your semen (v. 20a)

καὶ μετὰ ἄρσενος οὐ κοιμηθήσῃ κοίτην γυναικός[8]
and with a male you shall not lie down a lying down of a woman (v. 22a)

καὶ πρὸς πᾶν τετράπουν οὐ δώσεις τὴν κοίτην σου εἰς σπερματισμόν
and to any animal you shall not give your lying down unto semen (v. 23a)

The Greek text is a fairly literal rendering of the Hebrew, and the previous comments on the corresponding Hebrew Bible verses are applicable here as well. One small difference is that the Hebrew construct plural משכבי ("lyings down") in verse 22a has been translated by the Greek accusative singular κοίτην ("a lying down"); the same occurs in 20:15a as well.

Lev 20:11a, 12a, 13a, and 15a (LXX):

ἐάν τις κοιμηθῇ μετὰ γυναικὸς τοῦ πατρὸς αὐτοῦ
and if a man lies down with a wife of his father (v. 11a)

καὶ ἐάν τις κοιμηθῇ μετὰ νύμφης αὐτοῦ
and if a man lies down with his daughter-in-law (v. 12a)

καὶ ὃς ἂν κοιμηθῇ μετὰ ἄρσενος κοίτην γυναικός[9]
and if a man lies down with a male a lying down of a woman (v. 13a)

καὶ ὃς ἂν δῷ κοιτασίαν αὐτοῦ ἐν τετράποδι
and if a man gives his lying down with an animal (v. 15a)

Like the Greek verses from chapter 18, these are a fairly literal rendering of the Hebrew: the translator expressed the sense of the passages in the subjunctive mood. The previous comments on the corresponding Hebrew Bible verses are applicable here as well.

Lev 18:20a, 22a, and 23a (Vulg.):

cum uxore proximi tui non coibis
with the wife of your neighbor you shall not copulate (v. 20a)

cum masculo non commisceberis coitu femineo
with a male you shall not be joined in womanly copulation (v. 22a)

---

[8] NETS renders this as "And you shall not sleep with a male *as in* a bed of a woman" (emphasis added). In the Greek, no preposition is attached to κοίτην, which is a straightforward accusative direct object of κοιμηθήσῃ. The sense of κοιμηθήσῃ κοίτην is "lie down a lying down," corresponding to the Hebrew שכב משכב. The problem with the direct object κοίτην being translated as the object of a preposition also crops up in the NETS translation of 20:13.

[9] NETS incredibly renders this as "And he who lies with a male in a bed for a woman," leading the unwary reader to believe that the real offense here is not males engaging in anal sex per se but rather their doing so in a woman's bed!

cum omni pecore non coibis
with any animal you shall not copulate (v. 23a)

In verse 20a and verse 23a, the insertive man is enjoined not to copulate with his neighbor's wife or with an animal, the more concise *coibis* being used to render the Hebrew idiom "give a lying down (of semen) to." In verse 22a, the Hebrew "lie down lyings down of a woman" is rendered *commisceberis coitu femineo*, "be joined with in womanly copulation." Since the only way a woman can copulate is by being the receptive partner, it would appear that this is a prohibition against a man's allowing himself to be joined with another male as the receptive partner.

Lev 20: 11a, 12a, 13a, and 15a (Vulg.):

qui dormierit cum noverca sua
a man who sleeps with his stepmother (v. 11a)

si quis dormierit cum nuru sua
if a man sleeps with his daughter-in-law (v. 12a)

qui dormierit cum masculo coitu femineo
a man who sleeps with a male in womanly copulation (v. 13a)

qui cum iumento et pecore coierit
a man who with a beast or animal copulates (v. 15a)

In this group of verses all rendered in the subjunctive mood, verse 15a retains the sense of copulating (*coierit*) with a given entity as in 18:20a and 23a, while verses 11a and 12a employ the idiom "sleep with" (*dormierit cum*) to express the insertive agency of a man. Consistent with the Hebrew, "sleeps with a male" (*dormierit cum masculo*, v. 13a) directly parallels "sleeps with his stepmother" (*dormierit cum noverca sua*, v. 11a) and "sleeps with his daughter-in-law" (*dormierit cum nuru sua*, v. 12a). Although verse 13a should be able to stand alone with the meaning of "sleep with a male" in the sense of "sexually penetrate a male," it is consistent with the Hebrew in that it is followed by a curious qualifier, "in womanly copulation" (*coitu femineo*), which suggests that the man is not to have sex with a male the way a woman would, that is, as the receptive partner. There is a deviation from the Hebrew in verse 15a in that two creatures (*iumento* and *pecore*) are mentioned, whereas the Hebrew has only one (בהמה).

Lev 18:20a, 22a, and 23a (Early Wycliffe):[10]

With the wijf of thi neiȝbore thow shalt not goo togidir (v. 20a)

---

[10] Early Wycliffe and Later Wycliffe excerpts are from Josiah Forshall and Frederick Madden, eds., *The Holy Bible, Containing the Old and New Testaments, with the Apocryphal Books, in the Earliest English Versions Made from the Latin Vulgate by John Wycliffe and His Followers*, 4 vols. (Oxford: Oxford University Press, 1850), where the early and later versions appear in parallel columns.

With a maal thow shalt not be mengid, bi maner of goyng to gidere with womman (v. 22a)

With alle beestis thow shalt not goo to gidere

The Wycliffe translators used the Vulgate as their source and rendered the Latin for "copulate" and "copulation" as "go together (with)." The proscription in Latin of a male's being joined with another male in "womanly copulation"—*coitu femineo*, suggesting male receptivity—has, however, been recast as a proscription of a man's being joined with another male "by manner of going together with woman." The sense of the proscription is now altered so that it deals with the activity of the insertive party rather than the receptive party.

Lev 20:11a, 12a, 13a, and 15a (Early Wycliffe):

He that slepith with his stepdam (v. 11a)

If eny man sleepe with his sones wijf (v. 12a)

He that slepith with a maal, bi maner of goyng togidere with a womman (v. 13a)

He that with hows beeste or feelde beeste goth togider (v. 15a)

In the second group of verses, "go together with" has been retained as the idiom for sexual congress in verses 13a and 15a, "sleep with" appearing in verses 11a, 12a, and 13a. In verse 13a, "sleeping with a male" is followed up with "by manner of going together with a woman," leaving no doubt that the activity of the insertive party rather than the receptive party is being addressed. Thus, in the first preserved English translation of the Levitical proscriptions, there was a deviation from the suggestion of male receptivity in *coitu femineo*, the phrase instead being interpreted as describing the insertive agency of a man in relation to another male.

Lev 18:20a, 22a, and 23a (Later Wycliffe):

Thou schalt not do letcherie with the wijf of thi neiȝbore (v. 20a)

Thou schalt not be medlid with a man bi letcherie of womman (v. 22a)

Thou schalt not do letcherie with ony beeste (v. 23a)

The Later Wycliffe is a revision of the earlier translations undertaken by John Purvey and completed after Wycliffe's death. Quite significantly, Purvey takes a different tack on the Levitical prohibitions, bringing them back into line with the Latin. Here it is clear from verses 20a and 23a that "do letcherie with" is the translation of *coibis* ("copulate"). In verse 22a, being "medlid with a man bi letcherie of womman" is the translator's rendering of the Latin source's *commisceberis coitu femineo*, the translator attempting to convey the receptive role of the addressee suggested by the Latin.[11]

---

[11] The most recent edition of the Later Wycliffe parenthetically rephrases "bi letcherie of

Lev 20:11a, 12a, 13a, and 15a (Later Wycliffe):

If a man slepith with hys stepdamme (v. 11a)

If ony man slepith with his sones wijf (v. 12a)

If a man slepith with a man, bi letcherie of a womman (v. 13a)

He that doith letcherie with a greet beeste, ethir a litil beeste (v. 15a)

Again, the Later Wycliffe closely follows the Latin source; "slepith with" is a literal rendering of *dormierit cum* that clearly expresses the insertive agency of a man in verses 11a and 12a. Although "if a man slepith with a man" in verse 13a follows the formula of verses 11a and 12a and is enough by itself to express the insertive agency of a man in connection with another male, the addition of the qualifier "bi letcherie of a womman"—as in 18:22a—reflects the translator's understanding of *commisceberis coitu femineo* as describing the receptive role of the man who is the subject of the verse.

Lev 18:20a, 22a, and 23a (Tyndale):[12]

Thou ſhalt not lye with thy neghbours wife (v. 20a)

Thou ſhalt not lye with mankynde as with womankynde (v. 22a)

Thou ſhalt lye with no maner of beeſte (v. 23a)

In all three of these verses, the Tyndale translator consistently uses "lye with" to express the insertive agency of a man, and his use of "as with womankynde" in verse 22a underscores that perceived insertive agency. Although the Hebrew source of verse 22a literally states that the addressee is not to "lie down lyings down of a woman," the translator here apparently misconstrued "*of* a woman" as "*as with* womankind."

Lev 20:11a, 12a, 13a, and 15a (Tyndale):

Yf a man lye with his fathers wife (v. 11a)

Yf a man lye with his doughter in lawe (v. 12a)

Yf a man lye with the mankynde after the maner as with womã kynd (v. 13a)

Yf a man lye with a beeſt (v. 15a)

---

womman" as "like in fleshly coupling with a woman," tweaking it to apply to the insertive party instead of the receptive party (Terence P. Noble, ed., *Wycliffe's Old Testament Translated by John Wycliffe and John Purvey* [Vancouver: Terence P. Noble, 2010]). The same parenthetical rephrasing also occurs in 20:13.

[12] J. I. Mombert, ed., *William Tyndale's Five Books of Moses, Called the Pentateuch, Being a Verbatim Reprint of the Edition of M.CCCCC.XXX.* (New York: Randolph, 1884).

Again, "lye with" is consistently used in every verse to express the insertive agency of a man. The translator's choice of "after the maner as with womã kynd" in verse 13a underscores his interpretation of that verse as dealing with the activity of the insertive party. As noted above, the translator apparently misconstrued the Hebrew "*of* a woman" as "*as with* womankind."

In conclusion, Lev 18:22 and 20:13 are set in contexts where the prohibition of a man's sexual penetration of women or animals is expressed in straightforward terminology that should apply across the board to the penetration of males as well. Yet the Hebrew text and most of the early translations employ curious locutions and qualifiers where simple proscriptions directed to the insertive party ought to suffice, assuming that the insertive party was the intended subject of the verses. These locutions and qualifiers, however—lie down lyings down of a woman, lie down a lying down of a woman, be joined with in womanly copulation, sleep with in womanly copulation, be joined with by lechery of a woman, and sleep with by lechery of a woman—begin to make sense when understood as phraseology intended to change the focus of the verses from an insertive party to a receptive party. In the Early Wycliffe and Tyndale versions, however, the Latin and Hebrew sources were mistranslated as prohibiting a man's sexual congress with another male "by manner of going together with a woman" or "as with a woman," diametrically altering the meaning of the verses so that they apply to an insertive rather than a receptive party. This misunderstanding of the verses probably gained traction because of the proliferation of the Tyndale version via the printing press, and subsequent versions were duly influenced and followed suit.

The fact that the Early Wycliffe and the Tyndale versions rendered the passages in such a way as to refer to the insertive party indicates that there was a difference of opinion among some translators of the Latin and Hebrew. That being the case, however, modern adherents of the view that the passages deal with the insertive party need to account for the aforementioned locutions and qualifiers attached to the passages if they do in fact pertain to the insertive party. If, on the other hand, the passages refer to the receptive party, as argued here, certain exegetical consequences are bound to follow. Traditionally understood as referring to the insertive party, the passages have lent themselves to interpretations suggesting that they may have been directed in part against such practices as consorting with male temple prostitutes who played the receptive role. Understood as referring to the receptive party, however, the passages reflect a common taboo in antiquity against a male's assuming a female function; the coculpability of the insertive party in Lev 20:13 was probably a subsequent development.

Rabbinic Traditions in Jerome's Translation of the Book of Numbers

MATTHEW KRAUS
matthew.kraus@uc.edu
University of Cincinnati, Cincinnati, OH 45221

Although the possibility of rabbinic traditions informing Jerome's translation of the Bible "according to the Hebrews," the so-called Vulgate, has long been acknowledged, identification of these traditions remains a desideratum. Such identification involves challenging but manageable source-critical issues. We now know more about Jerome's more general methods from the works of Adam Kamesar, Hillel Newman, and Michael Graves. They indicate that Jerome's grammatically informed *recentiores*-rabbinic philology provides a basis for incorporating unreferenced oral rabbinic traditions in his translation. In this article, I examine several texts from the book of Numbers that reflect Jerome's practices, including his utilization of these Jewish traditions. In addition, I outline a method for securely determining rabbinic influences. Finally, the close textual analysis contributes to recent developments in translation studies and Hieronymian studies. Attention to the process of the translator offers a perspective that differs from a simple comparison between the source text and target text. Such a "thick" description of Vulgate Numbers shows how translation can create a bridge, not a wall, between Jews and Christians.

Jerome of Stridon (348–420 CE), who spent the bulk of his final years in Bethlehem, has long interested scholars of the history of Judaism because of his numerous references to Jews, Judaism, and Jewish traditions in his literary corpus. The most significant contribution in recent years has been Hillel Newman's doctoral dissertation from Hebrew University on Jerome and the Jews, in which he gathered and analyzed every explicit reference to Jews, the Hebrews, my Jewish teacher, and the like.[1] These attributions to Jewish informants include teachings

I am grateful for the helpful comments and suggestions of the anonymous *JBL* reviewer.

[1] Hillel Newman, "Jerome and the Jews" [in Hebrew] (PhD diss., Hebrew University, 1997). Other important studies include Moritz Rahmer, *Die "Quaestiones in Genesin,"* vol. 1 of *Die hebräischen Traditionen in den Werken des Hieronymus* (Breslau: Schletter, 1861); Rahmer, *Die Commentarii zu den zwölf kleinen Propheten*, vol. 2 of *Die hebräischen Traditionen in den Werken des Hieronymus* (Berlin: Poppelauer, 1902); Samuel Krauss, "The Jews in the Works of the Church

539

that appear in rabbinic literature. He did not directly read rabbinic texts but had access to oral traditions preserved in the targums, Midrash, and Talmud.[2] Newman further notes that discovering and analyzing the influences not explicitly assigned to Jewish sources remain a desideratum.[3] Many such influences have yet to be discovered in Jerome's translation of the Bible from Hebrew into Latin, the so-called Vulgate, which Jerome describes as the version "according to the Hebrews" (*iuxta Hebraeos*) based on the Hebrew truth (*Hebraica veritas*).[4] This study, in

---

Fathers," *JQR* 5 (1892): 122–57; 6 (1893): 82–99, 225–61; Louis Ginzberg, *Genesis*, vol. 2 of *Die Haggada bei den Kirchenvätern und in der apokryphischen Litteratur* (Berlin: S. Calvary, 1900); Jay Braverman, *Jerome's Commentary on Daniel: A Study of Comparative Jewish and Christian Interpretations of the Hebrew Bible*, CBQMS 7 (Washington, DC: Catholic Biblical Association of America, 1978); Pierre Jay, *L'exégèse de saint Jérôme d'après son 'Commentaire sur Isaïe'* (Paris: Études augustiniennes, 1985); Dennis Brown, *Vir Trilinguis: A Study in the Biblical Exegesis of Saint Jerome* (Kampen: Kok Pharos, 1992); Sarah Kamin, "The Theological Significance of the Hebraica Veritas in Jerome's Thought," in *Sha'arei Talmon: Studies in the Bible, Qumran, and the Ancient Near East Presented to Shemaryahu Talmon*, ed. Michael Fishbane and Emanuel Tov (Winona Lake, IN: Eisenbrauns, 1992), 243–53; Günter Stemberger, "Hieronymus und die Juden seiner Zeit," in *Begegnungen zwischen Christentum und Judentum in Antike und Mittelalter: Festschrift für Heinz Schreckenberg*, ed. Dietrich-Alex Koch and Hermann Lichtenberger, SIJD 1 (Göttingen: Vandenhoeck & Ruprecht, 1993), 347–64; Adam Kamesar, *Jerome, Greek Scholarship, and the Hebrew Bible: A Study of the Quaestiones hebraicae in Genesin*, OCM (Oxford: Clarendon, 1993); Benjamin Kedar-Kopfstein, "Jewish Traditions in the Writings of Jerome," in *The Aramaic Bible: Targums in Their Historical Context*, ed. D. R. G. Beattie and M. J. McNamara, JSOTSup 166 (Sheffield: JSOT Press, 1994), 420–30; Andrew S. Jacobs, *Remains of the Jews: The Holy Land and Christian Empire in Late Antiquity*, Divinations (Stanford, CA: Stanford University Press, 2004); Michael Graves, *Jerome's Hebrew Philology: A Study Based on His Commentary on Jeremiah*, VCSup 90 (Leiden: Brill, 2007); Megan Williams, "Lessons from Jerome's Jewish Teachers: Exegesis and Cultural Interaction in Late Antique Palestine," in *Jewish Biblical Interpretation and Cultural Exchange: Comparative Exegesis in Context*, ed. Natalie B. Dohrmann and David Stern (Philadelphia: University of Pennsylvania Press, 2008), 66–86; Hillel Newman, "How Should We Measure Jerome's Hebrew Competence?," in *Jerome of Stridon: His Life, Writings, and Legacy*, ed. Andrew Cain and Josef Lössl (Surrey, England: Ashgate, 2009), 131–40.

[2] Newman, "Jerome and the Jews," 70–74. Identifying the date and origin of a rabbinic pericope can be fraught with uncertainty (H. L. Strack and G. Stemberger, *Introduction to the Talmud and Midrash*, trans. Markus Bockmuehl [Minneapolis: Fortress, 1992], 50–66). Therefore, a Jewish tradition explicitly cited by Jerome establishes a late fourth-century Palestine provenance. See Matthew Kraus, "Christian, Jews, and Pagans in Dialogue: Saint Jerome on Ecclesiastes 12:1–7," *HUCA* 70–71 (1999–2000): 200–207.

[3] Newman, "Jerome and the Jews," 203.

[4] Brown, *Vir Trilinguis*, 87 n. 1. *Vulgate* is the conventional term for Jerome's translation directly from the Hebrew. In his own time, *Vulgate* would have referred to the Old Latin, whereas he described his own work as a translation "from the Hebrew" (*de hebraeo, Prol. Reg., Prol. in Pent., Prol. Job*) or "according to the Hebrews" (*iuxta Hebraeos, Prol. Job*). On Jerome's reliance on the *Hebraica veritas* ("Hebrew truth"), see Brown, *Vir Trilinguis*, 55–86; Stefan Rebenich, "Jerome: The 'Vir Trilinguis' and the 'Hebraica Veritas,'" *VC* 47 (1993): 50–77; and Christoph Markschies, "Hieronymus und die 'Hebraica Veritas': Ein Beitrag zur Archäologie des protestantischen

addition to recovering rabbinic traditions in Vulgate book of Numbers, establishes definitive criteria for verifying its Jewish exegetical sources.

I. Jerome and Jewish Exegetical Sources

Previous attempts to mine the Vulgate for rabbinic traditions have been sporadic and have lacked methodological precision.[5] Such studies assume that a "free"

Schriftverständnisses?," in *Die Septuaginta zwischen Judentum und Christentum*, ed. Martin Hengel and Anna Maria Schwemer, WUNT 72 (Tübingen: Mohr Siebeck, 1994), 131–81.

[5] Victor Aptowitzer, "Rabbinische Parallelen und Aufschlüsse zu Septuaginta und Vulgata," *ZAW* 29 (1909): 241–52; Friedrich Stummer, "Spuren jüdischer und christlicher Einflüsse auf die Übersetzung der grossen Propheten durch Hieronymus," *JPOS* 8 (1928): 35–48; Stummer, "Einige Beobachtungen über die Arbeitsweise des Hieronymus bei der Übersetzung des Alten Testaments aus der Hebraica Veritas," *Bib* 10 (1929): 3–30; Stummer, "'Convallis Mamre' und Verwandtes," *JPOS* 12 (1932): 6–12; Stummer, "Beiträge zur Lexikographie der lateinischen Bibel," *Bib* 18 (1937): 23–50; Stummer, "Beiträge zu dem Problem 'Hieronymus und die Targumim,'" *Bib* 18 (1937): 174–81; Stummer, "תכו = appropinquant: Ein Beitrag zur Erklärung der Vulgata von Dt 33b," in *Alttestamentliche Studien: Friedrich Nötscher zum sechzigsten Geburtstag, 19 Juli 1950, gewidmet von Kollegen, Freunden und Schülern*, ed. Hubert Junker and Johannes Botterweck, BBB 1 (Bonn: Hanstein, 1950), 265–70; Albert Condamin, "L'influence de la tradition juive dans la version de saint Jérôme," *RSR* 5 (1914): 1–21; Cyrus Gordon, "Rabbinic Exegesis in the Vulgate of Proverbs," *JBL* 49 (1930): 384–416, https://doi.org/10.2307/3259597; Felix Reuschenbach, *Hieronymus als Übersetzer der Genesis* (Limburg: Lahn, 1948). Regrettably, Reuschenbach did not include the discussion of rabbinic influences promised in the table of contents. See also Colette Estin, *Les psautiers de Jérôme à la lumière des traductions juives antérieures*, CBLa 15 (Rome: San Girolamo, 1984); Benjamin Kedar-Kopfstein, "The Vulgate as Translation" (PhD diss., Hebrew University, 1968); Kedar-Kopfstein, "The Latin Translations," in *Mikra: Text, Translation, Reading, and Interpretation of the Hebrew Bible in Ancient Judaism and Early Christianity*, ed. Martin Jay Mulder, CRINT 2.1 (Philadelphia: Fortress, 1988), 299–338; David Paul McCarthy, "Saint Jerome's Translation of the Psalms: The Question of Rabbinic Tradition," in *"Open Thou Mine Eyes ...": Essays on Aggadah and Judaica Presented to Rabbi William G. Braude on His Eightieth Birthday and Dedicated to His Memory* (Hoboken, NJ: Ktav, 1992).

There has been a recent upsurge of exegetical studies of the Vulgate: see John S. Cameron, "The Vir Triculus: An Investigation of Classical, Jewish and Christian Influences on Jerome's Translation of the *Psalter iuxta Hebraeos*" (PhD diss., Oxford, 2006); Cameron, "The Rabbinic Vulgate?," in Cain and Lössl, *Jerome of Stridon*, 117–30; Matthew Kraus, "The Late Antique Context of Jewish Exegetical Traditions in Jerome's Targum of the Bible," in *Midrash in Context: Proceedings of the 2004 and 2005 SBL Consultation on Midrash*, ed. Lieve Teugels and Rivka Ulmer (Piscataway, NJ: Gorgias, 2007), 17–37; Friedrich Avemarie, "Hieronymus und die jüdische Genesis: Hebraicae quaestiones und die Vulgata im Vergleich," in *Moderne Religionsgeschichte im Gespräch: Interreligiös, interkulturell, interdisziplinär; Festschrift für Christoph Elsas*, ed. Adelheid Herrmann-Pfandt (Berlin: EB-Verlag, 2010), 74–93; Sebastian Weigert, *Hebraica veritas: Übersetzungsprinzipien und Quellen der Deuteronomiumübersetzung des Hieronymus*, BWANT 207 (Stuttgart: Kohlhammer, 2016); Matthew Kraus, *Jewish, Christian, and Classical Exegetical Traditions in Jerome's Translation of the Book of Exodus: Translation Technique and the Vulgate*,

rendition of the Hebrew with a midrashic parallel constitutes direct rabbinic influence. The source of an exegetical rendering, however, could be one of Jerome's many *Vorlagen*—the Hebrew itself, the Septuagint, the Old Latin translation of the Septuagint, or the Greek recensions of Aquila, Symmachus, and Theodotion—or Christian, classical, or nonrabbinic Jewish literature.[6] The isolated comparison of the Latin target text with the Hebrew source text in Vulgate research stems from an early trend in translation studies to focus on the character and possibility of a translation.[7] These studies read the Vulgate more as an interpretation of the Hebrew language than as biblical commentary. Recent work in translation studies, however, has brought attention to translators as cultural mediators who, in the linguistic process of producing the target text from the source text, apply their historically situated background as interpretive tools.[8] For our purposes, this means entertaining the possibility that Jerome could use his Jewish knowledge and informants along with his *Vorlagen* as he engaged in biblical exegesis through the medium of biblical translation.[9] Just as he includes rabbinic traditions when recounting

---

VCSup 41 (Leiden: Brill, 2017). Rabbinic influence on the Vulgate is usually ignored in surveys of the history of biblical interpretation, as in Dennis Brown, "Jerome and the Vulgate," in *The Ancient Period*, vol. 1 of *A History of Biblical Interpretation*, ed. Alan J. Hauser and Duane F. Watson, 2 vols. (Grand Rapids: Eerdmans, 2003–2009), 364–71. In the more recent *From the Beginnings to 600*, vol. 1 of *The New Cambridge History of the Bible*, ed. Jean Carleton Paget and Joachim Schaper (Cambridge: Cambridge University Press, 2013), Pierre-Maurice Bogaert ("The Latin Bible," 505–26) and Adam Kamesar ("Jerome," 653–75) never refer to the Vulgate as a form of biblical interpretation.

[6] Cameron, "Vir Tricultus," 11–19; and Weigert, *Übersetzungsprinzipien und Quellen*, 83–214. The availability of such tools as the critical editions of the LXX (*Septuaginta, Vetus Testamentum Graecum Auctoritate Academiae Scientiarum Gottingensis editum*, 24 vols. [Göttingen:Vandenhoeck & Ruprecht, 1931–]) facilitates the consideration of his many *Vorlagen*.

[7] On traditional approaches to translation in general, see the essays in *Theories of Translation: An Anthology of Essays from Dryden to Derrida*, ed. Rainer Schulte and John Biguenet (Chicago: University of Chicago Press, 1992). On approaches to the Vulgate, see Werner Schwarz, *Principles and Problems of Biblical Translation: Some Reformation Controversies and Their Background* (Cambridge: Cambridge University Press, 1955); H. F. D. Sparks, "Jerome as a Biblical Scholar," in *From the Beginnings to Jerome*, vol. 1 of *The Cambridge History of the Bible*, ed. P. R. Ackroyd (Cambridge: Cambridge University Press, 1970), 513–15; Brown, "Jerome and the Vulgate," 359; and Eva Schulz-Flügel, "The Latin Old Testament Tradition," in *From the Beginnings to the Middle Ages (until 1300)*, vol. 1 of *Hebrew Bible/Old Testament: The History of Its Interpretation*, ed. Magne Sæbø (Göttingen: Vandenhoeck & Ruprecht, 1996), 642–62. The translation has been variously labeled as philological (Cameron, "Rabbinic Vulgate?" 125), theological (Schulz-Flügel, "Latin Old Testament," 644), rhetorical (Neil Adkin, "Biblia Catilinaria," *Maia* 55 [2003]: 93–98), and classical (Catherine Brown Tkacz, "*Labor tam utilis*: The Creation of the Vulgate," *VC* 50 [1996]: 42–72).

[8] See, e.g., Lawrence Venuti, *The Translator's Invisibility: A History of Translation*, 2nd ed. (London: Routledge, 2008) and the essays by various authors collected in *The Translation Studies Reader*, ed. Lawrence Venuti (London: Routledge, 2000).

[9] His Christian and classical learning also impact his translation. See Cameron, "Vir Tricultus," 69–124, 176–202; Kraus, "Late Antique Context," 17–37; Weigert, *Übersetzungsprinzipien und Quellen*, 25–67, 244–48; and Brown Tkacz, "*Labor tam utilis*," 42–72.

various exegeses in his commentaries, so too does he weigh rabbinic traditions when translating.[10] According to Adam Kamesar, Jerome outlines this method of "*recentiores*-rabbinic philology" in the *Quaestionum hebraicarum liber in Genesim*, a kind of preparatory work for his version "according to the Hebrews."[11] Whether he applies such an approach to his translation has rarely been comprehensively investigated.

Two recent studies comparing Vulgate Genesis to the *Quaestiones* and one study on Vulgate Deuteronomy have begun to address this lacuna.[12] In the *Quaestiones*, Jerome cites the textual versions of the Hebrew, LXX, Symmachus, Aquila, and Theodotion. Since he almost always provides a Latin translation of these versions (with or without the Hebrew and Greek), we can securely identify which option also appears in the Vulgate. According to C. T. R. Hayward, the Vulgate and *Quaestiones* agree ninety-nine times and disagree approximately eighty times, including twenty-four occasions where the Vulgate follows the LXX, even when Jerome shares concerns about the LXX.[13] Friedrich Avemarie and Sebastian Weigert agree that the *recentiores*-rabbinic philology of the *Quaestiones* influences the Vulgate, but not all of the time.[14] Despite such parallels between the Vulgate and *Quaestiones*, Hayward ultimately claims that the numerous differences between them, the omission of well-known textual cruxes, and the philological irrelevance of some Jewish traditions cited in the *Quaestones* all problematize Kamesar's contention that Jerome wrote the *Quaestones* to defend his new philological system for translating the Bible from Hebrew to Latin.[15] The purpose of the *Quaestiones* is not my concern here, although I am inclined to agree with Kamesar and Avemarie that the work develops his method for translation and promotes his version according to the Hebrew.[16] Rather, Hayward's claim that the Vulgate avoids Hebrew traditions valorized in the *Quaestiones* requires reconsideration.[17] For instance, the contention that "again, Aquila's rendering of $š^e lēmīm$ as 'perfect, complete' receives Jerome's

---

[10] Kamesar, *Jerome, Greek Scholarship*, 176–91; and Newman, "Jerome and the Jews," 130–219.

[11] Kamesar, *Jerome, Greek Scholarship*, 176–91.

[12] C. T. R. Hayward, *Saint Jerome's Hebrew Questions on Genesis*, OECS (Oxford: Clarendon, 1995); Avemarie, "Hieronymus und die jüdische Genesis"; and Weigert, *Übersetzungsprinzipien und Quellen*, 158–214.

[13] Hayward, *Saint Jerome's Hebrew Questions*, 11.

[14] Weigert, *Übersetzungsprinzipien und Quellen*, 23.

[15] Hayward, *Saint Jerome's Hebrew Questions*, 8–14.

[16] Avemarie, "Hieronymus und die jüdische Genesis," 76: "Das dürfte sich einerseits dadurch erklären, dass er mit den *Quaestiones* für sein späteres Übersetzungswerk nicht nur vorarbeiten, sondern vor allem auch werben wollte."

[17] It is true that the Vulgate does not always correlate with the *Quaestiones*. For example, on Gen 11:28, although Jerome positively mentions the legend of Abraham's being thrown into the fire by the Babylonians and the rendering of אור כשדים in Gen 15:7 as *ignis Chaldeorum*, the Vulg. has *Ur Chaldeorum* in both Gen 11:28 and 15:7. See Hayward, *Saint Jerome's Hebrew Questions*, 146.

unqualified approval in *Qu. hebr. Gen.* 34:20–21," but that Gen 34:21 Vulg. (*viri isti pacifici* [שלמים] *sunt*) follows the LXX's "peaceful" is based on a misreading of *Quaestiones*.[18] "From which it is clear that what we have said above about Salem is correct" (*Qu. hebr. Gen.* on 34:20–21) is not endorsing Aquila's rendition in favor of the LXX but rather is referring to Jerome's earlier claim (*Qu. hebr. Gen.* on 33:18) that Salem has two possible meanings, "complete, perfect" (*consummata, perfecta*) or "peaceable" (*pacifica*).[19] Similar questions could be raised by other examples highlighted by Hayward.[20] In some cases where Jerome cites Jewish traditions that, according to Hayward, shed no light on philological matters, the Vulgate in fact incorporates these traditions. For example, discussions about Gen 5:25–27 (Methuselah's age indicates that he survived the flood) and Gen 21:14 (Ishmael's age when he was expelled) dealing with chronological matters have philological implications, since the Vulgate resolves the chronological issues in accordance with the *Quaestiones*.[21] The issue for Gen 21:14 is more than a chronological matter. At stake is the age of Ishmael and whether it would be possible to put him on his mother's shoulders. Clearly, according to the Latin, only the bread and waterskin were put on her shoulders.[22] Therefore, we must reconsider the assertion that "such mismatches between *Qu. hebr. Gen.* and Vulg. must prompt the question whether the former can be regarded purely and simply as a philological defence of the

---

[18] Ibid., 11.

[19] See *Qu. hebr. Gen.* on 34:20–21: Ex quo perspicuum est verum esse illud, quod supra de Salem diximus. Cf. *Qu. hebr. Gen.* on 33:18: "for this word [Salem] means both things [perfect/complete and peaceable] if the accentuation is altered a little" (ibid., 71–72).

[20] Likewise for Gen 30:11, the Vulgate has *feliciter* for בגד, although the *qere* is בא גד. In *Qu. hebr. Gen.*, Jerome refers to Aquila's rendition of Gad as "a troop comes." Hayward claims this is a discrepancy between the *Quaestiones* and the Vulgate, but again Jerome is calling attention to two options. In *Qu. hebr. Gen.*, Jerome prefers to modify Aquila to the *ketiv* ("in arms") and explains that the homophone *ba* can mean "come" or "in." Jerome concludes, however: "therefore the son of Zelpha was called Gad either 'from 'chance' or from 'under arms'" (ibid., 65). Even if the Vulgate does not have the precise word endorsed by *Qu. hebr. Gen.*, Jerome still may be following Hebrew tradition. On Gen 4:8 Jerome says the LXX is superfluous, but, as Hayward notes, the Vulgate also follows *Epist.* 36.6 and targumic traditions (*Saint Jerome's Hebrew Questions*, 122). See also on Gen 6:3 (Hayward, 130), Gen 33:1 (the Vulg. has "divided" instead of Aquila's "halved," but the Vulg. appears to be referring to two rather than three groups), Gen 14:5 (follows LXX in reading בהם [*bāhem*], "with them," instead of בחם [*bāḥom*], "in Hom," but the MT has *bəham*, which could be read as *bāhem*).

[21] In both cases, Hayward acknowledges that the Vulg. follows the Hebrew (*Saint Jerome's Hebrew Questions*, 127, 175). See Avemarie, "Hieronymus und die jüdische Genesis," 77–78, 87–88.

[22] It might be more appropriate to use a late fourth-century CE definition of philology that incorporates an interest in realia and historia for which rabbinic traditions were a significant source. See Adam Kamesar, "The Evaluation of the Narrative Aggada in Greek and Latin Patristic Literature," *JTS* 45 (1994): 37–71.

latter."²³ Rather, the *Quaestiones* does indeed accurately reflect Jerome's method of translation, namely, a sporadic consideration of various possibilities.²⁴ A commentator can share different options, but the translator must make a final decision. The *Quaestiones* records the choices considered by the translator in each of the ninety-nine times in which the *Quaestiones* and the Vulgate agree and in which Jerome could be following the Hebrew, the LXX, Aquila, Symmachus, Theodotion, or a combination. Extrapolating from the comparison between the *Quaestiones* and Vulgate Genesis, we can posit that *recentiores*-rabbinic philology guided Jerome's translation as a whole.

This study concentrates on one aspect of this methodological question: how to ascertain rabbinic influence on the Vulgate in the absence of a commentary comparable to the *Quaestiones*.²⁵ I will be unpacking some selected examples from the book of Numbers that offer an approach for distinguishing between definite evidence of rabbinic influence and plausible evidence. The book of Numbers has received little attention in Hieronymian scholarship, and its rabbinic influences have not been identified.²⁶ While a number of studies have identified rabbinic influences on the Vulgate, there is still a need for more methodological precision beyond identifying an unusual rendering that has a parallel in rabbinic literature. I offer a

---

²³ Hayward, *Saint Jerome's Hebrew Questions*, 12. As Weigert has shown, Jerome regularly, but not universally, applies his *recentiores*-rabbinic philology to Vulgate Deuteronomy (*Übersetzungsprinzipien und Quellen*, passim).

²⁴ The notion that Jerome did not consistently apply a method to his translation is not new. See Georg Grützmacher, *Hieronymus: Eine biographische Studie zur alten Kirchengeschichte*, 3 vols. (Leipzig: Dieterich 1901–1908), 2:109; Sparks, "Jerome as a Biblical Scholar," 522–27; McCarthy, "Saint Jerome's Translation of the Psalms," 155–91; and Brown, *Vir Trilinguis*, 109.

²⁵ It could be argued that parallels to rabbinic literature reflect Jerome's general knowledge of Judaism rather than specific rabbinic traditions. Such a position is plausible, since, as Newman has demonstrated, Jerome's Jewish sources are primarily oral and he most often refers to his Hebrew teachers with the generic term *Hebraeus* (Newman, "Jerome and the Jews," 70–74). Nevertheless, the rabbinic provenance of these oral traditions is confirmed by his references to Jewish sources with distinctly rabbinic terms such as *deuterotes* (תנא), *scriba* (סופר), and *sapiens* (חכם; see Benjamin Kedar, "The Latin Translations," in Mulder, *Mikra*, 299–338, here 315) as well as *legis auctor* ("legal authority"; *Praef. ad Paral. ILXX*), and *praeceptor qui apud Hebraeos primas habere putabatur* ("a teacher highly regarded among the Hebrews"; *Prol. Hiob IH*). He also mentions specific rabbis (*Epist.* 121.10 and *Comm. Isa.* 8:11–15) and even describes a tradition that he learned from his Hebrew informant (*meus Hebraeus*), "who swore that Baracchiba [Rabbi Akiva], whom alone they [the Jews] especially admire, had transmitted [*tradisse*] this explanation about this section" (*Comm. Eccl.* 4:13–16). I am grateful to the anonymous reviewer for pushing me to clarify this point.

²⁶ Most of the examples cited by Niedermán Mór could be attributed to nonrabbinic sources (*A Vulgata Viszonya Az Agádához és Targúmokhoz* [Budapest: Neuwald Illés Utódai Könyvnyomda, 1915], 32–38). For instance, the source of *ariolus* ("soothsayer") for פתורה (Num 22:5) could be ὑφηγητής ("guide") from the hexaplaric textual tradition rather than פותר חלומות ("interpreter of dreams") preserved in Num. Rab. 20.7.

procedure for securely pinpointing a rabbinic tradition: establish a rendering as unusual; determine its relationship to the Greek textual tradition; find a comparable rabbinic tradition; and confirm Jerome's awareness of the Jewish tradition in his other writings. This last criterion, although relatively simple to analyze for Vulgate Genesis because we have the *Quaestiones*, is more challenging for other books. Despite many convincing examples of Jewish influence on Vulgate Deuteronomy, there is no evidence of familiarity with the Jewish tradition beyond the translation itself.[27] To be sure, there is a certain degree of subjectivity involved in assessing a rendering's uniqueness, Greek background, and similarity to a midrash.

The examples that follow clarify these criteria for identifying rabbinic interpretations in the Vulgate. The first set of examples, dealing with renderings for technical terms, distinguishes possible rabbinic traditions from exegetical influences mediated through the Hebrew itself and/or its *Vorlagen*. I start with these examples because interpretive renditions of technical terms are normative in a translation and these examples delineate the essential problems raised by trying to identify a rabbinic tradition. Here Jerome is turning to his sources to explain a specific term. Having established the possibility that the Vulgate incorporates traditions of Jewish teachers, the subsequent examples are exegetical renditions not demanded by the Hebrew text but represent interpretations that he weaves into his translation. I explore three aspects of this influence: rabbinically mediated combinations of his *Vorlagen* (*recentiores*-rabbinic philology), a rendition motivated by his late antique context, and differentiating between possible and definite rabbinic influence.

II. Examples

A. Technical Terminology

1. Numbers 1:52
MT וחנו בני ישראל איש על מחנהו ואיש על דגלו לצבאותם
The Israelite people shall encamp, each corps by itself and each *degel* by itself, according to their divisions.[28]

Vulgate
metabuntur autem castra filii Israhel unusquisque per turmas et cuneos atque exercitum suum
The children of Israel shall measure out the camps, however, each by cavalry squadrons and by wedge of troops as well by their army.[29]

---

[27] Weigert, *Übersetzungsprinzipien und Quellen*, 158–213. The commentaries on the prophetic books were in large part completed long after the biblical translation.

[28] Trans. Baruch A. Levine, *Numbers 1–20: A New Translation with Introduction and Commentary*, AB 4A (New York: Doubleday, 1993).

[29] All translations of the Vulgate are mine.

LXX
καὶ <u>παρεμβαλοῦσιν</u> οἱ υἱοὶ Ἰσραήλ, ἀνὴρ ἐν τῇ ἑαυτοῦ <u>τάξει</u> καὶ ἀνὴρ κατὰ τὴν ἑαυτοῦ <u>ἡγεμονίαν</u>, σὺν δυνάμει αὐτῶν.
And the sons of Israel shall <u>encamp</u>, a man in his own <u>unit</u> and a man according to his own <u>rank</u>, together with their force.³⁰

Targum Onqelos and Yerušalmi
וגבר על טִקְסֵהּ, and each by his standard³¹

A close reading of Vulgate Num 1:52 lays out the methodological problem of identifying a rabbinic exegetical tradition. After the census of the Israelite tribes, chapter 1 of Numbers concludes with a brief notice about Levites, who are exempt from the census, and explains the disposition of the tabernacle. The Levites encamp around the tabernacle while the rest of the Israelites camp around the Levites. Jerome's rendition strikingly differs from the Hebrew in three places. For וחנו he uses the periphrasitc expression *castra + metabuntur* ("they will measure out the camps"); for מחנהו, rather than repeat the cognate וחנו, he uses *turmas* ("squadron of calvary or infantry"); and for דגלו ("standard") he renders *cuneos* ("wedge, unit of thickly packed troops, several soldiers deep"). Here he clearly utilizes Latin technical military terminology that is suggested but not required by the context. Is this a "philological" or "exegetical" translation? Is Jerome offering what he considers the lexical equivalent of the word, or is he incorporating an exegetical explanation into his translation? A comparison beween Num 1:52 and Num 2:2 helps answer these questions.

2. Numbers 2:2

MT איש על <u>דגלו</u> באתת לבית אבתם <u>יחנו</u> בני ישראל מנגד סביב לאהל מועד יחנו

The people of Israel <u>shall encamp</u> each by <u>his own standard</u>, <u>with the ensigns</u> of their fathers' houses; they shall encamp facing the tent of meeting on every side.³²

Vulgate
Singuli <u>per turmas signa</u> atque <u>vexilla</u> et domos cognationum suarum <u>castrametabuntur</u> filiorum Israhel per gyrum tabernaculi foederis.
Each of the children of Israel <u>shall make their camps</u> by cavalry squadrons, <u>standards, flags</u> (or troops), and houses of their families in a circle around the tent of the covenant.

---

³⁰ All translations of LXX are from NETS, http://ccat.sas.upenn.edu/nets/edition.
³¹ All translations of targums are from volumes in the series The Aramaic Bible (ArBib), ed. Martin McNamara et al. (Wilmington, DE: Glazier, 1987–).
³² Translations are from the NRSV unless otherwise noted.

LXX

Ἄνθρωπος ἐχόμενος αὐτοῦ <u>κατὰ τάγμα</u>, κατὰ <u>σημέας</u>, κατ' οἴκους πατριῶν αὐτῶν, <u>παρεμβαλέτωσαν</u> οἱ υἱοὶ Ἰσραήλ· ἐναντίοι κύκλῳ τῆς σκηνῆς τοῦ μαρτυρίου παρεμβαλοῦσιν οἱ υἱοὶ Ἰσραήλ.

Let the sons of Israel <u>encamp</u>—a person next to him, <u>according to unit</u>, according to <u>ensigns</u>, according to their paternal houses—opposite round about the tent of witness let the sons of Israel encamp.

Since Jerome renders יחנו again with *castrametabuntur* and דגלו with *turmas*, he demonstrates lexical consistency as if these are the direct Latin equivalents of the Hebrew terms. This is not completely correct, however, since דגלו more precisely corresponds with *cuneos* in Num 1:52, not *turmas*. Nor is *turmas* the regular rendition of מחנה, which Jerome renders more accurately as *castra* in Num 2:9. In addition, Jerome uses two words, *signa* and *vexilla*, to render the one term אֹת. *Signa* is the technical term for the standards of a Roman army, and *vexilla* can refer to flags used to direct a battle or the troops under these banners. Rendering general Hebrew terms with additional, more specific, and technical Latin military terms, represents exegesis. Now is this rabbinic exegesis? On the one hand, from the context it is quite clear that this is a military census, so the application of military terms does not require a rabbinic basis. That having been said, however, there are two reasons to suggest a rabbinic provenance. First, both the LXX and Targum Onqelos render מחנהו in Num 1:52 with τάξις, the technical term for the order of battle or body of soldiers.[33] Jerome could be taking his cue from his Jewish sources to employ military terminology. Second, we do have two rabbinic traditions that correlate with Jerome's rendition of Num 2:2, Lev. Rab. 36:2 and Mek., Yitro 2:

Lev. Rab. 36:2

As the vine is not planted haphazardly but in regular rows [שורות שורות], so are Israel arranged under separate standards [דגלים דגלים], as is proved by the text, *by their fathers' houses; every man with his own standard, according to the ensigns*.[34]

Mek., Yitro 2

R. Hananiah the son of Gamaliel says: Why are all these figures stated? They were stated only in the second year when Moses was about to appoint magistrates' assistants [מבסיוטינוס] over Israel, as it is said: *By their fathers' houses, every man with his own standard, according to the ensigns*.[35]

---

[33] It can also refer to the infantry quota provided by tribes.

[34] *Midrash Rabbah Leviticus*, ed. H. Freedman and Maurice Simon, trans. Judah J. Slotki (London: Soncino, 1951).

[35] *Mekilta de Rabbi Ishmael*, trans. Jacob Z. Lauterbach (Philadelphia: Jewish Publication Society, 1933).

Leviticus Rabbah associates דגלו with דגלים דגלים and compares this to vines planted in rows, which parallels *per turmas*, while the Mekilta provides an early reference to use of a Greek technical military term. Using Num 2:2 as a prooftext, the Mekilta states that Moses appointed מבסיוטינוס, which Jastrow renders as ταξιῶτεις, magistrates or military officials.

3. Numbers 3:47

MT   ולקחת חמשת חמשת שקלים לגלגלת בשקל הקדש תקח עשרים גרה השקל

You shall take five shekels apiece; reckoning by the shekel of the sanctuary, <u>the shekel of twenty gerahs</u>, you shall take them.

Vulgate
Accipies quinque siclos per singula capita ad mensuram sanctuarii <u>siclus habet obolos viginti</u>.
You shall take five shekels for each person according to the measure of the sanctuary (<u>a shekel is worth 20 obols</u>).

LXX
καὶ λήμψῃ πέντε σίκλους κατὰ κεφαλήν κατὰ τὸ δίδραχμον τὸ ἅγιον <u>λήμψῃ εἴκοσι ὀβολοὺς τοῦ σίκλου</u>
You shall also take five shekels per head. You shall take according to the holy didrachma, <u>twenty obols to the shekel</u>.
Aquila: στατῆρες ... εἴκοσι ὀβολῶν τὸν στατῆρα, the stater to twenty obols
Symmachus: στατῆρες ... εἴκοσι νομισμάτων ... ὁ στατήρ, the stater to twenty coins
Theodotion: <u>εἴκοσι ὀβολοὶ ὁ σίκλος,</u> the shekel is twenty obols

A word of caution is appropriate here because use of a technical term may not be remarkable. For example, in Num 3:47, the Vulgate explains that "a shekel is worth 20 obols" rendering גרה as obol. If one follows the Greek here, it is difficult to believe that Jerome considered obol the literal meaning of a form of biblical currency. Rather, he is using a term that makes more sense to his late antique readers.[36] Here we do not have a case where the rendition reflects Hebrew philology or exegetical traditions. It is simply a "free" rendition into contemporary language, a typical feature of translations in general. It does reflect sensitivity to the experience of his late antique readers. Thus far, then, the evidence of technical terms indicates that Jerome may possibly, but not necessarily, have relied on rabbinic traditions.

---

[36] On the Latin usage, see Charlton Lewis and Charles Short, *A Latin Dictionary* (Oxford: Clarendon, 1879), s.v. "*obolus.*"

B. Rabbinic Exegetical Technique

Numbers 20:10

MT ויקהלו משה ואהרן את הקהל אל פני הסלע ויאמר להם שמעו־נא <u>המרים</u>
המן הסלע הזה נוציא לכם מים

And Moses and Aaron gathered the assembly together before the rock, and he said to them, "Hear now, you <u>rebels</u>; shall we bring forth water for you out of this rock?"

Vulgate

congregata multitudine ante petram dixitque eis audite <u>rebelles et increduli</u> num de petra hac vobis aquam poterimus eicere

After the crowd was gathered before the rock, he said to them, "listen you <u>rebellious unbelievers</u> whether we can bring forth water from this rock for you."

Old Latin

Audite me <u>increduli</u>: Numquid de petra ista educemus vobis aquam?

LXX

καὶ ἐξεκκλησίασεν Μωυσῆς καὶ Ααρων τὴν συναγωγὴν ἀπέναντι τῆς πέτρας καὶ εἶπεν πρὸς αὐτούς ἀκούσατέ μου οἱ <u>ἀπειθεῖς</u> μὴ ἐκ τῆς πέτρας ταύτης ἐξάξομεν ὑμῖν ὕδωρ

And Moyses and Aaron held an assembly of the congregation before the rock, and he said to them, "Listen to me, you <u>disobedient</u> people; we shall not bring forth water from this rock for you, shall we?"

Others: *recentiores*, οἱ <u>φιλόνεικοι</u>, "contentious"

In the famous section describing Moses's striking the rock, which results in his being barred from leading the Israelites into the promised land, Aaron and Moses gather the people and Moses says, "Hear now you rebels [מרים]." Jerome translates the one word מורים with two words: *rebelles* ("rebellious ones") and *increduli* ("unbelievers"). We can account for each individual rendition easily. *Rebelles* reflects the Hebrew and targum, while *increduli* follows the Greek tradition.[37] It is rabbinic tradition, however, that accounts for the double rendition of a single Hebrew word! According to Numbers Rabbah, המורים, meaning "fools," has multiple meanings: "'*Hammorim*' bears many interpretations. It may mean 'fools.'… It may signify 'teachers', trying to teach their instructors. It may denote archers" (Num. Rab. 19:9). So while the individual terms reflect Jerome's philological translation, the use of two terms to render one word exemplifies rabbinic exegesis.

---

[37] Targum Onqelos: "Then Moses and Aaron gathered the congregation together in front of the rock and he said to them, 'Hear now, you rebellious ones [סרבניא], Shall we extract water for you out of this rock?" The Greek ἀπειθεῖς can mean both "unbelieving" and "disobedient."

C. Rabbinic Exegesis in a Late Antique Context

Numbers 4:20
MT   ולא יבאו לראות כבלע את־הקדש ומתו
but they shall not go in to look upon the holy things <u>even for a moment</u>, lest they die.

Vulgate
<u>alii nulla curiositate</u> videant quae sunt in sanctuario <u>priusquam involvantur</u> alioquin morientur
Let not the <u>others out of curiosity</u> see the things which are in the sanctuary <u>before they have been wrapped</u> up lest they otherwise die.

Old Latin
et non intrent <u>de subito</u> [suddenly] videre sanctum

LXX
καὶ οὐ μὴ εἰσέλθωσιν ἰδεῖν <u>ἐξάπινα</u> τὰ ἅγια καὶ ἀποθανοῦνται
and they shall by no means enter in <u>suddenly</u> to see the holy things and die

In the case of Num 4:20, three additions to the Hebrew text cannot be explained as fuller renditions of Hebrew terms. The simple meaning of the Hebrew describes the function of the Kohathites, a Levite family charged with carrying the vessels of the sanctuary. It is clear (Num 4:15) that the Kohathites will die if they carry the vessels before the Aaronides cover up these holy objects. Then in Num 4:20 the Kohathites are cautioned against entering the sanctuary suddenly, which could also result in death. Jerome, however, first states that others (*alii*), not the Kohathites, should avoid entering the sanctuary. Second, he provides an explanation why they might enter, namely, curiosity (*curiositas*). Third, he provides a more precise time frame: do not enter "before the things in the sanctuary have been wrapped up." These are clearly exegetical renditions for which we can find rabbinic influence. The time frame correlates with Targum Onqelos's rendition, which also adds the detail of not seeing the holy vessels when they are being covered ("But let them not enter and look at the sacred vessels, <u>when they are being covered</u> that they not die," ולא יעלון למחזי כד מכסן ית מני קודשא לא ימותון). A passage from b. Yoma 54a preserves a tradition that those entering to see the holy objects were not the Kohathites but all Israel.

B. Yoma 54a
R. Kattina said: Whenever Israel came up to the Festival, the curtain would be removed for them and the Cherubim were shown to them, whose bodies were intertwisted with one another and they would be thus addressed: Look! You are beloved before God as the love between man and a women. R. Hisda raised the following objection: *But they shall not*

go in to see the holy things as they are being covered, in connection with which Rab Judah in the name of Rab said: It means at the time when the vessels are being put into their cases?—R. Nahman answered: That may be compared to a bride: As long as she is in her father's house, she is reserved in regard to her husband, but when she comes to her father-in-law's house, she is no more so reserved in regard to him.[38]

As for the curiosity that might kill the Kohathite, this might have been suggested by the tradition preserved in b. Yoma, which compares the sacred vessels to a bride, whom all would be curious to see. Curiosity also has an important late antique valence. It happens to be a key theme in Apuleius's *Metamorphoses* (the Golden Ass).[39] A popular work in late antiquity, it actually applies to the context of this biblical verse.[40] Sacrilegious curiosity is what gets the main character Lucius in trouble such that he turns into a donkey, and it is also a flaw of Psyche in the well-known story of Cupid and Psyche inset into the novel.[41] Lucius is ultimately healed from the effects of his curiosity through his conversion to Isis. And curiosity is associated with death as Psyche peeks at the box containing the beauty of Persephone and falls asleep in Hades, while Lucius's rebirth through Isis implies his previous "death" through curiosity.[42] It should also be noted that interest in seeing the holy of holies is not unprecedented.[43] Despite the strong circumstantial evidence for rabbinic influence mediated through a late antique trope, this reading typically raises the methodological question of overreading a text. How can we be certain that Jerome is relying on a midrashic tradition when we know he also can apply his own insight and creativity? What we need is indisputable evidence of reliance on rabbinic tradition.

---

[38] *The Babylonian Talmud*, ed. Isidore Epstein, trans. Leo Jung (London: Soncino, 1938).

[39] See Alexander Kirichenko, "Satire, Propaganda, and the Pleasure of Reading: Apuleius' Stories of Curiosity in Context," *HSCP* 104 (2008): 339–71; and Stefan Tilg, *Apuleius' Metamorphoses: A Study in Roman Fiction* (Oxford: Oxford University Press, 2014), 68–82, https://doi.org/10.1093/acprof:oso/9780198706830.001.0001.

[40] Augustine mentions the work in *Civ.* 18.18.

[41] Apuleius, *Metam.* 11.15.1: *curiositatis inprosperae sinistrum praemium reportasti*, "you reaped the perverse reward of your ill-starred curiosity" (Tilg, *Apuleius' Metamorphoses*, 68, 72–73). See also Kirichenko, who notes the ambiguity of "curiosity" in Apuleius's *Metamorphoses*. It has both positive and negative senses (intellectual curiosity or nosiness) ("Satire, Propaganda," 351–60).

[42] On the parallel "deaths" of Psyche and Lucius, see Tilg, *Apuleius' Metamorphoses*, 76–78, 141–45.

[43] E.g., Heliodorus (2 Macc 3:13–40) and Pompey (Josephus, *A.J.*, 14.4.4 §§71–73).

D. Proof of Rabbinic Exegesis?

1. Numbers 25:4

MT   ויאמר יהוה אל משה קח את כל ראשי העם <u>והוקע</u> אותם ליהוה נגד השמש וישב חרון אף־יהוה מישראל

And the Lord said to Moses, "Take all the chiefs of the people, and <u>hang</u>[44] them in the sun before the Lord, that the fierce anger of the Lord may turn away from Israel."

Vulgate
ait ad Mosen tolle cunctos principes populi et <u>suspende</u> eos contra solem in <u>patibulis</u> ut avertatur furor meus ab Israhel
And he said to Moses, "Raise the chiefs of the people and <u>hang</u> them before the sun on <u>wooden yokes</u> so that my wrath may be averted from Israel."

Old Latin
et dixit Dominus ad Moysen Accipe duces populi et <u>ostenta</u> eos Domino contra solem et auferetur ira animationis domini ab Israel

LXX
καὶ εἶπεν κύριος τῷ Μωυσῇ λαβὲ πάντας τοὺς ἀρχηγοὺς τοῦ λαοῦ καὶ <u>παραδειγμάτισον</u> αὐτοὺς κυρίῳ ἀπέναντι τοῦ ἡλίου καὶ ἀποστραφήσεται ὀργὴ θυμοῦ κυρίου ἀπὸ Ισραηλ
And the Lord said to Moyses, "Take the chiefs of the people, and <u>make an example</u> of them to the Lord before the sun, and the anger of the Lord's wrath shall be turned away from Israel."
Aquila (and other MSS): <u>ἀνάπηξον</u>, "impale"
Symmachus: <u>κρέμασον</u>, "hang"

At first glance, we may have our "smoking spear" in the story of the Israelites, the Moabites, the Midianite woman, and Phinehas, where the Vulgate has two renditions so radical that they must be exegetical. At first the Israelites fornicate with Moabite women, which leads to idolatrous worship of Baal Peor. God summons the leaders for punishment. While the people are weeping over this terrible turn of events, an Israelite enters an inner space with a Midianite woman. Phinehas, enraged, takes a spear, follows inside and impales both of them. Of interest in the Vulgate is how Jerome renders the punishment required of the leaders of the people for the sin with the Moabite women and the term for the inner space. In Num 25:4, Jerome renders the difficult והוקע as *suspende eos ... in patibulis* ("hang them on

---

[44] Baruch A. Levine translates as "impale" (*Numbers 21–36: A New Translation with Introduction and Commentary*, AB 4A [New York: Doubleday, 2000]).

fork-shaped yokes") and in Num 25:8, Jerome describes Phinehas as entering a *lupanar* ("whorehouse").

In Num 25:4, since we also find hanging as the punishment described in the targum it looks like we have a rabbinic exegesis.[45] Targum Yerušalmi reads:

> Then the Lord said to Moses: "Take all the chiefs of the people and appoint them judges and let them give capital judgments for people who go astray after Peor. You shall <u>crucify them on wood</u> [ותצלוב יתהון ... על קיסא] before the Memra of the Lord against the sun in the early morning and with the sinking of the sun you shall lower them and bury them." Then the great anger of the Lord will turn away from Israel.[46]

This tradition, however, is found also in Symmachus, who has κρέμασον, or "hang." This is the appropriate punishment for idolaters. It should be noted that the targumim use the root צלב ("crucify"), not תלה ("hang"), so Jerome's rendition could be technically more precise, as the *patibulum* ("wooden yoke") was part of the process of crucifixion.[47] In fact, Symmachus and Jerome could be interacting in different ways with the same tradition preserved in b. Sanh. 34b:

> R. Shimi b. Hiyya said: Scripture states, *And hang [we-hokaʾ] them up unto the Lord in the face of the sun*. Whence do we know that *hokaʾa* means hanging? — From the verse, *And we will hang them up [we-hokaʾanum] unto the Lord in Gibeah of Saul, the chosen of the Lord* (II Sam. 21.6).[48]

Symmachus agrees that והוקע must be rendered as "hang." Jerome's version "hang … on wooden yokes" is synonymous with his rendition of the same term (והוקענום)

---

[45] See Joseph Baumgarten, "Does *tlh* in the Temple Scroll Refer to Crucifixion?," *JBL* 91 (1972): 472–81, here 476, https://doi.org/10.2307/3263681.

[46] Cf. Tg. Neof. יצלבון על יצלבון, "They shall crucify on a cross." Cf. Sifre Balak 1: "And God said to Moses, take all the chiefs of the people. Judges. And they would crucify [צולבים] the sinners opposite the sun" (my translation).

[47] John Granger Cook, *Crucifixion in the Mediterranean World*, WUNT 327 (Tübingen: Mohr Siebeck, 2015), 16–32. Baumgarten contends that תלה does not refer to crucifixion ("*Tlh* in the Temple Scroll," 476–78).

[48] Adapted from *The Babylonian Talmud*, ed. Isidore Epstein, trans. Jacob Schachter (London: Soncino, 1938). See also Num. Rab. 20:23, "*And the Lord said unto Moses: Take all the chiefs of the people, and hang them up* (R. Judan says, he hanged [תלה] the chiefs of the people because they had not checked the people)." The legal meaning of תלה ("hang") has a long history beginning with Deut 21:22: "When someone is convicted of a crime punishable by death and is executed, and you hang him on a tree." In the Temple Scroll (11QT LXIV, 6–13), the order of Deut 21:22 is reversed: "you shall hang him also on the tree and he shall die." Hanging becomes a form of capital punishment rather than corpse humiliation as in Deuteronomy. צלב is the Aramaic translation of תלה and can refer to a form of capital punishment. Jerome renders Deut 21:22 as *adjudicatus morti adpensus fuerit in patibulo*, "after being condemned to death, he will be hung on a wooden yoke," which is closer to the tradition in 11QT. See Baumgarten, "*Tlh* in the Temple Scroll," 472–81. I am grateful to the anonymous reviewer for alerting me to this issue and the reference.

in 2 Sam 21:6 as *crucifigamus*, which happens to be the same biblical parallel that is cited in the Talmud. Thus, he accepts the principle that the הוקע in Numbers and 2 Samuel share the same meaning.[49] Nevertheless, we cannot rule out Symmachus as the exegetical source.

2. Numbers 25:7–8

MT ויכא פינחס בן אלעזר בן אהרון הכהן ויקם מתוך העדה ויקח רמח בידו
ויבא אחר איש־ישראל אל הקבה וידקר את שניהם את איש ישראל ואת האשה אל קבתה

When Phinehas the son of Eleazar, son of Aaron the priest, saw it, he rose and left the congregation, and took a spear in his hand [8] and went after the man of Israel into the <u>inner room</u>, and pierced both of them, the man of Israel and the woman, through her body.

Vulgate

quod cum vidisset Finees filius Eleazari filii Aaron sacerdotis surrexit de medio multitudinis et arrepto pugione 8 ingressus est post virum israhelitem in <u>lupanar</u> et perfodit ambos simul virum scilicet et mulierem in locis genitalibus

When Phinehas son of Eleazar son of Aaron the priest saw this, he arose from amidst the crowd, and, having snatched a short sword, he entered after the Israelite man into the <u>brothel</u> and impaled both the man and the woman simultaneously in the genital areas

LXX

καὶ ἰδὼν Φινεες υἱὸς Ελεαζαρ υἱοῦ Ααρων τοῦ ἱερέως ἐξανέστη ἐκ μέσου τῆς συναγωγῆς καὶ λαβὼν σειρομάστην ἐν τῇ χειρὶ 8 εἰσῆλθεν ὀπίσω τοῦ ἀνθρώπου τοῦ Ισραηλίτου εἰς τὴν <u>κάμινον</u> καὶ ἀπεκέντησεν ἀμφοτέρους τόν τε ἄνθρωπον τὸν Ισραηλίτην καὶ τὴν γυναῖκα διὰ τῆς μήτρας αὐτῆς...

And when Phinees son of Eleazar son of Aaron the priest saw it, he arose from the midst of the congregation. And he took a barbed lance in his hand, ⁸and he went in after the Israelite man into <u>the alcove</u> and pierced both of them, both the Israelite man and the woman through her womb.

Aquila: τέγος, "roof"

Symmachus: εἰς τὸ πορνεῖον, "brothel"; also Syro-Hexapla

It would seem that the strong possibility of a rabbinic tradition in the first part of the Phinehas story is confirmed by the appearance of *lupanar* ("whorehouse") in Num 25:8. There is nothing in the Hebrew קובה that suggests Jerome's *lupanar*,

---

[49] Alison Salvesen, *Symmachus in the Pentateuch*, JSSMS 15 (Manchester: University of Manchester, 1991), 137–39. The Greek for crucify (σταυρόω) does not appear in the LXX and versions.

which, therefore, must derive from an exegetical tradition.⁵⁰ Since in the Talmud קובה clearly connotes a brothel, we seem to have secure proof of a rabbinic source.⁵¹ Yet Symmachus also has brothel, and we find similar terminology in Origen (*Hom. Num.* 20.5: *prostibulum*, "brothel") and Philo (*Mos.* 1.302: πρὸς πορνήν, "to a prostitute"). Nevertheless, although conclusive evidence of rabbinic influence is lacking here, it does raise the question as to why Jerome adopts this particular rendition. I suggest that he appropriates an interpretive tradition that supports his overall reading of the passage. He refers to this story in his letters as the time of Israelite fornication.⁵²

E. Proof of Rabbinic Exegesis

Numbers 24:24
MT   וצים מיד כתים וענו אשור וענו עבר וגם הוא עדי אבד
But <u>ships shall come from Kittim</u>
and shall afflict Asshur and Eber;
and he also shall come to destruction.

Vulgate
<u>venient in trieribus de Italia</u> superabunt Assyrios vastabuntque Hebraeos et ad extremum etiam ipsi peribunt
<u>They will come in triremes from Italy</u>, they will conquer the Assyrians and destroy the Hebrews; even they themselves will ultimately perish.

LXX
<u>καὶ ἐξελεύσεται ἐκ χειρὸς Κιτιαίων</u> καὶ κακώσουσιν Ασσουρ καὶ κακώ-σουσιν Εβραίους καὶ αὐτοὶ ὁμοθυμαδὸν ἀπολοῦνται
<u>And one shall go forth from the hand of Kitieans</u>, and they shall harm Assour, and they shall harm Ebreans, and they too shall perish together.

⁵⁰ In fact, the Hebrew in question, אֶל־הַקֻּבָּה, is a *hapax legomenon* that probably means some kind of tent (Levine, *Numbers 21–36*, 287–88).

⁵¹ See b. 'Abod. Zar. 17b: "They sentenced … his daughter to be consigned to a brothel [קובה של זונות]." It could be objected that at stake is a lexical issue, not an exegetical one, and Jerome is following the normal definition of the word in his time. I would counter that the peculiarity of the Latin and its hermeneutical implications reflects an exegetical moment. Moreover, a single word may possess deep significance. Jerome's rendition of קיקיון (Jonah 4:6) as *hedera* ("ivy") rather than the traditional *cucurbita* ("gourd") caused a riot in North Africa (Augustine, *Ep.* 71.3; Jerome, *Epist.* 112.21), and the targumim, both Onqelos and the more expansive ones, include exegetical renditions of single words (see, e.g., Michael Klein, "The Aramaic Targumim: Translation and Interpretation," in *Michael Klein on the Targums: Collected Essays 1972–2002*, ed. Avigdor Shinan and Rimon Kasher, SAIS 11 [Leiden: Brill, 2011], 3–18).

⁵² Cf. e.g., *Epist.* 64.2; 78.43; and 147.5. His rendition of Ezek 16:24 ותבני לך גב ותעשי־לך רמה בכל רחוב, "you built yourself a platform and made yourself a lofty place in every square," as *et aedificasti tibi lupanar et fecisti tibi prostibulum in cunctis plateis* also renders the more general Hebrew "platform" and "lofty place" with the more specific "whorehouse."

Numbers 24:24 provides a certain example of a rendition based on a rabbinic interpretation because of explicit evidence external to the translation that confirms Jerome's awareness of Jewish tradition. As in the previous examples, a nonliteral translation alerts us to an exegesis that has parallels in rabbinic literature. For "but ships shall come from Kittim" Jerome has "they will come in triremes from Italy." The connection between Kittim and Romans appears already in Pesher Habakkuk, and we have references to Rome and Italy for Kittim in the targumim on Num 24:24.[53] What is unique about this rendition, however, is that Jerome explicitly attributes this to his Jewish sources.[54] In his commentary on Dan 11:30–31, Jerome explains his exegesis of a similar phrase in Dan 11:30 ובאו בו ציים כתים as "And triremes [or Italians] and Romans shall come":

> The Jews, however, would have us understand this as referring ... to the Romans, of whom it was earlier stated: "And triremes (or Italians) and Romans shall come and he shall be humbled." ... By the terms "siim" and "chetim", which we have rendered as "triremes" and "Romans," the Hebrews would have us understand "Italians" and "Romans."[55]

He explicitly attributes a connection between Kittim, Romans, and triremes to Jewish tradition.[56] Since Jerome wrote the commentary on Daniel in 407, he was aware of the Jewish tradition earlier when translating the Pentateuch and so he must have applied the rabbinic tradition both to his exegesis of Daniel and to his translation (he renders Dan 11:30 as *et venient super eum trieres et Romani*).[57] That Jerome attributes triremes and Italy/Romans to a Jewish tradition that happens to be preserved in the targumim is incontrovertible evidence that Num 24:24 is an exegetical, rabbinic translation.

---

[53] Timothy Lim, "Kittim," in *Encyclopedia of the Dead Sea Scrolls*, ed. Lawrence H. Schiffman and James C. VanderKam (Oxford: Oxford University Press, 2000 [e-book]). Targum Onqelos has "and the company/band shall be gathered from Rome"; Targum Yerušalmi I has "Now expeditions shall be summoned with implements of war and shall come out with great numbers from Lombarnia and from the *land of Italy* and be joined by legions who shall come out of Rome and Constantinople"; and Targum Neofiti renders "Numerous multitudes shall come forth in Liburnian ships of insolent language from the region of Italy."

[54] Mór notes the rabbinic basis of the Vulgate without reference to the *Commentary on Daniel* (*Vulgata Viszonya*, 37–38).

[55] Iudaei autem ... de Romanis intellegi volunt de quibus supra dictum est: *et venient trieres (sive Itali) atque Romani et humiliabitur* ... "siim" quippe et "chetim" quos nos "trieres" et "Romanos" interpretati sumus, Hebraei "Italos" volunt intellegi atque "Romanos" (trans. Braverman, *Jerome's Commentary on Daniel*).

[56] Ibid., 115–18. Braverman correctly notes that Jerome sides with Porphyry, who also attributes this to the Romans, specifically referring to Popilius Laenas.

[57] The translation of Daniel is dated to sometime between Jerome's completion of the prophets in 394 CE and the entire biblical translation by 404 CE (Bogaert, "Latin Bible," 515–16).

F. Moving the Argument Further

Numbers 10:5–7

MT ותקעתם תרועה ונסעו המחנות החנים קדמה: ותקעתם תרועה שנית ונסעו המחנות החנים תימנה תרועה יתקעו למסעיהם: ובהקהיל את־הקהל תקועו ולא תריעו:

When you blow an alarm, the camps that are on the east side shall set out. ⁶And when you blow an alarm the second time, the camps that are on the south side shall set out. An alarm is to be blown whenever they are to set out. ⁷But when the assembly is to be gathered together, you shall blow, but you shall not sound an alarm.

Vulgate

sin autem prolixior [more extensive (sound)] atque concisus clangor [short or broken sound] increpuerit movebunt castra primi qui sunt ad orientalem plagam ⁶in secundo autem sonitu et pari ululatu tubae [equal howling of the trumpet] levabunt tentoria qui habitant ad meridiem et iuxta hunc modum reliqui facient ululantibus tubis [and the rest will make the sound howling trumpets in this manner] in profectione ⁷quando autem congregandus est populus simplex tubarum clangor [plain sound of the trumpets] erit et non concise ululabunt [they will not howl briefly/brokenly].

Old Latin

et tuba canetis significationem primam et promovebant castra et constituentur ad orientem. ⁶et tuba canetis significationem secundam et promovebant castra et constituentur ad libanum. et tuba canetis significationem tertiam et promovebant castra et constituentur ad boream. et tuba canetis significationem quartam et promovebant castra et constituentur ad aquilonem: significationem tuba canent in pro motu eorum. ⁷et cum congregabitis synagogam, tuba canite et non significationem.

Aquila: ἀλαλαγμόν, "shouting" (for σημασίαν, "signal")

My final example includes the criteria of unusual translation, midrashic references, and evidence external to the translation itself. A comparison between the Vulgate and the Old Latin, which is very close to the Greek of the LXX, highlights Jerome's unique incorporation of various sounds of the horns. Numbers 10:5–7, which refers to military trumpets, must be read in conjunction with Num 10:10, which connects these trumpets to a liturgical context.[58] A careful reading of the Hebrew,

---

[58] Vulgate Num 10:10: si quando habebitis epulum et dies festos et kalendas canetis tubis super holocaustis et pacificis victimis ut sint vobis in recordationem Dei vestri ("Whenever you will have a feast and festival days and the kalends, you will sound with the trumpets over the burnt offerings and peace sacrifices so that they may be a remembrance of your God").

especially verse 7, indicates two types of trumpet sounds, *təqîʿâ* (תקע) and *tərûʿâ* (תרע).[59] Jerome not only detects this difference but exegetically explains the difference in his translation. He translates the sounds variously as *prolixior* ("more extended"), *concisus* ("short" or "broken up"), *pari ululatu* ("counter, equal howling"), *simplex tubarum clangor* ("the plain sound of the trumpets"), and *non concise ululabunt* ("they will not howl brokenly"). Based on his rendering of verse 7, *təqîʿâ* refers to the simple, plain, extended sound, and *tərûʿâ* refers to broken-up howling. This distinction parallels rabbinic traditions in the Mishnah and Pirqe Rabbi Eliezer about the shofar. According to m. Roš Haš. 4:9, "the length of the *təqîʿâ* is equal to three *tərûʿôt* and the length of a *tərûʿâ* to three *yəbābôt*."[60] What are *yəbābôt*? In Pirqe Rabbi Eliezer 32, *yəbābâ* is equated to ילל, which is cognate with the Vulgate's *ululate* (*ululabunt*):

> He [Samael] said to her: Thy husband, Abraham, has taken thy son Isaac and slain him and offered him up as a burnt offering upon the altar. She began to weep and to cry aloud three times [ומיללת שלשה יבבות], corresponding to the three sustained notes of the shofar [תקיעות], and she gave forth three howlings [יבבות יללות] corresponding to the three disconnected short notes [יבבות] [of the shofar] and her soul fled and she died.[61]

When Samael announced to Sarah about the binding of Isaac, she cried, literally ululating three *yəbābôt*, which is explicitly connected to the sounding of the shofar (תקיעת השופר). We learn from the Mishnah and Pirqe Rabbi Eliezer that a *təqîʿâ* is longer than a *tərûʿâ* and a *tərûʿâ* consists of ululations. This is the exact sense of the Vulgate, rendering תקע as *prolixior* (literally, "longer, more drawn out") and *simplex* ("plain") and תרע as a short, broken-up ululation/howling (*concise ululabunt*). Numbers 10:5–7, however, is referring to trumpets, so the connection to the shofar sounds on Roš Haššanah may seem farfetched. As early as Sifre, however, the passages from Numbers are already associated with Roš Haššanah and the shofar sounds.[62] In addition, a couple of references external to the Vulgate strongly suggest Jerome's awareness of the rabbinic tradition. He demonstrates familiarity with the current Jewish practice of sounding the shofar when he notes, "whence also as a sign of the ram that was sacrificed even today the Jews are accustomed to sound the horn."[63] In his commentary on Hosea, he defines the Hebrew שופר as a

---

[59] Cf. Sifre, Behaalotecha 16.

[60] M. Roš Haš. 4:9: שעור תקיעה כשלש תרועות. שעור תרועה כשלש יבבות (my translation). According to b. Roš Haš. 33b, *yəbābôt* can mean drawing a long sigh or short, piercing cries: מר סבר: גנוחי גנח, ומר סבר: ילולי יליל.

[61] *Pirke de Rabbi Eliezer*, trans. Gerald Friedlander (New York: Bloch, 1916).

[62] Sifre, Behaalotecha 19.

[63] Jerome, *Qu. hebr. Gen.* 22:14: Unde et in signum dati arietus solent etiam nunc cornu clangere. See Newman, "Jerome and the Jews," 165.

curved horn.⁶⁴ Thus, he may have actually heard and seen a shofar. It is possible that he saw artistic representations of the shofar, but his detailed knowledge of the sounds and the close textual parallels between the Vulgate and rabbinic passages prove a direct encounter with both the sound of the shofar and its rabbinic traditions.⁶⁵ Jerome does not actually associate the ram's horn with Roš Haššanah, and he has minimal knowledge of specific Jewish rituals of his own time.⁶⁶ So these explicit references to the shofar are all the more noteworthy. All of this correlates with a biblical translation here that reflects direct knowledge of the shofar without strong familiarity with the connection between the ram's horn and Roš Haššanah.

III. The "Hebrew Truth"

These examples shed light on a recent examination of Jerome's translation from a very different angle by Megan Hale Williams.⁶⁷ She reads Jerome's claims to rabbinic influence on his biblical translation in relation to Jerome's self-construction. The categories of constructed self-representation and objective analysis do not mutually exclude each other. Accounting for the apparent contradiction between Jerome's negative assessment of Jews and Judaism and his positive use of Jewish erudition, Williams argues that Jerome constructs and rejects Jewish learning and Jews as carnal in the process of fashioning himself as an ascetic.⁶⁸ In the course of her discussion, she makes an important methodological distinction between examining how Jerome explains his interactions with Jews and Jewish learning (the subject of her analysis) and the investigation of the actual parallels, which are interesting to pursue in their own right.⁶⁹ That is, explaining Jerome's

---

⁶⁴ Jerome, *Comm. Os.* 5:8–9: "Buccina" pastoralis est, et cornu recurvo efficitur; unde et proprie Hebraice "*sophar*," Graece κερατίνη appellatur.

⁶⁵ Depiction of the shofar was especially popular in the land of Israel. See Rachel Hachlili, *Ancient Jewish Art and Archaeology in the Land of Israel*, HdO 7.1 (Leiden: Brill, 1988), 256–66; Hachlili, *Ancient Jewish Art and Archaeology in the Diaspora*, HdO 1.35 (Leiden: Brill, 1998), 347–59; and Lee I. Levine, *Visual Judaism in Late Antiquity: Historical Contexts of Jewish Art* (New Haven: Yale University Press, 2012), 337–41. John Chrysostom condemns Christians flocking to the synagogue on Roš Haššanah to hear the sound of the trumpets (*Adv. Jud.* 1.5 and 7.1).

⁶⁶ Newman, "Jerome and the Jews," 155–66, esp. 164–65 on Roš Haššanah.

⁶⁷ Megan Hale Williams, *The Monk and the Book: Jerome and the Making of Christian Scholarship* (Chicago: University of Chicago Press, 2006); and Williams, "Lessons from Jerome's Jewish Teachers: Exegesis and Cultural Interaction in Late Antique Palestine," in Dohrmann and Stern, *Jewish Biblical Interpretation and Cultural Exchange*, 66–86.

⁶⁸ For example, in addition to erudition, Jerome's Jewish informants display a carnal venality because they receive payment for their scholarship (Williams, "Lessons," 82). Serious engagement with Jewish learning does not preclude disdain for Jews and Judaism.

⁶⁹ Ibid., 85.

apologetic descriptions, methodological discussions, and discursive uses of his translation *iuxta Hebraeos* to establish his identity, authority, and/or legitimacy simply represents a line of approach different from analyzing the translation process itself. As we have seen from the specific examples analyzed above, the separation between talking about translation and the actual translation may be overdrawn. Williams's conclusion that "Jerome's deployment of Jewish learning, then, and his descriptions of its exponents, construct not a bridge but a wall between 'the classic Jewish culture' and Latin Christendom" does not apply to Jerome's approach to translation.[70] His method of translation requires transgression of boundaries, so a close reading of his translation reveals evidence of a bridge, not a wall.[71] This complex attitude toward Jews and Jewish learning is not unique. Traffickers in Judaica such as Jerome as well as medieval and early modern Christian Hebraists express similarly ambiguous attitudes.[72]

---

[70] Ibid., 84.

[71] *Breach* may be a more apt term than the irenic *bridge*, for translation can engender violent engagement. In George Steiner's fourfold ethical classification of the translation process, the second stage after "trust" is "aggression" ("The Hermeneutic Motion," in Venuti, *Translation Studies Reader*, 186–97). Jerome himself uses the language of "captivity" to describe translation (*Epist.* 57.6.3). Aggression can move in both directions because when the target language incorporates the source language (stage 3), the appropriation affects the appropriators and their system of meaning. Steiner believes that ultimately this aggression can be transcended through reciprocity (stage 4), exchange between the source language and target language without loss (ibid., 189–90). Thus, Williams's observation that Jerome's disrespectful representation of Jews should not obscure Origen's more generous attitude can be interpreted as different stages in Steiner's hierarchy. Origen may have reached a reciprocity not achieved by Jerome. Williams rightly notes that the problem of Jerome's relationship with his Jewish interlocutors is symptomatic of a larger issue concerning how Jews and Christians in late antiquity interacted ("4 Lessons," 68–69). Williams quotes Peter Schäfer, who sees the interaction as active appropriation, explaining that "the recipient actively digests the transmitted tradition, transforms it, and creates something new" (Schäfer, *Mirror of His Beauty: Feminine Images of God from the Bible to the Early Kabbalah*, Jews, Christians, and Muslims from the Ancient to the Modern World [Princeton: Princeton Unviersity Press, 2002], 231–32). Although the boundaries between Judaism and Christianity are not considered closed, Schäfer, according to Williams (69), applies Harold Bloom's more extreme language that the process of re-creating involves "killing" of the transmitted.

[72] See, most recently, Jacobs, *Remains of the Jews*, 67–83; and Todd Berzon, "The Double Bind of Christianity's Judaism: Language, Law, and the Incoherence of Late Antique Discourse," *JECS* 23 (2015): 445–80, https://doi.org/10.1353/earl.2015.0045. On the ambivalence toward Jews and Jewish learning among Christian Hebraists of the early modern period, see, e.g., the various essays in Allison P. Coudert and Jeffrey S. Shoulson, eds., *Hebraica Veritas? Christian Hebraists and the Study of Judaism in Early Modern Europe*, Jewish Culture and Contexts (Philadelphia: University of Pennsylvania Press, 2004). I am grateful to the anonymous reviewer for observing the broader historical implications.

IV. Conclusion

The combined presence of the following three features securely identifies a rabbinic tradition in the Vulgate: an unusual discrepancy between the Hebrew and Latin, a unique and comparable tradition in rabbinic literature, and a reference external to the Vulgate indicating specific knowledge of this exegetical tradition. Since all three features appear in the Vulgate on Num 24:24 and 10:5–7, we know for a fact that Jerome uses Jewish exegetical traditions in his translation. He equates Kittim with Romans, which he explicitly connects to a Jewish tradition in his commentary on Daniel, and he adopts the mishnaic definition of different shofar sounds. This does not undermine previous claims of Jewish influence based solely on parallels between the Vulgate and rabbinic literature. On the contrary, I would argue that Jerome applies *recentiores*-rabbinic philology to biblical books besides Genesis and so the burden of proof lies in demonstrating a nonrabbinic source for a rabbinic parallel to the Vulgate. This means that cases such as Num 25:4 and 25:8 reflect the exegetical influence of Jerome's Jewish informants, not only lexicographical motivations.

Elucidating the process of the translator more than the character of the translations produces different results. For example, John Cameron claims that the Vulgate is not a targum.[73] If by targum he means something like Targum Yerušalmi with extensive midrashic additions, he is correct.[74] If we define the Vulgate as an essentially philological translation with occasional application of rabbinic exegesis similar to Targum Onqelos, then it is targumic, although *recentiores*-rabbinic is the more apt description.[75] Similarly, Williams's distinction between Jewish influences on Jerome's actual translation and the expression of Jewish influence as part of his self-construction requires rethinking. When Jerome mentions the Jewish tradition in his commentary on Daniel, he inscribes his rendition of Num 24:24 as a Jewish translation. Therefore, Jewish tradition is more than a tool leveraged in self-construction: it directly influences his scriptural exegesis. As a translator, he continued to rely on Jewish traditions despite his professed rejection of the carnal exegesis of Jews, just as he continued to pepper his writings with classical erudition despite his oath to forgo classical literature. Nevertheless, unlike his classical allusions, these incorporations of Jewish traditions would very likely be invisible to his readers.[76] For Jerome himself, however, and for those readers who accepted his

---

[73] Cameron, "Rabbinic Vulgate?," 118–20.

[74] Similarly, Avemarie, "Hieronymus und die jüdische Genesis," 91: "Zu behaupten, die Vulgata sei die Bibel der Rabbinen in lateinischem Gewand, ginge zu weit."

[75] C. T. R. Hayward, "The Aramaic Targums," in Paget and Schaper, *From the Beginnings to 600*, 218–21, 226–32.

[76] Harald Hagendahl, *Latin Fathers and the Classics: A Study on the Apologists, Jerome, and*

challenge to consult the Jews to verify his renditions, the translation became a bridge, not a wall.[77]

Other Christian Writers, AUG 64.2 (Göteborg: Elanders, 1958). More recently, Andrew Cain similarly detects numerous classical literary references in his commentary, *Jerome's Epitaph on Paula: A Commentary on the* Epitaphium Sanctae Paulae (Oxford: Oxford University Press, 2013).

[77] Jerome often invites his readers to consult the Jews. For example, "I am not at all aware that I changed anything from the Hebrew Truth ... but if at any rate you do not believe me, read the Greek and Latin volumes and compare with these only little works of mine and wherever you see the version disagreeing amongst themselves, go ask any of the Hebrews" (*Praef. in Reg.* 68–71: mihi omnino conscius non sim mutasse me quippiam de hebraica veritate ... certe si incredulus es, lege graecos codices et latinos et confer cum his opusculis, et ubicumque inter se videris discrepare, interroga quemlibet Hebraeorum). See also *Praef. in Pent.* 43, *In libro Ezrae* 31, *In libro Psalmorum* (IH) 28, *Comm. Ezech.* 10.33, and *Epist.* 112.20.

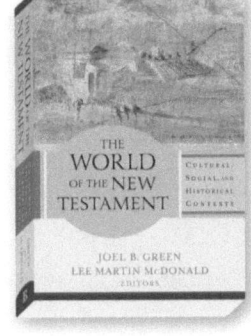

The Saga of Judah's Kings Continues: The Reception of Chronicles in the Late Second Temple Period

MIKA S. PAJUNEN
mika.s.pajunen@helsinki.fi
University of Helsinki, 00014 Helsinki, Finland

This article studies the early reception of Chronicles and its status in relation to its source texts in Samuel–Kings in the late Second Temple period. It has usually been supposed that Chronicles was less authoritative than its sources in Samuel–Kings. This dominant view is challenged in this study, especially regarding the status of these compositions in the second century BCE. I first present the evidence for the direct influence of Chronicles in later traditions by exploring the reception of the actual composition and then the influence of some of the central theological concepts and paradigms advocated in Chronicles. In the main part of the study, I analyze the impact of Chronicles on the interpretive traditions dealing with the kings of Judah. In these instances the differences between Chronicles and its sources are more marked than elsewhere, and most scholars would now agree that the majority of these differences come from the pen of the Chronicler. This means that the use of these features in later writings can fairly certainly be attributed to the direct influence of the traditions in Chronicles and can thus shed light on how later authors valued Samuel–Kings and Chronicles in relation to one another.

Louis Jonker has recently described Chronicles as the Cinderella of recent biblical studies who has lately shown herself to scholars as a glowing beauty because of her position as an early reader of the Torah.[1] The resurgence of scholarly interest in Chronicles has not yet reached its early reception, that is, how this early reader was welcomed by its own readers in the late Second Temple period. Apart from an article by Ehud Ben Zvi that represents the voice of the majority on this question

[1] Louis C. Jonker, "From Paraleipomenon to Early Reader: The Implications of Recent Chronicles Studies for Pentateuchal Criticism," in *Congress Volume: Munich 2013*, ed. Christl M. Maier, VTSup 163 (Leiden: Brill, 2014), 217–54, here 217–18, https://doi.org/10.1163/9789004281226_011.

and a recent monograph by Isaac Kalimi tracing the reception of Chronicles through the ages,[2] the early reception of Chronicles has not been studied in great detail.[3] It is usually supposed that Chronicles was viewed from early on, if not from the very beginning, as less authoritative than its sources in Samuel–Kings. I will challenge this dominant view in this study, especially regarding the status of these compositions in the second century BCE.

There has been a definite change in the evaluation of the relative status of these compositions in recent years. Looking at the current place of Chronicles in the canons of Scripture, one wonders why it was included at all. In Christian Bibles it is placed after Samuel–Kings as a kind of afterthought when the "proper" history has been read first. Many contemporary readers view it primarily as a long introduction to Ezra and Nehemiah. In the Hebrew Bible, 1 and 2 Chronicles are the last books of the entire corpus. This is hardly a coincidence and tells something of the status of the books in comparison to Samuel–Kings. The same is true of the Septuagint's designation of Chronicles as *Paraleipomena*, "the things omitted," which designates these books as a kind of supplement to Samuel–Kings.[4]

Why, then, is Chronicles in the canon of the Hebrew Bible? The traditional answer to this question has revolved around the idea of multiple witnesses to the same events, as, some argue, Samuel–Kings, Chronicles, Isaiah, and 1 Esdras provide in the Hebrew Bible or the four gospels in the New Testament. This idea of Chronicles as supplementary witness also fits with its LXX title. Particularly since the Qumran finds, however, it has become obvious that the process of transmitting traditions was more complex than was previously perceived. The Qumran corpus includes many works that present traditions found in canonical biblical books. These works typically aim to make the earlier traditions more useful in new situations and to change their theological and ideological focus. The existence of a large number of such works from the late Second Temple period has generated a lively discussion concerning the genre of such works and the processes involved in their composition. There is currently no consensus on which works should be placed in

---

[2] Ehud Ben Zvi, "The Authority of 1–2 Chronicles in the Late Second Temple Period," *JSP* 3 (1988): 59–88, https://doi.org/10.1177/095182078800000304 (a slightly modified version of the article appeared in Ben Zvi, *History, Literature and Theology in the Book of Chronicles*, BibleWorld [London: Equinox, 2006], 243–69); Isaac Kalimi, *The Retelling of Chronicles in Jewish Tradition and Literature: A Historical Journey* (Winona Lake, IN: Eisenbrauns, 2009).

[3] On the paucity of such studies, see Kalimi, *Retelling of Chronicles*, 9–11.

[4] It must be noted, however, that the most important Hebrew manuscripts from the medieval period, for example, the Aleppo Codex and Codex Leningradensis, have Chronicles as the first book of the Ketuvim, not the last. For the different nomenclature used for Chronicles in antiquity, see Gary N. Knoppers and Paul B. Harvey Jr., "Omitted and Remaining Matters: On the Names Given to the Book of Chronicles in Antiquity," *JBL* 121 (2002): 227–43, https://doi.org/10.2307/3268354.

this category of "rewritten scripture" or whether the term should be used to designate a literary genre, a compositional process, or neither.[5]

The Qumran evidence shows that Chronicles was in no way unique in offering a different perspective on earlier traditions. What does make Chronicles unique is that it is the only one of many such parallel traditions that was eventually included in the current Hebrew Bible. The uniqueness of Chronicles in this regard sharpens the question concerning its inclusion in the canon. Although this question cannot be answered in a single short study, some remarks offered here on the early reception of Chronicles might contribute to an answer. These observations point to the title of Chronicles in Codex Alexandrinus, "The Things Omitted regarding the Kings of Judah" (Παραλειπομένων Βασιλέων Ιουδα), being rather close to the mark.

Chronicles is usually treated by scholars as a rewriting of Samuel–Kings, which, in many ways, it certainly is.[6] Unlike most other writings typically placed under the rubric "rewritings" (e.g., Genesis Apocryphon and Jubilees), however, it radically contradicts its sources. All rewritings certainly offer new insights and interpretations as well as omit, adapt, and harmonize their sources, but Chronicles is novel in directly opposing its sources on a number of occasions, such as the case of Manasseh's reign (see 2 Kgs 21:1–18; 2 Chr 33:1–20). In these cases either the traditions in Samuel–Kings or those in Chronicles could be correct from the point of view of a later reader, but not both.

Chronicles' radical changes to the tradition represented by Samuel–Kings are due to the fact that Chronicles is a product of what Juha Pakkala would call a paradigm shift in the intellectual climate of Judean society.[7] Chronicles provided a new lens through which to view the traditions in Samuel–Kings, a lens strongly colored by the priestly concerns and theological convictions of the time of its composition. This lens subsequently became so essential for traditions of interpretation that it could no longer be removed.

Two particular thematic areas emphasized in Chronicles were very different from the source texts of Samuel–Kings and for this reason may have been especially influential: (1) matters related to the temple cult; and (2) modifications to narratives concerning the kings of Judah. The Hellenistic practice of the temple cult is presented as the proper manner of worship from the time of David onward. The changes in the narratives concerning the kings of Judah were implemented mainly

---

[5] See further Sidnie White Crawford, *Rewriting Scripture in Second Temple Times*, SDSSRL (Grand Rapids: Eerdmans, 2008); Molly M. Zahn, "Rewritten Scripture," in *The Oxford Handbook of the Dead Sea Scrolls*, ed. John J. Collins and Timothy H. Lim (Oxford: Oxford University Press, 2010), 323–36; Zahn, *Rethinking Rewritten Scripture: Composition and Exegesis in the 4QReworked Pentateuch Manuscripts*, STDJ 95 (Leiden: Brill, 2011).

[6] E.g., George J. Brooke, "Rewritten Bible," *EDSS* 2:777–81, here 778; Emanuel Tov, *Hebrew Bible, Greek Bible, and Qumran: Collected Essays*, TSAJ 121 (Tübingen: Mohr Siebeck, 2008), 69.

[7] Juha Pakkala, "Textual Development within Paradigms and Paradigm Shifts," *HBAI* 3 (2014): 327–42, https://doi.org/10.1628/219222714x14115480974934.

for reasons of theological consistency. These alterations aimed to demonstrate that the theological principles of divine justice advocated by the Chronicler(s) were the correct ones.

I will first present evidence for the direct influence of Chronicles on later traditions by exploring the reception of the actual composition and then the influence of some of the central theological concepts and paradigms advocated in Chronicles. In the main part of the study, I will analyze the impact of Chronicles on the interpretive traditions dealing with the kings of Judah. I will conclude with a short discussion of the implications of the study and some further factors that need to be more thoroughly considered in the future.

I. Chronicles: The Reception of the Composition

Many scholars have relied on the Qumran manuscripts as evidence that Chronicles was not important for the people who stored the scrolls, and they argue that the situation might have been similar in other groups as well.[8] It is true that only one tiny fragment among the over nine hundred Qumran manuscripts preserves a few words from Chronicles.[9] Naturally such a low figure cannot be entirely attributed to scroll preservation and happenstance. The situation of Chronicles, however, has to be seen in context alongside other "historical books."[10] Altogether only seven manuscripts preserve parts of Samuel (1QSam, 4QSam^{a-c}) or Kings (4QKgs, 5QKgs, 6QpapKgs). If Ezra and Nehemiah (4Q117) are added to the

---

[8] E.g., Ben Zvi, *History, Literature and Theology*, 251–54; George J. Brooke, "The Books of Chronicles and the Scrolls from Qumran," in *Reflection and Refraction: Studies in Biblical Historiography in Honour of A. Graeme Auld*, ed. Robert Rezetko, Timothy H. Lim, and W. Brian Aucker, VTSup 113 (Leiden: Brill, 2007), 35–48; Kalimi, *Retelling of Chronicles*, 111–14.

[9] The fragment is so small that the text might in theory derive from a quotation of Chronicles rather than from a manuscript of the actual book. Armin Lange argues—probably correctly—that the theory of quotation is unlikely because the fragment contains text from two different sections of Chronicles ("1–2 Chronicles: Ancient Hebrew Texts; Ancient Manuscript Evidence," in *The Hebrew Bible*, vol. 2 of *Textual History of the Bible*, ed. Armin Lange and Emanuel Tov [Leiden: Brill, 2016], 665).

[10] These compositions can be grouped together in the context of the Second Temple period because they claim to represent a history of Judah that is based in large part on supposed court annals. The narratives in these compositions are distinctly structured on the specific reigns of the kings and events that happened during those periods. They are also similar in that they rarely contain laws or prophecies, which could have been used and reinterpreted later. This is also how the historical books differ from apocalyptic histories: they explain parts of the supposed past from distinct theological viewpoints rather than offer a specific hidden message for the "future," except perhaps through the theological views they promulgate. Thus, they are firmly oriented toward interpreting and representing the past in order to build a common ancestry and background for the Jewish identity that was slowly beginning to form. They are the history of the exile, its reasons, and its continuing importance for the postexilic communities.

manuscripts preserving Samuel–Kings and Chronicles, all these scrolls would still only be about 1 percent of the entire Dead Sea Scrolls manuscript corpus. There are more manuscripts of the Community Rule alone. Clearly, the historical books were not nearly as popular at Qumran as the traditions in the Pentateuch or the Latter Prophets and Psalms. Chronicles is not unique in the paucity of its copies.[11]

Further, the number of quotations and allusions to Chronicles does not differ significantly from the use of the other "historical books" in this period. Moreover, the use of Samuel–Kings cannot always be distinguished from the use of Chronicles where the latter does not differ from its sources.[12] Thus, the direct reception of Chronicles does not reveal much about the influence of the work apart from the fact that it was in existence before 200 BCE and was particularly influential in the second century BCE. It has been used,[13] for example, in Daniel,[14] Ben Sira (see below), Greek Prayer of Manasseh, War Scroll (1QM),[15] 4Q252,[16] 4Q381,[17] 4Q522,[18] Temple Scroll[a] (11QT[a]),[19] 1–2 Maccabees,[20] and the Testament of Moses.[21] George Brooke has argued that Chronicles was neglected after this period, at least by the Qumran movement, because of its temple centrality and the Maccabean endorsement of it.[22] I will return to this argument briefly, but at this point I emphasize that there is no evidence that the Maccabees or the Hasmonean rulers would

---

[11] Similarly, the New Testament authors rarely use any of the "historical" books, but the Torah and the Prophets are frequently quoted and alluded to.

[12] See Armin Lange and Matthias Weigold, *Biblical Quotations and Allusions in Second Temple Jewish Literature*, JAJSup 5 (Göttingen: Vandenhoeck & Ruprecht, 2011).

[13] See Brooke, "Books of Chronicles," 43–47.

[14] Kalimi, *Retelling of Chronicles*, 17–20.

[15] Gary N. Knoppers, *I Chronicles 1–9: A New Translation with Introduction and Commentary*, AB 12 (New York: Doubleday, 2004), 110. The influence is found in the older parts of the War Scroll, not in the sectarian redactional layer(s) of it.

[16] Ibid.; Kalimi, *Retelling of Chronicles*, 116.

[17] Mika S. Pajunen, *The Land to the Elect and Justice for All: Reading Psalms in the Dead Sea Scrolls in Light of 4Q381*, JAJSup 14 (Göttingen: Vandenhoeck & Ruprecht, 2013), 214–16, 218–35, 253–54, https://doi.org/10.13109/9783666550607.

[18] Brooke, "Books of Chronicles," 44–45; Kalimi, *Retelling of Chronicles*, 118–19; Ariel Feldman, *The Rewritten Joshua Scrolls from Qumran: Texts, Translations, and Commentary*, BZAW 438 (Berlin: de Gruyter, 2014), 145–46.

[19] Yigael Yadin, *The Temple Scroll*, 3 vols. (Jerusalem: Israel Exploration Society, 1977–1983), 1:82–83; Yohanan Thorion, "Die Sprache der Tempelrolle und die Chronikbücher," *RevQ* 11 (1983): 423–28, here 423–26; Dwight J. Swanson, "The Use of Chronicles in 11QT: Aspects of a Relationship," in *The Dead Sea Scrolls: Forty Years of Research*, ed. Devorah Dimant and Uriel Rappaport, STDJ 10 (Leiden: Brill, 1992), 290–98; Swanson, *The Temple Scroll and the Bible: The Methodology of 11QT*, STDJ 14 (Leiden: Brill, 1994).

[20] Knoppers, *I Chronicles 1–9*, 110; Kalimi, *Retelling of Chronicles*, 75–76.

[21] The passage in question, T. Mos. 2:5–9, is typically dated to the second century BCE and is specifically influenced by Chronicles, not Samuel–Kings; so Ben Zvi, *History, Literature and Theology*, 247–48, 262.

[22] Brooke, "Books of Chronicles," 38–40; cf. Kalimi, *Retelling of Chronicles*, 111–14.

have endorsed Chronicles. On the contrary, they had their own heroes and stories to promulgate in 1 and 2 Maccabees. If someone continued to promote Chronicles expressly at this point, it would have been the institution and people whose power Chronicles tried to underline and emphasize, that is, the temple priesthood and the Levites.[23]

II. Chronicles: A Theological and Pragmatic Reception

An area of influence with more bountiful evidence than the reception of the actual composition is the impact of some of the central themes, conceptions, and theological ideas of Chronicles. The amount of evidence relating to this area of reception grows continually as scholars study individual books from the late Second Temple period. The difficulty is whether the theological convictions and conceptions, as well as some practical instructions, really derive directly from Chronicles or whether Chronicles is simply the earliest surviving literary source for them. The circles responsible for Chronicles probably wrote a number of texts with a similar theological outlook and undoubtedly used their influence in society to advance the use of these conceptions in other ways as well.

Furthermore, the Chronicler is attempting to root Second Temple practices in antiquity. The temple and priesthood, from which Chronicles probably emerged, were the central provincial power in Judean society in the Hellenistic period until the Maccabean revolt.[24] It is almost impossible to say, therefore, whether a certain ideology or practice comes from Chronicles, from other compositions authored by the same circles, or from the practices in place before Chronicles or instigated by it. Nevertheless, we can examine a few examples of such possibilities.

First, a practice encountered in the Qumran scrolls that has been argued to demonstrate the direct influence of Chronicles (1 Chr 24) is the division of priests into twenty-four service shifts to take care of the priestly duties at the temple (see 4Q322–325, 4Q328–329).[25] The manuscripts from Qumran correlate actual

---

[23] Chronicles also aligns well with a number of supposed Sadducean viewpoints, for example, retribution in the current life and an emphasis on Jerusalem and the priests. This demonstrates the difficulties with identifying a specific group that would have continued to favor Chronicles. Indeed, if it were not for the paucity of manuscript evidence, the early Qumran movement's emphasis on priests and Levites could be taken as an argument that they might well have regarded Chronicles highly. It is tempting to make a connection with a particular group and Chronicles, but too little is known of the actual groups active in the land in the late Second Temple period and even less about their views on Chronicles to make a convincing argument.

[24] See, e.g., Lester L. Grabbe, *The Coming of the Greeks: The Early Hellenistic Period (335–175 BCE)*, vol. 2 of *A History of the Jews and Judaism in the Second Temple Period*, LSTS 68 (London: T&T Clark International, 2008).

[25] See, e.g., Shemaryahu Talmon with the assistance of Jonathan Ben-Dov, "Calendrical Documents and Mishmarot," in *Qumran Cave 4.XVI: Calendrical Texts*, ed. Shemaryahu Talmon,

calendar dates for the Sabbaths and feasts with the different priestly service shifts, thus providing a practical example of the division into shifts provided by Chronicles. This indicates that the practice and, by extension, its legitimation in Chronicles held significant authority for the people in the movement. The practice, however, is probably the foremost authority in this instance. Although there were a number of significant modifications in relation to Chronicles,[26] the practice itself was preserved even though it differed from the solar calendar used by the Qumran movement.

Second, a priestly/Levitical emphasis is typical of Chronicles.[27] Many compositions from the late third to the late second century BCE have a similar emphasis, for example, the War Scroll, where the earliest editorial layer might have been a priestly manual of holy war; the Community Rule and especially the covenant renewal ritual in it; the Temple Scroll; Jubilees; the Aramaic Levi Document; and so forth.[28] That these writings all share the priestly/Levitical emphasis of Chronicles may mean no more than that the same circles were active for a longer period of time or were imitated by slightly later authors.

Third, a theological emphasis typical of Chronicles that is widely adopted later is repentance. According to Chronicles, there is always a possibility of repenting and turning back, which is a clear difference from Samuel–Kings.[29] This conviction about repentance is connected to the question of free will, which was debated particularly in second-century BCE wisdom writings, such as Instruction, Mysteries, Ben Sira, and 4Q185. Chronicles was probably part of the reason why this conviction of repentance became so widespread. This may be traced to the beginning of its reception when such a view was more novel than later, when people had already embraced this belief as a matter of course.

Jonathan Ben-Dov, and U. Glessmer, DJD XXI (Oxford: Clarendon, 2001), 8; Brooke, "Books of Chronicles," 45–46. It is intriguing that the Qumran calendrical documents move the beginning of the service shifts from the time of David all the way back to creation. This coincides with the tradition preserved in many second-century BCE texts in which the beginning of the liturgy is pushed back to creation, as well as the Qumran movement's slightly later tendency to expand this tradition in their own liturgies. For these traditions, see my recent study "The Praise of God and His Name as the Core of the Second Temple Liturgy," *ZAW* 127 (2015): 475–88, https://doi.org/10.1515/zaw-2015-0026.

[26] See, e.g., Brooke, "Books of Chronicles," 45–46.

[27] See, e.g., Knoppers, *I Chronicles 1–9*, 80.

[28] The family of Levi gained status as communicators of the divine will and as transmitters of it in written form; see Hanna Tervanotko, "Visions, Otherworldly Journeys and Divine Beings: The Figures of Levi and Amram as Communicators of Godly Will in the Dead Sea Scrolls," in *Crossing Imaginary Boundaries: The Dead Sea Scrolls in the Context of Second Temple Judaism*, ed. Mika S. Pajunen and Hanna Tervanotko, SESJ 108 (Helsinki: Finnish Exegetical Society, 2015), 210–38.

[29] For a somewhat programmatic statement of the Chronicler's notion of repentance, see 2 Chr 7:14. See Hugh G. M. Williamson, *1 and 2 Chronicles*, NCBC (Grand Rapids: Eerdmans, 1982), 389–93.

Chronicles' notion of repentance seems to emerge just before the institution of penitential prayer, a liturgical institution based on the concept of repentance that is frequently represented both in narrative works and in possible liturgical texts in the late Second Temple period.[30] This liturgical practice is grounded in the belief in the possibility of repentance emphasized in Chronicles. In fact, unlike Samuel–Kings, Chronicles lays the blame for the exile firmly on the last preexilic generation and their leaders, and more explicitly on their not repenting of their bad deeds (2 Chr 36:12–16). Thus, the practice of penitential prayer in the Second Temple period is linked with Chronicles' notion of the central importance of repentance, which is outwardly manifested in penitence. Similarly, the centrality of the concept of continuing exile in the penitential prayers is probably related to Chronicles' view of the exile as a punishment for the people's refusal to repent of their bad deeds.

There is, however, another theological emphasis of Chronicles that did not stand the test of time, and that is immediate divine retribution.[31] Soon after Chronicles was written, the idea gained ground that the reward or punishment for one's deeds was transferred to the afterlife. Nevertheless, the notion of immediate divine retribution did not disappear completely; see, for example, the Psalms of Solomon's treatment of Pompey's conquest of Jerusalem and his subsequent death (Pss. Sol. 2).

This evidence indicates that many of the ideas of the circles responsible for Chronicles were successfully implemented and continued to be influential, but this does not constitute evidence for the influence of the actual book of Chronicles. An area of investigation, however, where it can be shown that specific ideas of Chronicles were taken into account by later interpreters is the "historical" narration, particularly where Chronicles differs significantly from the accounts of Samuel–Kings. It is apparent that other sources were used in the genealogies at the beginning of Chronicles, and the genealogies of Chronicles have subsequently influenced the Gospel of Matthew, possibly 4Q245, LXX Job 42:17, and Jdt 8:1.[32] It is difficult to determine, however, whether Chronicles or its sources in Genesis, Joshua, and Psalms were used in these instances because the differences in the genealogies are so slight and there is always the possibility of a different *Vorlage* for the genealogy in Chronicles.[33] Thus, while the genealogies are possible further indicators of the influence of Chronicles, they do not unambiguously reveal how influential

---

[30] See Rodney Werline, *Penitential Prayer in Second Temple Judaism: The Development of a Religious Institution*, EJL 13 (Atlanta: Scholars Press, 1998), esp. 11–62.

[31] For immediate divine retribution in Chronicles, see Williamson, *1 and 2 Chronicles*, 391–93; Brian E. Kelly, *Retribution and Eschatology in Chronicles*, JSOTSup 211 (Sheffield: Sheffield Academic, 1996), 29–45; Sara Japhet, *The Ideology of the Book of Chronicles and Its Place in Biblical Thought*, trans. Anna Barber (Winona Lake, IN: Eisenbrauns, 2009), 129–37.

[32] Knoppers, *I Chronicles 1–9*, 106.

[33] For studies on the different genealogies and lists at the beginning of Chronicles, see, e.g., Gary N. Knoppers, "Sources, Revisions, and Editions: The Lists of Jerusalem's Residents in MT and LXX Nehemiah 11 and 1 Chronicles 9," *Text* 20 (2000): 141–68; Pancratius C. Beentjes, *Tradition and Transformation in the Book of Chronicles*, SSN 52 (Leiden: Brill, 2008), 17–29,

Chronicles was in relation to its source texts. In the representation of Judah's kings, however, the differences between Chronicles and its sources are more marked, and most scholars would now agree that the majority of these differences come from the pen of the Chronicler,[34] which means that the use of these features in later writings can be attributed to the direct influence of the traditions in Chronicles.

III. Reception of Traditions concerning Kings of Judah

The hypothesis that interpretive traditions concerning the kings of Judah formed gradually is based primarily on the following textual evidence presented here in a roughly chronological order:

1. Some form of Samuel and Kings and passages in Isaiah and Jeremiah related to the kings of Judah were in existence between 500 and 300 BCE.[35]
2. Chronicles was written in approximately 300–250 BCE.[36]
3. Ben Sira, Eupolemus, 4Q381, and 4Q522 derive from 200–150 BCE, and these sources are the focal point of this presentation. The dating of Ben Sira

---

https://doi.org/10.1163/ej.9789004170445.i-214. On Chronicles' use of pentateuchal sources, see Jonker, "From Paraleipomenon to Early Reader," 217–54.

[34] Chronicles is now typically considered to consist of one to three redactional layers, although some of the most recent scholarship suggests even more radical divisions. See, e.g., Reinhard G. Kratz, *Die Komposition der erzählenden Bücher des Alten Testaments: Grundwissen der Bibelkritik*, UTB 2157 (Göttingen: Vandenhoeck & Ruprecht, 2000). Nevertheless, the Chronicler is still usually seen as the author of the most important parts of the book, if not all of it, as reflected in book titles such as *The Chronicler as Author: Studies in Text and Texture*, ed. M. Patrick Graham and Steven L. McKenzie, JSOTSup 263 (Sheffield: Sheffield Academic, 1999). For studies arguing for the Chronistic origins of the major differences regarding the presentation of different kings, see, e.g., Sara Japhet, *I & II Chronicles: A Commentary*, OTL (London: SCM, 1993), 1041–44; Zipora Talshir, "The Three Deaths of Josiah and the Strata of Biblical Historiography (2 Kings XXIII 29–30; 2 Chronicles XXXV 20–5; 1 Esdras I 23–31)," VT 46 (1996): 213–36; Philippe Abadie, "From the Impious Manasseh (2 Kings 21) to the Convert Manasseh (2 Chronicles 33): Theological Rewriting by the Chronicler," in *The Chronicler as Theologian: Essays in Honor of Ralph W. Klein*, ed. M. Patrick Graham, Steven L. McKenzie, and Gary N. Knoppers, JSOTSup 371 (London: T&T Clark, 2003), 89–104; Ralph W. Klein, *1 Chronicles: A Commentary*, Hermeneia (Minneapolis: Fortress, 2006), 452, 516; Gary N. Knoppers, "Saint or Sinner? Manasseh in Chronicles," in *Rewriting Biblical History: Essays on Chronicles and Ben Sira in Honor of Pancratius C. Beentjes*, ed. Jeremy Corley and Harm van Grol, DCLS 7 (Berlin: de Gruyter, 2011), 211, https://doi.org/10.1515/9783110240948.211.

[35] It is acknowledged that especially the books of Samuel and Jeremiah continued to evolve in major ways after this, as witnessed by the Qumran and LXX evidence. Nevertheless, some recognizable form of them was in existence during this period.

[36] For a balanced account of the problems relating to the dating of Chronicles, see Knoppers, *I Chronicles 1–9*, 101–17.

to this period is commonly accepted.³⁷ The discussion of Ben Sira in this study will center on the Praise of the Ancestors (chs. 44–49).³⁸ Eupolemus was a Greco-Jewish historian writing in Greek around the middle of the second century BCE. He is the first known author to try to combine the accounts of Kings and Chronicles. This composition was apparently titled "Concerning the Kings of Judaea," but only a few passages of it have survived.³⁹ The author of 4QNon-Canonical Psalms B (4Q381) was another contemporary of Ben Sira and Eupolemus. The manuscript contains, among other psalms, five psalms expressly written from the viewpoint of different kings of Judah. The author of these psalms also knew both Samuel–Kings and Chronicles and has taken them into account in his composition.⁴⁰ Finally, 4QApocryphon of Joshua (4Q522) presents some events related to David's and Solomon's reigns as prophecies uttered in the time of Joshua and also utilizes both Samuel–Kings and Chronicles.⁴¹ All four authors clearly were aware of both of the earlier traditions, and their choices indicate which one they preferred to follow.

4. Finally, Josephus and some rabbinic sources from the period after the destruction of the Second Temple will be noted briefly in order to show the general way the traditions concerning kings of Judah continued to develop. The rabbinic evidence is much more complex and manifold than what is presented here.

I turn now to case studies of the influence of Chronicles, presenting accounts of six kings of Judah and how the lines of interpretation concerning them have changed in the course of time. The reception of the accounts of these kings is complex, but in each case certain details specific to the particular king continue to be discussed or highlighted in nearly all the sources. These controversial issues most clearly demand a choice between earlier sources and thus form the focal point of the following discussion. Each case deserves more detailed examination, but I concentrate on forming a general overview of Chronicles and its early reception.

---

³⁷ For details concerning the dating, see David S. Williams, "The Date of Ecclesiasticus," *VT* 44 (1994): 563–66.

³⁸ Ehud Ben Zvi did not find anything in Ben Sira's Praise of the Ancestors that would necessarily derive from Chronicles (*History, Literature and Theology*, 245–46), but in fact, as will be shown, it is clear that Ben Sira utilized both Samuel–Kings and Chronicles when composing this section of his composition.

³⁹ For an introduction to the surviving fragments and dating, see Ben Zion Wacholder, *Eupolemus: A Study of Judaeo-Greek Literature*, HUCM 3 (Cincinnati: Hebrew Union College–Jewish Institute of Religion, 1974), 1–26; Carl R. Holladay, *Historians*, vol. 1 of *Fragments from Hellenistic Jewish Authors*, SBLTT 20 (Chico, CA: Scholars Press, 1983), 93–97.

⁴⁰ For the text and dating of the psalms in 4Q381, see Pajunen, *Land to the Elect*, 182–273, 355–65.

⁴¹ For the text of 4Q522, see Feldman, *Rewritten Joshua Scrolls*, 128–67.

David: On the Road to Perfection

The traditions concerning David are rather straightforward in that they all move toward a more perfect portrait of David. In the books of Samuel, David is somewhat of a scoundrel who is described as a great warrior and leader (e.g., 1 Sam 17; 27; 30; 2 Sam 2; 5:17–25; 8). His greatest sins are his affair with Bathsheba and the taking of the census (2 Sam 11; 24). The overall picture becomes more idealized already in the final editorial layers of Kings, but Chronicles revises it more drastically. David becomes a paragon of virtue.[42] There is no Bathsheba episode, and Satan is responsible for the census (1 Chr 21). In Chronicles, David also becomes the formulator of liturgical practices (see, e.g., 1 Chr 25 and 29), which is an important change taken up in later texts, such as David's Compositions (11QPs[a] XXVII, 4–5), where he is credited with writing all the cultic songs used in the temple. The growing emphasis on David as a writer of large collections of psalms, visible particularly in 11QPs[a] and the Septuagint Psalter, may also be attributed to Chronicles' emphatic view of David as a creator of the liturgy. Ben Sira agrees with Chronicles' overall view of David: God has wiped away David's few errors and also glorified him as the organizer of the cult (Sir 47:9–10)—an emphasis obviously derived from Chronicles.[43]

Chronicles' accounts of David's battles, unlike the narratives in Samuel–Kings, bear a negative undertone. According to the Chronicler, David was not able to build the temple because his hands had been bloodied in the wars (1 Chr 22:7–8, 28:2–3). Eupolemus (frag. 2) agrees with this explanation for why David did not build the temple,[44] and David's role as a warrior on the battlefield is prominent in 4Q552, which has connections with 2 Chr 18–20 and prophesies David's capture of Jerusalem.[45] Some compositions, however, try to diminish David's battlefield role, perhaps because of the negative impact it had on his temple-building plans. 4Q381 and 11QPs[a] both describe David as the perfect humble person who no longer has an active role on the battlefield because God fights for him.[46] These descriptions elevate David above the bloodshed while underlining the concept of holy war—God fights on behalf of his righteous chosen ones.

Thus, Chronicles' view of David was accepted in all the earliest sources, and these writers tended to go even further than Chronicles in exalting David. But the

---

[42] Cf. Japhet, *Ideology of the Book of Chronicles*, 364–72.

[43] See Kalimi, *Retelling of Chronicles*, 81; Bradley C. Gregory, "The Warrior-Poet of Israel: The Significance of David's Battles in Chronicles and Ben Sira," in Corley and van Grol, *Rewriting Biblical History*, 79–96, https://doi.org/10.1515/9783110240948.79; Marko Marttila, "David in the Wisdom of Ben Sira," *SJOT* 25 (2011): 29–48, https://doi.org/10.1080/09018328.2011.568208.

[44] Wacholder, *Eupolemus*, 145; Kalimi, *Retelling of Chronicles*, 91.

[45] Knoppers, *I Chronicles 1–9*, 110.

[46] Pajunen, *Land to the Elect*, 182–97. See also Brent A. Strawn, "David as One of the 'Perfect of (the) Way': On the Provenience of David's Compositions (and 11QPs[a] as a Whole?)," *RevQ* 24 (2010): 607–26.

accounts in Samuel were not forgotten. David's sin over Uriah is mentioned in the Damascus Document as his only transgression, which was forgiven by God (CD V, 5–6). This small step back toward the depiction of David in Samuel is shared by Josephus, who states that Bathsheba was David's only sin. Nevertheless, the overall tradition concerning David does not change, and the rabbinic texts go so far as to state, "Whoever says that David sinned errs himself" (b. Šabb. 56a).

Solomon: A King Equaling His Father but a Youth in His Shadow

In Kings, Solomon is presented as a young, wise, and rich temple builder who has foreign wives, falls into idolatry in old age, and is the cause of the division of the kingdom (1 Kgs 1–11).[47] Chronicles enhances Solomon's image, as it did David's, by omitting the foreign concubines and the blame for the division of the kingdom.[48] As a king, Solomon becomes at least his father's equal in Chronicles, and his reign is characterized by peace and prosperity (1 Chr 22:9, 2 Chr 9). In contrast to the narrative in Kings, Chronicles diminishes Solomon's part in the main event of his reign, the building of the temple. In Kings he is a young, independent temple builder (1 Kgs 5–6), but in Chronicles he is overshadowed by the more glorified portrayal of David and becomes a son who only implemented his father's ready plans for the temple with the materials David had already gathered for the project (1 Chr 22).[49]

Ben Sira takes up details from both accounts (Sir 47:12–23). In Solomon's case he mostly follows the account in Kings by not omitting Solomon's wives or his blame for the division of the kingdom. He follows Chronicles in emphasizing peace as the hallmark of Solomon's reign. 4Q522 follows Chronicles in describing David's preparations for the building of the temple (4Q522 9 II, 4–6).[50] Moreover, Ariel Feldman has noted that the word שלום ("peace") is particularly emphasized in the version of Ps 122 preserved in the manuscript. The noun is used five times against three occurrences in the MT. Feldman further notes that in 4Q522 the context of the psalm includes other predictions concerning the times of David and Solomon.[51] The psalm presumes the existence of the Jerusalem temple, and its prophecy therefore cannot point to the time of David. It refers rather to Solomon, which also gives

---

[47] For further discussion on the development of traditions concerning Solomon, see, e.g., Pablo A. Torijano, *Solomon the Esoteric King: From King to Magus, Development of a Tradition*, JSJSup 73 (Leiden: Brill, 2002); the essays in *The Figure of Solomon in Jewish, Christian, and Islamic Tradition: King, Sage, and Architect*, ed. Joseph Verheyden, TBN 16 (Leiden: Brill, 2013); and Benjamin G. Wright III, "Solomon in Chronicles and Ben Sira," in Corley and van Grol, *Rewriting Biblical History*, 139–57.

[48] Japhet, *Ideology of the Book of Chronicles*, 372–81; Wright, "Solomon in Chronicles and Ben Sira," 144.

[49] Similarly Japhet, *Ideology of the Book of Chronicles*, 377–80.

[50] Feldman, *Rewritten Joshua Scrolls*, 145–46.

[51] Ibid., 142–48, 165.

a plausible explanation for the emphasis on peace, the hallmark of Solomon's time. This modification and interpretation of Ps 122 in 4Q522 might reflect the influence of Chronicles. Eupolemus (frag. 2) also strongly favors Chronicles not only regarding the building of the temple but in other details as well.[52] Eupolemus follows Chronicles for David's preparations for the building of the temple but interprets Kings such that Solomon must have been only twelve years old when his reign began, a view shared by LXX 3 Kgdms 2:12. Hence, in Eupolemus's account Nathan actually guides and supervises Solomon all through the building project, thus further diminishing Solomon's role in the building of the temple. Moreover, the details concerning the building project in Eupolemus and Solomon's peaceful succession of David also support Chronicles.[53]

Again, the early reception takes Chronicles seriously and relies on it more than on Kings. But it is Josephus who takes Kings more seriously. He follows Chronicles for the temple building but declares Solomon a sinner who broke the laws concerning mixed marriages and was responsible for the division of the kingdom in his senility.

Hezekiah: A Brave and Faithful King or a Coward?

The attitude toward Hezekiah in Kings is ambivalent (2 Kgs 18–20) because of the differences in the sources employed in the narrative. He is both a coward, emptying his treasury to please the Assyrians, and a king bravely trusting in God when threatened by the Assyrians. In Isaiah (chs. 36–37) only the brave king remains, and Hezekiah's complete trust in God is emphasized.[54] This picture of a brave king trusting utterly in God was further enhanced in Chronicles, which added mention of Hezekiah's encouragement of the people (2 Chr 32:7–8),[55] making trust and courage the central ideas of the account.[56] This line of tradition can be found also in 4Q381, in which Isa 35 is understood in terms of the oracle pertaining to Hezekiah in the following chapters, Isa 36–37.[57] Thus, bravery is one of the main character traits of Hezekiah in Chronicles, and both Ben Sira (Sir 48:17–22) and 4Q381 VI, 15–16 also mention bravery as a character trait of

---

[52] See Wacholder, *Eupolemus*, 248–53; Holladay, *Historians*, 95, 102.

[53] For details, see Wacholder, *Eupolemus*, 151–55; Kalimi, *Retelling of Chronicles*, 91–92.

[54] It is not relevant for the reception of Chronicles whether 2 Kings or Isaiah is the earlier representative of the tradition because both would have been available for the Chronicler(s) and for later authors. For the complexity of this question, see Robb Andrew Young, *Hezekiah in History and Tradition*, VTSup 155 (Leiden: Brill, 2012), 123–50, https://doi.org/10.1163/9789004229518_007.

[55] For the speech of Hezekiah as an addition deriving from the Chronicler(s), see, e.g., Japhet, *I & II Chronicles*, 977, 984–85; Young, *Hezekiah in History and Tradition*, 252.

[56] Simon J. De Vries notes that the thematic word root in the Hezekiah narrative in Chronicles is חזק (*1 and 2 Chronicles*, FOTL 11 [Grand Rapids: Eerdmans, 1989], 389).

[57] For a more extensive treatment, see Pajunen, *Land to the Elect*, 197–218. It is plausible that the author(s) of Chronicles also might have read Isa 35 in this way.

Hezekiah.[58] The emphasis on this positive quality is a departure from the more ambiguous depiction of Hezekiah in Kings. The line of tradition is quite clear, and rabbinic sources (e.g., b. Sanh. 94a–b, 99a) offer only praise of Hezekiah. Josephus, however, mentions the more negative aspects preserved in Kings and twice explicitly states that Hezekiah was a coward who was afraid of the Assyrians (*Ant.* 10.1.2 §§5, 8).[59]

Manasseh: A Heinous Sinner or a Repentant One?

Manasseh is perhaps the most controversial of Judah's kings.[60] He is depicted in the sources in markedly contrasting ways that are all but impossible to reconcile. In Kings, Manasseh is perhaps the most heinous ruler in the history of Judah (2 Kgs 21:1–18; cf. Jer 15:4). His sins exceed those of most of the other kings put together, and these sins are deemed terrible enough that even Josiah's later reform is not enough to absolve them (2 Kgs 23:26). Manasseh's sins are given as the main reason for God's final judgment of his chosen nation and its subsequent exile (2 Kgs 24:3–4). The account of Manasseh's reign in Chronicles is significantly different (2 Chr 33:1–20). It starts in the same way, listing Manasseh's sins, but then a complete reversal of the situation occurs. Manasseh is captured by some chiefs of the Assyrian king and taken to Babylon. He there repents of his evil deeds and prays to God for forgiveness. God answers him by allowing him to return to his throne. After this brief episode of captivity, Manasseh reverses his former deeds. Because these traditions are so different, there was no middle ground for later interpreters: either Manasseh repented or he did not.

Though one might expect both of these ideologically charged lines of tradition to find expression in later literature, the influence of Kings is witnessed only in late texts such as 2 Baruch, Mart. Isa. 2:1–6, and many rabbinic traditions. By contrast, the influence of Chronicles is found early on in two separate prayers written for Manasseh in 4Q381 VII, 17–VIII, 9 from the middle of the second century BCE[61] and the Greek Prayer of Manasseh from before the Common Era. In slightly later reception, Josephus uses both Chronicles and 4Q381 in his portrayal of Manasseh

---

[58] See Patrick W. Skehan and Alexander A. Di Lella, *The Wisdom of Ben Sira: A New Translation with Notes*, AB 39 (Garden City, NY: Doubleday, 1987), 538–39.

[59] See further Louis H. Feldman, *Studies in Josephus' Rewritten Bible*, JSJSup 58 (Leiden: Brill, 1998), 363–64, 367–71.

[60] See, e.g., Abadie, "From the Impious Manasseh," 89–104; Knoppers, "Saint or Sinner?," 211–29.

[61] See Mika S. Pajunen, "The Prayer of Manasseh in 4Q381 and the Account of Manasseh in 2 Chronicles 33," in *The Scrolls and Biblical Traditions: Proceedings of the Seventh Meeting of the IOQS in Helsinki*, ed. George J. Brooke et al., STDJ 103 (Leiden: Brill, 2012), 143–61, https://doi.org/10.1163/9789004231665_008; Pajunen, *Land to the Elect*, 218–35.

as a repentant sinner,⁶² and many rabbinic sources share this view.⁶³ The early reception, therefore, again favors Chronicles, whereas later works have a more balanced portrayal, including both the tradition in Kings and the one in Chronicles.

Josiah: A Virtuous King without a Proper Reward

Josiah is in all traditions seen as a great and virtuous king who reformed the cult, but his early death (2 Kgs 23:29) caused a problem for all interpreters, as it did not seem a just reward for his pious deeds. In Kings his death is explained through Huldah's prophecy as an act of mercy by God (2 Kgs 22:19–20). Josiah is spared by God from witnessing the sacking of Jerusalem by the Babylonians. Chronicles did not deem this a sufficient reason for Josiah's death because he seemed to have done nothing to deserve it. Chronicles resolved the question by blaming Josiah himself. His death was his own fault and was his expected punishment because he inadvertently did not obey God, who was acting through Pharaoh Neco.⁶⁴

All the early interpreters accept the Chronicles account as a starting point. Some, however, find the offered explanation inadequate, either because of uncertainty as to how Josiah would have known that it was his own God acting through Neco or because of the contrast between Josiah's violent death and Huldah's prophecy about Josiah dying in peace—or both. For 1 Esdras, both of these aspects were problematic. It first resolves the dilemma presented by the vague text of Chronicles by making it explicit that the God Neco is talking about is YHWH and further stating that Jeremiah is the one who delivers the message to Josiah (1 Esd 1:25–26). Thus, Josiah knowingly goes against God and his prophet and is punished.⁶⁵ The dilemma concerning Huldah's prophecy is in turn resolved in 1 Esdras by interpreting the word from the root חלה used for the wounding of Josiah (2 Chr 35:23) in its other well-attested meaning, "fall ill." Josiah is not wounded by Neco's archers as in Chronicles but rather falls ill during battle and is carried to Jerusalem, where he dies in peace as prophesied by Huldah (1 Esd 1:29).⁶⁶ Thus, 1 Esdras takes the

---

⁶²Pajunen, "Prayer of Manasseh in 4Q381," 156–61.

⁶³For Josephus's portrayal of Manasseh, see Feldman, *Studies in Josephus' Rewritten Bible*, 416–23. For the rabbinic traditions on Manasseh, see, e.g., Pierre Bogaert, "La légende de Manassé," in *Apocalypse de Baruch*, 2 vols., SC 144–45 (Paris: Cerf, 1969), 1:296–319; Feldman, *Studies in Josephus' Rewritten Bible*, 416–18.

⁶⁴Louis C. Jonker shows how this ending downplays the importance of Josiah and places more emphasis on the Passover ritual (*Reflections of King Josiah in Chronicles: Late Stages of the Josiah Reception in II Chr. 34f.*, Textpragmatische Studien zur Literatur- und Kulturgeschichte der Hebräischen Bibel 2 [Gütersloh: Gütersloher Verlagshaus, 2003], 14–33).

⁶⁵See Talshir, "Three Deaths of Josiah," 232–33; Ralph W. Klein, "The Rendering of 2 Chronicles 35–36 in 1 Esdras," in *Was 1 Esdras First? An Investigation into the Priority and Nature of 1 Esdras*, ed. Lisbeth S. Fried, AIL 7 (Atlanta: Society of Biblical Literature, 2011), 225–35.

⁶⁶Klein, "Rendering of 2 Chronicles 35–36," 228, 235.

Chronicles account as basically truthful and as its starting point. The interpretation, however, makes explicit that the God Josiah goes against is YHWH and understands a key term used in Chronicles in a way that allows Huldah's prophecy to be fulfilled.

Ben Sira, in his short description of Josiah (Sir 49:1–3), follows either Chronicles or, less likely, 1 Esdras.[67] The Hebrew and Greek versions differ in 49:2. The Hebrew (MS B) attests the verb נחל, which is most likely to be from the same verbal root discussed above (חלה) that is used in Chronicles and is behind the Greek account in 1 Esdras. Renate Egger-Wenzel argues that the use of this particular root indicates a dependence on 2 Chr 35:23, where the same root is used.[68] It cannot be established, however, whether Ben Sira read it as referring to the wounding of Josiah by archers, as in Chronicles, or to Josiah's falling ill, as in 1 Esdras. Alternatively, the word could be from the root חול with the meaning of being grieved, in anguish: "For he grieved over our betrayals."[69] This would align Ben Sira 49:2 closely with 1 Esdras, where the longest modification of Chronicles stresses Josiah's innocence and grief over the sins of the people.[70] The most probable source for the wording in Ben Sira, therefore, seems to be Chronicles, but a Hebrew *Vorlage* of 1 Esdras cannot be ruled out. Another noteworthy feature common to these three texts but lacking in most others is the explicit connection between Josiah and Jeremiah. Ben Sira places the blame for Josiah's death squarely on the shoulders of the people, not Josiah, and Chronicles blames the people and their transgressions directly for Josiah's death. Moreover, this accords well with the notion of Kings, thus combining the divergent accounts.

4Q381 is especially dissatisfied with the vagueness of the divine command that Josiah disobeyed and offers yet another attempt at solving the dilemma of Josiah's death (4Q381 VIII, 10–IX, 12).[71] This text takes the account and judgment of Josiah in Chronicles as a starting point and apparently agrees that Josiah's death was technically his own fault. The author, however, argues on the basis of the psalm attributed to Josiah himself that the king was led to err by the vague message and did not deserve to be punished. At the end of the psalm God seemingly agrees and consequently vindicates and rewards Josiah in the afterlife. This is a tradition that the rabbinic sources later explicitly reject, which suggests that it persisted for some time. The rabbinic sources (e.g., b. Taʿan. 22b) claim that Jeremiah was present when Josiah died and heard that Josiah did *not* pray to God to overturn the verdict but rather died quietly and faithfully.

---

[67] See Renate Egger-Wenzel, "Josiah and His Prophet(s) in Chronicles and Ben Sira: An Intertextual Comparison," in Corley and van Grol, *Rewriting Biblical History*, 231–56, https://doi.org/10.1515/9783110240948.231.

[68] Ibid., 236.

[69] Skehan and Di Lella, *Wisdom of Ben Sira*, 540.

[70] Klein, "Rendering of 2 Chronicles 35–36," 234–35.

[71] Pajunen, *Land to the Elect*, 235–56.

Josephus goes in a different direction by seeking to vindicate both God and Josiah. In his account God does not mislead Josiah nor does Josiah disobey God. Rather, it is destiny that drives Josiah to his death (*Ant.* 10.5.1 §§74–77).[72] Thus, Chronicles is one of the main voices in the tradition concerning Josiah's death and is taken seriously especially by the early interpreters. Nevertheless, the problems concerning Josiah's death persisted, and early interpreters felt the need to offer at least slightly modified ways of solving the dilemma.

Jehoiachin: A Bad King or a Suffering Servant?

The line of kings presented in this study will end here with a short discussion of Jehoiachin. Although this case might better be treated as an instance of the theological influence of Chronicles, it shows that Manasseh was not the only evil king who was later rehabilitated. Jehoiachin is mentioned only briefly in Kings and Jeremiah (2 Kgs 23:8–17; 24:27–30; Jer 22:26–27, 30; 52:31–34); he is described as an evil king who is taken to Babylon and put in prison but surprisingly released without apparent reason at the very end of Kings.[73] Chronicles reports only the capture and imprisonment of Jehoiachin (2 Chr 36:9–10), not the release. We can only speculate on the reasons for this seeming omission. This could be an intentional omission on the part of the Chronicler so as not to provide undue hope of the imminent return of the Davidic monarchy. Or, if Ronald E. Clements is correct and the passage in Kings about the release is a very late addition, it may not be an omission at all.[74]

Later authors were particularly intrigued by the reason why Jehoiachin was released from prison and on the dynastic succession. 4Q381 IX, 14–19 sees the explanation for Jehoiachin's release to be the same as Manasseh's, that is, repentance. The author of 4Q381 wrote a penitential prayer for Jehoiachin, depicting him as a sinner suffering for his acts who was released because of his repentance. Thus, the missing reason for the release in the account of Kings is provided by the theology of repentance so prominent in Chronicles.[75]

This rehabilitation of Jehoiachin continued in later traditions as well. Josephus (*Ant.* 10.7.1 §100) attributes to him the same character traits evident in Samuel and Josiah: Jehoiachin is kind and just, and his capture is transformed into a noble, selfless act of surrendering himself and his family in order to save the temple.[76] For the rabbis, Jehoiachin is a repentant forefather of the coming Messiah (see Matt

---

[72] Cf. Feldman, *Studies in Josephus' Rewritten Bible*, 425–30.

[73] For this episode, see Ronald E. Clements, "A Royal Privilege: Dining in the Presence of the Great King (2 Kings 25.27–30)," in Rezetko, Lim, and Aucker, *Reflection and Refraction*, 49–66.

[74] Ibid., 66.

[75] Pajunen, *Land to the Elect*, 256–71.

[76] For an analysis of Josephus's account of Jehoiachin, see Feldman, *Studies in Josephus' Rewritten Bible*, 437–49.

1:12), and they have only good things to say about him.⁷⁷ Thus, even though Chronicles itself does not rehabilitate Jehoiachin, this is accomplished later in accordance with Chronicles' own theological paradigm of repentance.

IV. The Influence of Chronicles in the Second Century BCE

The early reception of the traditions concerning the kings of Judah together with the quotations and allusions to Chronicles in works from the second century BCE demonstrate that Chronicles was most influential in this time period. In writings from this period, Chronicles frequently prevails over Kings in contradictory matters and is taken as the main starting point for further interpretations. In addition, it is possible that Chronicles influenced theological paradigms and conceptions from the third century BCE onward, together with other works from the same circles, whose impact can be seen, for example, in the widespread emphasis on Levites in sources from the third and the second centuries BCE. Chronicles seems to have been the most influential "historical" composition in the early Hellenistic period. If this suggestion is taken seriously and if, furthermore, 4QSamᵃ is seen as an edition of Samuel later than the (Proto-)MT, or even as a midrash,⁷⁸ this would mean that an edition of Samuel was modified toward Chronicles. The influence of Samuel–Kings on versions of Chronicles becomes true slightly later, but during the early Hellenistic period the editing of some versions of the books of Samuel toward the text of Chronicles might be a possibility in light of the influence of Chronicles just discussed.

The overall situation concerning the relative status of Samuel–Kings and Chronicles certainly changes at some point after the Hellenistic period. There is no discernible use of Chronicles by the Qumran movement, but this might be explained by their concentration on their own movement and its past rather than on the

---

⁷⁷ According to Feldman, there are many rabbinic sources that claim that the suffering experienced by Jehoiachin in exile led him to repent of his former deeds (ibid., 447).

⁷⁸ Alexander Rofé has proposed that 4QSamᵃ should be considered a later midrash of the book ("Midrashic Traits in 4Q51 [So-Called 4QSamᵃ])," in *Archaeology of the Books of Samuel: The Entangling of the Textual and Literary History*, ed. Philip Hugo and Adrian Schenker, VTSup 132 [Leiden: Brill, 2010], 75–90). Zipora Talshir in turn rightly refutes this designation and argues that 4QSamᵃ should still be considered a biblical manuscript, albeit a later edition than the (proto-)MT ("Texts, Text-Forms, Editions, New Compositions and the Final Products of Biblical Literature," in Maier, *Congress Volume: Munich 2013*, 49–60). Most scholars, like Brooke ("Books of Chronicles," 36–37), still consider 4QSamᵃ to be attesting in many instances an earlier *Vorlage* than the MT. This earlier *Vorlage* would have been used by the Chronicler, so that it would not have been the case that Chronicles influenced 4QSamᵃ. It seems, however, that the situation is much more complex and that more studies need to be conducted before firm conclusions on this matter can be made.

history of the nation preserved in the "historical" biblical books. Another sign of the declining influence of Chronicles is that sometime around the turn of the era the translation of the LXX Chronicles was modified toward Samuel–Kings.[79] The New Testament evidences very little use of Chronicles or Samuel–Kings, whereas Josephus takes into account both Samuel–Kings and Chronicles. Thus, Chronicles enjoyed a brief golden age in the early Hellenistic period shortly after it was written, but after this Chronicles was slowly eclipsed by Samuel–Kings.

V. Conclusions

Traditions concerning the kings of Judah developed mainly toward a certain ideal picture. The kings turned from the frequently more complex characters portrayed in Samuel–Kings toward a more black-and-white representation, though there are exceptions to this development in every tradition. Josephus is often the one to provide a new twist to a tradition, and Manasseh remains a controversial figure throughout antiquity.

It is clear that traditions did not develop in a straight line with a later text automatically building on a previous one. Rather, later interpreters from the second century BCE onward picked and chose between Samuel–Kings and Chronicles and typically inserted their own views into the developing traditions as well. Nevertheless, during the early Hellenistic period Chronicles seems to have been the dominant narrative. Traditions that preferred Samuel–Kings are "rediscovered" only later in Josephus, 2 Baruch, and the Martyrdom of Isaiah and similar texts. Thus, Chronicles was taken seriously from early on and probably had the backing of the priestly authorities.

It is not surprising that Chronicles was most influential from some point in the third century when it was written to the late second century BCE. Just as Deuteronomistic compositions were apparently most influential when the scribes had administrative power in the Persian period, so Chronicles, as a product of the temple priesthood, was most influential during the period of their strength. After the Hasmoneans gained power in the wake of the Maccabean revolt, the different factions of Judaism were mostly interested in their own literature and in interpreting earlier traditions from their own group-specific viewpoint. The groups for whom Chronicles would have had lasting importance were the priesthood and the Levites, from whom very little is extant from the first centuries BCE and CE. In this context, it may be that the Qumran movement and the Hasmoneans

---

[79] See Leslie C. Allen, *The Greek Chronicles: The Relation of the Septuagint of I and II Chronicles to the Massoretic Text*, 2 vols., VTSup 25, 27 (Leiden: Brill, 1974), 1:175–218. For much smaller but similar modifications made to the Hebrew text of Chronicles, see Mika S. Pajunen, "1–2 Chronicles: (Proto-) Masoretic Texts and Texts Close to MT," in Lange and Tov, *Hebrew Bible*, 665–69.

did not hold Chronicles or the other "historical" books in high regard. These groups had their own foundation myths in the Damascus Document, the Pesharim, the books of Maccabees and so forth. The same is true for Christians a century later. There is practically nothing of Chronicles or Samuel–Kings in the New Testament. The most important group history for the early Christians was written in their own gospels, not in Samuel–Kings or Chronicles. This general change in the setting of societal discourse created a favorable atmosphere for group-specific texts, whereas the larger histories concerning the identity of the entire people were of less interest in the fragmented Jewish society. There was renewed interest in these traditions, however, after the destruction of the temple when it was again necessary to highlight the unity of the people and hence also their common heritage.

Therefore, while Chronicles was perhaps never the easiest composition to use to explain changing contexts and settings, it is important because the practices, theological paradigms, and interpretations of earlier traditions that it preserves had a major influence in the late Second Temple period and beyond. Both Chronicles and Samuel–Kings, or traditions drawn from them, continued to be influential in all treatments of the kings of Judah. As it could no longer be decided which line of tradition was correct on all points, both traditions needed to be preserved.

A "Cryptic Phrase" in Haggai 2:6

MAX ROGLAND
rogland@erskine.edu
Erskine Theological Seminary, Columbia, SC 29201

This article reexamines the problematic phrase עוד אחת מעט היא in Hag 2:6 with a view to proposing a philologically and exegetically satisfying analysis of the MT. The phrase is universally understood as an adverbial modifier of the following participial clause referring to YHWH's "shaking" of the cosmos. Scholarly opinion is divided as to whether the Hebrew expression indicates a temporally imminent event ("yet a little while"), repetition of an event ("yet once more"), or a combination of the two. A closer grammatical examination indicates that none of these solutions is adequate. It is argued that עוד אחת מעט היא is best understood as a verbless clause, with עוד אחת ("one more thing") as the subject, מעט ("a little thing") as the predicate, with היא functioning as a copula. Accordingly, I propose that the clause be translated, "One more thing is a small matter." In the context of Hag 2, the utterance functions as part of a "greater-to-lesser" argument as the prophet urges the people to give generously to the rebuilding of the temple despite their impoverished circumstances. Verse 5 reminded the people of YHWH's power displayed in the deliverance from Egypt, and verse 6 assures them that it will be a small, trifling matter for him to do "one more thing," namely, to exert his power and bring the "desirable things of the nations" into the temple (vv. 7–8) so that it can be rebuilt.

כי כה אמר יהוה צבאות עוד אחת מעט היא ואני מרעיש את־השמים ואת־הארץ ואת־הים
ואת־החרבה

For thus says the LORD of hosts: Once again, in a little while, I will shake the heavens and the earth and the sea and the dry land. (Hag 2:6 NRSV)

It is widely agreed that מרעיש in Hag 2:6 is an instance of the participle indicating the imminent future (Joüon §121e): "And *I am going to shake* the heavens and the earth and the sea and the dry land." Such a use of the participle occurs regularly in prophetic utterances and suits the general context of Haggai's oracle.[1] The

---

[1] John Kessler, *The Book of Haggai: Prophecy and Society in Early Persian Yehud*, VTSup 91 (Leiden: Brill, 2002), 160 n. 12, 175; Frank Yeadon Patrick, "Haggai and the Return of YHWH" (PhD diss., Duke University, 2006), 174.

analysis of the verse is made more complicated, however, by the preceding עוֹד אַחַת מְעַט הִיא, which Peter Ackroyd has called with some justification a "cryptic phrase."[2] This is universally taken as an adverbial modifier of וַאֲנִי מַרְעִישׁ אֶת־הַשָּׁמַיִם וְאֶת־הָאָרֶץ וְאֶת־הַיָּם וְאֶת־הֶחָרָבָה, although there is disagreement over its meaning, with two main lines of interpretation proposed in the scholarly literature.

The first option is to understand עוֹד אַחַת מְעַט הִיא as marking temporal imminence or immediacy in accord with the participle מַרְעִישׁ expressing the *futurum instans*: "yet a little/in a little while."[3] As such, it is understood as functionally equivalent to the phrase עוֹד מְעַט encountered elsewhere (e.g., Exod 17:4, Isa 10:25, 29:17, Jer 51:33, Hos 1:4).[4] Hans Walter Wolff views עוֹד אַחַת מְעַט הִיא as an expansion of the standard idiom עוֹד מְעַט, with the addition of אַחַת underscoring the uniqueness of the "little while."[5] Ferdinand Hitzig does not appeal to the analogy of עוֹד מְעַט, but in the end he interprets the clause as having essentially the same meaning. Arguing that we are to understand עֵת ("Zeitalter") rather than פַּעַם ("Mal") as the referent of עוֹד אַחַת, he takes the phrase as referring to the period of time before the golden age of verses 7–8 begins, with מְעַט הִיא specifying that this will be of short duration: "noch eine Zeit, eine kleine … soll verstreichen."[6] Carol L. Meyers and Eric M. Meyers conclude that the phrase is a neologism intended to emphasize the imminence of the occurrence: "*In only a moment* I will shake.…"[7]

The second approach to the interpretation of עוֹד אַחַת מְעַט הִיא is represented by the LXX, which understands the phrase to be expressing repetition or addition and renders it with ἔτι ἅπαξ, "yet once more/once again."[8] Frank Yeadon Patrick,

---

[2] Peter Ackroyd, *Exile and Restoration: A Study of Hebrew Thought of the Sixth Century B.C.*, OTL (Philadelphia: Westminster, 1968), 153; cf. David L. Petersen, *Haggai and Zechariah 1–8: A Commentary*, OTL (Philadelphia: Westminster, 1984), 61.

[3] Patrick, "Haggai and the Return of YHWH," 173–74; Marvin A. Sweeney, *The Twelve Prophets*, 2 vols., Berit Olam (Collegeville, MN: Liturgical Press, 2000), 2:547–48; Petersen, *Haggai and Zechariah 1–8*, 62; cf. Ackroyd, *Exile and Restoration*, 153–54.

[4] See Wolfgang Richter, "Zum syntaktischen Gebrauch von Substantiven im Althebräischen am Beispiel von ʿōd: Ein Beitrag zur Partikelforschung," *ZAH* 7 (1994): 175–95, esp. 180, 192; Martin Hallaschka, *Haggai und Sacharja 1–8: Eine Redaktionsgeschichtliche Untersuchung*, BZAW 411 (Berlin: de Gruyter, 2011), 58 n. 294.

[5] Hans Walter Wolff, *Haggai: A Commentary*, trans. Margaret Kohl (Minneapolis: Augsburg, 1988), 70–71; see also Pieter Verhoef, *The Books of Haggai and Malachi*, NICOT (Grand Rapids: Eerdmans, 1989), 101–2.

[6] Ferdinand Hitzig, *Die zwölf kleinen Propheten* (Leipzig: Hirzel, 1881), 328.

[7] Carol L. Meyers and Eric M. Meyers, *Haggai, Zechariah 1–8: A New Translation with Introduction and Commentary*, AB 25B (Garden City, NY: Doubleday, 1987), 52.

[8] See Joüon §102f on the adverbial use of cardinal numbers; typically feminine numbers are used (Joüon §152g). Several scholars have drawn attention to the lack of מְעַט in the LXX, and some suggest that this was theologically motivated due to the lack of an apparently "immediate" fulfillment. See, e.g., Carroll Stuhlmueller, *Rebuilding with Hope: A Commentary on the Books of Haggai and Zechariah*, ITC (Grand Rapids: Eerdmans, 1988), 26; Wilhelm Rudolph, *Haggai-Sacharja 1–8 – Sacharja 9–14 – Maleachi*, KAT (Gütersloh: Mohn, 1976), 41; and Petersen, *Haggai*

for example, asserts that "this introductory comment suggests that YHWH will 'once again' act in a mighty way in order to bless the people."[9] An early witness to this approach can be found in Heb 12:26-28, which contrasts the earlier "shaking" of Mount Sinai with an eschatological "shaking" of the cosmos still to come. The NRSV simply combines this interpretation with the expression of temporal imminence discussed above by rendering two adverbial modifiers: "Once again, in a little while, I will shake the heavens and the earth...." A number of other scholars also view עוד אחת מעט היא as a combination or conflation of the two idioms and likewise render it with two adverbial phrases.[10]

It is obvious that differences remain over the correct interpretation of עוד אחת מעט היא, and neither view can claim a clear consensus. At the same time, it is evident that there is widespread agreement that the phrase is to be taken as some kind of adverbial modifier of ואני מרעיש את־השמים ואת־הארץ ואת־הים ואת־החרבה. Nevertheless, regardless of whether עוד אחת מעט היא is understood as one phrase or two, an adverbial analysis of the expression is problematic.

First, if the clause were intended to express an action occurring "once again" or "one more time," then the use of an auxiliary verb such as הוסיף or שוב would have been more idiomatic.[11] It is true that עוד occurs in phrases that are functioning adverbially, for example:

1 Kgs 12:5
Go away for another three days.   לכו עד שלשה ימים

Gen 7:4
For in another seven days I am   כי לימים עוד שבעה אנכי ממטיר
going to bring rain...

---

and Zechariah 1-8, 61. It is always possible that the LXX was working from a different *Vorlage*, of course, though the phrase מעט היא is attested in the Murabbaʿat manuscript and in the Targum and Vulgate. On the other hand, its absence could potentially be explained either as an abbreviation or simply as the translator's failure to understand the MT; see Anthony Gelston in *BHQ* 13:132*.

[9] Patrick, "Haggai and the Return of YHWH," 173. Some have objected to this on exegetical grounds, since it appears to presuppose an earlier "shaking," the referent of which is uncertain (Petersen, *Haggai and Zechariah 1-8*, 62; Hitzig, *Die zwölf kleinen Propheten*, 328). For discussion, see Kessler, *Book of Haggai*, 174-75; Patrick, "Haggai and the Return of YHWH," 172-73.

[10] E.g., Kessler, *Book of Haggai*, 160, 173-74: "One more time, and it will happen very soon, I will shake the heavens and the earth"; Rudolph, *Haggai-Sacharja 1-8*, 40-41: "Einmal noch – in Bälde! – erschüttere ich den Himmel und die Erde."

[11] A collocation involving פעם could conceivably have been employed as well (see BDB, s.v. "פעם"). But the expression פעם אחת (or simply אחת with פעם omitted, as in Lev 16:34; see Joüon §102f) refers *not* to repetition ("once more/again") but rather to a singular occurrence ("one time, once"); see, e.g., Josh 6:3, 11, 14; 10:42; 1 Sam 26:8; Isa 66:8; 4Q159 1 II, 7; 11Q19 XXII, 16; XXVII, 5.

Jonah 3:4
Another forty days and Nineveh will be overturned.   עוד ארבעים יום ונינוה נהפכת

In these and other instances, however, it would be more accurate to say that עוד is functioning as an adnominal modifier indicating "another X."[12] The adverbial notion is a function of the larger nominal phrase of which עוד is a part.[13] This adnominal function of עוד is particularly evident in a number of examples of verbless clauses. In the indirect question of Gen 43:6, for example, העוד לכם אח indicates "Do you have *another* brother?" and not "Do you *again/still* have a brother?" Likewise, 2 Kgs 4:6 אין עוד כלי means "There is *not another* vessel," not "There *is still* no vessel." Note also the following examples:

Gen 19:12
Do you have *anyone else* here?   עד מי־לך פה

Amos 6:10
Is there *another* (person) with you?   העוד עמך

Isa 45:5
"I am YHWH, and there is not *another* (deity) apart from me." (See also vv. 6, 14, 18, 21, 22; 46:9; Joel 2:27.)   אני יהוה ואין עוד זולתי

Jer 38:9
For there is *no other* bread in the city.   כי אין הלחם עוד בעיר

Qoh 9:5
And they do not have *another* reward.   ואין־עוד להם שכר

This can also be observed in examples of verbless clauses involving numerals:

Gen 45:6
For the famine (has been) in the midst of the land these two years, and (there are) *another five years* with neither plowing nor harvesting.   כי־זה שנתים הרעב בקרב הארץ ועוד חמש שנים אשר אין־חריש וקציר

Gen 45:11
For (there are) *another five years* of famine.   כי־עוד חמש שנים רעב

---

[12] In the examples just cited, the expression does not indicate "another three/seven/forty days (in addition to the current three/seven/forty days)" but rather "another X days (in addition to today)."

[13] See John C. L. Gibson, *Davidson's Introductory Hebrew Grammar: Syntax*, 4th ed. (Edinburgh: T&T Clark, 1994), 139 (§114).

Indeed, nowhere is עוֹד utilized with the number "one" to indicate repeated action. Rather, as argued above, it is used adnominally to indicate "one more/another" entity, for example:

Exod 11:1
I will bring *one more/another plague*   עוֹד נֶגַע אֶחָד אָבִיא
upon Pharaoh and Egypt.   עַל־פַּרְעֹה וְעַל־מִצְרַיִם

1 Kgs 22:8 (= 2 Chr 18:7)
There is *one more/another man*   עוֹד אִישׁ־אֶחָד לִדְרֹשׁ
from whom one may inquire of YHWH.   אֶת־יְהוָה מֵאִתּוֹ

In light of such examples, it is highly questionable whether עוֹד אַחַת in Hag 2:6 can legitimately be understood as "once again." Rather, it is best interpreted as "one more (thing)."[14]

Second, while עוֹד מְעַט is indeed used adverbially to indicate "yet a little/in a little while," the occurrence of the intervening element אַחַת in Hag 2:6 (עוֹד אַחַת מְעַט) must not be overlooked. This is the only time that a numeral occurs between עוֹד and מְעַט, and it begs the question to assume that this is functionally equivalent to the עוֹד מְעַט syntagm. As noted above, the usage of עוֹד with numerals suggests rather that we are to understand עוֹד אַחַת as "one more/another (thing)." It is of course possible that we are dealing with a neologism, as some have asserted, but such an explanation seems facile and can neither be proven nor disproven.

From this review it appears that the current adverbial analyses proposed for עוֹד אַחַת מְעַט הִיא are difficult to sustain.[15] As might be expected, text-critical emendations have been suggested as a way of resolving the issue. Hinckley G. T. Mitchell calls the text "evidently corrupt," being the confusion of the two adverbial idioms discussed above, and omits both אַחַת and הִיא, leaving simply עוֹד מְעַט.[16] The Minor

---

[14] The number אַחַת in Hag 2:6 is substantivized (see Joüon §100a); on the use of the feminine gender, see Joüon §152g.

[15] I would also argue that prosodic factors provide additional confirmation that עוֹד אַחַת מְעַט הִיא is best understood as a grammatically independent clause rather than as an adverbial modifier of וַאֲנִי מַרְעִישׁ אֶת־הַשָּׁמַיִם וְאֶת־הָאָרֶץ וְאֶת־הַיָּם וְאֶת־הֶחָרָבָה. The pattern is for עוֹד to stand as close to the verb as possible (see Christo H. J. van der Merwe, Jackie A. Naudé, and Jan H. Kroeze, *A Biblical Hebrew Reference Grammar*, Biblical Languages: Hebrew 3 [Sheffield: Sheffield Academic, 2002], 341 [§46.1.3.iia]). In Hag 2:6, however, the *athnach* in הִיא serves to create a major disjunction, which weighs against linking עוֹד אַחַת מְעַט הִיא with the clause that it is allegedly modifying. It is true that at times the accentuation of a verse runs contrary to its syntax (see Joüon §15e), and so this datum is merely suggestive rather than conclusive; but all things considered there is general validity to Israel Yeivin's assertion that accentuation "is a good guide to the syntax of a text" (*Introduction to the Tiberian Masorah*, trans. E. J. Revell, MasS 5 [Atlanta: Scholars Press, 1980], 158; see also Joüon §15j; *IBHS* §1.6.4a).

[16] Hinckley G. T. Mitchell, Julius A. Brewer, and John M. Powis Smith, *A Critical and Exegetical Commentary on Haggai, Zechariah, Malachi and Jonah*, ICC (New York: Scribner's Sons, 1912), 65.

Prophets scroll from Wadi Murabbaʿat (papMurXII), however, attests the pronoun היא.[17] A very different emendation is proposed by Arnold B. Ehrlich, who links עוד with the preceding verb אמר: "denn so sagt JHVH der Heerscharen *ferner*." Appealing to 2 Sam 12:8 ואם־מעט ואספה לך ("And if this were too little, I would add to you") for reading אם in place of אחת, he interprets היא as expressing a neuter/impersonal subject (see Joüon §152g), with מעט referring to the insignificant state of the temple. Thus he arrives at the translation "Wenn es unbedeutend ist, so will ich in Bewegung setzen...."[18] Yet there is no external textual data to support the proposed emendation, and such a use of עוד would be unique among the numerous attestations of the so-called messenger formula.[19] Meyers and Meyers aptly observe that the peculiarity of the expression speaks in favor of its originality.[20]

I would argue that there is an analysis of the MT of Hag 2:6 that is not only grammatically feasible but also exegetically fitting. For the reasons given above, עוד אחת מעט היא is to be taken as an independent verbless clause and not as adverbial to ואני מרעיש את־השמים ואת־הארץ ואת־הים ואת־החרבה.[21] As also noted previously, עוד אחת does not express "once (more)" but rather indicates "one more" of something. In this case the feminine gender is used for a neuter subject, that is, "one more (thing)," and the corresponding feminine pronoun היא functions as the equivalent of the copula.[22] Thus, we are dealing with a nominal clause, with מעט

---

[17] See Gelston, *Twelve Minor Prophets*, 132*.

[18] Arnold B. Ehrlich, *Randglossen zur hebräischen Bibel: Textkritisches, sprachliches und sachliches*, 7 vols. (Leipzig: Hinrichs, 1908–1914), 5:322.

[19] Note the use of עוד as part of the direct discourse introduced by the messenger formula in Jer 33:10, 12; Ezek 20:27; 36:37; Zech 1:17.

[20] Meyers and Meyers, *Haggai, Zechariah 1–8*, 52; see also Kessler, *Book of Haggai*, 160 n. 11.

[21] It would be difficult to take עוד אחת as a verbless clause in its own right, for עוד by itself is not easily understood as either the subject or predicate of a clause. Just possibly the phrase עוד אחת could be considered the predicate of a verbless clause with a subject pronoun omitted (Joüon §154b–c), for example, "(It is) one more thing." For reasons that will become clear, it is preferable to understand the entirety of עוד אחת מעט היא as a single tripartite nominal clause.

[22] See Meyers and Meyers, *Haggai, Zechariah 1–8*, 52; Kessler, *Book of Haggai*, 174–75. Richter argues that עוד can be interpreted as the copula in instances such as this one, but he offers no explanation for the function of היא in Hag 2:6 ("Zum syntaktischen Gebrauch," 180). One anonymous reviewer of this article suggested that the clause could also be construed as an instance of front dislocation: "One more thing—a small matter [is] it." Cf. Walter Gross, *Die Pendenskonstruktion im biblischen Hebräisch*, ATSAT 27 (St. Ottilien: EOS, 1987), 126; and Joüon, §154i. On the debate concerning the tripartite nominal clause, see Robert D. Holmstedt and Andrew R. Jones, "The Pronoun in Tripartite Verbless Clauses in Biblical Hebrew: Resumption for Left Dislocation or Pronominal Copula?," *JSS* 59 (2014): 53–89, https://doi.org/10.1093/jss/fgt035.

forming the predicate: "One more (thing) is מעט."²³ This could perhaps best be rendered, "One more thing is a little thing" or "one more thing is a small matter."²⁴

What is the meaning of this utterance in the context of Hag 2? A strong case can be made that verse 5 is, like 1:8–9, issuing a challenge to provide for the repair and reconstruction of the temple: "Do not fear the matter which I covenanted with you when you came out of Egypt, while my Spirit was abiding in your midst."²⁵ In fact, verse 5 appears to be referring intertextually to the directives given in the book of Exodus for the people to make offerings for the construction of the tabernacle (Exod 25:1–8, 35:4–11). The situational parallels with the prophet's hearers are not difficult to discern: "Haggai's post-Exilic audience is being urged not to be afraid of freely and generously making offerings for the rebuilding of the temple, just as the Israelites were directed to do for the construction of the original tabernacle."²⁶ Given the impoverished circumstances mentioned in the book (Hag 1:5, 9–11; 2:16–17), however, the oracle's addressees may very well lack confidence that they have sufficient means to carry out this charge. It is in this context that the prophet makes reference to the exodus event (v. 5: בצאתכם ממצרים, "when you came out of Egypt"). The exodus is frequently mentioned throughout the Tanak as the ultimate display of YHWH's power, and in Hag 2 it occurs as YHWH is about to assure the people that he can provide abundantly. The people need not hesitate in giving to the rebuilding, because YHWH is capable of summoning the "valuable things of the nations" to be brought to the temple (v. 7). YHWH is, after all, the one who possesses all the silver and gold (v. 8).

In this setting, then, I would argue that עוד אחת מעט היא forms part of a "greater-to-lesser" argument. If YHWH could deliver his people out of Egypt (who brought with them enough wealth to build the tabernacle), then, comparatively speaking, it will be a "little thing" to provide for the rebuilding of the temple as the people are returning from the exile. The phrase thus represents a kind of "boastful" statement meant to inspire confidence in YHWH's hearers: The shaking of the

---

²³ In this respect I agree with the analysis of Richter, who also takes מעט as the predicate of the clause ("Zum syntaktischen Gebrauch," 180). The lack of gender concord between מעט and both עוד אחת and היא is not an insuperable objection to this analysis. Not only is this sporadically attested in Biblical Hebrew (GKC §145r; Joüon §148b), but it occurs specifically with מעט in Eccl 10:1 (סכלות מעט, "a little folly") and Prov 6:10 (= 24:33) (מעט שנות מעט תנומות, "a little sleep, a little slumber"). Indeed, מעט never occurs in feminine forms and hardly even inflects for number, except for the masculine plural מעטים in Ps 109:8 and Eccl 5:1.

²⁴ Cf. Ackroyd's "yet one, and it is only a little one" (*Exile and Restoration*, 153–54), though he still understands the clause temporally.

²⁵ Haggai 2:5 is a notorious textual and exegetical problem that cannot be fully treated here. For a discussion of this rendering of the MT and its exegetical consequences, see Max Rogland, "Text and Temple in Haggai 2,5," *ZAW* 119 (2007): 410–15.

²⁶ Ibid., 414, with further discussion of the intended intertexts of verse 5.

cosmos and the ensuing time of prosperity are being presented as a trifling, easy achievement in comparison with the deliverance from Egypt.[27]

In light of the analysis proposed above, one final grammatical observation is in order. Specifically, it seems likely that the following verbal clause ואני מרעיש את־השמים ואת־הארץ ואת־הים ואת־החרבה is to be taken as explicative or epexegetical of the preceding עוד אחת מעט היא.[28] In other words, the participial clause specifies what the "little thing" is. As such, the entire verse may be rendered, "For thus has YHWH Tsevaot said, 'One more thing is a small matter, namely, I am going to shake the heavens and the earth and the sea and the dry land.'"

---

[27] An alternative suggestion by one anonymous reviewer of this article is that this could perhaps be viewed as an ironic comparison, as if YHWH is saying, "I'll do just one additional 'small thing' (like the 'small thing' I did in the past)." This is certainly possible, though by and large the book does not display irony elsewhere. In any event, this assumes the basic syntactical analysis of עוד אחת מעט היא proposed here.

[28] In many grammars the introductory conjunction ו would be considered an instance of the so-called explicative *vav*; see, inter alios, van der Merwe, Naudé, and Kroeze, *Biblical Hebrew Reference Grammar*, 300 (§40.8.2.vii); and Ronald J. Williams and John C. Beckman, *Williams' Hebrew Syntax*, 3rd ed. (Toronto: University of Toronto Press, 2007), 154 (§434). Though a full interaction with his views cannot be provided here, one should take note of the strong objections raised to such terminology by Richard Steiner, "Does the Biblical Hebrew Conjunction -ו Have Many Meanings, One Meaning, or No Meaning at All?," *JBL* 119 (2000): 249–67, esp. 264–65, https://doi.org/10.2307/3268486.

Translation of Horse Colors in Zechariah 1:8; 6:2–3, 6 Based on Textual and Material Evidence

DIANA ABERNETHY
diana.abernethy@duke.edu
Duke University, Durham, NC 27708

The first and final visions of Zechariah include the Hebrew Bible's only descriptions of horses in terms of their color. The color terms employed have long sparked debate about whether these horses have realistic or imaginative colors, the significance of these colors for the interpretation of Zechariah's visions, and whether technical or ordinary color terms are most appropriate for translating them today. Recent genetic studies of the coat color of ancient horses prompt a new consideration of these terms in Zechariah. This article combines Athalya Brenner's textual analysis of the color terms in the Hebrew Bible with a list of genetically probable horse coat colors in Iron Age Israel in order to produce working translations of these terms for American audiences. This list of genetically probable horse coat colors results from the integration of David Anthony's study of the initial domestication of horses with Arne Ludwig et al.'s genetic study of horse coat color in the ancient world. The evaluation of current genetic analyses of ancient horse coat colors in light of the broader use of color terms in the Hebrew Bible produces translations of these terms that are as precise as possible, given current genetic evidence, and sensitive to the contours of the source and target languages.

The Hebrew Bible describes the color of horses only in Zech 1:8 and 6:2–3, 6, in Zechariah's first and last visions; these colors constitute part of the *inclusio* in the imagery of the visions. The translation and significance of the colors have been widely debated, but the most compelling proposals suggest that these color terms reflect realistic horse colors and contribute to the interpretation of the passage. Athalya Brenner's textual analysis of the color terms in the Hebrew Bible can be combined with a list of genetically probable horse coat colors in Iron Age Israel to develop translations for the color terms describing horses in Zechariah for

American audiences familiar and unfamiliar with horses.[1] A list of genetically probable horse coat colors in Iron Age Israel will be deduced from David W. Anthony's account of horse domestication and trade patterns, which reveals how domesticated horses most likely entered ancient Israel, and Arne Ludwig et al.'s genetic study of coat colors present in ancient horse populations.[2]

In Zech 1:8, a man is riding one horse with more horses behind him: "In the night I saw a man riding on a red [אדם] horse! He was standing among the myrtle trees in the glen; and behind him were red [אדמים], sorrel [שרקים], and white [לבנים] horses" (NRSV). Zechariah 6:2–3 lists four chariots with differently colored horses: "The first chariot had red [אדמים] horses, the second chariot black [שחרים] horses, the third chariot white [לבנים] horses, and the fourth chariot dappled gray [ברדים] horses" (NRSV). The last word of Zech 6:3, אמצים, suggests that all of these horses are also "strong." In Zech 6:6, the groups of chariot horses head in different directions: "The chariot with the black [השחרים] horses goes toward the north country, the white ones [הלבנים] go toward the west country, and the dappled ones [הברדים] go toward the south country" (NRSV). The basic meanings of אדם, שחר, and לבן are, respectively, "red" or "brown," "black," and "white," but שרק and ברד are more obscure. שרק is a secondary term in the "red" range, and ברד refers to a type of speckled appearance.

I. Three Contested Issues

The debates about the color of the horses in Zechariah center on three issues: (1) whether these horse colors are realistic or visionary; (2) how significant these colors are to the interpretation of the text; and (3) whether technical terms or ordinary terms should be used to translate these horse colors into modern English.

Commentators have reached different conclusions about these issues.[3] Joyce

---

[1] The terminology for horse coat colors varies across the English-speaking world. My proposals use terms common in the United States.

[2] David W. Anthony, *The Horse, the Wheel, and Language: How Bronze-Age Riders from the Eurasian Steppes Shaped the Modern World* (Princeton: Princeton University Press, 2007); Arne Ludwig et al., "Coat Color Variation at the Beginning of Horse Domestication," *Science* 324 (2009): 485, https://doi.org/10.1126/science.1172750.

[3] William D. McHardy, "The Horses in Zechariah," in *In Memoriam Paul Kahle*, ed. Matthew Black and Georg Fohrer, BZAW 103 (Berlin: Töpelmann, 1968), 174–79; Joyce G. Baldwin, *Haggai, Zechariah, Malachi*, TOTC (Downers Grove, IL: InterVarsity Press, 1972), 95, 131, 138–40; David L. Petersen, *Haggai and Zechariah 1–8: A Commentary*, OTL (Philadelphia: Westminster, 1984), 136–60, 263–72; Carol L. Meyers and Eric M. Meyers, *Haggai, Zechariah 1–8: A New Translation with Introduction and Commentary*, AB 25B (Garden City, NY: Doubleday, 1987), 107–34, 316–36; Barry F. Peachey, "A Horse of a Different Colour: The Horses in Zechariah and Revelation," *ExpTim* 110 (1999): 214–16, https://doi.org/10.1177/001452469911000704; David J. Clark, "Red and Green Horses?," *BT* 56 (2005): 67–71. See also David J. Clark and Howard A.

Baldwin, David L. Petersen, Carol L. Meyers and Eric M. Meyers, and David Clark treat these colors as realistic for horses, while Barry Peachey argues that such an attempt is misguided because the horses are in Zechariah's visions and thus do not possess realistic coat colors.[4] Petersen and Meyers and Meyers maintain that horse color is an integral detail in the interpretation of the passage, while Baldwin and Peachey are skeptical that the precise colors bear on the text's interpretation.[5] Baldwin notes that the text does not ascribe specific meaning to the horse colors and suspects they were "merely background."[6] Peachey does not consider the colors significant because he does not know how much contact ancient Israelites had with horses.[7]

Petersen favors technical terms when translating these words, while Peachey and Clark prefer ordinary terms.[8] Because Peachey argues that the horses in Zechariah's visions do not necessarily have realistic colors, he contends that technical terms are not needed to translate these colors.[9] Clark recommends ordinary terms for translations that strive to use accessible language.[10]

II. Previous Translations

All of these scholars agree that "white" and "black" are good translations for לבנים and שחרים, respectively, but debate surrounds the other terms. ברדים is taken as "dappled" or "gray." Proposals for the translation of אדמים include "red" (McHardy and Meyers and Meyers), "bay" (Baldwin), "dark chestnut" or "bay" (Petersen), "chestnut" or "sorrel" (Peachey), and "brown" (Clark).[11] שרקים has been translated

---

Hatton, *A Handbook on Haggai, Zechariah, and Malachi*, UBS Handbook Series (New York: United Bible Societies, 2002), 161–62, 165.

[4] Baldwin, *Haggai, Zechariah, Malachi*, 95; Petersen, *Haggai and Zechariah 1–8*, 140–42; Meyers and Meyers, *Haggai, Zechariah 1–8*, 112–13; Peachey, "Horse of a Different Colour," 214; Clark, "Red and Green Horses?," 67.

[5] Petersen, *Haggai and Zechariah 1–8*, 140–42; Meyers and Meyers, *Haggai, Zechariah 1–8*, 112–13, 320–22; Baldwin, *Haggai, Zechariah, Malachi*, 139; Peachey, "Horse of a Different Colour," 215.

[6] Baldwin, *Haggai, Zechariah, Malachi*, 139.

[7] Peachey contends, "We do not know very much about the relationship of the *habiru* with equines, but we do know that in general in the ancient world the ownership of horses bespoke status" ("Horse of a Different Colour," 215).

[8] Petersen, *Haggai and Zechariah 1–8*, 141; Peachey, "Horse of a Different Colour," 215–16; and Clark, "Red and Green Horses?," 67. McHardy also uses "ordinary" color terms, but he does not state his motives for doing so. McHardy's essay focuses more on reconstructing the original lists of the horse colors than on proposing the best translations for the color terms themselves ("Horses in Zechariah," 174–79).

[9] Peachey, "Horse of a Different Colour," 216.

[10] Clark, "Red and Green Horses?," 67.

[11] McHardy, "Horses in Zechariah," 179; Meyers and Meyers, *Haggai, Zechariah 1–8*, 107; Baldwin, *Haggai, Zechariah, Malachi*, 95; Petersen, *Haggai and Zechariah 1–8*, 136, 141, 263; Peachey, "Horse of a Different Colour," 214; and Clark, "Red and Green Horses?," 67.

as "light bay" (Petersen), "sorrel" (Meyers and Meyers), "flea-bitten grey" (Peachey), and "grey" (Clark).[12] McHardy and Baldwin argue that אמצים is a color word; McHardy places it in the "yellow" range, and Baldwin renders it "bay."[13] Meyers and Meyers and Clark, however, argue that אמצים is from the root אמץ meaning "strong" and does not function as a color term here.[14] Table 1 summarizes the proposals for the translations of these terms in Zech 1:8 and 6:2–3.

TABLE 1. Translation Proposals for the Color Terms in Zech 1:8 and 6:2–3

Verse	1:8	1:8	1:8	1:8
Hebrew color word	אדם	אדמים	שרקים	לבנים
NRSV	Red	Red	Sorrel	White
McHardy	Red	Yellow[15]	Black[15]	White
Petersen	Dark Chestnut	Dark Chestnut	Light Bay	White
Meyers and Meyers	Red	Red	Sorrel	White
Peachey[16]	Chestnut/Sorrel	Chestnut/Sorrel	Flea-Bitten Gray	White
Clark	Brown	Brown	Gray	White
My proposal for an American audience familiar with horses	Chestnut	Chestnut	Chestnut Sabino/ Mealy Chestnut	Gray/ White
My proposal for an American audience unfamiliar with horses	Reddish Brown	Reddish Brown	Reddish Brown with White/ Lighter Areas	White

---

[12] Petersen, *Haggai and Zechariah 1–8*, 141; Meyers and Meyers, *Haggai, Zechariah 1–8*, 107; Peachey, "Horse of a Different Colour," 214; Clark, "Red and Green Horses?," 68.

[13] McHardy, "Horses in Zechariah," 174–77; and Baldwin, *Haggai, Zechariah, Malachi*, 138. Athalya Brenner argues that אמץ is a secondary color term that refers to "light reddish-brown" (*Colour Terms in the Old Testament*, JSOTSup 21 [Sheffield: JSOT Press, 1982], 112–14).

[14] Meyers and Meyers, *Haggai, Zechariah 1–8*, 107; Clark, "Red and Green Horses?," 68–69. See also Clark and Hatton, *Handbook on Haggai, Zechariah, and Malachi*, 162, 165.

[15] These proposals follow McHardy's textual emendations. McHardy argues that the lists in Zech 1:8; 6:2–3, 6 originally contained the same four colors and that these consistent lists diverged when the abbreviations in early texts were written fully in subsequent copies ("Horses in Zechariah," 174–79).

[16] These are the technical color terms that Peachey argues are closest to the Hebrew color terms rather than the ordinary terms he prefers for English translations ("Horse of a Different Colour," 214).

TABLE 1 (cont.)

Verse	6:2	6:2	6:3	6:3
Hebrew color word	אדמים	שחרים	לבנים	ברדים
NRSV	Red	Black	White	Dappled Gray
McHardy	Red	Black	White	Yellow[17]
Petersen	Bay	Black	White	Dappled
Meyers and Meyers	Red	Black	White	Dappled
Peachey[16]	Chestnut/Sorrel	Black	White	Gray
Clark	Brown	Black	White	Gray
My proposal for an American audience familiar with horses	Chestnut	Black	Gray/White	Dappled Gray/ Blue Roan
My proposal for an American audience unfamiliar with horses	Reddish Brown	Black	White	Speckled

III. Contested Issues Reevaluated

Brenner's analysis of how these color terms function in the Hebrew Bible provides a starting point for translating these terms in Zechariah. The terms that describe the horses in Zechariah refer to realistic horse colors because the Hebrew Bible elsewhere uses these terms to describe humans, animals, and objects that are part of the natural world.[18] Brenner concludes that אדם includes a range of colors from "'brown' through 'red' to 'pink.'" This term is particularly associated with blood, but it also refers to "animals' hides, lentils, blood, wine, [and] human complexion." The term לבן connotes "'bright,' 'clear,' 'hueless,' 'light,' 'pale,' [and] 'white.'" It is used to describe "animals' fleece, wood bark, teeth, גַּד-seed, hair, clothes, [and] the appearance of diseased skin." שחר refers to things that are "'dark-coloured' [or] 'black,'" and it is used of "human hair, human skin (complexion), [and] animals'

---

[17] This proposal corresponds to אמצים, which, according to McHardy, functioned as or replaced an earlier color word. He suggests that ברדים was a later gloss of אמצים ("Horses in Zechariah," 174–77). In contrast, Brenner proposes that ברדים was a "(mistaken) explanatory gloss" for אמצים (*Colour Terms*, 113).

[18] Brenner leaves open the question of whether the horses in Zechariah's vision have realistic or unrealistic colors (*Colour Terms*, 69–70, 114–15).

skin." Brenner identifies אדם, לבן, and שחר as primary color terms while שרק is a secondary term. שרק is "yellow-red," and related forms denote a type of vine. ברד is a pattern term that describes "a 'spotted' or 'speckled' appearance."[19]

The author of Zechariah would have been capable of describing horses with color terms applicable to other aspects of the natural world. Because agriculture and husbandry were prevalent in ancient Israel, color terms were likely used to describe animals regularly. Indeed, all of the color words used in Zechariah except שרק are used for other animals in the Hebrew Bible. Horses and chariots were used during the monarchy in Israel, and by the time Zechariah was written in the postexilic period, at least some Israelites would have had contact with Persians, whose use of horses was also advanced.[20] Ancient Israelites could apply everyday color terms to horses, which were colored similarly to other familiar animals, including goats, sheep, and cattle.

Because the Hebrew Bible uses color terms sparingly and in connection with horses only in Zechariah, these terms in Zechariah stand out as significant details in the text. Jacob and Laban's flocks in Gen 30–31 provide a helpful comparison. These texts describe the flocks with multiple color and pattern words, and Jacob distinguishes members of the flocks by their physical appearance as he sorts them.

---

[19] The quoted descriptions in this paragraph are from ibid., 69–71 and 179; 85 and 180; 181; 39–43; 114–15; and 112–13 and 169.

[20] Petersen, *Haggai and Zechariah 1–8*, 144–45. The presence of horses in Iron Age Israel is well established, as Gerald Klingbeil demonstrates. Klingbeil examined the use of equids in Iron Age I–II Palestine using a multidisciplinary approach that included the use of textual, iconographic, and paleozoological investigations. He considered the use of terms for equids in 1 and 2 Kings in contexts of military use, transportation, social-status markers, and religious practice. He also cataloged osteological remains, including four fragments of horse bones from Tel Dan and twenty from Hesban ("'Man's Other Best Friend': The Interaction of Equids and Man in Daily Life in Iron Age II Palestine as Seen in Texts, Artifacts, and Images," *UF* 35 [2003]: 259–89, esp. 259, 263–64, 269–70).

Extrabiblical textual evidence also supports the prevalence of horses during the monarchic period. In the ninth-century inscription on the Kurkh Monolith, Shalmaneser III declares that "Ahab the Israelite" contributed two thousand chariots and ten thousand foot soldiers to the coalition resisting him at Karkara (James B. Pritchard, ed., *The Ancient Near East: An Anthology of Texts and Pictures* [Princeton: Princeton University Press, 1958], 190). Additionally, in a seventh-century inscription, Sennacherib boasts of taking humans as well as "horses, mules, donkeys, camels, big and small cattle beyond counting" when he attacked Jerusalem and the surrounding area during the reign of Hezekiah (ibid., 200).

Deborah O'Daniel Cantrell argues that horses and chariots were the critical factors that allowed monarchic Israel to maintain its autonomy. As she examined monarchic Israel's six-chambered gates and architectural remains at Megiddo and Jezreel, she saw such extensive evidence of horses and chariots that Ahab's two thousand chariots mentioned in the Kurkh Monolith would be a realistic rather than an inflated number (*The Horsemen of Israel: Horses and Chariotry in Monarchic Israel [Ninth–Eighth Centuries B.C.E.]*, HACL 1 [Winona Lake, IN: Eisenbrauns, 2011], 35–38, 76–113, 142–43).

Jacob also controls the color of their offspring by placing certain rods in front of mating pairs. This Genesis text demonstrates that ancient Israelites could distinguish individual goats and sheep by coat color and possibly tried to influence the color of their offspring.[21]

Even if it is not as explicit as the role of the colors of the flocks in Gen 30–31, the colors of the horses in Zechariah have interpretive significance. Nogah Hareuveni, Meyers and Meyers, and Petersen explore how the significance of the horses' colors could have been obvious to the original audience of Zechariah's prophecy in view of their cultural knowledge. Hareuveni and Meyers and Meyers argue that the horse colors in Zech 1:8 would blend into the colors of vegetation at the time of year specified in Zech 1:7, and they assume that the color of seasonal vegetation was well known at the time when Zechariah was written.[22] Petersen quotes an Arabian proverb to suggest that horse colors were linked to other attributes.[23] In this case, the colors themselves would convey additional details about

---

[21] This episode is only loosely connected to the horses in Zechariah; Gen 31:10, 12 contain the only other occurrences in the Hebrew Bible of the sole pattern term used of Zechariah's horses, ברדים. This term describes the goats in Jacob's dream after he successfully manipulated the color of Laban's flocks.

[22] For Hareuveni, the explicit date in Zech 1:7, "the twenty-fourth day of the eleventh month, the month of Shebat," points to a specific time of year characterized by certain colors of wild vegetation on uncultivated land. He says, "Towards the middle of *Shvat*, the almond tree adorns the landscape in a blaze of snowy white blossoms, white and red anemones sparkle in the fields." The horse colors blend into this landscape: "the horses which return from scouting out the land are 'red, purple and white,' as though they were carrying the very colors which, in this season, characterize the wild fields which have lain fallow 'these seventy years'" (Nogah Hareuveni, *Nature in Our Biblical Heritage*, trans. Helen Frenkley [Kiryat Ono, Israel: Neot Kedumim, 1980], 115–17). Meyers and Meyers follow Hareuveni's proposal about the seasonal vegetation and horses in Zechariah's first vision (Meyers and Meyers, *Haggai, Zechariah 1–8*, 112–14).

[23] Petersen underscores the differences between the imagery of the two visions. The significance of the colors lies in the horses themselves in the first vision, while the colors in the latter vision distinguish the chariots going toward each compass point. The Arabian proverb, which is of indeterminate date, is an example of the kind of association between the color of a horse and its other attributes that would have been possible in the ancient Near East: "The fleetest of horses is the chestnut, / the most enduring the bay, / the most spirited the black, / and the most blessed the white." Petersen suggests that these kinds of associations guided the meaning of the horse colors in the first vision (*Haggai and Zechariah 1–8*, 142, 268–69).

Some links between coat colors and other horse attributes have a genetic basis, and geneticists are beginning to explore these connections. Anna Stachurska and P. Jansen contend, "Horse breeders have always believed that coat colour was associated with a horse's performance. Such a connection would result from genes which control the coat colour and simultaneously are linked with genes responsible for the performance" ("Crypto-Tobiano Horses in Hucul Breed," *Czech Journal of Animal Science* 60 [2015]: 1, https://doi.org/10.17221/7905-CJAS). One such documented example is the connection between horses with leopard spotting and congenital stationary night blindness in horses homozygous for the leopard-spotting gene (Rebecca R. Bellone et al., "Fine-Mapping and Mutation Analysis of *TRPM1*: A Candidate Gene for Leopard

the horses. For these scholars, the significance of the horse colors emerges in their connection to now-lost background knowledge about seasonal vegetation and horse traits.

The importance of the color terms necessitates care in translating them, and different color vocabularies in Biblical Hebrew and modern English affect the rendering of these terms in the target language. Color terms are notoriously difficult to translate because various languages divide the color spectrum in different ways. Horse color terms present additional difficulty for translation into modern English because it has a separate set of technical terms used specifically for horses, while Biblical Hebrew uses the same color terms for a range of everyday animals and objects as well as for the horses in Zechariah. This requires one translation in modern English for those who are familiar with horses and a different translation for those who are not. Although some modern English speakers have a much wider range of experience with horses and other livestock than did ancient Israelites, others have minimal interaction with horses and farm animals. Modern English speakers who are familiar with horses use an extensive vocabulary to describe the associated colors, equipment, movement, ailments, and so on; they learn this vocabulary through their experiences in subcultures that arise around different equine practices.

As a result, technical horse color terms are appropriate for translations aimed at a modern audience well acquainted with horses. Their use shows that the author of Zechariah was using color terms that were both realistic and as precise as were available to him. The use of ordinary color terms for such an audience, however, might mistakenly communicate that the author of Zechariah did not know how to describe horse color or that he saw horses that did not have realistic colors. Conversely, ordinary color terms are appropriate for modern audiences unfamiliar with horses because such terms are the clearest way to describe horses. The use of technical terms for this audience could wrongly communicate that the horses did not have colors readily known by the average person. The diversity of experience with horses among modern English speakers requires different translations to convey the precise and realistic colors of the horses in Zechariah.

Complex [LP] Spotting and Congenital Stationary Night Blindness in Horses," *Briefings in Functional Genomics* 9 [2010]: 193, https://doi.org/10.1093/bfgp/elq002).

Likewise, D. Phillip Sponenberg notes, "A small collection of European research is beginning to verify that horses of specific colors tend to react somewhat predictably in certain situations and that these reactions vary from color to color. A general trend seems to be that horses of darker colors are livelier than lighter ones, but the breeds in which this was determined were not noted, so the range of colors is likewise uncertain.… Even though the relationships of behavior and color are speculative, they are an interesting part of the art of horse breeding and horse keeping" (*Equine Color Genetics*, 3rd ed. [Ames, IA: Wiley-Blackwell, 2009], 9). Even as the connections between specific colors and qualities remain tentative, the Arabian proverb that Petersen quotes also, interestingly, links darker horses with livelier qualities.

IV. Assessing the Genetic Evidence

Examining the available material evidence of horse coat colors in ancient Israel will help produce more precise translations of the terms used to describe them in Zechariah. Anthony's study of early horse domestication can be combined with Ludwig et al.'s genetic study of horse coat color in ancient populations to establish, according to the best evidence available at present, which coat colors were most likely present in Iron Age Israel.

In *The Horse, the Wheel, and Language*, Anthony uses archaeology, anthropology, and historical linguistic reconstructions of Proto-Indo-European to trace the initial migrations of speakers of Proto-Indo-European from their homeland in the Pontic-Caspian steppe. Herders in the Pontic-Caspian steppe domesticated horses as a source of winter meat as early as 4800 BCE and were riding them by 4300–4000 BCE. Horseback riding allowed these groups to become formidable raiders; to shepherd larger herds of sheep and cattle across more grazing land; to engage in long-distance metal trade; and to spread domesticated horses into Europe, the eastern steppe, Central Asia, Mesopotamia, the Near East, and Egypt. If Anthony's migration and trade patterns are correct, the domesticated horses in ancient Israel descended from wild horses initially domesticated in the Eurasian steppe.[24]

Anthony's account of the diffusion of domesticated horses from the Eurasian steppe into the ancient Near East traces at least three possible paths: through western Anatolia, through the Caucasus Mountains, and through Central Asia. First, domesticated and ridden horses entered western Anatolia from the Danube River valley in the third or fourth millennium BCE.[25] No clear evidence connects these early horses with the Near East, but by the second millennium BCE, groups in Anatolia had horse-trading relationships with the Near East. Second, the Maikop culture persisted in the Caucasus Mountain region from 3700 to 3000 BCE and rode steppe horses. Maikop maintained trade relationships with Mesopotamia during this period, but domesticated horses did not move into the Mesopotamian lowlands until later.[26] Third, groups derived from Sintashta in the Ural Mountains and eastern steppe brought horses and chariots into Central Asia and from there into well-attested trade routes with the Near East around 2100–1900 BCE.[27] Domesticated horses probably entered the Near East and ancient Israel by multiple routes, but the domesticated horse populations in the surrounding regions all descended from those in the Eurasian steppe.[28]

---

[24] Anthony, *Horse, the Wheel, and Language*, 182–85, 216, 220–24, 237, 460–63.
[25] Ibid., 260–62.
[26] Ibid., 282–99.
[27] Ibid., 397–427.
[28] After the Ice Age, ten thousand to fourteen thousand years ago, wild horses survived primarily in the Eurasian steppe; small populations may have persisted "in Europe, central

Ludwig et al.'s genetic study of the color of horses in Eastern Europe and Siberia definitively reveals coat colors present in domesticated horse populations ancestral to and contemporaneous with those in ancient Israel.[29] The performance of genetic studies like those of Ludwig et al. on horse remains from archaeological sites in ancient Israel would provide more conclusive evidence about coat colors in the domesticated horse population there. In the absence of such studies, however, genetic studies of domesticated horse populations ancestral to and descended from the same initial groups as those in ancient Israel indicate coat colors that are likely present among the domesticated horses there. Of course, it is possible that not all colors in the ancestral population were part of the population in ancient Israel, and it is also possible that new coat colors arose in populations there or elsewhere. Furthermore, because the genetic control of some horse coat colors is still unknown, ongoing work in equine coat color genetics will also refine the identification of colors in ancient horse populations.[30]

Ludwig et al.'s Tartas I and Lchashen sites fit most directly into Anthony's routes from the Eurasian steppe to ancient Israel. Tartas I lies in western Siberia near the border with Kazakhstan.[31] Ludwig et al.'s horses from Tartas I lived after migrations brought horseback riding to the nearby Botai-Tersek cultures around

---

Anatolia (modern Turkey), and the Caucasus Mountains," but there is no evidence for wild horses in Mesopotamia after this climatic shift. Mitochondrial DNA and Y chromosome studies indicate that domesticated populations were supplemented with other wild horses, particularly mares, from the Eurasian steppe at many points (Anthony, *Horse, the Wheel, and Language*, 196–98; and Sebastian Lippold et al., "Discovery of Lost Diversity of Paternal Horse Lineages Using Ancient DNA," *Nature Communications* 2 [2011]: article no. 450, https://doi.org/10.1038/ncomms1447). Vera Warmuth et al.'s population genetics study concurs with Anthony's proposal that domesticated populations spread from the steppe in "modern-day Ukraine and northwest Kazakhstan" and were primarily supplemented with wild mares ("Reconstructing the Origin and Spread of Horse Domestication in the Eurasian Steppe," *Proceedings of the National Academy of Science* 109 [2012]: 8202–6, https://doi.org/10.1073/pnas.1111122109).

[29] Ludwig et al., "Coat Color Variation," 485. Genetics determine the pigmentation of a horse's coat, but environmental factors, including diet and exposure to sunlight, can affect how brilliant or dull a coat appears (Sponenberg, *Equine Color Genetics*, 27–28).

[30] Genetic studies of horse coat colors are continuing with promising results. For example, see Bellone et al., "Fine-Mapping and Mutation Analysis," 193–207; Melanie Pruvost et al., "Genotypes of Predomestic Horses Match Phenotypes Painted in Paleolithic Works of Cave Art," *Proceedings of the National Academy of Science* 108 (2011): 18626–30, https://doi.org/10.1073/pnas.1108982108; Emma Svensson et al., "Coat Colour and Sex Identification in Horses from Iron Age Sweden," *Annals of Anatomy* 194 (2012): 82–87, https://doi.org/10.1016/j.aanat.2011.11.001; Bianca Haase et al., "Accumulating Mutations in Series of Haplotypes at the *KIT* and *MITF* Loci Are Major Determinants of White Markings in Franches-Montagnes Horses," *PLoS One* 8 (2013): e75071, https://doi.org/10.1371/journal.pone.0075071; Regula Hauswirth et al., "Novel Variants in the *KIT* and *PAX3* Genes in Horses with White-Spotted Coat Colour Phenotypes," *Animal Genetics* 44 (2013): 763–65, https://doi.org/10.1111/age.12057; and Stachurska and Jansen, "Crypto-Tobiano Horses in Hucul Breed," 1–9.

[31] Ludwig et al., "Coat Color Variation," supplementary online text 5, 15, and 17.

3500 BCE. The Petrovka offshoot of Sintashta incorporated some descendants from the earlier Botai cultures and spread into Central Asia around 1900 BCE.[32] Thus, the horses from Tartas I were likely part of populations ancestral to the horses traded into the Near East through Central Asia.

Ludwig et al.'s Lchashen site in Armenia lies in the Caucasus Mountain region where the Maikop culture rode steppe horses around 3700–3000 BCE. By the mid-second millennium, the Mitanni dynasty south of Lchashen had become skilled trainers of chariot horses and provided another connection between domesticated steppe horses and trade networks in the ancient Near East.[33]

At Tartas I, Ludwig et al. found three bay horses, three black horses, a chestnut horse, and a bay sabino horse dating between 3000 and 2500 BCE, and at Lchashen,

---

[32] Anthony, *Horse, the Wheel, and Language*, 237, 264–65, 441–57. The presence of horse milk on Botai pottery from 3500 BCE provides additional strong evidence that the Botai culture had domesticated horses during this period (John Travis, "Trail of Mare's Milk Leads to First Tamed Horses," *Science* 322 [2008]: 368a, https://doi.org/10.1126/science.322.5900.368a).

[33] The Mitanni group spoke an Indo-European language, possessed sophisticated chariot skill and technology, migrated from Central Asia, and conquered "a Hurrian-speaking kingdom in north Syria about 1500 BCE" (Anthony, *Horse, the Wheel, and Language*, 50, 403, 412, 454). Mitanni maintained a kingdom in northern Syria until the Hittite ruler Suppiluliuma I defeated them around 1350 BCE (Ann Nyland, *The Kikkuli Method of Horse Training* [Armidale, Australia: Presto Print, 1993], 9; and Gerard F. Probst, *The Kikkuli Text on the Training of Horses* [Lexington, KY: King Library, 1977], 2). Around this time, the Hittites commissioned Kikkuli, a Mitanni horse trainer, to record his method of conditioning chariot horses. Kikkuli's text remains the earliest known written horse-training manual. Written in a cuneiform Hittite, this text describes a 214-day program for developing a horse's endurance, including the time of day for exercise; the distance the horse should be driven or ridden; how much grain, hay, and water the horse should consume; and instructions for bathing the horse in the river (Probst, *Kikkuli Text*, 2–3 and i–xxxviii; and Nyland, *Kikkuli Method*, 8). Nyland re-created Kikkuli's method with ten horses in 1991 and found it to be very effective in achieving peak fitness and in preserving overall health and soundness. Kikkuli's method uses the principles of interval training, which are employed by human athletes today (*Kikkuli Method*, 10).

The Kikkuli text does not describe horses in terms of color but demonstrates that the earliest known text about horse training is very sophisticated and was produced by an Indo-European language speaker whose group came from the Eurasian steppe via Central Asia. The Ugaritic hippiatric texts reflect a similarly sophisticated knowledge of horses in their description of remedies for a range of horse ailments. These texts were discovered at Hattusa and date not long after the Kikkuli text (Chaim Cohen and Daniel Sivan, *The Ugaritic Hippiatric Texts: A Critical Edition*, AOS Essays 9 [New Haven: American Oriental Society, 1983], 2, 10).

When the Hittites conquered Mitanni, they could participate in the already flourishing horse trade in the ancient Near East. The Hyksos had previously introduced horses from the north into Egypt, and Egypt in turn became another source of horses for the Hittites (Nyland, *Kikkuli Method*, 10). Likewise, during monarchic Israel, the Israelites acquired horses from Egypt, Kue (southeast of Anatolia), and Beth-Togarmah (in Armenia). Even if the dates remain uncertain, Deut 17:16, 1 Kgs 10:26–29, 2 Kgs 18:23–24, 2 Chr 1:14–17, 9:28, Isa 31:1–3, and Ezek 27:14 preserve memories of this horse trade (Cantrell, *Horsemen of Israel*, 44–46).

they found a chestnut sabino horse dating between 1410 and 1250 BCE.[34] The bay color consists of a mostly brown coat with black regions covering the lower legs, ear rims, mane, and tail.[35] Bay horses range from reddish brown to almost black, but rarer genetically black horses also exist.[36] Chestnut horses are entirely reddish brown.[37] The sabino pattern consists of large white spots overlaying a base coat color of bay, chestnut, black, or brown.[38] Sabinos characteristically have speckled areas and extensive white markings on their legs and head. The extent of white spotting in sabino horses varies, and those with maximal spotting can have white over almost all of their body.[39]

Anthony's account connects the population of initially domesticated horses in the western Eurasian steppe with populations of domesticated horses in Siberia and Armenia that were in turn traded into the Near East. Therefore, the coat colors that Ludwig et al. identified in Siberia and Armenia comprise the list of probable coat colors in Iron Age Israel: bay, black, chestnut, bay sabino, and chestnut sabino.

V. Combining Textual and Material Evidence for Translations

When combined with Brenner's catalogue of the ranges of the color terms used in the Hebrew Bible, this list of probable coat colors in Iron Age Israel provides

---

[34] Ludwig et al., "Coat Color Variation," supplementary online text 15 and 17.

[35] Horses with a bay coat possess at least one dominant allele of the gene for the agouti-signaling protein, ASIP (Sponenberg, *Equine Color Genetics*, 17–20). Ancient wild horses were predominantly bay and black, likely with a dun dilution. The dun dilution causes a base color to appear lighter and is controlled by a genetic mechanism separate from those that control base coat colors. The dun dilution gene, however, has not been identified. The diversity of coat colors increased markedly after humans domesticated and started breeding horses (Pruvost et al., "Genotypes of Predomestic Horses," 18627–28; and Sponenberg, *Equine Color Genetics*, 40–46).

[36] The genetic control of whether bays have a lighter or darker shade is not yet characterized, but genetically black horses possess two recessive alleles for the *ASIP* gene (Sponenberg, *Equine Color Genetics*, 19–20, 26–28).

[37] Chestnut horses have two recessive alleles with mutations in the gene that codes for the melanocyte-stimulating hormone receptor, or *MC1R*. Because the genetic control of the chestnut color is epistatic to the *ASIP* gene, a horse with two alleles for the chestnut color will be chestnut regardless of whether it carries genes for bay or black color at the *ASIP* gene (Sponenberg, *Equine Color Genetics*, 20).

[38] Brown horses that are not bay or chestnut are rare. The gene that causes the uniform chocolate-brown color of dogs and other animals does not affect horse coat colors; other genes cause brown horse colors (Sponenberg, *Equine Color Genetics*, 23, 26).

[39] Horses with white spotting have a base color controlled by the *ASIP*, *MC1R*, etc. genes, and additional genes affect the white markings. The *KIT* gene codes for the mast cell growth factor, and mutations at this gene are responsible for several different white patterns. One type of sabino pattern is caused by a single base pair change in the *KIT* gene, and Ludwig et al. used this mutation, called *sabino-1*, to test for sabino horses in their archaeological samples (Sponenberg, *Equine Color Genetics*, 73–74, 97–102; and Ludwig et al., "Coat Color Variation," supplementary online text 13).

a way to translate more precisely the color terms used for horses in Zechariah.[40] Brenner argues that אדם includes a range from brown to red to pink. Of the genetically probable coat colors, chestnut lies most clearly within this range, which likely also encompasses lighter bays. From prehistoric times to today, bay remains one of the most common horse colors, and it would be unlikely, although not impossible, for the lists in Zechariah to omit bay horses.[41] Lighter bays fall closer to the range of אדם than to that of the other color terms used for Zechariah's horses. אדם is likely a larger category than chestnut or light bay, so an exact category correspondence between it and a modern English technical horse color term is impossible. "Chestnut" best renders אדם for an audience familiar with horses because it conveys both the reddish and brown nuances of אדם. For audiences unfamiliar with horses, "reddish brown" is an appropriate translation because it includes both chestnuts and lighter bays, as אדם does.

For Brenner, שרק is a secondary red color term, and, like Brenner, Meyers and Meyers suggest that it is related to the Arabic word ʿašpar, "which designates horses that have a ruddy tinge over white."[42] Chestnut and light bay sabino are the only colors from the genetically probable list that adequately fit into this range. Several other colors, however, would be appropriate for the combination of a reddish color over or in addition to white or lighter regions, as designated by שרק. The genetic mechanism for several of these coat patterns, including roan and mealy, remains unknown. Roan coats consist of white hairs interspersed with a base coat color.[43] D. Phillip Sponenberg describes the mealy pattern as having "pale red or yellowish areas on the lower belly and flanks, behind the elbows, inside the legs, on the muzzle, and over the eyes."[44] Tobiano and leopard-spotted horses could also be included in the range of שרק. In the tobiano pattern, large white spots with definite edges overlay a base coat color, and the base coat color covers the head.[45] Horses with leopard spotting appear to have small colored spots against a white background,

---

[40] The following translations are of the color terms in the MT rather than those of the various textual emendations proposed. For a discussion of ancient translations of the coat colors in Zech 1:8; 6:2–3, 6, see Garrick V. Allen, "Zechariah's Horse Visions and Angelic Intermediaries: Translation, Allusion, and Transmission in Early Judaism," *CBQ* 79 (2017): 222–39.

[41] Sponenberg, *Equine Color Genetics*, 17; and Pruvost et al., "Genotypes of Predomestic Horses," 18627.

[42] Meyers and Meyers, *Haggai, Zechariah 1–8*, 113. Brenner similarly deems a "reddish-brown colour of horses" a good rendering of שרק in Zech 1:8 (*Colour Terms*, 114–15).

[43] Sponenberg, *Equine Color Genetics*, 80.

[44] American terminology varies for mealy chestnuts. Draft-horse breeders call mealy chestnuts "sorrel," but quarter horse breeders use "sorrel" for lighter chestnuts regardless of whether they exhibit the mealy modification. Sponenberg also indicates that the mealy modification was likely present in wild-type horses, which makes its presence in ancient horse populations probable (*Equine Color Genetics*, 32–35).

[45] Ibid., 90–93. Ludwig et al. found a bay tobiano in Miciurin, Moldova, dating between 1500 and 1000 BCE, but this area is farther away from trade routes into the ancient Near East ("Coat Color Variation," supplementary online text 17).

and this pattern can extend from the haunches to the entire body.⁴⁶ שרק probably included at least horses with sabino, roan, mealy, tobiano, or leopard-spotted patterns in addition to a base coat color of chestnut or light bay if they were present in Iron Age Israel. Given the current genetic evidence, a good translation of שרק for audiences familiar with horses would be "chestnut sabino" or "mealy chestnut" because both of these suggest a lighter modification of base reddish-brown color and were likely present in ancient populations. As with אדם, the modern English technical categories are probably narrower than the range שרק designates. Although a bit cumbersome, "reddish brown with white/lighter areas" is a precise translation for audiences unfamiliar with horses.⁴⁷

לבן includes light colors as well as white in Brenner's catalog. לבן probably included both genetically white and gray horses if they were present in Iron Age Israel.⁴⁸ The only color from the list of genetically probable coat colors in Iron Age Israel that could fit into this range is a maximally expressing sabino, which would appear almost completely white. Further genetic studies are needed to determine

---

⁴⁶ Sponenberg, *Equine Color Genetics*, 110–20. Ludwig et al. did not include leopard spotting in their study, but Pruvost et al.'s subsequent study tested for its presence in some of the Copper Age and older samples from Ludwig et al.'s study. Pruvost et al. found two leopard-spotted horses around 3650–3380 BCE in Mayaki, Ukraine, shortly before the Usatovo culture appeared in that region around 3300 BCE with domesticated horses ("Genotypes of Predomestic Horses," 18627–28; and Anthony, *Horse, the Wheel, and Language*, 302, 349–52). Further testing of later Iron Age samples would provide clearer connections to Anthony's trade routes into the Near East and would illuminate whether leopard-spotted horses were likely present in Iron Age Israel.

⁴⁷ This explanation of the color terms in Zechariah focuses on precise descriptions; however, literary translations would elicit more artful renderings.

⁴⁸ Although adult white and gray horses can appear similar, they differ genetically. Genetically white horses are born with pink skin underneath a white coat; they have pigmented eyes and are not albino. Genetically gray horses are born with gray skin under a black coat that becomes whiter with age. Some gray horses appear completely white with age while others exhibit a flea-bitten pattern of small brown dots throughout their coat. As their coats lighten, gray horses can go through a dappled stage in which white spots intersperse throughout their darker coats. Genetically gray horses are much more prevalent than white horses. Gray horses have a mutation in the *STYX17* gene, but several mutations in the *KIT* gene produce white horses. Because multiple mutations can cause white horses, it is hard to identify and test for all types of genetically white horses in ancient populations (Sponenberg, *Equine Color Genetics*, 74–77, 100, 109–10; and Haase et al., "Allelic Heterogeneity at the Equine *KIT* Locus in Dominant White [*W*] Horses," *PLoS Genet* 3 [2007]: e195, https://doi.org/10.1371/journal.pgen.0030195).

Ludwig et al.'s study did not test for white or gray horses, but textual evidence suggests the presence of white, gray, or both colors of horses in ancient populations. Herodotus and Xenophon remember the Persians ascribing cultic significance to white horses, as did the Assyrians (Petersen, *Haggai and Zechariah 1–8*, 141). Augusto Azzaroli also says, "White horses are mentioned in writings since the second millennium B. C. and were frequently selected for sacrifices; among Indo-European tribes the cult to the twin god-heroes and riders, the Dioskours, was celebrated with the sacrifice of a black and a white horse" (*An Early History of Horsemanship* [Leiden: Brill, 1985], 166).

if "gray" or "white" is a more accurate translation for audiences familiar with horses. "White" is certainly an appropriate translation for audiences unfamiliar with horses.

Brenner indicates that שחר includes both dark colors and black. Black horses are genetically probable and certainly part of the range of this term. Dark bays are probably also included in the range of שחר. Nonetheless, "black" is an appropriate translation for audiences familiar and unfamiliar with horses because it is often difficult to determine the difference between a genetically black horse and very dark bay based on visual appearance alone.

According to Brenner, the pattern ברד refers to some kind of speckled appearance. Clark connects this color term with a word from the same root that denotes "hail," and he links it to "the speckled appearance of the ground after hail has fallen."[49] It is difficult to determine if this pattern is limited to or independent of certain base coat colors in its use in Biblical Hebrew. None of the colors that are genetically probable in Iron Age Israel fits into this category. ברד could include a range of speckled patterns, including dappled grays, flea-bitten grays, roans, and leopard-spotted horses. Blue roans have a black base coat color with the roan pattern and bear a striking similarity to hail on the ground in Israel.[50] Given the current genetic uncertainty, "dappled gray" or "blue roan" is an adequate translation for an audience familiar with horses, and "speckled" is appropriate for audiences unfamiliar with horses.

VI. Conclusion

Brenner's analysis has been combined with the genetically probable colors determined from Anthony's migration routes and Ludwig et al.'s genetic study to unite the textual context of the color descriptions of horses in Zechariah with the best available material evidence about the appearance of horses in Iron Age Israel. This combination produces probable color ranges for each of the color terms in Zech 1:8; 6:2–3, 6 and permits more precise translations of these terms. The translations of these terms for both audiences familiar with horses and those unfamiliar convey their realistic nature. Even though these texts in Zechariah do not explicitly state the significance of the horse colors, their contribution to the visions' imagery was likely clearer in light of cultural background assumptions at the time. Further work can be done to refine the list of genetically probable horse coat colors in Iron Age Israel and to clarify the use of the color terms in Zech 1:8; 6:2–3, 6.

---

[49] Clark, "Red and Green Horses?," 68.
[50] Eric Meyers, comment in course, 12 October 2011.

# The Wisdom of Solomon, Ruler Cults, and Paul's Polemic against Idols in the Areopagus Speech

DREW J. STRAIT
drew.strait@gmail.com
St. Mary's Ecumenical Institute, Baltimore, MD 21210

Despite recent attempts to read Luke-Acts as subverting Roman imperial ideology and power, the Areopagus speech in Acts 17:16–34 remains politically elusive. If Luke's attitude toward Rome was negative, one would expect to find anti-imperial motifs in Paul's *Missionsreden*, especially in Athens, where we know imperial cult media existed and where Luke most explicitly criticizes Greco-Roman religion. In this study, I investigate the political referents of the Areopagus speech through (1) an examination of the hybrid material representation of gods and kings in the urban spaces of empire, including Roman Athens; and (2) a comparative analysis of the Areopagus speech with the Wisdom of Solomon's polemic against imperial cult media (Wis 14:16–21). In contrast to scholars who read the Areopagus speech as a critique of the traditional gods *sensu stricto*, I suggest that Paul's polemic against *sebasmata* ("objects of worship," Acts 17:23) and precious materials (Acts 17:29) critiques the iconic spectacle underlying the visibility and euergetism of gods and imperial authority.

The cultural survival of Second Temple Jews hinged on their ability to manage external political authority and foster allegiance to the law of Moses. The crises of exile, in particular, brought the need for resistance literature to the fore. Under the hegemony of Babylonian captivity, Isaiah developed the icon parody to resist Jews' assimilation with the habitus and iconic culture of the ruling power (Isa 40:18–20; 41:5–7, 21–29; 42:8, 17; 45:16–17, 20–21; 46:1–7; 48:5).[1] By rendering the ritual practices and media of Babylon's idols powerless and deaf, the icon parodies functioned as "political acts of power" to classify the iconic spectacle of gods and political authority as inanimate and idolatrous.[2] In so doing, the icon parody legitimated

[1] Nathaniel B. Levtow, *Images of Others: Iconic Politics in Ancient Israel*, BJSUCSD 11 (Winona Lake, IN: Eisenbrauns, 2008), 57–72.
[2] Ibid., 16.

Jewish conceptions of divine identity, especially Jews' allegiance to one God whose image and rule over the nations are incompatible with the worship of other gods and their material representation.

The utility of the icon parody as a form of resistance literature is evident in its adoption and adaptation in the "cultural and religious equipment" of early Judaism and Christianity.[3] It is widely accepted that Isaiah's polemic against idols influenced the composition of the Areopagus speech.[4] What is less understood is the relationship between the Areopagus speech and Hellenistic Jewish sources that recontextualized Isaiah's polemic to confront the material culture of the ruling power. The Wisdom of Solomon's *digressio* on pagan idolatry (Wis 13:1–15:19), for example, represents the most sophisticated use of the topoi in early Judaism.[5] Ps.-Solomon's polemic against idols in Augustan Egypt is innovative: for the first time in the tradition, the Isaianic icon parody is recontextualized explicitly to censure the origins and material representation of deified political authority (Wis 14:16–21).[6] Ps.-Solomon's explicit critique of the Roman imperial cults raises unexplored questions about the allusive political referents inherent in the bulk of Jewish and Christian icon parodies. Indeed, when early Jews and Christians parodied the hybrid material culture used to honor gods and kings without giving the referents identification—as Paul does in Athens—what were the objects of resistance?

In what follows, I suggest that Paul's criticism of σεβάσματα ("objects of worship," Acts 17:23) and listing of precious materials (Acts 17:29) is *not* a politically innocuous speech act when read alongside the Wisdom of Solomon. In the Areopagus speech, Luke confronts the iconic spectacle of gods and imperial authority with the gospel of the Lord of all—a worldview that is incompatible with the euergetic visual culture underlying the visibility of gods and kings.

I. Hybrid Iconography and the Icon Parody's Referential Polyvalency

The influence of Homer on artists' imaging of the gods is reflected in Dio Chrysostom's *Olympic Discourse*. Dio employs *prosopopoeia* to allow the famous

---

[3] James C. Scott, *Weapons of the Weak: Everyday Forms of Peasant Resistance* (New Haven: Yale University Press, 1985), 331.

[4] See David W. Pao, *Acts and the Isaianic New Exodus*, WUNT 2/130 (Tübingen: Mohr Siebeck, 2000), 193–97.

[5] So Maurice Gilbert, "Trois chapitres du livre de la Sagesse (13–15) forment le dévelopement le plus important que l'Ancien Testament consacre à la critique des manifestations religieuses du paganisme," in Gilbert, *La critique des dieux dans le Livre de la Sagesse (Sg 13–15)*, AnBib 53 (Rome: Biblical Institute Press, 1973), xiii.

[6] Some exceptions exist; see Bel 6; Sib. Or. 3:652–656; Ep Jer 6:52, 56, 65; 3 Macc 4:16.

sculptor Phidias to defend his anthropomorphic chryselephantine colossus of Zeus in Athens by telling his detractors that they should "be angry with Homer first" (*Or.* 12.62). As Phidias's interlocutors indicate, the representation of the divine in human form was provocative. Yet the human body, for "lack of a better illustration," provided artists with a dynamic medium through which to communicate what is "invisible and unportrayable" (*Or.* 12.59).[7] In Pliny the Elder's account of the first gilded statues made of bronze, on the other hand, Pliny provides important insight into the era in classical Greece when artists began representing powerful humans with anthropomorphic statuary (in contrast to reserving this practice for the gods alone). According to Pliny, no fewer than three times did an athlete have to achieve victory at the Olympic games in order to receive a statue with an "exact resemblance" (*Nat.* 34.9). This caution, according to Pliny, changed to *temeritas* in 510 BCE when the tyrant slayers Harmodius and Aristogiton freed Athens of tyrannical kings. Artistically speaking, the result was transformative: for the first time in Greek art, the ruling power was represented anthropomorphically in public space, creating what Peter Stewart calls the "potential for elision" between gods and political authority.[8]

The potential for elision between gods and kings came to full expression in the aftermath of Alexander's conquests. Although the story of the emergence of the Hellenistic cult of rulers is complex and diverse—and there "was no such thing as *the* imperial cult"[9]—we know that local traditions of cult and religion provided an important hermeneutical framework for subjects in the Greek East to interpret and cope with external political authority.[10] As Karl Galinsky recently warned biblical scholars, deified rulers were not stand-alone deities.[11] Rather, Alexander the Great's successors and the Roman imperial cults were embedded in a "hybrid iconography"[12] with honors like the gods (ἰσόθεοι τιμαί; *SEG* 41.75), as temple-sharing gods (σύνναος θεός; *OGIS* 332) and, in at least one case, as σύνθρονος ("enthroned") with the gods (*OGIS* 383).[13] Additionally, role-playing (e.g., Plutarch, *Adul. amic.*

---

[7] Unless otherwise noted, all translations of classical sources are from the Loeb Classical Library.

[8] Peter Stewart, *Statues in Roman Society: Representation and Response*, Oxford Studies in Ancient Culture and Representation (Oxford: Oxford University Press, 2003), 33.

[9] Mary Beard, John North, and Simon Price, eds., *Religions of Rome*, 2 vols. (Cambridge: Cambridge University Press, 1998), 1:318.

[10] Simon R. F. Price, *Rituals and Power: The Roman Imperial Cult in Asia Minor* (Cambridge: Cambridge University Press, 1984), 29–30, 234–35, 247–48.

[11] Karl Galinsky, "The Cult of the Roman Emperor: Uniter or Divider?," in *Rome and Religion: A Cross-Disciplinary Dialogue on the Imperial Cult*, ed. Jeffrey Brodd and Jonathan L. Reed, WGRWSup 5 (Atlanta: Society of Biblical Literature, 2011), 4–5.

[12] I borrow the phrase "hybrid iconography" from Robert Turcan, *The Cults of the Roman Empire*, trans. Antonia Nevill, Ancient World (Oxford: Blackwell, 1996), 27.

[13] Aside from Antiochus I of Commagene, Alexander's father, Philip, was considered

12.56–57; Philo, *Legat.* 78–79) and cosmogonic associations (e.g., Plutarch, *Alex.* 2–3; *OGIS* 219, line 25; Suetonius, *Aug.* 94.4) reinforced the Hellenistic kingship ideal, namely, "that a king is something resembling the divine" (ὅτι θεόμιμόν ἐντι πρᾶγμα βασιλεία, Stobaeus 4.7.61).[14]

Although rare, it was possible for imperial statuary to stand alone apart from the traditional gods such as the colossus of Domitian in Ephesus or that of Hadrian in Athens (Pausanius, *Descr.* 1.18.6).[15] The design of the colossi, however, imitated the architectural patterns of the traditional gods in order to associate the emperor with the numinous, making imperial sanctuaries, in the words of Paul Zanker, "otherwise indistinguishable in their outward appearance."[16] Josephus reflects how the aesthetic design *and* location of imperial statuary could associate the emperor with the numinous. In his description of the temple of Augustus and Roma in Caesarea, Josephus writes that Augustus's colossus "was in no way inferior to [Phidias's] Olympian Zeus, *which it was designed to resemble*" (*J.W.* 1.22.7 §414). Likewise, in accord with Augustan policy, his statue was set up alongside Roma (Suetonius, *Aug.* 52; Cassius Dio 51.20.6). Herein lies our hermeneutical problem: If a Hellenistic Jew or early Christian employed the icon parody allusively to critique statuary and precious material in Caesarea, would the referent be Augustus, Olympian Zeus, or Roma?[17]

The hybridity of imperial art is reflected also in Philo of Alexandria. Philo observes, "the whole world gives honors to Augustus equal to those of the Olympian gods" (πᾶσα ἡ οἰκουμένη τὰς ἰσολυμπίους αὐτῷ τιμὰς ἐψηφίσαντο, *Legat.* 149). When Philo critiques the hubris of Gaius, it is often overlooked that Gaius did not

---

σύνθρονος with the Olympian gods (Diodorus Siculus 16.92). On the emperor's sharing cult space with the traditional gods, see Arthur D. Nock, "Σύνναος θεός," *HSCP* 41 (1930): 1–62; and B. Schmidt-Dounas, "Statuen hellenistischer Könige als Synnaoi Theoi," *Egnatia* 4 (1993–1994): 71–141. On divine associations more broadly, see Julien Tondriau, "Comparisons and Identifications of Rulers with Deities in the Hellenistic Period," *RR* 131 (1949): 24–47. It is worth observing that Paul critiques the Greco-Roman notion of ἰσόθεοι τιμαί in Phil 2:6; see Erik M. Heen, "Phil 2:6–11 and Resistance to Local Timocratic Rule," in *Paul and the Roman Imperial Order*, ed. Richard A. Horsley (Harrisburg, PA: Trinity Press International, 2004), 125–54.

[14] See Holger Thesleff, ed., *The Pythagorean Texts of the Hellenistic Period*, AAAbo.H 30.1 (Åbo: Åbo Akademi, 1965), 75, line 16. For an English translation of the Pythagorean fragments, see Kenneth Sylvan Guthrie, *The Pythagorean Sourcebook and Library: An Anthology of Ancient Writings Which Relate to Pythagoras and Pythagorean Philosophy* (Grand Rapids: Phanes, 1988).

[15] For the colossus at Ephesus, see Steven J. Friesen, *Twice Neokoros: Ephesus, Asia, and the Cult of the Flavian Imperial Family*, RGRW 116 (Leiden: Brill, 1993), 59–62, pls. VI–VII.

[16] Paul Zanker, *The Power of Images in the Age of Augustus*, Jerome Lectures 16th Series (Ann Arbor: University of Michigan Press, 1988), 298.

[17] As Nock observes, these associative honors of assimilation "make it impossible to know sometimes whether he [the king] and the god in question were treated as separate entities" ("Σύνναος θεός," 12).

intend to erect a statue of himself in Jerusalem; rather, he conspires to erect a colossus of Zeus in the Jerusalem temple (*Legat.* 265) that included a dedicatory inscription "Gaius, the New Zeus Made Manifest" (Διὸς Ἐπιφανοῦς Νέου χρηματίζῃ Γαΐου, *Legat.* 346; cf. also 188). Moreover, the opposing embassy, upon winning their case, honored Gaius "by the titles of all the gods" (*Legat.* 354).[18] Gaius's associations with Zeus remind us that the colossi are not justification for interpreting the Roman imperial cults as a phenomenon abstracted from the representation and cosmic framework of the traditional gods, as if the emperor stood apart from the "functional polytheism" of Greco-Roman religion.[19]

We have evidence of Jews employing the icon parody to critique images "in human form" as early as the Babylonian exile (כתבנית איש; μορφήν ἀνδρός, Isa 44:13). But when Hellenistic and Roman Jews recontextualized Isaiah's polemic against anthropomorphic images under the shadow of ruler cults, the referents could evoke a political dimension (e.g., Let. Aris. 134–136; Wis 13:13; 14:15; 15:16; Bar 6:11; Sib. Or. 3:29–34, 721–723; Philo, *Prov.* 2.15; *Spec.* 1.10; Josephus, *C. Ap.* 2.17 §167). The same point applies to the critique of precious materials, which constitutes the bulk of Jewish idol polemic (Let. Aris. 135, Dan 5:4, Wis 13:10, 14:21, 15:9, etc.).[20] Without an adjectival descriptor for *what* gold, silver, or stone object an author is critiquing, the referent becomes polyvalent—open to interpretation by the audience. We see this referential polyvalency in Philo's comments on the second commandment in *De decalogo* and *De specialibus legibus*, wherein Philo employs the icon parody to critique precious materials without providing a direct referent (*Decal.* 4, 7, 66, 71; *Spec.* 1.21–22). That Philo could have had in mind an imperial referent is evident in the *Legatio ad Gaium*, where he openly critiques Gaius's threat to erect in Jerusalem "a gilded statue of superhuman size" (κολοσσιαῖον ἀνδριάντα ἐπίχρυσον, *Legat.* 203, trans. Smallwood; see also *Legat.* 337). The integration of gods and kings in shared cult media and anthropomorphic representation placed the Hellenistic and Roman Jewish icon parodies in a new hermeneutical context—one that did not critique religion *sensu stricto* but could simultaneously resist the iconic spectacle underlying the divine honors conferred on political authority. How, then, did the relationship between gods and kings materialize in the built environment of Roman Athens?

---

[18] English translation from E. Mary Smallwood, *Philonis Alexandrini Legatio Ad Gaium* (Leiden: Brill, 1961).

[19] I borrow the phrase "functional polytheism" from John Scheid, *An Introduction to Roman Religion*, trans. Janet Lloyd (Bloomington: Indiana University Press, 2003), 159.

[20] Johannes Tromp, "The Critique of Idolatry in the Context of Jewish Monotheism," in *Aspects of Religious Contact and Conflict in the Ancient World*, ed. Pieter W. van der Horst, UTR 31 (Utrecht: Utrechtse Theologische Reeks, 1995), 105–20, here 112.

Athens and the Roman Imperial Cults

Rome's transformation of Athens's civic space is well attested.[21] Given Athens's siding with Antony, the embedding of Rome in Athens—to borrow a phrase from Nancy Evans—held special ideological significance for Augustus's conquest of the East.[22] After Actium, Athens acquiesced to Roman power by building a small round temple to Augustus and Roma in a prominent location on the Acropolis (east of the Parthenon on its main axis, with a diameter of over eight meters and nine columns of the Ionic order).[23] The placement of the *tholos* on the axis of the Parthenon inserted Augustus into the center of Athenian politics and religion. Notably, on the architrave of the temple, Augustus was hailed as "Savior" (*IG* II², 3173). The statues in the temple of Augustus and Roma are no longer extant; however, Helene Whittaker notes that the architectural design of the structure most closely resembles the Philippeion at Olympia, which held chryselephantine sculpture to honor Philip II of Macedon and his family (Pausanius, *Descr.* 5.20.9–10).[24]

From the Julio-Claudian period alone, forty-three dedicatory inscriptions on statue bases and altars have been found in Athens honoring the emperor or a member of his family.[25] Twelve inscriptions in the lower city honor Augustus with the following titulary: Αὐτοκράτορος Καίσαρος Θεοῦ υἱοῦ Σεβαστοῦ (*IG* II², 12764).[26] A front-row seat in the theater of Dionysus has the inscription "(seat) of the

---

[21] Antony Spawforth argues that evidence for the imperial cult is better for Athens than any other city in old Greece (except for Corinth) ("The Early Reception of the Imperial Cult in Athens: Problems and Ambiguities," in *The Romanization of Athens: Proceedings of an International Conference Held at Lincoln, Nebraska [April 1966]*, ed. Michael C. Hoff and Susan I. Rotroff, Oxbow Monograph 94 [Oxford: Oxbow, 1997], 183–202, here 183). The city of Athens was exposed to the ruler cult well before its Romanization. In 307 BCE, for example, the city of Athens hailed Demetrius Poliorcetes (306–283 BCE) as σωτήρ and εὐεργέτης for liberating Athens from tyrants and for bestowing benefits of grain and lumber on the populace (Plutarch, *Demetr.* 8–10; *OGIS* 6, lines 10–34). The honors accorded to Demetrius included annual sacrifices, the weaving of his image into the *peplos* of Athena, and a bronze equestrian statue in the marketplace next to personified Democracy with epigraphic honors (*Inscriptiones Atticae Supplementum Inscriptionum Atticarum*, ed. A. N. Oikonomides [Chicago: Ares, 1976], 256–62; Frederick Danker, *Benefactor: Epigraphic Study of a Graeco-Roman and New Testament Semantic Field* [St. Louis: Clayton, 1982], no. 30). The extravagant honors conferred on Demetrius are corroborated in the ithyphallic hymn sung to Demetrius in 291 BCE (*FGH* 76 F 13).

[22] Nancy Evans, "Embedding Rome in Athens," in Brodd and Reed, *Rome and Religion*, 83–98.

[23] Helene Whittaker, "Some Reflections on the Temple to the Goddess Roma and Augustus on the Acropolis at Athens," in *Greek Romans and Roman Greeks: Studies in Cultural Interaction*, ed. Erik Nis Ostenfeld, Aarhus Studies in Mediterranean Antiquity 3 (Aarhus: Aarhus University Press, 2002), 25–39, here 25.

[24] Ibid., 26.

[25] Geoffrey C. R. Schmalz, *Augustan and Julio-Claudian Athens: A New Epigraphy and Prosopography*, MnemosyneSup 302 (Leiden: Brill, 2009), nos. 113–56.

[26] See Anna Benjamin and Antony E. Raubitschek, "Arae Augusti," *Hesperia* 28 (1959): 65–85, https://doi.org/10.2307/147339.

priest and high priest of *Sebastos Kaisar*" (*IG* II², 5034), which may indicate the introduction of Roman games to the Athenian theater.[27] The embedding of Augustus in the cults of the traditional gods is evident also in the Agora, where a two-chambered annex was built onto the Stoa of Zeus Eleutherios that likely housed emperor worship.[28] Moreover, a dedicatory inscription on a statue base honored Augustus as the "New Apollo" ([Σεβαστὸ]ν Καισ[αρα νέον Ἀ]πόλλωνα; *IG* II² 3262 + 4725; Schmalz, no. 127). The association of the Roman imperial family with traditional gods in Athens is summarized in the following chart adapted from Fernando Lozano.[29]

Identification of Emperors and Members of the Imperial Family with Traditional Divinities in Athens			
Identities	Divinity	Cult Location	Testimony (Selected)
Augustus	New Apollo	Athens	*SEG* 17, 34
	Zeus *Boulaio*	Bouleuterion at Eleusis	*SEG* 47, 218
Livia	Augustus Higea	Acropolis	*IG* II² 3240
	Artemis *Boulaia*	*Tholos* or Southwest Temple in the Classical Agora	*SEG* 22, 152
	Pronoia	Roman Agora	*IG* II² 3238
	Vesta-Hestia	Monopteros in the Acropolis and *Tholos* in the Classical Agora	*IG* II² 5097
Gaius Caesar, son of Julia and M. Agrippa	New Ares	Temples of Ares	*IG* II² 3250
Drusus Caesar, son of Tiberius	New Ares	Temples of Ares	*IG* II² 3257
Drusilla	New Aphrodite	?	*SEG* 34, 180
Claudius	Apollo *Patroos*	Temple of Apollo *Patroos*	*IG* II² 3274 + *SEG* 22, 153
Nero	New Apollo	Temple of Apollo *Patroos*?	*IG* II² 3278 *SEG* 22, 34, 44, 165, 182, 252

---

[27] For English translation, see Spawforth, "Early Reception," 183.

[28] Homer Thompson, "The Annex to the Stoa of Zeus in the Athenian Agora," *Hesperia* 35 (1966): 171–87. There is disagreement over the dating of the addition of the annex, which could have been built under Augustus or Tiberius. See Spawforth, "Early Reception," 186.

[29] Fernando Lozano, *La religión del poder: El culto imperial en Atenas en época de Augusto y los emperadores Julio-Claudios*, BARIS 1087 (Oxford: Archaeopress, 2002), 98.

The imperial family's cosmogonic associations with traditional gods in Athens illustrate how Paul's allusive rhetoric could include a political dimension. Though it is difficult to tell how the average Athenian responded to the imperial cults' impact on civic space—or whether they even cared—it is clear that, by the time of Claudius and Nero, "the political Romanization of the Athenian elite" had been achieved.[30]

The entrance of Paul into the city of Athens in the mid-first century CE put him in close contact with emperor worship. The imperial cult's embedding in a forest of idols is not reason to diminish its presence in Athens, as Colin F. Miller recently argued.[31] Though the theology of the Areopagus speech is refracted through the monotheism of an altar to an unknown god, its criticism—within its own narrative framework—is ultimately toward all gentile religiosity.[32] We have more inscriptional evidence for the Roman imperial cults than we do for altars to an unknown god in Athens. Given the integration of politics and religion into the built environment of Athens, how is one to interpret Paul's criticism of the system of euergetic visual honors that gods and kings shared: idols (Acts 17:16), objects of worship (17:23), altars (17:23), epigraphy (17:23), temples (17:24), precious materials for figurative representation (17:29), and the τέχνη ("skill") of the artisan's hands (17:29)?

Although these motifs are typical referents of the icon parody, the ritual and material culture that Paul criticizes closely parallels Aristotle's definition of euergetic τιμαί ("honors"). Aristotle suggests that sacrifices (i.e., temples), monuments in verse and in prose (i.e., epigraphic honors), first seats (in theaters), tombs, and statues are conferred especially on benefactors who provide benefits (μάλιστα οἱ εὐεργετηκότες, Rhet. 1.5.9). For Aristotle, these benefits can materialize in the form of "rescue" (εὐεργεσία δὲ ἢ εἰς σωτηρίαν, Rhet. 1.5.9). Luke is the only author in the New Testament to employ the entire euerg- family (εὐεργέτης [Luke 22:25]; εὐεργεσία [Acts 4:9]; εὐεργετέω [Acts 10:38]).[33] For our purposes here, it is striking

---

[30] Spawforth, "Early Reception," 194. The term Romanization has been criticized in recent years because it oversimplifies Greeks' diverse responses to Roman power. Despite the semantic difficulties associated with the word, I employ it here to indicate Athens's acculturation and adoption of Roman customs especially related to cult and religion by local elites. For discussion, see Susan E. Alcock, "The Problem of Romanization, the Power of Athens," in Hoff and Rotroff, Romanization of Athens, 1–8.

[31] Colin F. Miller, "The Imperial Cult in the Pauline Cities of Asia Minor and Greece," CBQ 72 (2010): 314–32, here 329.

[32] See C. Kavin Rowe, World Upside Down: Reading Acts in the Graeco-Roman Age (New York: Oxford University Press, 2009), 27–29.

[33] See Frederick W. Danker, Benefactor: Epigraphic Study of a Graeco-Roman and New Testament Semantic Field (St. Louis: Clayton, 1982), 323–24. The words εὐεργέτης and εὐεργετέω in Luke are hapax legomena in the New Testament. The word εὐεργεσία, however, also occurs in 1 Tim 6:2. Luke also shows awareness of the important related epithet σωτήρ (Luke 1:47; 2:11; Acts 5:31; 13:23).

that Luke employs the substantive εὐεργέτης (Luke 22:25) and the verb εὐεργετέω (Acts 10:38) to critique gentile power dynamics.³⁴ This point adds impetus to a reading of the Areopagus speech that fits into Luke's larger narratological agenda to reorient his audience's imaginative faculties away from the magnetism of idols and deified benefactors toward the resurrected and ascended Christ. Paul's polemic, therefore, is no mere critique of religion *sensu stricto*. Rather, Paul's polemic is an act of discursive resistance that sought to undermine euergetic τιμαί for objects of power that distracted the auditor from the worship of the one true God. Moreover, the allusive nature of such discourse could evoke multiple referents, thereby creating a space for the speaker's safety. Further evaluation of the Areopagus speech and the Wisdom of Solomon will help to illuminate Paul's allusive cult referents.

II. Ps.-Solomon's Polemic against Gods and Kings

The Wisdom of Solomon is traditionally divided into three sections: 1:1–6:21 (Book of Eschatology); 6:22–10:21 (Book of Wisdom); and chapters 11–19 (Book of History).³⁵ A recurring motif in all three sections is a negative portrayal of gentile rulers, including a criticism of Roman hegemony through a mini-apocalyptic scenario (Wis 5:17–23); a censure of rulers' embellished ontological status through the example of Solomon (7:1–10);³⁶ and a polemic against rulers' cultic media (14:16–21). That Ps.-Solomon directs his criticism toward the Roman imperial cults becomes acute in the Book of History's *digressio* on pagan idolatry (13:1–15:19). In reaction to the ethnic tensions that Alexandrian Jews experienced after Augustus's annexation of Egypt, Ps.-Solomon embeds his criticism of Rome within a larger parody of various forms of Greco-Egyptian idolatry. For Ps.-Solomon, emperor worship did not have a preeminent place in Greco-Egyptian religion—rather, it stood alongside the superstition associated with nature worship (13:1–9), Egyptian theriolatry (13:14), Castor and Pollux (14:1), hero cults (14:15), Dionysus (14:23) and the τέχνη of the idol artisan (15:9, etc).³⁷

The danger of idols for the Jew was their power to stimulate what Moshe

---

³⁴ See Craig A. Evans, "King Jesus and His Ambassadors: Empire and Luke-Acts," in *Empire in the New Testament*, ed. Stanley E. Porter and Cynthia Long Westfall, MNTS (Eugene, OR: Pickwick, 2011), 120–39.

³⁵ See Addison Wright, "The Structure of the Book of Wisdom," *Bib* 48 (1967): 165–84; and Maurice Gilbert, "The Literary Structure of the Book of Wisdom," in *The Book of Wisdom in Modern Research: Studies on Tradition, Redaction, and Theology*, ed. Angelo Passaro and Giuseppe Bellia, Deuterocanonical and Cognate Literature Yearbook 2005 (New York: de Gruyter, 2005), 19–32.

³⁶ See Maurice Gilbert, "Your Sovereignty Comes from the Lord," in Gilbert, *La Sagesse de Salomon: Recueil d'etudes*, AnBib 189 (Rome: Biblical Institute Press, 1973), 121–40, here 127.

³⁷ See Marie Françoise Baslez, "The Author of Wisdom and the Cultured Environment of Alexandria," in Passaro and Bellia, *Book of Wisdom in Modern Research*, 83–116.

Halbertal and Avishai Margalit call "an improper conception of God in the mind of the worshiper."[38] The power of idols' visual stimulation (ὄψις; see Wis 13:7, 14:17, 15:5) is criticized by Ps.-Solomon in his etiological reflection on the origins of idolatry (14:12–21). Remarkably, Ps.-Solomon criticizes the erotic stimulation of cult images by arguing that "the invention of idols was the beginning of *porneia*" (ἀρχὴ γὰρ πορνείας ἐπίνοια εἰδώλων, Wis 14:12a).[39] After a euhemeristic attribution of the origins of idolatry to a father who honors an image of a dead child (14:15), Ps.-Solomon redirects his argument toward the Roman imperial cults in 14:16–21:[40]

> (16) Then, when the impious custom had grown strong with time, it was kept as a law, and at the command of princes [τυράννων][41] carved images were worshipped. (17) When people could not honor them in their presence because they lived far off, they imagined their appearance from afar and made a visible image [ἐμφανῆ εἰκόνα] of the king [βασιλέως] whom they honored, that through diligence they might flatter the absent one as though present [ἵνα ὡς παρόντα τὸν ἀπόντα κολακεύωσιν διὰ τῆς σπουδῆς]. (18) But the ambition [φιλοτιμία] of the craftsman impelled even those who did not know the king to a higher pitch of worship. (19) For he, perhaps wishing to please his ruler, skillfully forced the likeness into a more beautiful form, (20) but the multitude, drawn by the charm of his work, now counted as an object of worship [σέβασμα] the one whom a little before had been honored as a human being. (21) And this became a trap for human life, because people, enslaved either by misfortune or tyranny [ὅτι ἢ συμφορᾷ ἢ τυραννίδι δουλεύσαντες ἄνθρωποι], bestowed on objects of stone and wood the incommunicable name. (NETS)

Ps.-Solomon's criticism of monarchs who "lived far off" and subjects who "flatter the absent one as though present" (14:17) provides an unmistakable reference to the Roman era. David Winston takes the phrase "at the command of princes" (14:16) as a reference to the antics of Caligula (Philo, *Legat.* 133–134).[42] Winston fails to recognize, however, that the imperial cult was set up from above and locally

---

[38] Moshe Halbertal and Avishai Margalit, *Idolatry*, trans. Naomi Goldblum (Cambridge: Harvard University Press, 1998), 2.

[39] For fuller discussion, see Jason von Ehrenkrook, *Sculpting Idolatry in Flavian Rome: (An)Iconic Rhetoric in the Writings of Flavius Josephus*, EJL (Atlanta: Society of Biblical Literature, 2012), 55–58; von Ehrenkrook, "Image and Desire in the *Wisdom of Solomon*," *Zutot* 7 (2011): 41–50, https://doi.org/10.1163/187502111795240467.

[40] For Euhemerus's theory, see Diodorus 6.1.2–10.

[41] Ps.-Solomon highlights the absolute sovereignty of the monarch by using the flexible yet potentially subversive title τύραννος (6:9, 21; 8:15; 12:14; 14:17). Though τύραννος is typically translated as "monarch," the early Jewish usage of this word shows that Jews could employ it in the truly tyrannical sense. See, e.g., 4 Macc 5:1; Philo, *Legat.* 350; *Alleg. Interp.* 3.79; Wis 6:9, 21; 14:17.

[42] David Winston, *The Wisdom of Solomon: A New Translation with Introduction and Commentary*, AB 43 (Garden City, NY: Doubleday, 1979), 23.

organized in Egypt already during the Augustan era.⁴³ The efficacy of the imperial image for inducing awe and, consequently, honor from the imperial subject is evident in verses 19–20, where the artisan redesigns the imperial image to take on more beautiful form. The aesthetic quality of the imperial image blurs the distinction between human and divine, thus leading the multitudes to deify their ruler, who "a little before had been honored as a human being [τιμηθέντα ἄνθρωπον]" (v. 20).

To resist divine honors, Ps.-Solomon recontextualizes Isaiah's polemic against idols for a new imperial context in Roman Egypt. The lexical and thematic overlap between the Wisdom of Solomon and the Areopagus speech, along with their departure from the Hebrew Bible through their shared rhetorical and philosophical convictions, places these two texts in unique relationship to each other, as the table on the following page illustrates.

These lexical and thematic associations are not meant to downplay the significance of Isaiah for Luke-Acts' intertextual repertoire. Additionally, it is possible that Luke learns these literary conventions from early Christian sources (e.g., Rom 1:18–32 stands out). As Luke's use of Paul becomes more accepted among scholars, an intratextual analysis of Acts' polemic against idols with Paul's letters may be useful.⁴⁴ Here, however, my aim is not to prove Luke's direct dependence on Wisdom; rather, it is to show that the Areopagus speech's diction of polemic against idols is not politically innocuous when read alongside the literary culture of early Judaism. Although critical motifs 1–8 all evoke a hypothetical denunciation of deified political authority, in what follows I will focus particular attention on critical motif 1 (images on σέβασμα) and critical motif 6 (precious materials).

Critical Motif 1: Cultic Objects on σέβασμα

Ps.-Solomon's assiduous choice of the word σέβασμα in verse 20 to depict objects of worship rather than the more typical ἄγαλμα or εἰκών evokes a neologism from the reign of Augustus coined after the appellation Augustus (= σεβαστός; see Suetonius, *Aug.* 7.2).⁴⁵ The only two occurrences of σέβασμα in the LXX are in Wis

---

⁴³ Inscriptional evidence shows that Augustus and local elites had direct oversight of the imperial cult in Egypt before the reign of Caligula (e.g., *OGIS* II, 656 = *I Alex.* 2). See also Géza Alföldy's reading of a palimpsest on a third obelisk from Augustus's *Sebasteion* in *Der Obelisk auf dem Petersplatz in Rom: Ein historisches Monument der Antike*, SHAW.PH 1990.2 (Heidelberg: Winter, 1990), 41–42. For further comment, see Gregory S. Dundas, "Pharaoh, Basileus and Imperator: The Roman Imperial Cult in Egypt" (PhD diss., University of California Los Angeles, 1994), 41–96.

⁴⁴ See David Moessner et al., eds., *Paul and the Heritage of Israel: Paul's Claim upon Israel's Legacy in Luke and Acts in the Light of the Pauline Letters*, LNTS 452 (London: T&T Clark, 2012).

⁴⁵ On the title σεβαστός, see Pausanias, *Descr.* 3.11.4; Res gest. divi Aug. 34.2. The adjective σεβαστός implies divinity through its adjectival descriptors of one who is "'stately, 'dignified' and 'holy'" (Zanker, *Power of Images*, 98).

Lexical and Thematic Parallels in Wisdom and the Areopagus Speech		
Critical Motif	The Book of Acts	Wisdom of Solomon
1. Images	ἀναθεωρῶν τὰ σεβάσματα ὑμῶν (17:23)	τὸ δὲ πλῆθος ἐφελκόμενον διὰ τὸ εὔχαρι τῆς ἐργασίας τὸν πρὸ ὀλίγου τιμηθέντα ἄνθρωπον νῦν σέβασμα ἐλογίσαντο (14:20; see also 15:17).
2. Made by Human Hands	οὐκ ἐν χειροποιήτοις ναοῖς κατοικεῖ (17:24)	τὸ χειροποίητον δέ ἐπικατάρατον (14:8)
3. Works of Human Hands	οὐδὲ ὑπὸ χειρῶν ἀνθρωπίνων θεραπεύεται (17:25)	ταλαίπωροι δὲ καὶ ἐν νεκροῖς αἱ ἐλπίδες αὐτῶν οἵτινες ἐκάλεσαν θεοὺς ἔργα χειρῶν ἀνθρώπων (13:10; see also 13:19; 15:17).
4. Humans Have Breath, Idols Do Not	αὐτὸς διδοὺς πᾶσι ζωὴν καὶ πνοὴν καὶ τὰ πάντα (17:25)	15:15–17; 2:2
5. Seeking the Invisible God —Natural Theology	ζητεῖν τὸν θεόν, εἰ ἄρα γε ψηλαφήσειαν αὐτὸν καὶ εὕροιεν (17:27)	ἀλλ' ὅμως ἐπὶ τούτοις μέμψις ἐστὶν ὀλίγη καὶ γὰρ αὐτοὶ τάχα πλανῶνται θεὸν ζητοῦντες καὶ θέλοντες εὑρεῖν (Wis 13:6); also, οὔτε δάκτυλοι χειρῶν εἰς ψηλάφησιν (15:15)
6. Precious Materials	γένος οὖν ὑπάρχοντες τοῦ θεοῦ οὐκ ὀφείλομεν νομίζειν χρυσῷ ἢ ἀργύρῳ ἢ λίθῳ (17:29)	χρυσὸν καὶ ἄργυρον τέχνης ἐμμελέτημα καὶ ἀπεικάσματα ζῴων ἢ λίθον ἄχρηστον χειρὸς ἔργον ἀρχαίας (13:10; see also 14:21; 15:9).
7. Skill of Idol Artists	χαράγματι τέχνης καὶ ἐνθυμήσεως ἀνθρώπου (17:29)	ὁ μὲν γὰρ τάχα κρατοῦντι βουλόμενος ἀρέσαι ἐξεβιάσατο τῇ τέχνῃ τὴν ὁμοιότητα ἐπὶ τὸ κάλλιον (14:19); and ταλαίπωροι δὲ καὶ ἐν νεκροῖς αἱ ἐλπίδες αὐτῶν οἵτινες ἐκάλεσαν θεοὺς ἔργα χειρῶν ἀνθρώπων χρυσὸν καὶ ἄργυρον τέχνης ἐμμελέτημα καὶ ἀπεικάσματα ζῴων ἢ λίθον ἄχρηστον χειρὸς ἔργον ἀρχαίας (13:10)
8. Human Ignorance	τοὺς μὲν οὖν χρόνους τῆς ἀγνοίας ὑπεριδὼν ὁ θεός (17:30)	ἀλλὰ καὶ ἐν μεγάλῳ ζῶντες ἀγνοίας πολέμῳ (14:22)

14:20 and 15:17. Both references criticize cultic images and stress the gap between the human and the divine. Philo refers to the colossal statue of Augustus in Alexandria as τὸ λεγόμενον Σεβαστεῖον (*Legat.* 151), and Josephus records Augustus renaming Samaria "Sebaste" (*J.W.* 1.21.2 §403).[46] As Winston and others have noted, given the literary context in which the word is employed, Ps.-Solomon's polemic takes on an "Augustan" aura. In extrabiblical tradition, the word σέβασμα occurs in only five authors, always with a cultic meaning but never with direct reference to the imperial cults.[47] In a political prophecy about the emperor Hadrian in the Sibylline Oracles, the Sibyl prophesies that Hadrian will erect an image of his lover Antinous as a god and "will destroy all objects of reverence" (ἅπαντα σεβάσματα λύσει, Sib. Or. 8:57). Aside from Acts, the only other occurrence of σέβασμα in the New Testament is in 2 Thess 2:4, where the author associates the "lawless one" with one who "exalts himself above every so-called god or object of worship [σέβασμα]." Though the lawless one is composite, the author of 2 Thessalonians juxtaposes σέβασμα with an individual who seeks to usurp the power of God, a sense that is not far removed from Ps.-Solomon's criticism of the superhuman status of the Roman emperor (Wis 14:20).

Although the word σέβασμα does not occur in Athens's epigraphic record, of the forty-three dedicatory inscriptions in Athens to the imperial family, twenty-eight employ the appellation Σεβαστός or, when referring to Livia or Julia, Σεβαστή.[48] The table on the following page organizes these inscriptions by dedicatory type and highlights when a Julio-Claudian emperor is associated with a god.[49]

The σεβαστός inscriptions create a context that is not devoid of political connotations when Luke depicts Paul in the guise of a Socratic *periegesis* "observing carefully" (ἀναθεωρέω) Athens's objects of worship (τὰ σεβάσματα, Acts 17:23) in the *captatio benevolentiae* of the speech proper:

Σταθεὶς δὲ [ὁ] Παῦλος ἐν μέσῳ τοῦ Ἀρείου πάγου ἔφη· ἄνδρες Ἀθηναῖοι, κατὰ πάντα ὡς δεισιδαιμονεστέρους ὑμᾶς θεωρῶ. διερχόμενος γὰρ καὶ ἀναθεωρῶν τὰ σεβάσματα ὑμῶν εὗρον καὶ βωμὸν ἐν ᾧ ἐπεγέγραπτο· Ἀγνώστῳ θεῷ. ὃ οὖν ἀγνοοῦντες εὐσεβεῖτε, τοῦτο ἐγὼ καταγγέλλω ὑμῖν.

---

[46] Adolf Deissmann draws attention to eight ostraca that speak of taxes paid on the "Sebaste Day," which, for Deissmann, creates the "possibility that the distinctive title 'Lord's Day' may have been connected with conscious feelings of protest against the cult of the Emperor with its 'Augustus Day'" (*Light from the Ancient East: The New Testament Illustrated by Recently Discovered Texts of the Graeco-Roman World*, 4th ed. [London: Hodder & Stoughton, 1910], 358–61).

[47] See Dionysius of Halicarnassus, *Ant. rom.* 1.30; Bel 27; Josephus, *Ant.* 18.9.5 §344; Strabo, *Geogr.* 3.3.8; 12.8.6; and Ps.-Clementine *Homilies* 10, 21, and 22.

[48] Notably, the masculine form σεβασμός is employed in the so-called great inscription that Antiochus I ordered for his sacred *Nomos*, which was inscribed in stone on the east and west sides of the *tumulus* monument at Nemrud Dagh in order to be "unassailable to the ravages of time" (ἀπόρθητον χρόνου λύμαις; *OGIS* 383, line 36; English trans. Danker, no. 41).

[49] This table is compiled based on Schmalz, *Augustan and Julio-Claudian Athens*, nos. 113–56.

Occurrences of Σεβαστός and Σεβαστή in Athens's Epigraphic Record During the Julio-Claudian Period			
Emperor/ Empress	Inscription	Dedication Type	Association?
1. Augustus	SEG 29 (1979) no. 178	Statue	
2. Augustus	SEG 47 (1997) no. 218	Statue	
3. Augustus	IG II² 3227	Altar	
4. Augustus	IG II² 3228 (lines 1–3)	Altar	
5. Augustus	SEG 18 (1962) no. 73	Altar	
6. Augustus	SEG 18 (1962) no. 74	Altar	
7. Augustus	SEG 18 (1962) no. 75	Altar	
8. Augustus	SEG 18 (1962) no. 76	Altar	
9. Augustus	SEG 18 (1962) no. 77	Altar	
10. Augustus	SEG 18 (1962) no. 78	Altar	
11. Augustus	SEG 18 (1962) no. 79	Altar	
12. Augustus	IG II² 3262+4725	Statue	Augustus as "New Apollo"
13. Gaius	IG II² 3250	Statue	Gaius Caesar as "New Ares"
14. Livia	IG II² 3242	Temple	
15. Livia	SEG 22 (1967) no. 152	Statue	
16. Livia	IG II² 3238	Statue	
17. Livia	IG II² 3239	Statue	
18. Julia	IG II² 3239	Statue	
19. Julia	SEG 47 (1997) no. 220	Monumental	
20. Julia	SEG 47 (1997) no. 156	Statue	
21. Julia	SEG 47 (1997) no. 156	Building	
22. Tiberius	IG II² 4209	Monumental	
23. Tiberius	IG II² 3261	Monumental	
24. Caligula	SEG 34 (1984) no. 182	Altar	
25. Caligula	SEG 34 (1984) no. 180	Statue	With Drusilla as "New Goddess Aphrodite"
26. Caligula	IG II² 3266	Statue	
27. Caligula	SEG 25 (1971) no. 208	Statue	
28. Nero	SEG 32 (1982) no. 252	Altar	Nero as "New Apollo"

Then Paul stood in front of the Areopagus and said, "Athenians, I see how extremely religious you are in every way. For as I went through the city and looked carefully at the objects of your worship, I found among them an altar with the inscription, 'To an unknown god.' What therefore you worship as unknown, this I proclaim to you." (Acts 17:22-23 NRSV)

We know from Paul's recitation of an inscription to "an unknown god" that Paul occupied himself with reading epigraphic dedications on at least one altar ("an altar with the inscription" βωμὸν ἐν ᾧ ἐπεγέγραπτο, Acts 17:23). We also know that Luke is the only author in the New Testament to use the word σεβαστός—first when Paul appeals to the emperor (i.e., "imperial majesty," Acts 25:21, 25) and, second, when Paul is transferred to a centurion of the "Augustan cohort" (σπείρης Σεβαστῆς, 27:1). In David Gill's background article on the Areopagus speech he rightly recognizes that, although "the word [σέβασμα] may merely reflect the numerous altars and visual images related to cult at Athens, it also resonates with the worship of the imperial family, usually in a Sebasteion."[50] Gill, however, misses the lexical overlap with the Wisdom of Solomon, an oversight that is also committed by several scholars who do cite Wis 14:20 and 15:17 as parallels to Acts 17:23 but do not explore the context in which Ps.-Solomon employs the word.[51]

The high degree of lexical and thematic overlap between Wis 13:1–15:19 and the Areopagus speech produces the literary relationship one would expect for an intertextual allusion. Yet if Luke did intend for his audience to imagine images of the imperial cults embedded in Athens through his use of σέβασμα, he certainly does not dwell on it long. Just as Luke seems to direct his gaze toward imperial cult media—especially after the disciples are accused of acting contrary to the decrees of the emperor in Thessalonica (Acts 17:7)—he abruptly changes directions to an altar to an unknown god. But the embedding of the imperial cults in Athens, along with Ps.-Solomon's clear use of σέβασμα in correlation with the deified Augustus, precludes one from reading Paul's criticism of gentile religiosity in Athens as a criticism of Greco-Roman religion that is separate from the politics of Luke's day.

---

[50] David Gill, "Achaia," in *The Book of Acts in Its Graeco-Roman Setting*, vol. 2 of *The Book of Acts in Its First Century Setting*, ed. David Gill and Conrad Gempf (Grand Rapids: Eerdmans, 1994), 433–54, here 447.

[51] For scholars who cite Wis 14:20 but miss the context, see Ernst Haenchen, *The Acts of the Apostles: A Commentary* (Philadelphia: Westminster, 1971), 521; Luke Timothy Johnson, *The Acts of the Apostles*, SP 5 (Collegeville, MN: Liturgical Press, 1992), 314; Ben Witherington III, *The Acts of the Apostles: A Socio-rhetorical Commentary* (Grand Rapids: Eerdmans, 1998), 520; Darrell L. Bock, *Acts*, BECNT (Grand Rapids: Baker Academic, 2007), 565. Jacob Jervell is certainly correct that "Paulus hat in Athen viele Heiligtümer gefunden, σεβάσματα, 'Gegenstände religiöser Verehrung,' was hier nicht näher bestimmt wird, warscheinlich Götterbilder und Götterstatuen" (*Die Apostelgeschichte*, KEK 3 [Göttingen: Vandenhoeck & Ruprecht, 1998], 445). Jervell, however, does not cite the Wisdom of Solomon and, in accord with most commentaries, his exegesis focuses on the altar to an unknown god (17:23b).

Critical Motif 6: The Critique of Precious Materials

The luster, value, and aesthetic beauty of precious metals provided the material stuff for theologizing about gods and kings in the Greco-Roman world (Dio Chrysostom, *Or.* 12.44). In Greek culture, literary evidence supports the use of precious materials for iconic purposes by ca. 1200 BCE, when Homer talks about gold and silver dogs by Hephaistos (*Od.* 7.90).[52] Tacitus observes how Jews' aniconic monotheism could conflict with the iconic culture of the ruling power: "Therefore they set up no statues in their cities, still less in their temples; this flattery is not paid their kings, nor this honour given to the Caesars" (*non regibus haec adulatio, non Caesaribus honor, Hist.* 5.5.4). Recent archaeological evidence has shown Jewish tolerance for images.[53] The presence of precious metals even on aniconic objects related to Roman imperial authority, however, could evoke a strong response from Jewish subjects, especially within or near the vicinity of Jerusalem (e.g., Josephus, *Ant.* 18.3.1 §§55–59; *J.W.* 2.9.2–3 §§169–174; Philo, *Legat.* 299–305).[54]

Philo reflects the hierarchy of materials used to theologize about divinity when he repudiates silver and gold because they "are esteemed the most honorable of all materials" (*Spec.* 1.22). Josephus also understands the hierarchy of materials: "The artists who are the most admired use ivory and gold as the material for their constant innovations" (*C. Ap.* 2.36 §252).[55] In contrast to gentile iconic culture, Josephus suggests that "no materials, however costly, are fit to make an image of Him; no art [ἄτεχνος] has skill [τέχνη] to conceive and represent him" (*C. Ap.* 2.23 §191). Although gold and ivory were the premier materials used to honor the gods in antiquity, in the discussion that follows, stone and wood are included under the rubric "precious materials" because of their utility as an effigy that could stand alone or be encased with precious metals (notably, all of the extant colossal statues of Roman emperors are acroliths with a wooden core of cypress).[56]

The use of precious materials to exploit the elision of gods and kings occurs

---

[52] Of the extant archaeological evidence, a gold statue of a goddess from Ephesus—possibly identified as Artemis—can be dated to ca. 600 BCE (Vermeule, no. 1). See C. C. Vermeule, *Greek and Roman Sculpture in Gold and Silver* (Boston: Museum of Fine Arts, 1974).

[53] See E. R. Goodenough, *Jewish Symbols in the Greco-Roman Period*, 13 vols., Bollingen Series 37 (New York: Pantheon, 1953–1968).

[54] Helen K. Bond, "Standards, Shields and Coins: Jewish Reactions to Aspects of the Roman Cult in the Time of Pilate," in *Idolatry: False Worship in the Bible, Early Judaism and Christianity*, ed. Stephen C. Barton (London: T&T Clark, 2007), 88–106.

[55] Trans. John M. G. Barclay, *Against Apion: Translation and Commentary*, Flavius Josephus Works 10 (Leiden: Brill, 2006).

[56] See Barbara Burrell, *Neokoroi: Greek Cities and Roman Emperors*, Cincinnati Classical Studies NS 9 (Leiden: Brill, 2004), 318.

early on in the Hellenistic period. Pliny goes out of his way to make it known that Augustus was not the first ruler to receive honors with precious metals:

> It is generally believed, but erroneously, that silver was first employed for making statues of the deified Emperor Augustus, at a period when adulation was all the fashion: for I find it stated, that in the triumph celebrated by Pompeius Magnus there was a silver statue exhibited of Pharnaces, the first king of Pontus, as also one of Mithridates Eupator, besides chariots of gold and silver. (Pliny, *Nat.* 33.54)

According to Pliny, the tradition of representing deified rulers with precious materials arose well before the Roman principate. Here I limit the discussion to a few examples. We know that Demetrius Poliorcetes was honored with a gold statue in Athens (Diodorus 20.46.1–4) and a bronze statue in the marketplace near personified Democracy (*IASIA* 256–62; Danker, no. 30). In Alexandria, Ptolemy Philadelphus (283–246 BCE) oversaw a royal procession with a gold statue of Alexander juxtaposed with Athena and Victory on a chariot drawn by elephants (Callixeinus, apud Athenaeus 5.202a).[57] The Canopus Decree instructs the Egyptian priesthood to honor the princess Berenice with a gold agalma in "all the temples" (ἐν ἅπασι τοῖς κατὰ τὴν χώραν ἱεροῖς, *OGIS* 56, lines 54–64); the Raphia decree records that "many people brought [Ptolemy IV] ... a gold crown" (Austin, no. 276); Ptolemy II Philadelphus commissioned chryselephantine statues of his parents Ptolemy I Soter and Berenice I as "savior gods" (Theocritus, *Idylls* 17.121–128); and the Rosetta Stone praises Ptolemy V Epiphanes (204–180 BCE) for lavishing decorations of "precious gold, silver and stones" on the temple of Apis (Χρυσίο[υ] τε κ[αὶ ἀργυρί]ου καὶ λίθων πολυτελῶν, *OGIS* 90, line 34).[58] Rather strikingly, the order of the precious materials in the Rosetta Stone reflects verbatim the order of Paul's critique of precious materials in the Areopagus speech (χρυσῷ ἢ ἀργύρῳ ἢ λίθῳ, Acts 17:29).

In contrast to the practice of Hellenistic kings, the use of precious material to honor Roman emperors was considered incompatible with Roman cultural ideals.[59] As Kenneth Scott observes, "Almost every emperor deemed it necessary to promulgate a policy of either accepting or refusing statues in precious metals."[60] While

---

[57] For further discussion, see Kenneth Scott, "The Significance of Statues in Precious Metals in Emperor Worship," *TPAPA* 62 (1931): 101–23, here 115, https://doi.org/10.2307/282968.

[58] For further examples, see Kenneth D. S. Lapatin, *Chryselephantine Statuary in the Ancient Mediterranean World*, Oxford Monographs on Classical Archaeology (Oxford: Oxford University Press, 2001), 138–51. The English translation of the Raphia decree is from Michel Austin, *The Hellenistic World from Alexander to the Roman Conquest: A Selection of Ancient Sources in Translation*, 2nd ed. (Cambridge: Cambridge University Press, 2006), https://doi.org/10.1017/CBO9780511818080.

[59] On Rome's purported aniconicism, see Plutarch, *Num.* 8.7–8; Varro in Augustine, *Civ.* 4.31.

[60] Scott, "Significance of Statues in Precious Metals," 101.

Scott may embellish the ubiquity of this policy, Augustus intentionally embodied vestiges of the past by appeal to a public image of *moderatio* and *pietas*. In the Res gestae, Augustus writes of an event in 31 BCE when he refused statues in precious metals:

> After my victory I reinstated into temples of all cities in Asia the dedications which the enemy against whom I had prevailed had plundered and was holding in his possession. Nearly eighty silver pedestrian and equestrian statues of me and statues in chariots had been set up in the city, which I myself removed, and from this money I set up golden dedications in the temple of Apollo both in my name and in the name of those who honored me with these statues [ἐκ τούτου τε τοῦ χρήματος ἀναθέματα χρυσᾶ ἐν τῶι ναῶ(ι) τοῦ Ἀπόλλωνος τῶι τε ἐμῶι ὀνόματι καὶ ἐκείνων, οἵτινές με (τ)ούτοις τοῖς ἀνδριᾶσιν ἐτείμησαν, ἀνέθηκα]. (Res. gest. divi Aug. 24.1–2)[61]

As Stewart suggests, the offerings are unprecedented in the city of Rome and most likely were "set up in or near temples."[62] Augustus interprets the gestures as hubris and redirects the offerings toward the gods. Cassius Dio also reflects the Roman tradition of *moderatio* when he has Maecenas exhort Augustus to reproduce his image in his subjects through benefaction rather than through gold or silver images (Cassius Dio 52.35).[63] Similarly, Plutarch suggests that the ideal ruler who animates law needs no Phidias, "but by his virtue [δι' ἀρετῆς] he forms himself in the likeness of God [εἰς ὁμοιότητα θεῷ] and thus creates a statue [ἀγαλμάτων] most delightful of all to behold and most worthy of divinity" (*Princ. iner.* 780EF).

Despite Augustus's *pietas* toward his patron god Apollo, he was quickly absorbed into the cults of the traditional gods in the winter of 30/29 BCE when he permitted honors of himself in the Greek East (with the expectation that his image be set up alongside Roma and he not be worshiped as a god [Suetonius, *Aug.* 52]).[64] Augustus's move toward accepting divine honors is evident as early as ca. 30 BCE when, according to Appian, a gold statue was set up in the Forum (*Bell. civ.* 5.130).[65] Likewise, after Augustus's death and apotheosis, Dio records that "they placed a

---

[61] Translation from Allison E. Cooley, *Res Gestae Divi Augusti: Text, Translation, and Commentary* (Cambridge: Cambridge University Press, 2009). Cassius Dio also alludes to the melting of the statues but suggests that the overture was used to fund new roads (53.22.3). Suetonius writes that the golden offerings were tripods (*Aug.* 52). See figs. 69, 193, and 209 in Zanker, *Power of Images*, 86.

[62] Stewart, *Statues in Roman Society*, 172.

[63] Tacitus records a similar tradition when he has Tiberius claim that his subjects represent his temples and statuary (*Ann.* 4.37.3 and 4.38).

[64] Zanker, *Power of Images*, 302.

[65] See also Augustus's claim in the Res gestae that golden shields were set up in his honor in the Curia Julia (Cassius Dio 50.5).

golden image of him on a couch in the temple of Mars" (Cassius Dio 56.46).[66] In Roman Egypt, to illustrate the honors given to Augustus in Alexandria, Philo records a detailed description of Augustus's Sebasteion inlaid with precious metals of silver and gold overlooking the harbor of the city and, presumably, the porticoes he acknowledges are built of stone (*Legat.* 151). The Sebasteion provides a partial extratextual background for Ps.-Solomon's polemic against cult images in precious materials.

The use of silver and gold was not lost on the so-called mad emperors (e.g., Caligula [Suetonius, *Cal.* 21–23; Philo, *Legat.* 79, 203], Nero [Cassius Dio 63.6, 9; Tacitus, *Ann.* 14.12], and Domitian [Cassius Dio 8.1; Suetonius, *Dom.* 13; Pliny, *Pan.* 52]). In contrast to Caligula's hubristic acceptance of statues in precious metals, Claudius's policy appears intentionally more modest: "At first he accepted only one portrait, and that merely of silver, and two statues, one of bronze and one of stone, which were voted to him" (Cassius Dio 60.5.4–5). Notwithstanding the diverse imperial cult media that existed in first-century Athens, there is no extant sculptural or literary evidence of imperial cult images cast in gold or silver. From the second century, however, Pausanias records in his description of Greece that a colossal statue of Hadrian encased with ivory and gold was located before the entrance to the sanctuary of Olympian Zeus in Athens (*Descr.* 1.18.6). The proliferation of Hadrian's image in Athens is evident also in his construction of the massive Olympieion, where no fewer than 136 portraits of Hadrian stood in the *temenos* from every Greek city.[67]

Ps.-Solomon's Polemic against Precious Materials

There are three passages in the Wisdom of Solomon that criticize precious materials (13:10, 14:21, 15:9). One could add to this list Ps.-Solomon's paragon of the ideal ruler, where the wise Solomon refuses to represent Lady Wisdom with precious material (Wis 7:1–10). Wisdom 13:10 and 15:9 do not have an explicit imperial target; however, Gilbert and others have persuasively shown that the main section of the *digressio* on idolatry (13:10–15:13) is structured in a concentric design, where 13:10–19 and 15:1–13 frame Ps.-Solomon's etiology of idols (Wis 14:12–21) with traditional biblical icon parodies.[68] One can take it as axiomatic, then, that images in gold or silver—whether of a beast, a planet, or an imperial portrait—are implicitly criticized in 13:10 and 15:9. Criticism of precious materials moves from implicit to explicit critique of imperial cult media in Wis 14:21. The cluster of words used for "honoring" the distant ruler in verses 16–21—ἐτίμησεν

---

[66] In addition, Cassius Dio notes that Augustus's coffin was made of ivory and gold (56.34.1).
[67] Susan E. Alcock, *Graecia Capta: The Landscapes of Roman Greece* (Cambridge: Cambridge University Press, 1993), 181.
[68] See Gilbert, *La critique des dieux*, 245–57.

(v. 15c), τιμᾶν (v. 17a), τιμωμένου (v. 17c), φιλοτιμία (v. 18b), and τιμηθέντα (v. 20b)—heightens Ps.-Solomon's criticism of the imperial cults' euergetic system of honors.[69]

In an attempt to expose the honors that undergird the emperor's power, Ps.-Solomon calls imperial honors a "trap for human life" among those "enslaved by misfortune or tyranny" (τυραννίδι δουλεύσαντες, v. 21). With resonances of Isa 42:8, Ps.-Solomon proceeds to attack those who give the name of the one God "that ought not to be shared" to objects of "stone and wood" that represent the Roman emperor (v. 21: τὸ ἀκοινώνητον ὄνομα λίθοις καὶ ξύλοις περιέθεσαν). It is crucial to recognize that, like Luke, Ps.-Solomon recontextualizes Isaiah's icon parody by placing it within the persuasion strategies of Greco-Roman rhetoric (a concept foreign to the thought world of Isaiah).[70] Moreover, in contrast to Isaiah, both Wisdom and Luke employ the icon parody in an apologetic context to condemn the philosophical shortcomings of pagan religiosity rather than the Israelite community per se.[71] More importantly for my purposes here, however, both Wisdom's and Luke's evocations of the icon parody coincided with Greco-Roman philosophical criticism of religion and the angry tyrant—an additional *Gesprächspartner* foreign to Isaiah.[72]

The Philosophical Critique of Precious Material

The philosophical critique of honors in precious materials finds a striking precedent in the Platonic Socrates. Socrates urged his pupils to avoid public τιμή in precious material because philosophers have "gold and silver ... of the divine quality from the gods always in their souls" (Plato, *Resp.* 416e–417a). For Plato, the soul already comprises the quality of precious materials, thereby making wealth and numismatic representation a potential for "many impious deeds" (*Resp.* 417a). In Plutarch's comments on this passage, he condemns the "love of honors" (φιλοτιμία) within a robust euergetic framework. Because the soul is made of gold, philosophers have an innate honor—"a gold uncorrupted, undefiled, and unpolluted."

---

[69] See ibid., 130.

[70] See Leo G. Perdue, "Rhetoric and the Art of Persuasion in the Wisdom of Solomon," in *Text, Image, and Christians in the Graeco-Roman World: A Festschrift in Honor of David Lee Balch*, ed. Aliou Cissé Niang and Carolyn Osiek, Princeton Theological Monograph Series 176 (Eugene, OR: Pickwick, 2012), 183–98.

[71] As Joshua Jipp recently argued, Luke exalts the Christian movement as a superior and more consistent philosophical form of knowledge by blending Jewish and Greco-Roman traditions ("Paul's Areopagus Speech of Acts 17:16–34 as *Both* Critique *and* Propaganda," *JBL* 131 [2012]: 567–88, here 568, https://doi.org/10.2307/23488255).

[72] See Harold W. Attridge, *First-Century Cynicism in the Epistles of Heraclitus*, HTS 29 (Missoula, MT: Scholars Press, 1976), 3–13.

Therefore, according to Plutarch, "we have no need of honours painted, modeled, or cast in bronze" (*Praec. ger. rei publ.* 820B). The pursuit of unbridled power and φιλοτιμία makes one "top-heavy and weighty ... like ill-proportioned statues, quickly overturned" (*Praec. ger. rei publ.* 820F). For Plutarch, the ideal ruler should represent oneself by the logos of philosophy—not the "art of statuary" and "lifeless images" (*Max. princ.* 776CD).[73] Strikingly, Plutarch's criticism is not against a particular piece of statuary or the imperial cults per se. Rather, he attacks the larger system of visual euergetism that leads to self-indulgence. In Plutarch's biographical sketch of Demetrius, he notes that "the most paltry evidence of the people's good will towards kings and rulers is excess of honors [ὑπερβολὴ τιμῶν]" (*Dem.* 30.4). Luke and Ps.-Solomon would certainly be in agreement. Ps.-Solomon, for example, condemns the artisan's love of honors (φιλοτιμία, a *hapax legomenon* in the LXX), which visually impels "those who did not know the king to intensify their worship" (Wis 14:18 NRSV).

That Plutarch could critique the precious materials of the ruling power's iconography explicitly is evident elsewhere. In *De superstitione*, Plutarch critiques the superstitious "who give credence to workers in metal, stone, or wax, who make their images of gods in the likeness of human beings, and they have such images fashioned, and dress them up, and worship them" (*Superst.* 167E). Although Plutarch's criticism of anthropomorphic images and precious material does not have an explicit referent, Suetonius recalls a golden statue of Caligula being dressed every day (*Cal.* 21–22). A few passages later Plutarch compares the superstitious with those who "give welcome to despots [τυράννους], and pay court to them, and *erect golden statues* in their honour, but in their hearts they hate them and shake the head" (*Superst.* 170E). The passage is remarkably subversive; just as worshipers alleviate their fear of the gods through visual honors and ritual, so also do subjects who mollify the ruling power by erecting chryselephantine sculpture.

Plutarch's criticism of tyrants' iconography in precious material is even more explicit in his treatise *To an Uneducated Ruler*. Here Plutarch parodies rulers who imitate the gods through colossal statues rather than through law and philosophy, "but inside *are full of clay, stone, and lead*" (*Princ. iner.* 2). The passage explicitly associates the critique of precious materials with imperial statues. The flattery (κολακεύω) of artists, poets, and subjects is no true mark of the ideal ruler, whose metric for ruling properly is predicated on law and philosophical acumen rather than visual ostentation (*De se ipsum laud.* 543DE; *Alex. fort.* 330F–331A). In a similar way, Ps.-Solomon caricatures those who "flatter the absent one as though present" (ἵνα ὡς παρόντα τὸν ἀπόντα κολακεύωσιν, 14:17), and Philo ridicules those

---

[73] Geert Roskam, "Α ΠΑΙΔΕΙΑ for the Ruler: Plutarch's Dream of Collaboration between Philosopher and Ruler," in *Sage and Emperor: Plutarch, Greek Intellectuals, and Roman Power in the Time of Trajan (98–117 A.D)*, ed. Philip A. Stadter and Luc van der Stockt, Symbolae Facultatis Litterarum Lovaniensis A.29 (Leuven: Leuven University Press, 2002), 175–89, here 178.

who erected images of Caligula in Alexandrian synagogues as "flattery" (κολακεία, *Legat.* 133–134). Although the philosophical critique of images in precious material tended to be universal in focus (Epictetus, *Diatr.* 2.8.13–14; Plutarch, *Is. Os.* 171; Ps.-Heraclitus, *Ep.* 4.10–18, 20–21; Lucian, *Philops.* 20; *Jupp. conf.* 8; *Sacr.* 11; and *Pro imag.* 23), Plutarch shows that (1) the philosophical critique of precious materials could evoke a political dimension, and (2) philosophers' polemic against images could encompass a critique of φιλοτιμία (and, hence, euergetic τιμαί).

What Is Divinity Like?

The archaeological record and the Hellenistic-Jewish and philosophical critique of precious materials illuminate the political referent of Acts 17:29. Luke's dramatic audience is already familiar with the critique of anthropomorphic images before the Areopagus speech proper. In Lystra, locals attempt to apotheosize Paul and Barnabas for their benefaction toward a crippled man by claiming, "The gods have descended in the likeness of human beings [ὁμοιωθέντες ἀνθρώποις]!" (Acts 14:11). Paul corrects the Lystrans' attempt at deification (and assimilation with Zeus and Hermes), arguing that human benefactors' ontological status is "like the nature" (ὁμοιοπαθεῖς) of mere mortals—*not* gods (Acts 14:15). This logic carries over into the Areopagus speech; but here the learned audience of Athens provides Paul with an opportunity to explicate philosophically what divinity—τὸ θεῖον rather than τὸν θεόν—is "like" (ὅμοιον, 17:29).[74] By appeal to the Stoic concept that God pervades humanity (Aratus, *Phaen.* v. 5), Luke argues that it is illogical to think that human art (τέχνη) and imagination (ἐνθύμησις) can manipulate divinity in human form with gold, silver, and stone (because humanity already properly embodies the image of and, hence, *metaphysical representation* of God).

The listing of materials reflects the hierarchy of materials used to theologize about divinity in antiquity. Eckhard J. Schnabel and Craig S. Keener are certainly correct to recognize an implicit critique of Phidias's gold and ivory Athena (Pliny, *Nat.* 34.19.54; Pausanias, *Descr.* 1.24.5–7).[75] But I suggest we can go further: to articulate that divinity is incompatible with gold, silver, and stone in the heart of Romanized Athens is to undermine the system of honors that upholds the visibility of gods *and* imperial families (a point that would certainly not be lost on Luke's dramatic audience).

If Luke intends to target the Roman imperial cults through his criticism of precious materials, his Stoic audience would surely have been sympathetic. In his

---

[74] C. K. Barrett, *A Critical and Exegetical Commentary on the Acts of the Apostles*, 2 vols., ICC (London: T&T Clark, 1998), 2:848.

[75] Eckhard J. Schnabel, *Acts*, Zondervan Exegetical Commentary on the New Testament 5 (Grand Rapids: Zondervan, 2012), 738; Craig S. Keener, *Acts: An Exegetical Commentary*, 4 vols. (Grand Rapids: Baker, 2012–2014), 3:2667.

seminal study on opposition to the Roman Empire, Ramsay MacMullen argued that Stoicism "sharpened the impulse and the courage to say what one felt [against the emperors]."[76] Luke's philosophical convictions, however, are not driven by Stoic philosophy alone. Rather, Luke's theopolitical imagination is funded by the story of Israel coming to completion in YHWH's eschatological act in Jesus's resurrection (Acts 17:30–31). In accord with the Wisdom of Solomon, Luke recontextualizes the Jewish icon parody to censure images cast in precious materials—*which includes political objects of power*—but only insofar as the imperial cults are understood as an integrated component of the larger polytheistic system of the religions of Rome.

III. Conclusion

Hans Conzelmann memorably wrote that Athens was the "museum of classical culture for the Hellenistic world."[77] Within this urban museum stood the *sebasmata* of gods and kings. The iconological impact of these media on the eye was mediated by a plastic language of signs shaped and molded by the hands of the artisan. Depending on how the artisan shaped the object—or what material the object was made of—the syntax of signs could communicate different meanings of social, religious, and political reality. The same can be said of the rhetorical art of the Areopagus speech. Depending on where you are standing in Athens's forest of idols, Paul's idol polemic is carefully sculpted to evoke polyvalent angles of criticism upon the visual theology of a city full of idols. As Jaś Elsner writes, in the Roman world, "art was power."[78] In continuity with Luke's criticism of benefactors who lord their power over subjects (i.e., οἱ βασιλεῖς τῶν ἐθνῶν, Luke 22:25), the Areopagus speech censures the false divinity of gods and kings from a different direction, that is, the (mis)representation of their power concretized in art.

To achieve this rhetorical end, Luke recontextualizes the strategies of resistance developed by his Hellenistic Jewish predecessors, such as the Wisdom of Solomon, who blended Old Testament idol polemics with Greco-Roman philosophical reflections on God. In a world where gods posed as kings and kings posed as gods, Luke censures the hybrid material culture that communicated divinity, power, and benefaction to the watching world. Luke, therefore, maintains the

---

[76] Ramsay MacMullen, *Enemies of the Roman Order: Treason, Unrest, and Alienation in the Empire* (Cambridge: Harvard University Press, 1966), 53, https://doi.org/10.4159/harvard.9780674864962.

[77] Hans Conzelman, "The Address of Paul on the Areopagus," in *Studies in Luke–Acts: Essays Presented in Honor of Paul Schubert*, ed. Leander E. Keck and J. Louis Martin (Nashville: Abingdon, 1966), 217–32, here 218.

[78] Jaś Elsner, *Imperial Rome and Christian Triumph: The Art of the Roman Empire, AD 100–400*, Oxford History of Art (Oxford: Oxford University Press, 1998), 53.

aniconic monotheism of his Jewish heritage but reorients the controlling narrative of Judaism around the ascended Christ. This theopolitical conviction is by no means inherently anti-imperial in the sense of a call for sedition; it is, rather, a call for gentiles to repent of trinket gods and theopolitical superstition. Although the Areopagus speech cannot account for the totality of Luke's political vision, Luke's presentation of Paul in Athens presents an alter-cultural vision of monarchy, monotheism, and representation that is at odds with the religions of the Roman Empire—including emperor worship.

Celebrating the New Year with the Israelites: Three Extrabiblical Psalms from Papyrus Amherst 63

KAREL VAN DER TOORN
k.vandertoorn@uva.nl
University of Amsterdam, 1012WX Amsterdam, Netherlands

Papyrus Amherst 63 is a fascinating extrabiblical source shedding light on the religion of the Israelites. This collection of Aramaic texts written in demotic characters contains three Israelite psalms, only one of which is known through the Hebrew Bible. The three songs have a common focus on the rites of the New Year. They corroborate and supplement the biblical data on this festival as it was celebrated in Israel. The conjunction of such themes as the harvest, the new wine, a meal of plenty in the presence of God, and the celebration of YHWH's kingship leave no doubt about the original ritual context of these psalms.

This study presents three Israelite psalms that are not in the Bible. They were found in an Egyptian papyrus with Aramaic texts written in demotic characters. Though the papyrus is from the mid-third century BCE, the material it contains is considerably older. I will show that the three psalms come from the northern kingdom at the time it was still a distinct polity. One of the texts was reworked by Judean editors and ended up in the Hebrew Bible as Ps 20. These three extra-biblical psalms—extrabiblical in spite of the obvious echoes of the first psalm in Ps 20—derive their logic, coherence, and sequence from the connection between the new wine (the autumn harvest), the new moon (ḥdyš), the New Year, and the renewal of Yaho's enthronement in the heavenly council. They are New Year psalms, preserving the memory of an Israelite festival among the Jewish diaspora in Egypt.

My work on these psalms has benefited from an unpublished paper by Tawny Holm (Pennsylvania State University) given at the SBL Annual Meeting in San Diego, California, in 2014. In addition, I am indebted to Tawny Holm for her comments on an earlier version of this paper.

I. The Date of the Psalms

Papyrus Amherst 63, now in the collections of the Pierpont Morgan Library, was discovered around 1890 in Luxor (ancient Thebes). It was part of a lot of papyri dated to the third century BCE. In the 1890s Lord Amherst acquired the lot and had them catalogued, as a result of which the papyrus is now known as Papyrus Amherst 63. It is an extraordinary document. The scribes who produced the papyrus used demotic characters, but the language of the texts they wrote down is Aramaic. The analysis of the papyrus shows that it is a library of sorts. The twenty-three columns, most of them running about twenty lines or more, contain texts from the stream of tradition: hymns, divine love lyrics, historical narrative, and sundry other materials.[1] Since the papyrus was produced in Egypt, the general assumption is that it reflects elements of the cultural heritage of Syrian expatriate communities. Most of those communities consisted of mercenaries in the service of the Egyptian, and later the Persian and Ptolemaic, armies. Among these Syrians, there were Jews too. We know about them from the Elephantine papyri and written evidence from various other places in Egypt (Memphis, the Nile Delta).

If Papyrus Amherst 63 was written in the third century BCE, the material it contains is often considerably older. The three Israelite psalms in columns xii and xiii (xii 11–19; xiii 1–10; xiii 11–17) are a case in point. Since one of the three psalms has a close biblical parallel, it allows us to appraise the difference between the earlier and the later version. Psalm 20 is the later version; the Amherst papyrus presents its forerunner.

The discovery of an Aramaic parallel to Ps 20 was made in the early 1980s. At that time, Richard Steiner (New York) and Jan Wim Wesselius (Amsterdam) were both working on the Amherst papyrus. Independently of each other, they discovered that the second half of column xii (column xi by the count of Steiner, who takes column v as ivb) contained an Aramaic prayer that bore a striking resemblance to Ps 20.[2] Steiner was the first to bring the find to the notice of the general

---

[1] For an introduction to Papyrus Amherst 63 and a general description of its contents, see Richard Steiner, "Papyrus Amherst 63: A New Source for the Language, Literature, Religion and History of the Aramaeans," in *Studia Aramaica: New Sources and New Approaches; Papers Delivered at the London Conference of the Institute of Jewish Studies, University College London, 26th–28th June 1991*, ed. Markham J. Geller, Jonas C. Greenfield, and M. P. Weitzman, JSSSup 4 (Oxford: Oxford University Press on behalf of the University of Manchester, 1995), 199–207; Ingo Kottsieper, "Aramaic Literature," in *From an Antique Land: An Introduction to Ancient Near Eastern Literature*, ed. Carl S. Ehrlich (Lanham, MD: Rowman & Littlefield, 2009), 393–444, esp. 427–29. For a translation of the entire papyrus, "with many uncertainties and controversial elements," see Richard Steiner, "The Aramaic Text in Demotic Script," *COS* 1.99: 309–27; quotation from 310.

[2] See Charles F. Nims and Richard C. Steiner, "A Paganized Version of Psalm 20:2–6 from the Aramaic Text in Demotic Script," *JAOS* 103 (1983): 261–74, https://doi.org/10.2307/601883;

public. In an interview with the *New York Times*, he presented the Aramaic text as an adaptation of the biblical psalm—and not merely as a neutral adaptation but as a pagan one, since the Aramaic version introduced foreign gods into the text (Bethel and Baal-Shamayin).[3] Should Steiner be correct, the historical priority would lie with the biblical psalm. Yet a close comparison between the Aramaic and Hebrew shows that the Aramaic is actually older; that is, the Hebrew text, which the Aramaic version has adapted, reflects an earlier stratum of Ps 20 than the version available in the MT of the Hebrew Bible.

Below is my transliteration of the papyrus based on two sets of photographs, followed by my translation of the Aramaic.[4] The transliteration follows the system developed by Sven Vleeming and Wesselius, as outlined in the second volume of their *Studies in Papyrus Amherst 63*, allowing for some slight adaptations for the convenience of the reader.[5] Multiconsonantal signs are underlined; capitals stand for determinatives (such as G for "God"); the subscript numbers distinguish different signs for the same consonant. It should be noted, moreover, that the script does not distinguish between D/T/Ṭ; G/K/Q; Z/S; and L/R (though r_2 is consistently used for R only). As will be seen, the transliteration implies choices and represents an interpretation of the demotic notation.

11   y^{ᶜ}n^{ɔ}n^{ɔ} | yhwG b^{ɔ}m^{ɔ}ṣw$_2$r$_2$yn^{ɔ} |
12 y^{ᶜ}n^{ɔ}n^{ɔ} | $^{ɔ}_2$d^{ɔ}ny | b^{ɔ}mṣw$_2$r$_2$yn^{ɔ} | h^{ɔ}y^{ɔ} + qš^{ɔ}t | b^{ɔ}š^{ɔ}myn |
13 s^{ɔ}hr$_2$^{ɔ} | š^{ɔ}l^{ɔ}h^{ɔ} | ṣ$_3$y^{ɔ}r$_2$^{ɔ}k | mn^n k^{ɔ}l | $^{ɔ}_2$r$_2$^{ɔ}š^{ɔ}H w^{ɔ}mn + ṣ$_3$p^{ɔ}n^{ɔ} |
14 yhwG y^{ɔ}s^{ᶜ}d^{ɔ}n^{ɔ} | y^{ɔ}m^{ɔ}t^{ɔ}n + $^{ɔ}_2$l^{ɔ}n^{ɔ} | yhwG k^{ɔ}bl^{ɔ}b^{ɔ}n^{ɔ} | y^{ɔ}mt^{ɔ}n^{ɔ} |
15 $^{ɔ}_2$l^{ɔ}n^{ɔ} | mry.C | k^{ɔ}bl^{ɔ}b^{ɔ}n | k$_2$l | y^{ᶜ}ṣ^{ɔ}t^{ɔ} | yhwG yh^{ɔ}m^{ɔ}ly | yh^{ɔ}mly yhwG
    l + yḫ^{ɔ}{|}
16 s^{ɔ}r$_2$^{ɔ} | $^{ɔ}_2$d^{ɔ}ny | k$_2$l | m^{ɔ}š$^{ɔ}_2$l +<l>^{ɔ}b^{ɔ}n^{ɔ} | ^{ɔ}l + b^{ɔ}qšt | ^{ɔ}l+ b^{ɔ}ḥ^{ɔ}nt^{ɔ} | ^{ɔ}r$_2$
17 $^{ɔ}_2$nḥ^{ɔ}n^{ɔ} | mry.Cy + ^{ɔ}lhn^{ɔ}nH yhwG yhw$_2$ + t^{ɔ}r$_2$^{ɔ}n^{ɔ} | ^{ᶜ}ymn^{ɔ}n^{ɔ} |
    y^{ᶜ}n^{ɔ}^{ɔ}n|
18 m^{ɔ}ḥr$_2$^{ɔ} ⌜|⌝ byt^{ɔ}l | b^{ɔ}lG šmynG mry.C yb$_2$^{ɔ}r$_3$^{ɔ}k$_2$^{ɔ} | l^{ɔ}[ḥ]^{ɔ}sy^{ɔ}/d$_2${|}
19 dyk^{ɔ} | b$_2$^{ɔ}r$_3$k^{ɔ}t^{ɔ}k^{ɔ} | sp.C

May Yaho answer us in our anxiety,
May Adonay answer us in our anxiety,
Crescent, be a bow in heaven!

Sven P. Vleeming and Jan W. Wesselius, "An Aramaic Hymn from the Fourth Century B.C.," *BO* 39 (1982 [the issue actually appeared spring 1983]): 501–9.

[3] "Aramaic Papyrus a Riddle No More," *New York Times*, 11 October 1982.

[4] My transliteration of Papyrus Amherst 63 is based on the Chicago photographs of 1901 (courtesy John A. Larson Jr.) in combination with more recent photographs of the text (2012 or 2013) made at the Pierpont Morgan Library (courtesy John Vincler, Head of Reader Services).

[5] Sven P. Vleeming and Jan Wim Wesselius, *Studies in Papyrus Amherst 63: Essays on the Aramaic Text in Aramaic/Demotic Papyrus Amherst 63* (Amsterdam: Juda Palache Instituut, 1990), vol. 2.

Send your messengers from all of Rash!
May Yaho sustain us from Zaphon.
May Yaho give to us our heart's desire,
May the Lord give to us our heart's desire.
May Yaou fulfill every plan, may Yaho fulfill!
Let Adonay not withhold any wish of our heart.
Some by the bow, some by the spear,
But as to us—the Lord is our God, Yaho!
Our Bull shall be with us.
May Bethel answer us tomorrow.
Baal Shamayin shall bless the Lord.
I bless you for your mercies! End.

There are several reasons to claim chronological priority for the version extant in Papyrus Amherst. A general consideration is the difference in length; Ps 20 is longer than the Aramaic prayer; verses 4, 6a, 7, and 9 of Ps 20 have no equivalent in the Aramaic text. In textual criticism one of the rules of thumb is *lectio brevior probabilior*; that is, the shorter reading is to be preferred (as being closer to the original).[6] The same rule is valid with respect to redaction criticism: normally the shorter text is earlier than the longer one: *brevior anterior*, as indicated by comparison between the Old Babylonian and the Standard Babylonian version of Gilgamesh, or between the book of Jeremiah in the MT and the LXX/Qumran version (4QJer[b]).[7] A closer look at the expansions made by the Judean scribe indicate that he was reframing the prayer so as to bring it in line with the messianic ideology: "Now I know that Yahweh will give victory to his Messiah; he will answer him from his holy heavens, by the mighty victory of his right hand" (Ps 20:7). This verse is absent from the Aramaic version; in the Judean edition of the psalm it has become the angle that commands the perspective of the entire psalm. That is why the "we" of the Aramaic psalm has become the single "you" in the MT; where the "we" has not been suppressed, the collective has become a witness to the victory given to the Messiah (Ps 20:6, 10).

The priority of the Aramaic psalm is indicated also by the theological corrections performed by the Judean editor. A striking example is found in Ps 20:3: "May he send you help from the sanctuary, and from Zion may he sustain you." The translation of the pertinent Aramaic phrases sounds very different: "Send your messengers from all of Rash! And from Zaphon may Yaho sustain us." A comparison of the Hebrew and the Aramaic shows more affinities than the translation suggests: *mn kl ʾrš* ("from all of Rash") // מקדש ("from the sanctuary"); *ṣyrʾk* ("your

---

[6] See Ralph W. Klein, *Textual Criticism of the Old Testament: The Septuagint after Qumran*, GBS (Philadelphia: Fortress, 1974), 75.

[7] See Karel van der Toorn, *Scribal Culture and the Making of the Hebrew Bible* (Cambridge: Harvard University Press, 2007), 125–32.

messengers") // עזרך ("your help"); wmn ṣpʾn ("and from Zaphon") // ומציון ("and from Zion"). The Judean scribe changed the meaning but tried to retain the sound of the text. The content of the changes proves that he was correcting the Aramaic text (or, rather, its Hebrew *Vorlage*), rather than the other way around. The change from Zaphon to Zion is traditional but could have been performed in both directions.[8] The phrase "from the sanctuary," however, is far less specific than "from all of Rash," since Rash is the name of a particular topographical area (the Lebanon mountains, in view of the parallel מן לבנן // mn rš in P.Amh. 63 xi 1); and "your messengers" is also more specific than "your help" (meaning help for you). A similar shift from the particular to the general has occurred toward the end of the text. "Tomorrow" (*mḥr*) has become "on the day we call" (ביום־קראנו).

If the chronological priority of the Amherst prayer over the MT of Ps 20 is accepted, the fact remains that the papyrus has an Aramaic text over against the Hebrew of the Bible. That is why it has been necessary to specify that the chronological priority belongs to the Hebrew original on which the Amherst papyrus is based. It is not necessary, however, to assume a huge linguistic gap between the Hebrew and the Aramaic. In fact, the Aramaic of the three Israelite psalms in the Amherst papyrus is a thin veneer rather than a complete recast. As Wesselius pointed out in 1985, the language of the three hymns is a mix of Hebrew and Aramaic.[9] Some words are clearly Hebrew (נזבח instead of *ndbḥ*, xiii 2, "we will sacrifice"; מא כאבא [= מי] for *mn kʾkʾ*, xiii 12, "who is like you?"—compare the correct form in xi 17; ישב for *ytb*, xiii 16). In several instances the form of the words is Aramaic, but the meaning derives from the underlying Hebrew (מצורינא in the forerunner of Ps 20 is a case in point). Since the gap between the Hebrew text and its Aramaic restyling is minimal, there is no real need speculatively to restore the lost original before we might attempt an interpretation.

II. Psalm No. 2: Celebrating the New Year

Psalm no. 1 has been discussed many times and by many people;[10] by comparison, Pss nos. 2 and 3 have received little attention.[11] Undeservedly so, for, as

---

[8] Cases where "Zion" is likely to be a substitute for "Zaphon" include Pss 9:12, 50:2, 74:2, 133:3.

[9] See Vleeming and Wesselius, *Studies in Papyrus Amherst 63*, 1:46–47.

[10] For a recent treatment, see Raik Heckl, "Inside the Canon and Out: The Relationship between Psalm 20 and Papyrus Amherst 63," *Sem* 56 (2014): 359–79, with references to much of the earlier literature.

[11] Martin Rösel devoted an article to the three psalms in 2000 ("Israel's Psalmen in Ägypten," *VT* 50 [2000]: 81–99) but had to depend entirely on the translation of these psalms by others (primarily by Wesselius in *TUAT* 2:933–34). For Rösel's discussion of Pss nos. 2 and 3, see 93–97. He emphasizes the parallel between parts of Ps no. 2 and Ps 75:8–10 but fails to observe that there

the analysis will show, they do in fact contain the key for the correct understanding of Ps no. 1. As the second psalm is both the longest and the most explicit in its references to a ritual context, it offers a good starting point for our study of the three texts. Below is my transliteration of the photographs of Papyrus Amherst, followed by my translation of the text, col. xiii, lines 1–10.

1 ⸢š⸣m'ʿny | ʾl [...] ʾ [ʾ₂]ʾrmʾrʾy | šʾpr | k[..] | [..]zʾ |
2 nʾzʾbʾḥ | lʾkʾ | bʾʾlhnʾnH q₂rʾtʾn | ʾ₂ʾlʾkʾ | mnⁿ ʾ₂dʾ₂ry | ʿm |
3 ʾ₂ʾdny | lʾkʾ | mnⁿ ʾdʾ₂rʾy ʿm | (rest of line is left blank)
4 ʾ₂ʾdny | ybʾ₂rʾ₃kʾkʾ | ʿm + sʾdʾrʾ₂tʾ | šʾntʾkʾ | nʾqʾḥ |
5 mnⁿ kʾd | rʾ₂ʾwʾy + ʾl | lʿʿlm | yʾgʾd | mʾgdlʾ | rʾb |
6 mrḥm | yhwG mʾšpʾly | šʾḥʾ | yʾynʾ | mʾzʾgw₂ + bʾg₂ʾlʾn |
7 bʾg₂ʾlʾn | bʾḥdyšʾnʾ | šty.C | yhwG bʾṭʾb + ʾlʾʾpʾ | ṣ₃⸢ʿ⸣ʾ |
8 r₂wy | ʾ₂ʾdny | bʾṭb + ʾ₂ʾnšy | yq₂w₂mn₃.C ʿl.C mry.C šwrn.C šʾr + nbʾl |
9 šrʾ + kʾnʾrʾ₂ʾ | nʾšʾrʾ₂ʾnʾkʾ₂ | šr + kʾnrʾ₂ | ṣ₃dny |
10 wḥlyʾynʾ | bʾʾ₂ʾdʾny | bq₂ʾrʾ₂ʾty | ʾ₂ʾdʾm | sp.C

Listen to me, my God [...]
Fine lambs [...]
We will sacrifice for you among the gods,
Our banquet is for you among the Mighty Ones of the people,
For you, Adonay, among the Mighty Ones of the people.
The people will bless you, Adonay,
We will perform your annual rites.
Quench yourself from the jar, my God!
Let it be announced forever:
The Merciful One exalts the great,
Yaho brings down the lowly one.
They have mixed the wine in our jar,
In our jar, at our New Moon festival.
Drink, Yaho, from the bounty of a thousand bowls![12]
Be satiated, Adonay, from the bounty of humanity.
May the musicians stand in attendance before Mar,
The player of the harp, the player of the lyre;
We will perform for you
The song of the Sidonian lyre—
Pleasant sounds in his ears,
At the banquets of humankind. End.

---

is a significant difference between a deity pouring out mixed wine for all the wicked of the earth to drink (Ps 75) and a god invited to be satiated with wine himself (Ps no. 2).

[12] For ṣᶜ, see Ugaritic ṣᶜ ("washbasin" > "bowl"); Arabic ṣāᶜ ("drinking vessel"); and Ethiopian ṣĕwāᶜ ("goblet").

Psalm no. 2 is a communal hymn; it belongs more specifically to the genre of New Year psalms as defined by Sigmund Mowinckel. Adducing Ps 81 as his main evidence, Mowinckel observed that "in early times the harvest feast (Tabernacles) was also the new year festival."[13] This extrabiblical psalm corroborates his view. The cultic occasion on which this psalm was chanted was a "banquet" (קרת) at which sacrifices were brought (נזבח).[14] Despite the reference to animal sacrifice, the psalm focuses on the offerings of wine. "They have mixed the wine in our jar...: Drink, Yaho, from the bounty of a thousand bowls!" The mixing of the wine (verb to be read as either Aramaic *mzg* or Hebrew *msk*) consists of the addition of spices and honey; such additions were normally made in larger containers after which the mixed wine (Hebrew מסך; see Ps 75:9; compare מזג in Cant 7:3) was drunk from cups.[15] The expression *gln* in lines 6 and 7 is best interpreted as "our *gl*," the *gl* being a jar or a large bowl.[16] In the Kirta Epic it is mentioned in the context of offerings on a rooftop: *yṣq . b gl . ḥtt . yn / b gl . ḥrṣ . nbt*, "He poured wine into a silver bowl, honey into a bowl of gold" (*KTU* 1.14 iv:1–2).

Two expressions put this sacrificial banquet with its generous supply of wine in a seasonal perspective. The celebrations are referred to as "your annual rituals" (sʾdʾr₂ʾtʾ | šʾntʾkʾ, line 4), and they occur "at our *ḥdyš*" (bʾḥdyšʾnʾ, line 7). The term *sdrt*, from the root *SDR*, implies the notion of order and appropriateness. It here refers to the ritual acts that are appropriate to the year; the pronominal suffix indicates the recipient of the rites: "the annual rituals for you." Two interpretations are possible: the singer of the psalm could be implying that the community was committed to the observance of the ritual calendar with its succession of annual festivals, or he could be referring more particularly to one of those festivals, namely, the "regular festival" of the New Year, on the understanding that *šnh* refers to "the turn of the year," as the Hebrew expression goes (Exod 34:22, 2 Chr 24:23; compare the variant "turning point of the days," 1 Sam 1:20).

Both Steiner and Tawny Holm translate the second expression, "at our *ḥdyš*," as "at our wedding (feast)," on the basis of Akkadian *ḫadaššūtu*. It is true that

---

[13] See Sigmund Mowinckel, *The Psalms in Israel's Worship*, trans. D. R. Ap-Thomas, 2 vols. (Oxford: Blackwell, 1962; based on *Offersang og Sangoffer* [Oslo: H. Aschehoug, 1951]), 1:95.

[14] The word *qrt* is best understood in light of Akkadian *qerītu* ("banquet, festival"); see *CAD* 13:240–42. The noun may also occur in Ugaritic; see *KTU* 1.14 ii:28: ʿ*db / akl . l qryt / ḥtt . l bt . ḥbr*, "He prepared food for the banquet, wheat for the house of din/ale-house" (compare Hebrew בית חבר in Prov 21:9, 25:24).

[15] See Patrick E. McGovern, *Ancient Wine: The Search for the Origins of Viticulture* (Princeton: Princeton University Press, 2003), 308–12; Mark S. Smith and Wayne T. Pitard, *The Ugaritic Baal Cycle*, vol. 2, VTSup 114 (Leiden: Brill, 2009), 112; Carey Ellen Walsh, *The Fruit of the Vine: Viticulture in Ancient Israel*, HSM 60 (Winona Lake, IN: Eisenbrauns, 2000), 203–5; Philip J. King and Lawrence E. Stager, *Life in Biblical Israel*, LAI (Louisville: Westminster John Knox, 2001), 102, 346.

[16] Another possibility would be to read *qrn* ("horn"), familiar to the Israelites as a container of oil. The "horn," however, is never mentioned in connection with wine.

Papyrus Amherst 63 has some divine love lyrics (as in xvii 7–14); however, nothing indicates that the cultic community is celebrating a sacred marriage here. In fact, the Ugaritic and the Hebrew have a word that perfectly fits in this context: the ḥdyš is the ḥdṯ or ḥōdeš: the new moon or new moon festival.[17] We are in the presence, then, of a combination of "the rites of the year" and "the new moon (festival)."[18]

In order to illuminate the cultic context of the Aramaic psalm it is helpful to take a look at some of the biblical and Ugaritic evidence in connection with the New Year festivities. The usual Hebrew term for the festival is זבח הימים ("annual sacrificial feast"), a term also used in Phoenician sources.[19] Alternatively, the New Year festival could simply be called "the festival" (החג), as it was the most important one of the annual celebrations. Some of the most significant biblical data about the festival are to be found in 1 Samuel. Three passages deserve particular attention: chapters 1, 9–10, and 20. The books of Samuel open with a description of the annual pilgrimage of a man from the hill country of Ephraim and his two wives to Shiloh. They go to worship, to bring sacrifice, and to give thanks for the wine harvest; hence they come each year with a bull (פרה), some flour (קמח), and "a jar of wine" (נבל יין; see 1 Sam 1:1–3, 24). All the participants in the annual feast consume meat and wine (1:9), so much that the main priest of the temple presumes the woman engaged in a silent prayer to be drunk (1:12–19). This is the picture of a harvest New Year festival in a northern sanctuary.

The events surrounding Saul's anointment as king also reflect a range of activities connected with the autumnal New Year festival (1 Sam 9–10). The anointment itself takes place at Ramah, in the hill country of Ephraim, in the early morning after the celebration of the yearly sacrifice at the shrine (1 Sam 9:12).[20] That very day Saul relates three signs: he meets two men at the tomb of Rachel; he encounters three men making a pilgrimage to God at Bethel, carrying three kids (גדיים), three loaves of bread, and "a jar of wine" (נבל־יין); and he ends up among "a band of prophets coming down from the shrine, preceded by lyres [נבל], timbrels [תוף], flutes [חליל], and harps [כנור], in a state of frenzy" (1 Sam 10:1–13). The conjunction of these events is not a coincidence; the narrative is set in the time of the New Year festival. Throughout the hill country of Ephraim, people gathered at local

---

[17] See Dennis Pardee, *Ritual and Cult at Ugarit*, WAW 10 (Atlanta: Society of Biblical Literature, 2002), no. 41: "During the six days of the new-moon festival (ḥdṯ)"; cf. Ps 81:4: "Blow the horn on the new moon [חדש], on the full moon [כסה] for our feast day [ליום חגנו]."

[18] Wesselius translates "our goblet," suggesting that the unknown word ḥtš means goblet, without any real support for this conjecture.

[19] See *KAI* 26 A III 1//*KAI* 26 C V 4: *zbḥ ymm*.

[20] The Hebrew has כי זבח היום לעם בבמה, generally translated as "For today there is a sacrifice for the people at the shrine." I have emended *hayyôm* into *hayyāmîm* (haplograhy of the *mem*) in view of the expression זבח הימים ("annual sacrifice") in the comparable context of 1 Sam 20:6 כי זבח הימים שם לכל־המשפחה, "For there is the annual sacrifice there for the entire clan") and because the events occurring in 1 Sam 10 (the three signs foretold by Samuel) fit the context of the annual harvest festival.

sanctuaries offering animals, bread, and wine; music was part of the festivities, as was prophetic ecstasy under the influence of the spirit of God—aided, no doubt, by the consumption of wine.[21]

The relevance of the third text (1 Sam 20) lies in the connection between "the annual sacrifice" (זבח הימים, 20:6) and the "new moon festival" (חדש). The days of the new moon mark the beginning of "the annual sacrificial meal for the entire clan." The period of the new moon lasted several days, since the text speaks of "the second (day of the) new moon" (v. 27) and "the third day (of the new moon)" (vv. 19–20). Psalm 81:4 confirms that the new moon is the start of "the day(s) of our festival." At this point the Ugaritic evidence on the New Year festival merits our attention.[22] The ritual texts from Ugarit mention several new moon festivals; the New Year festival took place at the new moon following month XII, Raʾšu-yêni, "First-of-the-wine."[23] The evidence confirms the connection between new wine, new moon, and the celebration of the New Year.

In light of both the biblical and the Ugaritic evidence, the combination of references to the "new moon" and "annual rites," plus the presentation of large quantities of wine, indicates that Ps no. 2 had its setting in the celebration of the New Year in autumn. On the basis of that conclusion, the most appropriate translation of the expression *sdrt šntk* is "your annual festival," that is, the New Year festival. The rites the psalm describes and the terminology it employs are helpful for reconstructing the typical celebration of the New Year among the early Israelites.

The psalm emphasizes the fact that the sacrifices and wine offerings are meant for Yaho alone. He is singled out from "among the gods" (*bʾlhn*, line 2) and "from among the Mighty Ones of the people" (2x, *mn ʾdry ʾm*, lines 2, 3). These "Mighty Ones" (Hebrew אדירים) are not human beings; the preposition *mn* does not indicate the provenance of the sacrificial banquet but has to be read in direct connection with *(ʾ)lk*, "for you" (3x, lines 2, 3). Here I find myself in agreement with Steiner's understanding of the text: "for you (alone) out of all the supreme beings" (COS 1.99:318). The *ʾdry ʾm* stand in a synonymous parallelism with "the gods," in the same way that the אדירים* of Ps 16:3 stand in parallelism with the "Holy Ones" (קדושים); both terms refer to deities.[24] The comparison with Ps 16 is instructive for the correct understanding of the Aramaic hymn. In the biblical psalm, too, the emphasis falls on the exclusive worship of YHWH ("I will not perform their bloody libations, nor will I take their names on my lips—YHWH (alone) is my allotted share and portion," Ps 16:4b–5a). The parallels between Ps 16 and Ps no. 2 of the

---

[21] For the use of wine to induce a state of prophetic frenzy in Mesopotamia and elsewhere in the ancient Near East, see Jean-Marie Durand, "In vino veritas," *RA* 76 (1982): 43–50.

[22] For an introduction to the subject, see Johannes C. de Moor, *New Year with Canaanites and Israelites*, 2 vols., Kamper Cahiers 21–22 (Kampen: Kok, 1972).

[23] See Pardee, *Ritual and Cult at Ugarit*, no. 15, pp. 56–65.

[24] So correctly Mitchel Dahood, *Psalms: Introduction, Translation, and Notes*, 3 vols., AB 16 (Garden City, NY: Doubleday, 1966–1970), 1:87–88.

Amherst papyrus reinforce the hypothesis of the Israelite background of the Aramaic psalms. On the basis of a linguistic analysis, Gary Rendsburg has pointed out the northern origin of Ps 16—a conclusion confirmed by the presence of the parallel pair "Holy Ones" and "Mighty Ones."[25]

In line with the psalm's focus on Yaho as sole recipient of the sacrificial banquet, the author throws into relief Yaho's power to exalt and to bring down. The expression of this idea differs from the forms it usually takes in the Hebrew Bible; there the focus is on the reversal of fortunes brought about by God. "Men once sated must hire out for bread; Men once hungry hunger no more.... Yahweh ... brings down and lifts high; he raises the poor from the dust" (1 Sam 2:4–9; see also Pss 113:5–9, 147:6). Here, on the other hand, the emphasis is entirely on God's power to bring down and to lift up; humans are "great" (*rb*) or "lowly" (*šḥ*) only as a result of Yaho's initiative to exalt or to bring down. A close parallel of this idea is found in Ps 75:8, "For God is (the only) judge: he brings down one man, he lifts up another." While the beginning of Ps no. 2 presents Yaho as eminently worthy of receiving worship, the middle of the psalm emphasizes his power to determine human destinies. At the Babylonian New Year festival, there was a ritually staged session of the assembly of the gods during which the chief god (in this case Marduk/Bel), seated upon the "throne of destinies" (*parak šīmāti*), inscribed the decisions about the coming year upon "the tablet of destinies" (*ṭuppi šīmāti*).[26] It is known from the biblical psalms that the New Year festival included the celebration of YHWH's kingship—or the renewal of his kingship, as he once more ascended the throne. The determination of the destinies for the year to come aptly fits the context.[27]

The references to "musicians," the "player of the harp" and "the player of the lyre," "the song of the Sidonian lyre," and the mention of "pleasant sounds" are entirely in keeping with the biblical allusions to musical performances at the New Year festival (see, e.g., 1 Sam 10:5, Pss 47:6–7, 81:3). They also fit with the mythological background of the Israelite New Year festival. In anticipation of the discussion of Pss nos. 3 and 1, it may be observed that the banquet of plenty Yaho is enjoying is full of echoes of the victory feast of the divine warrior. Once Baal returns

---

[25] See Gary A. Rendsburg, *Linguistic Evidence for the Northern Origin of Selected Psalms*, SBLMS 43 (Atlanta: Scholars Press, 1990), 29–33. For *ʾdr* as a divine adjective and, on occasion, the epithet of a deity in Phoenician, see *DNWSI* 1:18–19, s.v. "*ʾdr*"; for *qdšn* as a substantivized adjective, "the holy ones" = "the gods," see the references in *DNWSI* 2:996.

[26] See Julye Bidmead, *The Akītu Festival: Religious Continuity and Royal Legitimation in Mesopotamia*, Gorgias Dissertations: Near Eastern Studies 2 (Piscataway, NJ: Gorgias, 2004), 8–92; Jacob Klein, "Akitu," *ABD* 1:138–40. For the possible influence of the Babylonian New Year festival on Jewish conceptions, see Stephanie Dalley et al., *The Legacy of Mesopotamia* (Oxford: Oxford University Press, 1998), 77.

[27] Note that the most extended elaboration of the motif of God's power to exalt and to bring down is found in the Hymn of Hannah (1 Sam 2:1–10; cf. the parallel lines in Ps 113), a text that has the autumn harvest feast as its setting.

victorious from his battle with Yamm, he is served a meal at which he drinks wine from a thousand pitchers; all the while, singers chant his praises (*KTU* 1.3 i:2–22, esp. 15–16). In the Hebrew Bible there is not a single reference to YHWH's drinking wine—although new wine "gladdens God and men" (Judg 9:13) and Ps 75:8 pictures YHWH with a cup of foaming wine in his hand. In the Israelite Ps no. 2 of the Amherst papyrus there is no censorship against the idea of God enjoying wine—just as Baal and El enjoy wine in the Ugaritic literature.

III. Psalm No. 3: The Council of Heaven Proclaims Yaho's Kingship

The third Israelite psalm of the Amherst papyrus can be read as an independent piece of religious poetry; however, it yields its full meaning only when read in conjunction with Ps no. 2. This is the text.

11 mn' | b'l'h'nH b'd'm | yhwG mn' | b'l'h'nH | b'm'lk' | bl | m'lk' |
12 m' | k'k' | yhwG b'l'h'nH mn^n š'r$_2$w + 'd'ny | n$_2$'q'm | l'q'ryk' |
13 °m + d$_5$ry.C by'n | °q'b'n | w't'b | w'n'ny | l't'ḥtyk' | yhwG
14 l't'ḥtyky | '$_2$'dny | d'r$_2$' | š'mynH k'h'w$_2$l' | yhwG d'r$_2$' š'mynG
15 q'r'w' + ln + m'r$_2$'t'k' | byn | °q'b'n | wt'b | '$_2$'w'n'ny | b°lG mn s$_3$p'n |
16 yhwG yb$_2$r$_3$'k' | q$_2$'m | yhwG l'yl'n | y'š'b{w$_2$} '$_2$'d'ny | ꜥ.C t$_3$'sl't' | mry.C
17 q$_2$'m ⌐¬ yhwG t'n'ṭr'{k'} | k'dy$_2$ mry.C t'nt'r' | mn^n °t'q't | ꜥm'k' | sp.C

Who among the gods, among humankind, Yaho;
Who among the gods, among king and commoner,
Who is like you, Yaho, among the gods?
Take revenge, Adonay, from Siryon,
On behalf of those that invoke you, the people of old.[28]
Take note of our pursuer and make me strong again!
Beneath you, Yaho, beneath you, Adonay,
The heir of heaven is like sand, Yaho,
The heir of heaven proclaims to us your kingship.
Take note of our pursuer and make me strong again!

---

[28] Instead of "from Siryon," Steiner suggests "from Shur" (*COS* 1.99:318) and Wesselius (*Studies in Papyrus Amherst*, 1:75) proposes "from the beginning" (Aramaic *šêrûy*, compare Akkadian *šurrû*, "beginning"). Neither solution is entirely satisfactory, as the authors concede. I prefer to identify *š'rw* with Siryon, another name for (part of) Mount Hermon. Siryon occurs in a Ugaritic text as *šryn*, in synonymous parallelism with "Lebanon" (*KTU* 1.4 vi:18–21); in the Old Babylonian version of Gilgamesh as *sa-ri-a* (OB Ishchali [Nērebtum] tablet).

Let Baal from Zaphon bless Yaho.
Arise, Yaho, to our rescue!
Let Adonay pay attention to my prayer![29]
Mar, arise! Yahu, you will protect,
As you have protected, Mar, your people since of old. End.

Although Ps no. 3 presents a few difficult passages, its main thrust is not in doubt. The central message of the text is in lines 13–15: "Beneath you, Yaho, beneath you, Adonay, the heir of heaven is like sand, Yaho, the heir of heaven proclaims to us your kingship." The "heir of heaven" or "the council of heaven" (*dr šmyn*) is "like sand" (*khwl*); the term *sand* is unproblematic, but Steiner and Holm prefer the more unusual sense of "phoenix" (on the basis of Job 29:18, "I thought ... I would multiply my years like the phoenix [כחול]"). This is possible only by linking *khwl* of line 14 with the plea to "make me [for: us?] strong again" in line 13, which leads to an awkward construction of the intervening phrases.[30] There is a simpler solution. The inhabitants of heaven are the stars. The comparison with sand highlights their large number. "I will multiply your offspring like the stars of heaven and like the sand on the shore of the sea" (Gen 22:17). The sheer number of stars underscores Yaho's preeminence, since they are all subordinate to him.

In order to grasp the full implication of the term *dr šmyn* it is helpful to take into account that Ugaritic texts put "the council of the heavens" (*dr dt šmm*) in synonymous parallelism with "the assembly of the stars" (*pḫr kkbm*) and "the sons of El" (*bn il*), meaning the gods.[31] So if the council of heaven "proclaims" (QRʾ) the "lordship" (*mārût*) of Yaho, it is a way of saying that the assembly of the gods is acclaiming Yaho as their king.[32] The celebration of Yaho's kingship commands the logic of the rest of the psalm. The incomparability of Yaho ("Who is like you among the gods?" [cf. Ps 86:8, "None is like you (כמוך) among the gods, Adonay"]; see also Pss 71:19 ["Who is like you...?"] and 89:6–9) provides the rationale of his kingship. The reference to "king and commoner" (lit., king and nonking, *mlk blmlk*) echoes a phrase from Ugaritic mythology. As Mot threatens to undermine Baal's kingship, Baal defiantly asks whether anyone, "whether king or commoner" (*umlk ublmlk*), would dare to establish a dominion that would rival his own (KTU 1.4 vii:43–44). Here Yaho has taken Baal's place; he has no peer among either gods or humans, whether they be king or nonking; in the end, there is only one King, and that is

---

[29] Although the writing of the *ṣade* is unusual (normally t/t₃ and s are not separated by *aleph*), the reading *ṣlw* ("prayer") seems assured.

[30] Steiner translates, "And make us strong again, beneath you, *Horus*; beneath you, Adonai, Resident of Heaven."

[31] *KTU* 1.10 i:3–5. See the discussion by E. Theodore Mullen Jr., *The Divine Council in Canaanite and Early Hebrew Literature*, HSM 24 (Chico, CA: Scholars Press, 1980), 195–96.

[32] See *DNWSI* 691 s.v. "*mrt*," with references to further literature; see also Marcus Jastrow, *A Dictionary of the Targumim, the Talmud Babli and Yerushalmi, and the Midrashic Literature*, 2 vols. (London: G. P. Putnam, 1903), 840, s.v. "מָרוּת" and "מָרוּתָא."

Yaho. Precisely because no one compares to Yaho, he is the rightful lord of the gods. Even Baal Zaphon, traditionally acknowledged as king of the gods, must pay tribute to the new ruler. "May Baal from Zaphon bless Yaho" (lines 15–16). The theme of Yaho's kingship adds a further dimension to the celebrations of the New Year alluded to in Ps no. 2. It neatly fits in with the theory, propounded by such scholars as Paul Volz, Hermann Gunkel, and Sigmund Mowinckel, that the New Year festival in Israel was simultaneously the festival of YHWH's enthronement.[33]

IV. Psalm No. 1: Waiting for the New Moon

Let us return to Ps no. 1—the Aramaic restyling of the Hebrew forerunner of Ps 20. Properly speaking, this psalm is not a hymn but a communal intercession. The Judean editor turned it into an intercession for the king, for which reason Gunkel, Mowinckel, and many others have placed the psalm in the category of royal psalms.[34] In the prebiblical version of the psalm, however, there is no king; there is only a group of Yaho devotees praying as a community ("we" throughout the text) for Yaho to answer them in their anxiety. What is the nature of their "anxiety"? Ever since the first publications on this text in the 1980s, the perspective of the biblical Ps 20 has determined, to a greater or lesser extent, the analysis of the Aramaic text. Yet without its references to the messianic king and Zion (additions by the Judean editor) the prayer seems a bit bland: people are in trouble; they ask God for help and for the fulfillment of their desires; and they finish by expressing confidence that tomorrow God will answer. But they do not say what their trouble is, nor do they specify their heart's desire. Is this a multipurpose text, its vagueness a deliberate device to make it do duty for a great many different occasions? Hardly so. In fact, the Aramaic text does contain some very specific hints that allow us to put it in a particular context.

There are three hints that deserve particular attention: (1) the reference to the moon crescent as a "bow in heaven"; (2) the plea for "messengers" to be dispatched from Rash; and (3) the presence of Baal Shamayin blessing the Lord, Mār.

1. Lines 12–13 read *hyʾ qšt bšmyn šhr*. Neither the reading of the signs nor the reconstruction of the phrase poses particular problems. The only word that is not entirely clear is at the beginning. It is here translated as an imperative from *hyh*,

---

[33] See Paul Volz, *Das Neujahrsfest Jahwes: Laubhüttenfest*, Sammlung gemeinverständlicher Vorträge und Schriften aus dem Gebiet der Theologie und Religionsgeschichte 67 (Tübingen: Mohr, 1912); Hermann Gunkel, *Einleitung in die Psalmen: Die Gattungen der religiösen Lyrik Israels*, 4th ed. (Göttingen: Vandenhoeck & Ruprecht, 1985; 1st ed., 1933]), 94–116; Mowinckel, *Psalms in Israel's Worship*, 1:106–92.

[34] Gunkel, *Einleitung in die Psalmen*, 140; Mowinckel, *Psalms in Israel's Worship*, 1:47; Hans-Joachim Kraus, *Psalmen*, 2 vols., 5th ed., BKAT 15 (Neukirchen-Vluyn: Neukirchener Verlag, 1978), 1:309.

"be!," on the assumption that it is a Hebraism (for in Aramaic the term would be *hwh*). Others (Steiner, Holm) prefer to read it as an exclamation: "Oh!" But the difference in translation of this word does not really affect the meaning of the phrase. That there is mention of the "moon crescent" (*shr*) is undisputed; the reference to a "bow in the sky" (*qšt bšmyn*) also is unproblematic. Though Wesselius prefers to read *yqšṭ bšmyn shr*, "he adorns the moon in the sky," the presence of the expression *qšṭ bšmyn* in column xvi 14 favors the more usual understanding of our passage.[35] The meaning of the words is clear; but what is the meaning of the phrase as such? In xvi 14, the reference to the "bow in the sky" occurs in the context of a hymn to Eshem-Bethel depicted as a divine warrior; the bow is one of his weapons. On the strength of the parallel, the "bow in the sky" might be a weapon here too, this time of Yaho. The bow in the sky, however, is here identified with the moon. Normally the heavenly bow is associated with the rainbow, a fitting weapon of a storm god. What does it mean if the moon is asked to be a bow in the sky?

My suggestion is to interpret the metaphor of the "bow in the sky" as a reference to the appearance of the moon as a thin sliver of silver in the shape of a bow—that is, the way the moon looks at its first appearance after a period of invisibility. The line refers to the first sighting of the new moon. My interpretation assumes that there is a connection between the communal prayer in xii 11–19 and the two Israelite hymns of column xiii. The hymn of xiii 1–10 is quite specific about the liturgical occasion of the text: it is a celebration that takes place "at our new moon festival" (*bḥdyšn*, line 7). The mood of the hymn is festive throughout; there is no anxiety any longer. On the assumption that the three Israelite psalms are thematically connected, we may pin down the "anxiety" of the communal petition as the anxiety of the time just preceding the appearance of the new moon. The night(s) of the *bubbulu*, as Babylonians called the phenomenon of the invisibility of the moon, were fraught with danger. The moon was believed to be in the underworld; that is why the time of the new moon (the חדש, as it is called in the Hebrew Bible, a term covering both the invisibility of the moon and its first appearance) was eminently suited for offerings to the dead. The anxiety will be dispelled only at the first sighting of the moon returning: the small bow-shaped crescent in the morning sky.

The interpretation of the "bow in the sky" as image for the new moon (the "crescent," *shr*) assumes that the songs here discussed were to be chanted after sunset. The crescent is to rise like a bow in heaven; the festival being celebrated is that of the "new moon" (*ḥdyš*). In line with this nocturnal setting, the central message of Ps no. 3 looks at the night sky: the heir of heaven is "underneath" (*ltḥt*) Yaho. Though *dr šmyn* might be translated as "council of heaven," the image is astral. Preference should therefore be given to the translation "heir of heaven." As the Ugaritic texts show, there is no contradiction, for the stars are "the Sons of El." This

---

[35] See Vleeming and Wesselius, *Studies in Papyrus Amherst*, 1:51–53.

astral imagery suggests that Yaho is understood to manifest himself in the guise of the moon crescent. The stars bow to the moon. There is a parallel in a hymn to Bethel in Papyrus Amherst 63 ix 1–x 8, where the god is called "our Crescent" (sʾ[h]r₂ʾn, ix 18; cf. ʾ₂sʾhrʾ in line 19). There, too, the liturgical context is an evening festival—with particular attention, however, to the appearance of the evening star as embodiment of the queen of heaven. The Israelite hymns have no reference to a goddess; their sole focus is on the kingship of Yaho as it manifests itself in the rise of the moon crescent and its dominance over the stars.

2. The second hint about the context of our prayer is the reference to "messengers." Steiner and Holm offer a different interpretation of this line. They take ṣyrʿk (ṣ₃yʾr₂ʾk) as a noun in the singular, and instead of kl ʾrš, "all of (the land of) Rash," they read <ʾ>gr ʾrš, "Send your emissary/envoy from the temple of Rash." The emendation of kl rš into ʾgr rš is unnecessary in view of the occurrence of kl rš in xi 3: "You dwell in all of Rash, the land of our god."[36] Apparently, Steiner resorts to the reading "the temple of Rash" in order to obtain a closer parallel with the first colon of Ps 20:3: "May he send you help from the sanctuary." Yet the parallel is deceptive. The crucial difference is in the expression ṣyrʿk ("your messenger[s]"), transformed in the biblical psalm into עזרך ("your help"). This is one of the instances where it is clear that the biblical version depends on the Aramaic one (more precisely, its Hebrew Vorlage, but at this juncture the difference between the two must have been minimal) rather than the other way around. The phrasing of the biblical psalm retains the acoustic image of the original but gives the phrase a very general twist. "Help" (for you, the king) is far less specific than "messengers" (from you, the God). For a ṣîr is not just an "emissary" (Steiner) or "envoy" (Holm) but really someone charged to deliver a message. Steiner and Holm turn the messenger into a delegate from the God sent out to help somehow, thus obtaining in substance something analogous to "help."

What is the connection between the moon appearing as "a bow in the sky" and the God dispatching his "messengers from all of Rash"? At first sight, there is none. Where there is a bow, one might expect arrows. It is possible to emend the text so as to obtain these arrows. Read the line as šlḥ <ḥ>ṣy{r}k mn kl ʾrš, and the deity is asked to send his arrows from all of Rash. But that solution is a little too ingenious; moreover, the emendation feels too much like a surgery of the text. The line speaks about messengers—not arrows, nor envoys, nor emissaries. What is their message? It must be related to the appearance of the new moon. As argued above, the "bow in the sky" is here not a weapon in the hands of a divine warrior but a reference to the form of the moon at its first appearance. This sighting of the moon is apparently the sign of some other event to be announced by messengers. What event?

---

[36] Steiner's translation in COS 1.99 shows that he does read bkl rš in xi 3: "you dwell throughout the land of Rash."

Taken as an ensemble, the three Israelite psalms of the Amherst papyrus allow for an informed guess. The working hypothesis says that the three psalms belong together as liturgical texts to be recited on the occasion of the autumnal harvest festival celebrated at the time of the new moon. In addition to their liturgical occasion, the three texts share an emphasis on the preeminence of Yaho. It is most explicit in Ps no. 3. "Who among the gods, among humankind, Yaho; who among the gods, among king and commoner; who is like you, Yaho, among the gods?" (xiii 11–12). The same idea, voiced more implicitly, is in Ps no. 2. "Among the gods, our festival banquet is for you; among the Mighty Ones of the people, Adonay, it is for you, among the Mighty Ones of the people" (xiii 2–3). A similar logic, taken from a different angle, inhabits Ps no. 1. "Some by the bow, some by the spear, but as to us—the Lord is our god, Yaho!" (xii 16–17). Psalm no. 3 shows that the preeminence of Yaho means primacy over all other gods. "Under you, Yaho, under you, Adonay, the heir of heaven is like sand, Yaho; the heir of heaven proclaims to us your kingship" (xiii 13–15). The heir of heaven—or the "council of heaven" (*dr šmyn*)—proclaims Yaho's "rule" or "kingship" (*mrt*);[37] the celebration of Yaho's preeminence is the celebration of his kingship.

The messengers to be dispatched from all of Rash, then, go out to announce Yaho's kingship. The theme of divine messengers, mostly sent as a pair, is familiar from Ugaritic mythology. Gods communicate through messengers.[38] This ancient mythological motif is here applied to Yaho: the appearance of the new moon marks the renewal of his kingship; messengers are sent out to announce it. The three Israelite psalms of Papyrus Amherst 63 conform to the patterns of the enthronement festival of YHWH as delineated by Volz, Gunkel, and Mowinckel.[39] The beginning of the new year coincided with the autumn harvests and provided the context for the celebration of YHWH's ascent to the throne.

3. At this point it is appropriate to take note of the third hint present in the forerunner of Ps 20. Toward the end of the text there is a reference to Baal Shamayin. It is a short phrase that allows of two translations: "May Baal-Shamayin, the Lord, bless" (so Steiner and Holm), or "May Baal Shamayin bless the Lord" (*b'l šmyn mr ybrk*, xii 18). If Mār is taken in apposition to Baal Shamayin, it implies the identification of Baal with Bethel, since Mār, throughout Papyrus Amherst 63, refers to Bethel. A very similar phrase occurs at the end of the third Israelite psalm: *b'l mn ṣpn yhw ybrk* (xiii 15–16). Here Holm translates, "May Baal from Ṣapon bless Yahu" (Steiner construes the sentences differently). This seems indeed the correct

---

[37] See *DNWSI* 691, s.v. "*mrt*," with references to further literature; Jastrow, *Dictionary of the Targumim*, 840, s.vv. "מָרוּת" and "מָרוּתָא."

[38] See Mullen, *Divine Council*, 209–26; Samuel A. Meier, *The Messenger in the Ancient Semitic World*, HSM 45 (Atlanta: Scholars Press, 1989), 124–28.

[39] See Volz, *Das Neujahrsfest Jahwes*; Gunkel, *Einleitung in die Psalmen*, 94–116; Mowinckel, *Psalms in Israel's Worship*, 1:106–92.

interpretation, and it should be applied to the same turn of phrase in the forerunner to Ps 20: "May Baal Shamayin bless the Lord [Mār]." This is not about the identification of two gods; it is the acknowledgment by the one god of the superiority of the other. Who blesses whom? The lower-ranking deities greet the higher-ranking one; the superior god benignly accepts the blessing. What is at stake here, then, is the question who will reign as king of the gods: is it Baal or Yaho? By casting Baal (Baal Shamayin and Baal Zaphon are two designations of the one god Baal) in the role of the one who initiates the blessing, he is made implicitly to acknowledge his subordination to Yaho. In the ancient Near East, the notion of blessing has the connotations of greeting and congratulating. Baal congratulates Yaho on the occasion of his enthronement.

V. Conclusion

By a strange twist of fate, an Egyptian papyrus from the third century BCE has brought us in touch with three Israelite psalms unknown from the Bible. One of them was later recast in the form of Ps 20, but the version available in the Amherst papyrus is older. The three psalms belong together, and they owe their coherence and sequence to the liturgical occasion of the New Year festival in autumn. At the time of the wine harvest, the rise of the new moon signified the reenthronement of Yaho over the other gods, which meant that the new year had begun. The Israelite character of these psalms is hardly open to doubt, as the title "our Bull" demonstrates (xii 17). The implied identity between Yaho and Bethel (xii 18) is another indication of a Samarian origin of the text (cf. Jer 48:13). It is possible that an Aramean editor secondarily added some references to Mār, "the Lord."[40] In essence, however, these texts provide valuable insight into the religious life of Israel before the fall of Samaria.

---

[40] Note xii 17 and xiii 16, 17, where mry.C seems to be an addition burdening the rhythm of the text. In xii 18 and xiii 8, mry.C may have been a substitute for Yaho or Adonay.

SBL PRESS

New and Recent Titles

SARGON II, KING OF ASSYRIA
Josette Elayi
Paperback $41.95, 978-1-62837-177-2   310 pages, 2017   Code: 061722
Hardcover $56.95, 978-0-88414-224-9 E-book $41.95, 978-0-88414-223-2
Archaeology and Biblical Studies 22

EARLY JEWISH WRITINGS
Eileen Schuller and Marie-Theres Wacker, editors
Paperback $44.95, 978-1-62837-183-3   316 pages, 2017   Code: 066006
Hardcover $59.95, 978-0-88414-233-1 E-book $44.95, 978-0-88414-232-4
The Bible and Women 3.1

HOUSEHOLD AND FAMILY RELIGION IN PERSIAN-PERIOD JUDAH
An Archaeological Approach
José E. Balcells Gallarreta
Paperback $33.95, 978-1-62837-178-9   208 pages, 2017   Code: 062822
Hardcover $48.95, 978-0-88414-226-3 E-book $33.95, 978-0-88414-225-6
Ancient Near East Monographs 18

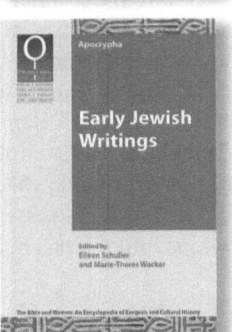

UNCOVERING ANCIENT FOOTPRINTS
Armenian Inscriptions and the Pilgrimage Routes of the Sinai
Michael E. Stone
Paperback $34.95, 978-1-62837-173-4   202 pages, 2017   Code: 069024
Hardcover $49.95, 978-0-88414-216-4 E-book $34.95, 978-0-88414-215-7

TEXTS AND CONTEXTS OF THE BOOK OF SIRACH / TEXTE UND KONTEXTE DES SIRACHBUCHES
Gerhard Karner, Frank Ueberschaer, and Burkard M. Zapff, editors
Paperback $50.95, 978-1-62837-182-6   342 pages, 2017   Code: 060467
Hardcover $70.95, 978-0-88414-230-0 E-book $50.95, 978-0-88414-229-4
Septuagint and Cognate Studies 66

SBL Press • P.O. Box 2243 • Williston, VT 05495-2243
Phone: 877-725-3334 (toll-free) or 802-864-6185 • Fax: 802-864-7626
Order online at www.sbl-site.org/publications

Mary's Magnificat (Luke 1:46b–55) and the Price of Corn in Mexico

DAVID L. BALCH
dbalch@plts.edu
Pacific Lutheran Theological Seminary/California Lutheran University,
Berkeley, CA 94704

The article has three parts. First, I sketch debates concerning the origins, function, and history of religions context of the Lukan birth narrative and its canticles. Second, I outline the urban–rural conflict between patricians/aristocrats and plebeians in Rome as narrated by Dionysius of Halicarnassus. Dionysius's Greek terminology is identical to the vocabulary of Mary's Magnificat in Luke 1, including the contrasts between the proud rich and the hungry humble. I then glance at Carol Wilson's recent model of how poor persons scratched out a living in the Roman Empire and how changes in their circumstances would drive them below subsistence level. Dionysius's narrative and Wilson's model correspond to an amazing degree. Given this economic interpretation of the Magnificat, I record how contemporary corporations' investments in Mexico deprive farmers of their land and living, generating migration through poverty, a significant parallel to Dionysius's narrative, Wilson's model, and the Magnificat.

This article concerns the reception and meaning of the Magnificat in Greco-Roman culture, for example, by those who read or heard the Gospel of Luke in Ephesus or Rome, where scholars argue that Luke(-Acts) was written.[1] As an introduction (I.A) to the main part of the article, I sketch scholars' observations about the Magnificat's origins in *Judean* circles, either Pharisaic, Baptist, or early Jewish Christian.[2] Next I note scholars' contrasting theories of the hymn's function,

---

I presented the second and third sections of this paper to the Postcolonial Section, International SBL, Buenos Aires, Argentina (24 July 2015). Now I dedicate the essay to Leo G. Perdue in memoriam (1946–2017).

[1] Richard Pervo, "Acts in Ephesus (and Environs) c. 115," *Forum*, third series 4.2 (2015): 125–51; and M. Eugene Boring, *An Introduction to the New Testament: History, Literature, Theology* (Louisville: Westminster John Knox, 2012), chapter 24.

[2] Raymond E. Brown classifies the Magnificat as a hymn of praise, not an eschatological hymn (*The Birth of the Messiah: A Commentary on the Infancy Narratives in the Gospels of Matthew and Luke*, 2nd ed., ABRL [New York: Doubleday, 1993], 355, 652–53). Stephen Farris argues that

idealistic or economic (I.B). Since the second major portion of the article (II) displays verbal parallels between the Magnificat and a Greek author narrating Roman history, I comment on the history of religions question (I.C), whether the birth narratives and the canticles are wholly Jewish or whether we might also consider Greco-Roman contexts.

The first question, regarding sources, has not been resolved. In this article I contribute primarily to the second question, regarding function, by focusing on how the reversals and key verbs would have been heard and interpreted politically and economically in Greco-Roman culture (II). Dionysius of Halicarnassus's narrative of the first secession in Rome, that is, of conflict between patricians/aristocrats/the proud, on the one hand, and plebeians/the humble, on the other, employs values and vocabulary that are significantly similar to those in the Magnificat (II.B). I conclude (II.C) that comparing economic/political conflict in Rome with the vocabulary of the Magnificat yields an economic interpretation. Therefore, I employ Carol Bakker Wilson's model of how people got access to food in the Roman world (II.D). This leads me to compare economic conflicts in ancient imperial Rome with poverty, hunger, and emigration in the contemporary United States and Mexico (III).

I. THE MAGNIFICAT (LUKE 1:46B–55): ORIGINS, FUNCTION, HISTORY OF RELIGIONS

A. Origins

Luke prefaced the Markan material with an infancy narrative, which was neglected by Hans Conzelmann when he characterized Lukan theology but which Joseph A. Fitzmyer calls an overture to the whole opus.[3] The infancy narrative never

---

the Lukan hymns and Phil 2:6–11 are quite different: the former are eschatological and were composed in the Palestinian, perhaps the Jerusalem, church, while the latter is a declarative psalm of praise used in the diaspora church (*The Hymns of Luke's Infancy Narratives: Their Origin, Meaning and Significance*, JSNTSup 9 [Sheffield: JSOT Press, 1985], 68–97). Eschatological hymns are "unqualifiedly Jewish" (Farris, 69). Gunter Kennel suggests that the Magnificat is a literary hymn and Phil 2:6–11 is a hymnic confession (*Frühchristliche Hymnen? Gattungskritische Studien zur Frage nach den Liedern der frühen Christenheit*, WMANT 71 [Neukirchen-Vluyn: Neukirchener Verlag, 1995], 273, 276). Brown (*Birth of the Messiah*, 654) cites A. Contri, "Il 'Magnificat' alla luce dell'inno cristologico di Filippesi 2,6–11," *Marianum* 40 (1978): 164–68, who judges the Magnificat and Pauline *kenōsis* hymns to be similar because of the theme of humiliation-exaltation, with which I agree.

[3] Joseph A. Fitzmyer, *The Gospel according to Luke: Introduction, Translation, and Notes*, 2 vols., AB 28, 28A (Garden City, NY: Doubleday, 1981, 1985), 1:184. Also Brown, *Birth of the Messiah*, 239–45, 620–21; Robert C. Tannehill, *The Gospel according to Luke*, vol. 1 of *The Narrative Unity of Luke-Acts: A Literary Interpretation*, FF (Philadelphia: Fortress, 1986–1991), xiii, 8, 15,

became part of the early kerygma, except perhaps in Rom 1:3–4.[4] According to Fitzmyer, Luke freely composed the narrative utilizing (a) a Jewish-Christian source: the canticles (Magnificat, Benedictus, perhaps the Nunc Dimittis), and perhaps the final scene of chapter 2, and (b) an earlier Baptist source: the announcement of his birth (1:5–25) and the story of his birth, circumcision, and manifestation (1:57–66b).[5] Fitzmyer accounts for the Hebraisms in the story as Luke's imitation of Septuagintal Greek style, denying Hebrew or Aramaic sources.[6] Yet, given close parallels between Jewish poetry in the Magnificat and the Psalms of Solomon, which is probably Pharisaic, François Bovon prefers a Pharisaic origin for the hymn, not one in the Baptist or Jewish Christian movements.[7]

The Lukan infancy narrative discovers christological themes in the Old Testament: the dawning of messianic times, temple piety, and the beginnings of Christian faith, but the canticles themselves are only loosely related to the story.[8] Still, the Magnificat is similar to the canticle of Hannah in 1 Sam 2:1–10: both Hannah and Mary praise God for choosing them to be instruments of God's saving intervention in Israel's history.[9] In her preceding prayer,[10] Hannah refers to herself as God's "humble slave woman" (ἐπιβλέψῃς ἐπὶ τὴν ταπείνωσιν τῆς δούλης, 1 Sam 1:11), a designation with which Mary begins her canticle (Luke 1:48b).[11] In the canticle itself, Hannah praises God's reversals (1 Sam 2:2–9); contrasts include none righteous/holy God, mighty/weak (Luke 1:52a), full of bread/hungry (Luke 1:53), the barren one/woman bears seven, death/life, Lord brings down to Hades/brings

---

19–20, 26, 29–32; and Bernhard Heininger, "Magnificat," in *RPP* 7:725–26. For discussion of hymns in Second Temple Judaism and in the Greco-Roman world, see Matthew E. Gordley, *The Colossian Hymn in Context: An Exegesis in Light of Jewish and Greco-Roman Hymnic and Epistolary Conventions*, WUNT 2/228 (Tübingen: Mohr Siebeck, 2007).

[4] Brown, *Birth of the Messiah*, 29–32, 272, 311–16.

[5] Fitzmyer, *Gospel according to Luke*, 1:309, 357. According to Brown the closest parallels are Jewish hymns in 1 Maccabees, Judith (16:11, "humble ones"), 2 Baruch, 4 Ezra, Qumran Hodayot (1QH^a II, 27; X, 36; XIII, 16, 18, 22), War Scroll, and 4QpPs 37 (4Q171 I, 8–9) (*Birth of the Messiah*, 346–55, 645). See Ulrike Mittmann-Richert, *Magnifikat und Benediktus: Die ältesten Zeugnisse der judenchristlichen Tradition von der Geburt des Messias*, WUNT 2/90 (Tübingen: Mohr Siebeck, 1996), 66–67, 70–76, 82–89 (a dissertation directed by Martin Hengel). Importantly, the Lukan canticles resemble the speeches in Acts (Brown, 347), which, I note, are *not* from Judea.

[6] Fitzmyer, *Gospel according to Luke*, 1:312; Brown, *Birth of the Messiah*, 622–23; differently John Nolland, *Luke 1–9:20*, WBC 35A (Dallas: Word, 1989), 21–22, 42–46, 57.

[7] François Bovon, *Luke 1: A Commentary on the Gospel of Luke 1:1–9:50*, trans. Christine M. Thomas, Hermeneia (Minneapolis: Fortress, 2002), 56–57. Cf. Bovon, *Luke the Theologian: Fifty-Five Years of Research (1950–2005)*, 2nd rev. ed. (Waco, TX: Baylor University Press, 2006), chapter 3 ("Christology"), esp. 138, 163, 183, 219–23; and Brown, *Birth of the Messiah*, 643.

[8] Fitzmyer, *Gospel according to Luke*, 1:314–16; Brown, *Birth of the Messiah*, 497–99.

[9] Brown, *Birth of the Messiah*, table 12, 358–60.

[10] For connections between prayer and hymnic attitudes, see Lutz Käppel, "Hymn," in *RPP* 6:354–55, with bibliography.

[11] Mittmann-Richert, *Magnifikat und Benediktus*, 10.

up (cf. Luke 16:19–31; Acts 2:31–32), poor/rich, the Lord humbles and raises up (ταπεινοῖ καὶ ἀνυψοῖ, the Lord raises up the poor and makes them inherit a throne). Mary's praise of God's reversal of the conditions of the proud (διεσκόρπισεν ὑπερηφάνους) and the humble (ὕψωσεν ταπεινούς, Luke 1:51–52), key terms in the Magnificat,[12] is prefigured in Hannah's song of praise.[13]

B. Idealistic or Political?

John Nolland is an example of an interpreter who recognizes but strictly limits the political/economic meaning of the Magnificat.[14] The hymn should not be spiritualized away but must be seen only in juxtaposition to the ethico-religious (esp. vv. 50–51), the socioeconomic (vv. 52–53), and the ethnic or national situations (vv. 54–55); each interprets the other.

> Values from none of the spheres can be allowed to stand alone. Due weight must also be given to the use of stereotyped OT language here, which should not be

---

[12] For both "proud" and "humble" with reversals, see Ps 17:29 LXX; Prov 3:34; for both terms without reversals, see Ps 88:11; Isa 1:25; 2:12; 13:1; Sir 13:20; Jdt 6:19; Esth 14:1, 8, 16 (C12). For the terms singly, see Pss. Sol. 5:14 with 2:2, 29; 4:24; 17:6, 13, 23, 41. Bovon observes that the reversal of conditions is a familiar topos in Greek literature (*Luke 1*, 62 n. 75, with references), citing Luise Schottroff, "Das Magnificat und die älteste Tradition über Jesus von Nazareth," *EvT* 38 (1978): 298–312, https://doi.org/10.14315/evth-1978-jg29. See also Brown, *Birth of the Messiah*, 361, on "low estate," and 363 on the real poverty of the Jerusalem Christians—surprisingly brief discussions. Mittmann-Richert (*Magnifikat und Benediktus*, 209) denies this Greek context and interprets God's "scattering the proud" (1:51) of the universal, eschatological final judgment (204–5); Luke 1:52–53, she claims, refers not to revolutionary political reversal, not to external political relationships but rather to the relativizing of human authority structures (210). On the social character of these reversals, contrast Mittmann-Richert's assertions with Stephanie Buckhanon Crowder, "The Gospel of Luke," in *True to Our Native Land: An African American New Testament Commentary*, ed. Brian K. Blount et al. (Minneapolis: Fortress, 2007), 158–85, here 158, 161–62.

[13] See Mittmann-Richert, *Magnifikat und Benediktus*, 13–14, 21, who also cites the royal Ps 88:2–4, 9, 11a: "It is you who humbled a proud one." This reversal, humiliation/exaltation, also appears in the *kenōsis* hymn: "[Christ Jesus] humbled himself [ἐταπείνωσεν ἑαυτόν] ... and God highly exalted him" (ὁ θεὸς αὐτὸν ὑπερύψωσεν, Phil 2:8a, 9a). This hymn, however, is typically assigned a *Hellenistic* (Jewish) origin. See Ralph P. Martin, *A Hymn of Christ: Philippians 2:5–11 in Recent Interpretation and in the Setting of Early Christian Worship* (Downers Grove, IL: InterVarsity Press, 1997; orig. 1967), 297–311, 317; and John Reumann, *Philippians: A New Translation with Introduction and Commentary*, AYB 33B (New Haven: Yale University Press, 2008), 335, 361–62: "This [claim for epideictic rhetoric] fits with authorship by converts in Philippi, an assertion for the Greco-Roman world about Christ and God, used in witnessing to neighbors"; also 365: "2:6–11 is a composition by the Philippians, not 'pre-' but 'para' Pauline." Mittmann-Richert distinguishes the Lukan from the Pauline hymn; the Magnificat represents the beginning of Christian hymnody, which continued to develop (*Magnifikat und Benediktus*, 191–92).

[14] Nolland, *Luke 1–9:20*, 72. Michael Wolter refers to a common "utopian or eschatological" expectation (*Das Lukasevangelium*, HNT 5 [Tübingen: Mohr Siebeck, 2008], 104).

pressed [as, he suggests, is done by Schottroff] to drive a wedge between Luke's attitude to poverty and riches and that brought to expression here in the Magnificat:[15] the Magnificat is a soteriological statement in traditional terms and reflects on poverty and riches solely within that framework. One may speak similarly in relation to the nationalism of vv. 54–55. Luke never denies the appropriateness of Israel's national hope, but he establishes a cosmic framework for its fulfillment and opens it up for the inclusion of the Gentiles.[16]

Richard Horsley gives a more political interpretation: he doubts the modern theoretical separation of religion from politics and economics.[17] He critiques Brown's and Fitzmyer's depoliticizing spiritualization of the Magnificat and Mary, making her an ideal believer who abandons herself to God's will in absolute self-surrender. Horsley contrasts Brown and Fitzmyer with the Freudian Otto Rank, who constructed the myth of the birth of a hero utilizing Oedipus, Theseus, Romulus, Jesus, and Lohengrin, but the Bible is not primarily myth of the gods. The fundamental conflict in biblical stories rather concerns hero legends: the current ruler is threatened by the birth of the hero, a future liberator who seeks to eliminate him (Exod 1–2, Luke 1–2). A century ago scholars focused on parallels from Hellenistic religion, but recently more careful exploration has focused on Palestinian Jewish literature.[18] Luke 1 includes the fulfillment of the promises to Abraham, a liberator of Israel, and Samuel, a prototypical prophet. The stories refer to particular historical circumstances, to real historical events, to Herod the Great, and Augustus Caesar and should therefore be called "historical legends." The main thrust of the infancy narratives, according to Horsley, is that God delivers Israel from Herod and Roman rulers, who terrorized their subjects. Herod was the paradigm of tyranny: he impoverished his Jewish subjects for his own and Caesar's glory.

Horsley also critiques Brown's theory that the canticles have their source in Jewish Christian Anawim (the poor) piety, which included devout observation of

---

[15] See, however, Mittmann-Richert, *Magnifikat und Benediktus*, 131–32, who traces an original Hebrew hymn back to the earliest Jerusalem church.

[16] Nolland, *Luke 1–9:20*, 72–73. Conflict in Luke-Acts is indeed engendered by the change from God's election of one ethnic/religious group, Judeans, to God's accepting "all nations," as promised already to Abraham, but Nolland's argument that this change in election/ethnicity qualifies and limits Luke's social attitudes toward the economic hopes of the poor is not a valid analogy/argument. Attitudes toward social factors such as ethnicity, gender, economic class, and sexual orientation are not always consistent.

[17] Richard A. Horsley, *The Liberation of Christmas: The Infancy Narratives in Social Context* (New York: Crossroad, 1989), x. For the discussion in this paragraph, see 9–19, 25–32, and 46.

[18] See Claudia Janssen and Regene Lamb, "Gospel of Luke: The Humbled Will Be Lifted Up," in *Feminist Biblical Interpretation: A Compendium of Critical Commentary on the Books of the Bible and Related Literature*, ed. Luise Schottroff and Marie-Theres Wacker (Grand Rapids: Eerdmans, 2012; German 1999), 645–61.

the law and participation in the temple cult.[19] There is little evidence for Jewish Christian Anawim, unless it would be the older prophet Anna. Among the few female models for Anna are Miriam and Deborah. This points to an alternative for Brown's milieu: many of the psalms in which the Anawim appeal to God are directed against foreign or domestic oppressive rulers (Pss 25, 34–35, 40–41, 86, 109, 140, 149). The humble are the people of Israel over against their rulers, foreign or domestic. The births of John and Jesus are for the deliverance of the people (Luke 1:17, 68, 77; 2:10, 25, 32) and of Israel (1:16, 33, 54; 2:25, 32), a people who could not pay their debts. One of the first acts of Jewish rebels in Jerusalem in 66 CE was to burn debt records (Josephus, *J.W.* 2.17.6 §427). In this social context, Jesus blessed the poor (Luke 6:20–21) and taught his disciples to pray, "Forgive us our sins as we forgive everyone indebted [ὀφείλοντι] to us" (Luke 11:4ab). Horsley places these words in the context of large social movements headed by popularly acclaimed kings and of Jewish longings for liberation; he denies that this refers to eschatological redemption.[20] Finally, Horsley (ch. 7) draws an analogy to the contemporary North American empire and its client regimes in Central America.[21]

Bovon also emphasizes the political and liberative meaning of the Magnificat.[22] The hymn derives from an older psalm, which the evangelist has Christianized only slightly. Like the speeches in Acts, Luke attaches great importance to the song, which interprets the events theologically. The key to interpretation is the beatitude in verse 45: Mary is blessed and believing, awaiting the fulfillment of God's promise in faith.[23] Luke knows that Deutero-Isaiah has interpreted hymns eschatologically. Luke's aorist tense verbs in the Magnificat function prophetically; "Luke knows more than Mary and lives *after* Jesus' mission, cross, and resurrection. He knows how God *has* attended to … Israel in Jesus Christ." But tension remains, because the rich and the rulers have not lost their power. "The song's prerequisite, according to vs. 45, is faith: Christians believe that the resurrected one reigns *now*, and they do sometimes see the oppressed gaining their dignity through God's action. The reversal of conditions has already begun in the form of a sign."[24] "The

---

[19] For material in this paragraph, see Horsley, *Liberation of Christmas*, 63–80 (ch. 4, "To All the People").

[20] Some scholars contrast Jewish hopes for vengeance with Christian emphases on mercy, as in the textually problematic prayer in Luke 23:34, a contrast problematized by Shelly Matthews, *Perfect Martyr: The Stoning of Stephen and the Construction of Christian Identity* (Oxford: Oxford University Press, 2010), https://doi.org/10.1093/acprof:oso/9780195393323.001.0001.

[21] Horsley, *Liberation of Christmas*, 127–43 (ch. 7, "A Modern Analogy").

[22] For this paragraph, see Bovon, *Luke 1*, 64–65.

[23] Mary's faith is matched by Mary Magdalene and other women in Luke 24:8–10. The male priest Zechariah's doubt (Luke 1:18–20) is matched by the male apostles' disbelief in 24:11, a female/male contrast that frames the gospel. See Turid Karlsen Seim, "The Gospel of Luke," in *A Feminist Commentary*, vol. 2 of *Searching the Scriptures*, ed. Elisabeth Schüssler Fiorenza (New York: Crossroad, 1994), 733, 754, 758, 761.

[24] Bovon, *Luke 1*, 64 (Bovon's italics).

song extols the threefold activity of God on religious, sociopolitical, and ethnic levels," a God who stands on the side of the poor.[25] God's compassion for the humble and weak must come into conflict with the mighty of this world. The Magnificat "is one of the New Testament texts with the most strongly political and liberating content. It calls on us to take the words totally concretely, and to fight against oppression in order to take seriously the Lord of history."[26]

C. History of Religions

A number of contemporary scholars, perhaps the majority, insist that the birth narratives of Jesus, including the Lukan canticles, are Jewish, not Greco-Roman.[27] Without discussing the long history of this binary, I note that it is socially unrealistic, as unrealistic as attempting to separate American Jews, Italian Catholics, or Saudi Muslims into binary categories. I mention this because the second major part of this article quotes a Greek author narrating Roman history, Dionysius, to clarify the Lukan Magnificat.[28]

Bovon's reading is more realistic.

> Luke 1:26–38 and Matt 1:18–25 are not alien to NT christology. The conception of the Messiah through the divine Spirit is a development of Jewish messianism and earliest christology, that, though subject to foreign influences, is not a foreign element. The virgin birth, like the preexistence of the Messiah, is intended to attest, in a narrative manner, the divine origin of the Son. The terminology of both [Luke 1:] vv. 31–33 and 34–35 is thoroughly Jewish; but Jewish messianism—as can be shown to be the case with minorities—expressed its identity polemically, in foreign categories.[29]

---

[25] Ibid.

[26] Ibid., 65.

[27] See, e.g., Nolland, *Luke 1–9:20*, 57–58, explaining 1:26–38, and Mittmann-Richert, *Magnifikat und Benediktus* (see nn. 10–13, 15 above).

[28] I present thirty-two significant similarities, also terminological, between Dionysius's story of Roman origins and Luke's story of the origin of the church in "Founders of Rome, of Athens, and of the Church: Romulus, Theseus, and Jesus: Theseus and Ariadne with Athena Visually Represented in Rome, Pompeii and Herculaneum (with 6 figs.)," in *Seeing the God: Image, Space, Performance and Vision in the Religion of the Roman Empire*, ed. Marlis Arnhold, Harry O. Maier, and Jörg Rüpke (Tübingen: Mohr Siebeck, forthcoming 2017). One of these thirty-two similarities concerns founders' extraordinary births; another commonality is their violent deaths. On the other hand, I contrast Rome's and Christ's lordship in "Violence in Pompeian/Roman Domestic Art as a Visual Context for Pauline and Deutero-Pauline Letters," in *Early Christianity in Pompeian Light: People, Texts, Situations*, ed. Bruce Longenecker (Minneapolis: Fortress, 2016), 123–65, with figs. 5.1–11. See also David L. Balch, "Paul's Mission to Rome's Enemies the Gauls: Faith Welcoming Foreigners," *Journal of Lutheran Ethics* 15/10 (Nov.–Dec. 2015), with five figures, http://elca.org/JLE/Articles/1124.

[29] Bovon, *Luke 1*, "Excursus: The Virgin Birth and the History of Religions," 43–47, here 47,

Bovon emphasizes Egyptian sources of the birth narratives, which I have also discussed.[30]

In summary, scholars debate the Magnificat's origins, its function, and its history of religions context. In the Roman Empire neither the Magnificat's origins nor its history of religions context can be barricaded exclusively within early forms of Judaism to only one ethnic/religious group. The second part of this article demonstrates that there are close terminological and conceptual links between the Magnificat and Greco-Roman economic hopes and conflicts.

II. Economic Conflicts in the Roman World between the Humble and the Proud, the Poor and the Rich

The Magnificat's vocabulary reflects urban–rural conflict in the Roman Empire,[31] which I will demonstrate in relation to the contrasting terms *rich* and *hungry*, *proud* and *humble*. Given this economic context, I then glance at Carol Bakker Wilson's recent model of how poor persons scratched out a living in the Roman Empire and how changes in their circumstances would drive them below subsistence level. Finally, I show that both the Magnificat and Wilson's model have a close parallel in contemporary Mexico (III).

A. Mary's Magnificat: Urban–Rural Conflict between Rich and Hungry, Proud and Humble

Mary believes what was spoken to her by the Lord, chanting:

> My soul magnifies the Lord, and my spirit rejoices in God my Savior, for he has looked with favor on the humility of his slave woman [ἐπὶ τὴν ταπείνωσιν τῆς δούλης αὐτοῦ].... He ... has scattered the proud [ὑπερηφάνους] in the thoughts of their hearts. He has brought down the powerful [δυνάστας] from their thrones and lifted up the lowly [ὕψωσεν ταπεινούς]; he has filled the hungry [πεινῶντας]

---

citing Eduard Norden, *Die Geburt des Kindes: Geschichte einer religiösen Idee*, SBW 3 (Leipzig: Teubner, 1924).

[30] Bovon, *Luke 1*, 46. See also David L. Balch, *Roman Domestic Art and Early House Churches*, WUNT 228 (Tübingen: Mohr Siebeck, 2008), chapter 5, citing Thomas Schneider, "Die Geburt des Horuskindes: Eine ägyptische Vorlage der neutestamentlichen Weinachtsgeschichte," *TZ* 60 (2004): 254–71; and Balch, *Contested Ethnicities and Images: Studies in Acts and Art*, WUNT 345 (Tübingen: Mohr Siebeck, 2015), chapter 17.

[31] See Balch, *Contested Ethnicities and Images*, chapters 4 and 6, which this article develops; and, for further observations, Balch, "Two Mothers: Veturia and Mary; Two Sons: Coriolanus and Jesus," in *Bodies, Borders, Believers: Ancient Texts and Present Conversations; Festschrift for Turid Karlsen Seim*, ed. A. N. Grung, M. B. Kartzow, and A. R. Solevåg (Eugene, OR: Wipf & Stock, 2015), 342–74. Cf. Douglas E. Oakman, *Jesus and the Peasants*, Matrix 4 (Eugene, OR: Cascade, 2008), part 1 ("The Political Economy").

with good things and sent the rich [πλουτοῦντας] away empty. (Luke 1:46b-55; NRSV modified and shortened)

The root ταπειν- ("humble") is fundamental to this story; it may have psychological overtones, but it primarily refers to political and economic status. In Mary's hymn the opposite of humble is proud (ὑπερήφανος), and these terms are synonyms for the "poor" and the "rich."

B. Dionysius's Narrative of the First Secession in Rome, Conflict between Patricians/Aristocrats and Plebeians

As a political/economic parallel that uses identical Greek terminology, I narrate Dionysius's story of the first secession in Rome, conflict between the patricians and the plebeians, who "inhabit two cities, one of which is ruled by poverty [πενίας] ... and the other by satiety and insolence, but modesty, order, and justice [δίκη] ... remains in neither of these two cities.... Like wild beasts we choose to destroy our enemy ... rather than, by consulting our own safety, to be preserved [σεσῶσθαι] together with our adversary" (Dionysius, *Rom. ant.* 6.36.1 [Cary, LCL]). Poverty revolts against wealth, the humble against the proud (πενία πρὸς πλοῦτον ἐστασίασε καὶ ταπεινότης πρὸς ἐπιφάνειαν), who act arrogantly, as in nearly all states (6.54.1). Lucius Junius (Brutus) gives a speech (6.72-80) referring to the arrogant (οἱ ὑπερήφανοι, 6.72.4), who deceive and do not fulfill promises (6.73.2; 6.76.3; 6.77.2). Brutus repeatedly gives examples from Roman history (6.74.1, 4, 6; 6.75.3; 6.80.1-3). Will the senators promise a benefit, honors, magistracies, or relief from poverty (ἐπανόρθωσιν ἀπορίας, 6.78.1)? Some advantages of the humble (τοὺς ταπεινούς) and obscure (6.79.1) have been destroyed by wars, consumed by the scarcity of the necessities of daily life (ἡ τῶν καθ'ἡμέραν ἀναγκαίων); others have been robbed by these haughty money lenders (ὑπερηφάνων δανειστῶν), who then treat the poor like wild beasts (6.79.2-3). The proud rich are "unwilling to associate as fellow-citizens and to share your blessings with those of a humbler estate [ἀπολίτευτα καὶ ἀκοινώνητα πρὸς τοὺς ταπεινοτέρους]" (6.80.4). During this urban–rural conflict, Brutus, speaking for the poor, persuades the Roman senate to create the office of tribunes to protect the poor (6.88-89).

The peasants, however, had left their farms during the winter solstice when corn is planted, and the land was destitute of people (7.1.1). Slaves deserted, and animals disappeared; the peasants had no store of corn for seed or food (7.1.3). The poor accused the rich of treachery for the dearth of corn, declaring that they had secretly hoarded corn and had money to buy (7.14.3-4). Still, the poor did not attack the houses of the rich where they suspected they would find stores, nor did they raid the public markets; rather, without money, they used roots and grass for food (τὰς ἐκ γῆς ῥίζας τε καὶ βοτάνας σιτούμενοι, 7.18.2). The following year the consuls were able to supply the city with corn, believing that the harmony of the masses depended on it (7.20.1).

Roman ambassadors successfully bought corn from Sicily, fifty thousand bushels of wheat (πυρῶν), half bought at a low price, the other half a free gift from Sicily.³² When ships arrived laden with corn (σιτηγῶν), the patricians debated how to distribute it to the plebeians, whether to sell to them at a low price (σῖτον ὀλίγης αὐτοῖς ἀπεμπολῆσαι τιμῆς), which moderates the animosity of the poor against the rich (ἐπιεικέστεραι πρὸς τοὺς εὐπόρους αἱ τῶν πενήτων ὀργαί), or to make the provisions as costly as possible (τιμίας ὡς ἔνι μάλιστα ποιεῖν), so that the poor might become more moderate (σωφρονέστεροι, 7.20.3–4). Marcius, surnamed Coriolanus, was of the latter opinion. Conflict, including significant debates, followed.

As tribune, Decius persuaded the senate to pass a decree for the trial of the famous general, Coriolanus, accusing him of trying to dissolve the bonds between the senate and the people (7.44.1). "Giving to the liberty of the poor [πενήτων] the name of insolence, and to equality that of tyranny, he [Coriolanus] advised you to deprive us of them" (7.44.2). But a "multitude of poor men [ἀπορίας], when deprived of the necessities of life" (πένητες ἄνθρωποι τῆς ἀναγκαίου τροφῆς ἀποκλειόμενοι), will either leave the city and perish or, calling on the divinities to witness their sufferings, attack those who keep the price of corn (σιτία) high, no longer regarding them as friends (7.44.3–4). He advises Coriolanus to descend from his haughtiness (ὑπερηφάνων), to assume the humble and piteous demeanor (σχῆμα ταπεινὸν καὶ ἐλεεινόν) of one who has erred (ἡμαρτηκότος) and is asking pardon (7.45.4). The senator Manius Valerius also advises Coriolanus to change his way of life to a humble deportment (σχῆμα ταπεινὸν μεταλαβεῖν, 7.54.5). At the trial, the people of Rome vote for Coriolanus's perpetual banishment (7.64.6). Coriolanus then goes to Rome's enemies, the Volscians, and describes himself as forsaken, exiled, and humbled (ἔρημος καὶ ἄπολις καὶ ταπεινός, 8.1.6). Does this not suit the God whom Mary praises in the Magnificat?

C. Conclusions

In sum, (1) Mary/Luke and Dionysius employ the same complex of Greek roots: "rich/proud" (πλουτέω/ὑπερήφανος)³³ and "hungry/humble" (πεινάω/ταπείνωσις; Luke 1:48, 51, 52).³⁴ This story also narrates (2) the proud Coriolanus's being humbled and (3) the humble Brutus attaining the powerful office of Roman tribune. The political reversal named second and third is also proclaimed in the

---

³²M. Kokoszko, K. Jagusiak, and Z. Rzeznicka, *Cereals of Antiquity and Early Byzantine Times* (Lódz: Wydawnictwo Uniwersytetu kódzkiego, 2014), ch. 1.

³³I give the verbal or nominal forms as they occur in the Magnificat. For "poor" Luke once (21:2) employs the adjective πενιχρός, ά, όν, but otherwise uses πτωχός, πτωχεύω, πτωχεία. Dionysius writes πενία, πενητεύω.

³⁴See also René Krüger, "Conversion of the Pocketbook: The Economic Project of Luke's Gospel," in *God's Economy: Biblical Studies from Latin America*, ed. Ross Kinsler and Gloria Kinsler (Maryknoll, NY: Orbis, 2005), 169–201.

Magnificat: "he [God] has brought down the powerful from their thrones and lifted up the humble" (ὕψωσεν ταπεινούς, Luke 1:52). (4) Whether those without corn will be fed remains uncertain in the Coriolanus narrative, but Mary's Magnificat affirms this of God: "God has filled the hungry [πεινῶντας] with good things and sent the rich [πλουτοῦντας] away empty" (Luke 1:53). The rich/proud Roman general Coriolanus refuses to provide corn/wheat at a low price for the hungry, but Mary in the Magnificat praises God, who cares for the humble hungry.

D. Carol Bakker Wilson's Model of How People Got Access to Food

Wilson has constructed a model that describes access to food, especially grain (corn and wheat) in the first-century Roman world.[35] Wilson's model and Dionysius's narrative of Coriolanus and Brutus correspond to an amazing degree. Her model is necessarily complex; I emphasize only those aspects that illuminate Dionysius's story. Wilson modifies John Kautsky's model, which addresses the demands of aristocrats on rural peasants in villages in the form of tributes and rents. The aristocrats' exploitative practices resulted in loss of life because the peasants did not have sufficient food.[36] One of Wilson's theses is that aristocrats "in the first century Roman East made decisions and took actions condoned by the dominant entitlement system that undermined the critical survival mechanisms" used by peasants "to keep from slipping below subsistence level," survival "mechanisms that helped them stave off starvation."[37] Wilson cites Gerhard Lenski's argument that the aristocrats' political and economic control of distribution displayed and produced marked social inequality.[38] Wilson outlines food production, distribution, preparation, consumption and clean-up, emphasizing distribution, which was overtly political.[39] Who got how much was closely related to how much rent and taxes aristocrats demanded. An increase in taxes took a surplus that did not exist.[40] Or aristocrats could store the grain until they could sell it at a higher price.[41] They sometimes diverted peasant land, which the latter used for food and household needs, to generate cash crops for their more ostentatious lifestyles.[42] The result was less available grain to eat locally, which caused artificial food shortages in the cities

---

[35] Carol Bakker Wilson, *For I Was Hungry and You Gave Me Food: Pragmatics of Food Access in the Gospel of Matthew* (Eugene, OR: Pickwick, 2014).

[36] Ibid., 53; see also John Kautsky, *The Politics of Aristocratic Empires* (Chapel Hill: University of North Carolina Press, 1982; repr., New Brunswick, NJ: Transaction, 1997).

[37] Wilson, *For I Was Hungry*, 3.

[38] Ibid., 1–3; see also Gerhard Lenski, *Power and Privilege: A Theory of Social Stratification* (New York: McGraw-Hill, 1966).

[39] Wilson, *For I Was Hungry*, 44, 58, 60–61, 69.

[40] Ibid., 61.

[41] Ibid., 9, 22, 70–71, 78, 102–6, 187–210.

[42] Ibid., 57, 67, 72, 75.

and a decrease in the cultivation of nongrain foods grown to feed peasants. When the situation was dire, peasants would take their livestock and leave their land to join their pastoralist relatives, described as "migration through poverty," or, hoping for doles, would move to cities.[43]

Wilson refers to the debate over the relationship of the city to the rural population, whether the city is a pariah or the two are in a reciprocal relationship.[44] In the light of Dionysius's late first-century BCE narrative, it seems that Jim Grimshaw underplays tensions between city and country, between urban aristocrats and rural peasants, even though it is Dionysius's thesis that in Rome, differently from Greece, the two dialogue with each other so that their "mutual hatred" does not lead to irreparable mischief (ἀνήκεστον, 7.18.1; 7.21.1; 7.34.2–5; 7.66.1), that is, to mutual murder (contrast *Rom. ant.* 2.11 on Gaius Gracchus).[45]

III. A Significant Social Parallel

The contemporary economic exploitation of Mexican peasants by Mexican presidents and by wealthy Canadian and North American corporations presents a modern analogy to the economic situation described here.[46]

A. Mexican Presidents and the Constitution

The situation of Mexican farmers is complex, of course; I point only to those aspects of contemporary social conflict analogous to those in the Roman world as described by Dionysius and modeled by Wilson. Like King Herod, the Mexican government can give away farmers' land for foreigners to exploit.[47] David Bacon affirms that it is federal policy virtually to give away Mexico's mineral wealth.[48] In

---

[43] Ibid., 79 n. 82, 101 n. 125, 119 n. 251, 120–22; quotation from 101 n. 125. Wilson cites Øystein S. LaBianca, "Subsistence Pastoralism," in *Near Eastern Archaeology: A Reader*, ed. Suzanne Richard (Winona Lake, IN: Eisenbrauns, 2003), 116–25, here 118. See also Balch, *Contested Ethnicities and Images*, chapter 4.2, for similar narratives by Isocrates and Dionysius.

[44] Wilson, *For I Was Hungry*, 50.

[45] Jim Grimshaw, "Luke's Market Exchange District: Decentering Luke's Rich Urban Center," *Semeia* 86 (1999): 33–51.

[46] For further comments on the USA/Mexican border, see David L. Balch, "Jesus and the Samaritan/Judean Border," in *Borders: Terms, Ideologies, and Performances*, ed. A. Weissenrieder, WUNT 366 (Tübingen: Mohr Siebeck, 2016), 61–76.

[47] Wilson, *For I Was Hungry*, 9 n. 25, 61, 166.

[48] David Bacon, *The Right to Stay Home: How US Policy Drives Mexican Migration* (Boston: Beacon, 2013), 45, with significant bibliography (289–91), including online resources. For this reference I thank the Rev. Kim Erno (ELCA), Convergencia Resistencia (creamericas@gmail.com). For historical and economic contexts, see Thomas Weaver et al., eds., *Neoliberalism and Commodity Production in Mexico* (Boulder: University of Colorado Press, 2012), chapters 5, 6, 11,

1992 Mexican president Carlos Salinas de Gortar modified the country's mining law, and in the same year he also changed Mexico's land reform law to allow the sale of former communal lands held by indigenous peoples. This legal change conflicts with the United Nations' International Labor Organization's Convention 169, Article 14, on indigenous and tribal peoples' ownership and possession of land.[49] By the end of President Vincente Fox's term in 2006, the federal government had conceded 61 million acres, and that more than doubled to 126 million acres by the end of Felipe Calderon's term (2006–2012), who granted foreign and domestic corporations almost 10 million acres for US $20 million, which made the corporations US $15 billion.[50]

After the Mexican Revolution of 1910–1920, the nationalist government of Lázaro Cárdenas (1934–1940) established the Mexican Constitution, which mandates using natural resources for social benefits, creating equitable distribution of public wealth, which led to improved conditions of life for the Mexican people.[51] After World War II, Mexico adopted a policy of industrialization: factories produced products for the domestic market, and imports were limited. Large state-owned enterprises employed hundreds of thousands of workers, and unions were strong. Under successive administrations of the Institutional Revolutionary Party (PRI), the gulf widened between the political and economic elite—who managed the state's assets in their own interests—and the workers and farmers. President Carlos Salinas's mining law of 1992 gives preference to the exploitation of resources over all other considerations; the law prohibits local governments from imposing fees on mining activities or taxes even for the use of roads. Foreign concession holders can demand that land used for growing food be vacated. North American companies promise jobs and economic development, but the result is negative environmental and economic consequences and the exodus of displaced farmers.[52]

B. Giving Away Farmers'/Indigenous Peoples' Land

Bacon gives specific examples of giving away land; for example, Vancouver-based Fortuna Silver began explorations in the Mexican state of Oaxaca in 2006 and went into full production in 2011. Gold ore is treated with cyanide, a strong poison that bonds with the gold; when the gold is separated out, it leaves cyanide-laced wastewater, which is held in huge open-air ponds. In 2012 the silver and gold

---

and 13 on Oaxaca. See also Guadalupe Correa-Cabrera, *Democracy in "Two Mexicos": Political Institutions in Oaxaca and Nuevo León* (New York: Palgrave Macmillan, 2013), https://doi.org/10.1057/9781137263032.

[49] See www.ilo.org/.
[50] Bacon, *Right to Stay Home*, 46.
[51] For the discussion in this paragraph, see ibid., 41, 42, 44, 46, 110.
[52] See Jonathan Fox and Libby Haight, "Subsidizing Inequality: Mexican Corn Policy since NAFTA," Woodrow Wilson Center, 2010, 2011, www.wilsoncenter.org.

mines yielded US $23.3 million, and they anticipate that annual profits will reach US $39 million. Several nearby indigenous towns had already lost more than half their population to migration. The company distributed its largess by giving local people energy-saving stoves and ecological toilets.[53] Five hundred thousand indigenous people have migrated from the Mexican state of Oaxaca to the US, three hundred thousand of them to California. "Migration means not having to manhandle a wooden plough behind an ox, for growing corn that cannot be sold for what it costs to grow it."[54] In Mexico 9.4 percent of the people are illiterate, and 28.4 percent do not finish elementary school; in Oaxaca 45.5 percent never complete elementary school. Half of Mexican workers make less than ten dollars a day.[55]

For another example, Goldcorp Resources, with headquarters in Vancouver, proposed the Caballo Blanco mine in the state of Veracruz during the term of Governor Fidel Herrera (2004–2010), and the federal government virtually gave them a concession of seventy-seven square miles.[56] The mine uses four hundred million cubic feet of water per year, depleting the aquifer on which rural farming communities depend. The mine produces a hundred thousand ounces of gold a year, valued at $1,660 an ounce, which in 2012 yielded $166 million. People in nearby towns protested that they have been threatened in order to get them to sell their land to Goldcorp, protests that have been criminalized.[57]

C. Conclusions

Instead of utilizing Mexico's natural resources to give social benefits to Mexicans, for example, to support farmers growing corn, to provide transportation, clean water, education, and jobs, as the Mexican constitution mandates, Bacon affirms that the Mexican presidents are virtually giving away those natural resources and farmers' land to foreign, mostly North American, corporations.

IV. Social/Economic Parallels between Mary's Magnificat, Dionysius's Narrative, Wilson's Model, and Contemporary Latin and North America

The first part of this article argued that we may not limit the values of the Magnificat to various forms of early Judaism even though the hymn originated in Judea. Mary's hymn praising God has diverse sources and a complex history of

---

[53] Bacon, *Right to Stay Home*, 55.
[54] Ibid., 56.
[55] Ibid.
[56] Ibid., 42–43.
[57] Ibid., 44.

religions context. The second part of the article examines similar terminology and comparable values between the Magnificat and conflicts in Roman society between the humble and the proud, the hungry and the rich. The Magnificat continued to communicate and legitimate similar values also in Ephesus and/or Rome.

Social conflicts between the humble hungry and the proud rich in ancient Rome and in contemporary America have significant parallels, among which I note the following. (1) In Dionysius's narrative, in Wilson's model, and in contemporary Mexico, the price of grain (corn, wheat) is high for rural peasants and indigenous peoples, who rely on grain to sustain life. (2) There is high tension (in Dionysius's language, "hatred," and in the Magnificat contrasts between proud and powerful and the humble and hungry) between patricians/aristocrats and plebeians, urban rich and rural poor. (3) In Dionysius, in Wilson's model, and in contemporary Mexico, the rich store grain, speculating that they can then sell it later for a higher price, which results in hunger among peasant farmers. (4) Wilson observes that the high price of grain is also directly related to decisions made by the powerful rich about taxes and rents for the poor farmers. In contemporary Mexico the presidents' decisions have resulted in peasants losing land to wealthy corporations. (5) In Dionysius, in Wilson's model, and in contemporary Mexico, the high price of grain leads to "migration through poverty."[58]

Mary's Magnificat rather praises the God who opposes such social, political, and economic exploitation of the humble and hungry for the benefit of the arrogant and wealthy, whether in ancient Rome or in contemporary North America.[59]

---

[58] See Mary Bauer and Meredith Stewart, *Close to Slavery: Guestworker Programs in the United States* (Southern Poverty Law Center, www.splcenter.org, 2013). J. B. Greenberg et al., "Conclusion: Structural Adjustment, Structural Violence," in Weaver et al., *Neoliberalism and Commodity Production in Mexico*, 315–41, here 319–21: "Among the [Mexican] revolution's crowning achievements was land reform, enshrined in Article 27 of the 1917 constitution, which formed the legal basis for communal land tenure and a system of *ejidos* that distributed lands to deserving peasants and rural communities. In Mexico, neoliberalism constitutes a regressive about-face and a betrayal of many of the Mexican Revolution's values." NAFTA has imposed conditions on Mexican rural producers under which competition is so unfair that maize farmers and coffee producers prefer to abandon their fields and migrate to Mexico's urban centers or seek work in the United States (see chapters by González Ríos, Greenberg, Sesia, and Alvarez, in this same book). Now see Joerg Rieger, ed., *Religion, Theology, and Class: Fresh Engagements after Long Silence* (New York: Palgrave Macmillan, 2015). Also U. Duchrow, D. Beros, M. Hoffmann, and H. G. Ulrich, eds., *Radicalizing Reformation/Die Reformation radikalisieren*, 7 vols. (Berlin: LIT, 2015). Vol. 6 is *Radicalizing Reformation: North Ameircan Perspectives*, ed. K. Bloomquist, C. L. Nesson, and H. G. Ulrich; vol. 7 is in Spanish.

[59] Historical-critical exegesis is often said to alienate contemporary readers from ancient sacred texts; this historical-critical exegesis brings the two into dialogue.

SBL PRESS

New and Recent Titles

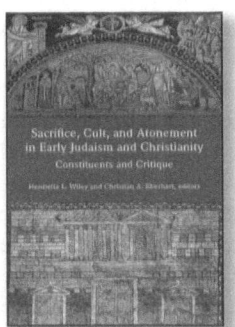

PEDAGOGY IN ANCIENT JUDAISM AND EARLY CHRISTIANITY
Karina Martin Hogan, Matthew Goff, and Emma Wasserman, editors
Paperback $49.95, 978-1-62837-165-9 424 pages, 2017 Code: 063548
Hardcover $64.95, 978-0-88414-208-9 E-book $49.95, 978-0-88414-207-2
Early Judaism and Its Literature 41

SACRIFICE, CULT, AND ATONEMENT IN EARLY JUDAISM AND CHRISTIANITY
Constituents and Critique
Henrietta L. Wiley and Christian A. Eberhart, editors
Paperback $56.95, 978-1-62837-155-0 434 pages, 2017 Code: 060393
Hardcover $76.95, 978-0-88414-191-4 E-book $56.95, 978-0-88414-190-7
Resources for Biblical Study 85

THE BOOK OF THE TWELVE AND BEYOND
Collected Essays of James D. Nogalski
James D. Nogalski
Paperback $49.95, 978-1-62837-164-2 380 pages, 2017 Code: 062631
Hardcover $64.95, 978-0-88414-206-5 E-book $49.95, 978-0-88414-205-8
Ancient Israel and Its Literature 29

REDESCRIBING THE GOSPEL OF MARK
Barry S. Crawford and Merrill P. Miller, editors
Paperback $89.95, 978-1-62837-163-5 708 pages, 2017 Code: 064520
Hardcover $109.95, 978-0-88414-204-1 E-book $89.95, 978-0-88414-203-4
Early Christianity and Its Literature 22

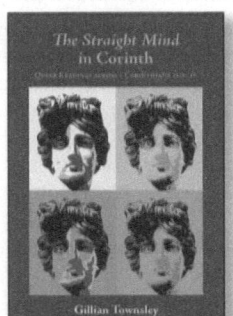

THE STRAIGHT MIND IN CORINTH
Queer Readings across 1 Corinthians 11:2–16
Gillian Townsley
Paperback $43.95, 978-1-62837-147-5 366 pages, 2017 Code: 060685
Hardcover $58.95, 978-0-88414-176-1 E-book $43.95, 978-0-88414-175-4
Semeia Studies 88

SBL Press • P.O. Box 2243 • Williston, VT 05495-2243
Phone: 877-725-3334 (toll-free) or 802-864-6185 • Fax: 802-864-7626
Order online at www.sbl-site.org/publications

You Can't Hear "Aeneas" without Thinking of Rome

MICHAEL KOCHENASH
michael.kochenash@gmail.com
Los Angeles, California

The long-standing connection between the Trojan Aeneas and Rome was advertised throughout the empire in various ways, but scholars rarely draw from this cultural capital when interpreting Acts 9:32–35, an account of Peter healing a man named Aeneas. They often assume both that Aeneas is well attested as a personal name during the first and second centuries of the Common Era (it is not) and that Luke inherited this name from a source (which is possible but insufficient). Acts 9:31 is a summary statement on the progress of the church in Judea, Samaria, and Galilee. Readers who recall Jesus's commission in Acts 1:8 will wonder about "the end of the earth." Given the proximity of the Aeneas pericope to Luke's summary statement and the fact that the narrative of Acts ends in Rome, I argue that the story of Aeneas can be read as a literary signpost for Rome (comparable to Luke 9:51–53 and Jerusalem). Luke's use of "Aeneas" as a structuring device works in tandem with "Joppa" in Acts 9:36–43, which signals the inclusion of gentiles by evoking the thought world of Jonah. The balance of Luke's narrative consists of negotiating and expanding the gentile mission and progressively moving toward the city of Rome. In this way, two proper nouns function as metonymic signposts to foreshadow the direction of the narrative, in both ethnic and geographic terms.

In Acts 9:32–35, Peter heals a man named Aeneas. It is unusual for recipients of healing miracles to be identified by name in Luke-Acts. In the Gospel of Luke, not a single recipient of healing is named; Luke even omits a name found in his source: "Bartimaeus" (18:35–43; cf. Mark 10:46–52).[1] The book of Acts contains only a handful of exceptions: Saul (9:17–18; 22:12–13)/Paul (28:3–6), Aeneas (9:32–35), Tabitha/Dorcas (9:36–43), and Eutychus (20:9–12). In each of these cases, the name of the healed individual is significant either because of who the

---

[1] Healing narratives with unnamed recipients include: Luke 4:31–37, 38–39; 5:12–13, 18–25; 6:6–10; 7:1–10, 11–17; 8:26–39, 43–48, 49–56; 9:37–42; 11:14; 13:11–13; 14:1–4; 17:11–19; 18:35–43; 22:50–51; Acts 3:1–10; 14:8–10; 16:16–18; 19:11–12; 28:8–10.

person is or what the name means. Paul is, of course, one of Luke's protagonists and was well known outside of Luke's narrative; the name Saul—regardless of whether it was used by the historical Paul—identifies him with the first king of Israel, who persecuted David (cf. Acts 13:21). Eutychus is "lucky" to survive a three-story fall (Acts 20:9–12).[2] Tabitha's name (Dorcas/"deer") must also be significant since Luke provides a Greek translation of her Aramaic name that he already transliterated.[3] Aeneas's name is likewise significant, and I will argue that its significance is due not to Aeneas's being an individual known to Luke's audience but rather to the cultural freight carried by the name in the Mediterranean world for hundreds of years before and after the composition of Luke's narrative: its association with Rome.

Scholars often assume that Aeneas is well attested as a personal name during the first and second centuries of the Common Era and/or that Luke inherited this name from a source.[4] Both assumptions are misguided. In the first case, the name Aeneas was demonstrably uncommon in the Greek-speaking Mediterranean generally and remarkably rare in the regions of Syria and Palestine specifically. The accuracy of the second assumption is less clear, but it is nevertheless unable to explain why Luke does not omit Aeneas's name as he does that of Bartimaeus. I will address both of these assumptions, first the latter, then the former.

Commentators commonly identify the Petrine healing narratives featuring Aeneas (in Lydda) and Tabitha (in Joppa) as tralatitious, asserting that Luke integrated received traditions into his narrative. According to Josephus, however, both Lydda and Joppa were burned to the ground in the Jewish War and then resettled by the Romans.[5] Thus, if the miracle stories concerning Aeneas and Tabitha were traditions incorporated by Luke, it is improbable that they were *local* traditions that

---

[2] See Dennis R. MacDonald, "Luke's Eutychus and Homer's Elpenor: Acts 20:7–12 and *Odyssey* 10–12," *Journal of Higher Criticism* 1 (1994): 5–24; MacDonald, *The Gospels and Homer: Imitations of Greek Epic in Mark and Luke-Acts*, New Testament and Greek Literature 1 (Lanham, MD: Rowman & Littlefield, 2015), 223–29.

[3] An argument for a particular interpretation lies beyond the purview of this article; see Michael Kochenash, "Political Correction: Luke's Tabitha (Acts 9:36–43), Virgil's Dido, and Cleopatra," *NovT*, forthcoming. I suggest that a credible reading should make sense of both the meaning of the names Tabitha and Dorcas and also the close proximity of this narrative to one about Peter healing a man named Aeneas. For the possible relationship of "Tabitha" in Acts 9:40 to the Aramaic command in Mark 5:41, see C. K. Barrett, *A Critical and Exegetical Commentary on the Acts of the Apostles*, 2 vols., ICC (Edinburgh: T&T Clark, 1994–1998), 1:485; Richard I. Pervo, *Acts: A Commentary*, Hermeneia (Minneapolis: Fortress, 2009), 254.

[4] Two exceptions merit attention here: Dennis R. MacDonald and Patrick Henry Reardon (see also n. 14 below). Reardon, in only three sentences, asserts that the name points to a Roman destination ("Homing to Rome: The *Aeneid* and the Acts of the Apostles," *OiC* 38 [2003]: 45–55). MacDonald argues that Acts 9:32–35 imitates Homer's Aeneas from *Il.* 5 (*Gospels and Homer*, 47–48).

[5] *J.W.* 2.19.1 §§513–516 (4.8.1 §444); 2.18.10 §§507–508 (3.9.2–3 §§414–427). Cf. Pervo, *Acts*, 252 n. 10; Joseph A. Fitzmyer, *The Acts of the Apostles: A New Translation with Introduction and Commentary*, AB 31 (New York: Doubleday, 1998), 443.

retained the names because the transmitters were familiar with them. In that case the stories would have perished along with the inhabitants of these cities.[6] Therefore, either Luke's tradition included the name—for an unclear reason—and Luke made a decision to retain it, or Luke added the name himself. In either case, more stands to be gained by attending to the rhetorical effect of the inclusion/retention of Aeneas's name, especially that which is derived from its cultural freight in the Roman Mediterranean and its position within Luke's narrative, than by speculating further about the contents of a hypothetical source.[7]

When commentators give any attention to Aeneas, they typically foreground issues surrounding his identity: whether he was a Jew or a gentile, a Christian or a non-Christian.[8] Matthew Sleeman describes this focus of modern scholarship as the "commentators' perennial concern with Aeneas' spiritual status."[9] If a decision must be made on this issue, then surely it is more credible to suppose that Aeneas is a Jew or a Jewish Christian. If Aeneas had any other spiritual status, then Luke's placement of this narrative just prior to the Cornelius episode would be nonsensical. Nevertheless, when commentators do discuss Aeneas's *name*, they generally treat it as unremarkable.[10] Richard I. Pervo, in a footnote citing Margaret H. Williams, simply says, "Names are usually secondary details. 'Aeneas' is attested for Palestinian Jews from the second century B.C.E. to the fourth century C.E."[11] Although Pervo reports the range of attestation presented by Williams accurately, his phrasing is misleading. In fact, Williams is able to muster only one attestation each for the second century BCE and the first century CE, and both come from Josephus (*Ant.* 14.10.22 §248; *J.W.* 5.8.4 §§326–328).[12] The only inscriptional

---

[6] This observation obtains whether we date Acts to circa 85 CE, with the majority of scholars, or to circa 115 CE, with a growing contingent of Lukan specialists.

[7] For a review of proposals regarding possible traditions behind Acts 9:32–43 and Luke's compositional contributions, see Pervo, *Acts*, 251–52.

[8] See Barrett, *Acts of the Apostles*, 1:477, 480; Fitzmyer, *Acts of the Apostles*, 444; F. F. Bruce, *The Book of the Acts*, rev. ed., NICNT (Grand Rapids: Eerdmans, 1988), 197–98; Robert C. Tannehill, *The Narrative Unity of Luke-Acts: A Literary Interpretation*, 2 vols. (Minneapolis: Fortress, 1990), 2:125; Jacob Jervell, *Die Apostelgeschichte*, KEK 17 (Göttingen: Vandenhoeck & Ruprecht, 1998), 295; Craig S. Keener, *Acts: An Exegetical Commentary*, 4 vols. (Grand Rapids: Baker Academic, 2012–2015), 2:1706.

[9] Matthew Sleeman, *Geography and the Ascension Narrative in Acts*, SNTSMS 146 (Cambridge: Cambridge University Press, 2009), 219, https://doi.org/10.1017/CBO9780511635540.

[10] Some commentators are silent on the apparent incongruence of the name here, e.g., Ernst Haenchen, *The Acts of the Apostles: A Commentary* (Oxford: Basil Blackwell, 1971), 337–42.

[11] Pervo, *Acts*, 253 n. 16. He cites Margaret H. Williams, "Palestinian Jewish Personal Names in Acts," in *The Book of Acts in Its Palestinian Setting*, vol. 4 of *The Book of Acts in Its First Century Setting*, ed. Richard Bauckham (Grand Rapids: Eerdmans, 1995), 79–113.

[12] In both instances, Josephus uses the more popular spelling for the first century, Αἰνείας, instead of Luke's Αἰνέας.

evidence—and, as it should happen, the only other attestation she provides—is one occurrence of the name in the fourth century CE.[13]

Perhaps commentators assume that Aeneas was a popular name in the first two centuries of the Common Era because of the overwhelming popularity of Virgil's *Aeneid*. After all, it is common to name children after popular public figures. Nevertheless, even scholars who exhibit awareness of the *Aeneid* rarely treat Aeneas's name in Acts 9:32–35 as noteworthy.[14] Ken Dowden does acknowledge the heroic nature of the name Aeneas: "It may seem curious that so elevated a name should be assigned to the cripple in Acts 9:33–34, but Greek culture … was unlikely to have taken cognizance of a Latin text such as Virgil's. It is best regarded as a solid, traditional name dignified by its bearer in Homeric epic."[15] Dowden then notes that, according to the *Lexicon of Greek Personal Names* (*LGPN*), there are very few occurrences of the name Aeneas after the time of Christ, but he discounts this

---

[13] See Williams, "Palestinian Jewish Personal Names," 110.

[14] Ben Witherington III writes, "Aeneas is a familiar name, especially to anyone who knew something of Virgil's epic about those who survived the Trojan War (the *Aeneid*)" (*The Acts of the Apostles: A Socio-rhetorical Commentary* [Grand Rapids: Eerdmans, 1998], 329). Witherington applies this insight only to the question of whether Aeneas is supposed to have been a Jew or a gentile: the "commentator's perennial concern." Reardon and MacDonald (see n. 4 above) do account for the cultural significance of Aeneas's name in their interpretations. Reardon writes, "Before ever narrating the journeys of Paul, Luke sounded the Roman theme already in the ministry of St. Peter, whose baptism of the centurion Cornelius, the first official representative of Rome to become a Christian (Acts 10), was a crucial event in the whole mission of the Church and its movement to Rome. Just prior to that event, furthermore, Luke suggested its immense significance by describing Peter's healing of … Aeneas! Of the many persons healed through the ministry of Peter (3:7; 5:15–16), it is noteworthy that only Aeneas and Dorcas are named (9:32–41). In the case of Aeneas, the name already suggests a subtle connection to the Rome-ward motif of the Acts of the Apostles" ("Homing to Rome," 54–55; ellipsis original). The quoted material comprises the extent of Reardon's discussion of Aeneas in Acts 9:32–35. Reardon makes this connection by comparing Acts with Virgil's *Aeneid*; in this article, I make the same connection by drawing from a larger body of evidence: the cultural capital of "Aeneas" in the Roman Mediterranean world.

MacDonald suggests that Luke might be imitating a Homeric episode featuring Aeneas (*Gospels and Homer*, 47–48). In book 5 of the *Iliad*, Diomedes hurls a massive boulder at Aeneas, striking his hip (*Il.* 5.302–310). The bard says he would have died were it not for the assistance both of his divine mother, Aphrodite, and of Apollo, who rescued him after Aphrodite herself was injured (*Il.* 5.311–313, 445–448). Although the parallels between Acts 9:34–35 and *Il.* 5.512–515 are few and the verbal similarities are not particularly striking, the mental images evoked by each of these narratives are remarkably similar: a crippled man named Aeneas is healed through divine agency. In MacDonald's reading, Luke refers to an iconic Trojan-Roman figure in a familiar state of injury (Aeneas is similarly injured and divinely healed in the *Aeneid* [12.385–429]) and substitutes Jesus (via Peter) for the Olympian deities, the conventional healers of Aeneas. The present article builds on the insistence of Reardon and MacDonald that the Aeneas narrative needs to be interpreted within the matrix of the name's signification in the Roman Mediterranean.

[15] Ken Dowden, "Aeneas," in *DDD*, 11–12, here 11.

observation as "probably a sampling error."[16] Dowden's assessment suffers, however, from faulty logic: the heroic nature of Aeneas's name was well known among non-Latin-speaking Greeks long before Virgil's epic. Thus, Luke's readers need not have "taken cognizance of a Latin text such as Virgil's" in order to understand the freight carried by "so elevated a name." His evaluation is also disadvantaged by a lack of data; he had access to only the first volume of *LGPN* when the first edition of *DDD* was published. Six additional volumes are now available (and three more are forthcoming with data accessible through the editors).

The newer editions of *LGPN* confirm the results that Dowden attributed to a sampling error in the first volume: Aeneas was not a popular name in the first and second centuries CE in the Roman Mediterranean.[17] Although the *LGPN* volume covering Syria, Palestine, and Trans-Euphrates has yet to be published, the data collected from these regions, made available to me by the editors, suggest unequivocally that Aeneas was *never* a popular name in these regions: there exist six attestations of the name Aeneas in Palestine (one of which is Acts 9:33–35 [!]) and only one in Syria within the entire chronological purview of the *LGPN* project, from the emergence of written Greek until the sixth century CE.[18] It may be noteworthy that Luke's choice of spelling—Αἰνέας—is less common at the time of the composition of Luke-Acts than the other (less Latinized) spelling of the name, Αἰνείας. Αἰνέας was the preferred spelling in the first century BCE, coinciding with the reigns of Julius Caesar and Augustus; in the first century CE, the name Aeneas had declined in popularity overall, but the preferred spelling, by however small a margin, was Αἰνείας (see table 1).[19] There was thus no increase in the first century CE of parents naming their children after the hero of Virgil's *Aeneid* (at least not among those with Greek names).[20]

Given how rare the name Aeneas was as a personal name, there is good reason to examine the cultural freight it carried in the Roman Mediterranean world—its

---

[16] Ibid. See P. M. Fraser et al., eds., *A Lexicon of Greek Personal Names*, 5 vols. in 7 (to date) (Oxford: Clarendon, 1987–).

[17] The only exception is, unsurprisingly, coastal Asia Minor. In the published *LGPN* volumes, there are 202 attestations of Aeneas (both spellings: Αἰνείας and Αἰνέας); ninety of them are located in the coastal regions of Asia Minor. In these regions, Luke's spelling (Αἰνέας) is preferred (49:41) but only due to the name's popularity in the second century BCE, where twenty of the attestations of Αἰνέας occur.

[18] I obtained data from the forthcoming *LGPN* part 2 in response to an e-mail request to the *LGPN* staff. Richard Catling, assistant editor for *LGPN*, reported this data on 5 September 2012.

[19] It should be noted, however, that three of the five (non-Acts) attestations of Aeneas in Palestine are Αἰνέας, not Αἰνείας. Nevertheless, from a literary perspective it is not clear whether there is any significance in Luke's choice of spelling. Whether the name was spelled Αἰνέας or Αἰνείας, the audience would have heard "Aeneas."

[20] Interestingly, there *is* a dramatic spike in the popularity of the name Aeneas in the second century BCE, after it had been associated with Romans in interstate discourse for about a century.

TABLE 1. Attestations of the Name Aeneas by Century according to
the *Lexicon of Greek Personal Names*

The numbers listed represent the total number of attestations of the name Aeneas (spelled Αἰνέας or Αἰνείας) with the attestations of Luke's spelling (Αἰνέας) in parentheses.

	2nd BCE	2nd/1st BCE	1st BCE	1st BCE/ 1st CE	1st CE	1st/2nd CE	2nd CE +
The Aegean Islands, Cyprus, and Cyrenaica (*LGPN* 1)	4 (4)	1 (1)	9 (7)	2 (1)	2 (–)	–	5 (2)
Attica (*LGPN* 2)	4 (2)	1 (1)	5 (–)	–	1 (–)	–	2 (–)
The Peloponnese, Western Greece, Sicily, and Magna Graecia (*LGPN* 3A)	2 (2)	1 (1)	3 (3)	–	1 (1)	–	1 (1)
Central Greece: from Megarid to Thessaly (*LGPN* 3B)	7 (7)	–	1 (1)	–	2 (2)	–	2 (2)
Macedonia, Thrace, and the northern shores of the Black Sea (*LGPN* 4)	–	1 (–)	2 (–)	1 (1)	–	–	–
Coastal Asia Minor: Pontos to Ionia (*LGPN* 5A)	3 (2)	2 (–)	–	2 (1)	1 (–)	1 (1)	10 (4)
Coastal Asia Minor: Caria to Cilicia (*LGPN* 5B)	19 (18)	6 (6)	4 (1)	3 (3)	4 (1)	2 (1)	25 (4)

association with Rome—and to consider whether such capital might account for Luke's inclusion or retention of the name in Acts. The antiquity of Aeneas's connection to Italy can be demonstrated by a survey of his role in Homeric literature and by noting interstate relations during the Roman Republic. In order to establish the ubiquity of this association, I will cite a number of examples from the first centuries BCE and CE that testify to it.

The Trojan hero named Aeneas appears in Homer's *Iliad*;[21] his escape from the Greek destruction of Troy was apparently narrated by Arctinus in the now lost

---

[21] In the *Iliad*, Homer almost always spells Aeneas's name with an extra *iota*: Αἰνείας. There is one exception: *Il.* 13.541. In this scene, the Trojans and the Greeks are sparring over the bodies of fallen comrades. Amid the chaos, Aeneas (spelled Αἰνέας as in Acts) is said to slay the Greek Aphareus, who had been turned toward him at the time. It is a short but graphic account of Aphareus's death. This spelling anomaly is insignificant when it comes to interpreting Acts 9, however: there are no shared distinctives that would suggest an intertextual connection aside from the spelling of Aeneas's name.

Iliupersis. In the *Iliad*, Aeneas "is uninteresting and unmemorable, [but] not unimportant."[22] He is saved from death by the gods twice: once by Aphrodite and Apollo (*Il.* 5) and once by Poseidon (*Il.* 20). According to the bard, Aeneas was saved by the gods because of his future, prophesied by Poseidon, as the king of the Trojans (20.307–308).[23]

The Roman connection with Aeneas was most commonly invoked, beginning in the third century BCE, in the political context of the Roman Republic's relations with Greek cities. According to Jan N. Bremmer and Nicholas M. Horsfall, in 281 BCE with the attack of Pyrrhus, "Rome's Trojan origins were born ... in a national sense."[24] In the Pyrrhic War, Pyrrhus, the ruler of Epirus, appropriated the legacy of Achilles, identifying the Romans as Homer's Trojans by default. Of course, by 275 BCE, these new "Trojans" had prevailed. Few if any classics scholars, however, believe that the Trojan identity of Rome originated with Pyrrus.[25] Paramount in this discussion is the witness of the Greek historian Timaeus, who, in the aftermath of the Pyrrhic War, writes as if Roman identification with ancient Troy was already well established.[26] Later, in the First Punic War (264–241 BCE), the city of Segesta created an alliance with Rome on the basis of their common claim of descent from Aeneas.[27] In 238 BCE, not long after Rome's first war against Carthage, "the Acarnanians applied for a tax exemption from Rome ... on the grounds that they had not participated in the Trojan War as had the rest of Greece (Justin, *Hist. Philippicae* 28.6)."[28] Neither this appeal nor Segesta's alliance makes sense apart from the legend of Aeneas's travel to Italy.

Jane DeRose Evans observes that Romans in general began to identify

---

[22] Jan N. Bremmer and Nicholas M. Horsfall, *Roman Myth and Mythography*, Bulletin Supplement 52 (London: University of London Institute of Classical Studies, 1987), 12.

[23] Cf. Homeric Hymn 5, to Aphrodite. Erich Gruen notes that these ancient passages initially inhibited the association of Aeneas with the Romans among Greeks: Homer says Aeneas will rule over *Trojans* (implying that this will happen in *Troy*). Gruen writes, "When the link between Aeneas and the origins of Rome had been forged, the Homeric lines became an embarrassment" (*Culture and National Identity in Republican Rome*, CSCP 52 [Ithaca, NY: Cornell University Press, 1992], 12).

[24] Bremmer and Horsfall, *Roman Myth*, 21; see also Gruen, *Culture and National Identity*, 44.

[25] Gruen, *Culture and National Identity*, 27. He subsequently writes, "The Greeks hoped to capitalize on the legend; the Romans merely engaged in response and reaction" (46), which suggests that the evidence indicates, at least in the fourth and third centuries BCE, that the Aeneas–Trojan connection to Rome was emphasized not by the Romans but by the Greeks.

[26] See Gruen's extensive discussion in *Culture and National Identity*, 6–51. For Timaeus's witness, see the works cited by Gruen on 27 n. 97. According to Gruen, Timaeus's "researches aimed at confirmation and demonstration of accepted tenets" (27).

[27] Ibid., 45. See also the primary texts cited there.

[28] Jane DeRose Evans, *The Art of Persuasion: Political Propaganda from Aeneas to Brutus* (Ann Arbor: University of Michigan Press, 1992), 37. See also Gruen, *Culture and National Identity*, 45.

themselves as corporate descendants of Aeneas as early as the second century BCE.²⁹ Among the evidence she cites is a bold statement made by Rome toward the end of the Hannibalic War (218–201 BCE). With victory all but assured, the Romans moved the cult of Magna Mater, "a protective deity of the Trojans," from Mount Ida, "the birthplace of Aeneas, his refuge, and a place of assemblage before his departure," to the Palatine in Rome.³⁰ This transfer occurred in 205 BCE. According to Erich Gruen, "Allusions to Troy and the [Aeneas] legend in interstate relations cease abruptly after the early second century. They reappear only at the end of the Republic in very different circumstances."³¹ These "different circumstances" involved a shift from national to individual identification with Aeneas.

The appropriation of Aeneas's legacy and of Trojan identity reappeared during the reign of Julius Caesar. Caesar is said to have so emphasized his descent from Venus, Aeneas's mother, that "even Caesar's enemies substituted 'the descendant of Venus' for Caesar's personal name."³² By 48 BCE, after Caesar's decisive victory in the Battle of Pharsalus to end the civil war and the so-called First Triumvirate, "Caesar combined this propaganda [of descent from Venus] with a claim of descent from Aeneas, heretofore only implied in the Julian propaganda."³³ Evans notes the apparent non sequitur in this claim: "We still must answer how he managed to transform Aeneas from a generalized founder of the Roman people (as in Flamininus's inscription) to the founder of a specific family." She suggests, "The most attractive answers are Caesar's force of personality, the insistence of his claim, and the readiness of the Roman people to accept this personalized version of their national foundation story."³⁴

With the formation of the Second Triumvirate, ending the Roman Republic, the Roman state was governed by Octavian, Mark Antony, and Marcus Aemilius Lepidus. Although Octavian associated himself with Apollo, he also began advertising his descent from Aeneas during this period.³⁵ As Augustus, he not only expanded this propaganda to include public monuments in Rome, but he also promoted his genealogy throughout the empire in at least two other ways: (1) by depicting Aeneas carrying Anchises out of Troy on the reverse of coins that featured his own likeness on the obverse; and (2) by commissioning several court poets to disseminate his descent from Aeneas.³⁶ Two literary figures who were active during Augustus's reign merit special attention in this context: Virgil, for composing the

---

²⁹ Evans, *Art of Persuasion*, 37.
³⁰ Gruen, *Culture and National Identity*, 47.
³¹ Ibid., 50.
³² Evans, *Art of Persuasion*, 40. Cf. Cicero, *Fam.* 8.15; Suetonius, *Jul.* 6.1.
³³ Evans, *Art of Persuasion*, 40.
³⁴ Ibid.
³⁵ Ibid., 41–42.
³⁶ Ibid., 41–44. The poets Augustus commissioned included Virgil, Horace, Ovid, and Varro.

iconic and authoritative version of Aeneas's establishment of the Trojan people in Italy, and Dionysius of Halicarnassus, for his inability to deny it.

In the *Aeneid*, Latin's answer to Greek's *Iliad* and *Odyssey*, Virgil narrates the sea voyages of Aeneas and a remnant of Trojans across the Mediterranean and their war with the Latins in Italy. The bard explicitly identifies Augustus as the descendant of Aeneas and as the heir to the promise of an eternal empire (6.792–793; cf. 1.278–279). Virgil's epic poem enjoyed immense popularity soon after it was published in 19 BCE following the poet's premature death. "The *Aeneid* made Aeneas a national hero at Rome in a way far beyond the reach of the diplomacy and propaganda of earlier generations."[37] Outside the Roman royal court, Greek historian and rhetorician Dionysius of Halicarnassus wrote about the history of Rome; his intention, as a Greek, was to present Rome as the *Greek* city he believed it to be.[38] As such, he narrates the Hellenic origins of several Latin peoples, including some established by Heracles himself (*Ant. rom.* 1.41–44).[39] Clearly, Dionysius would have omitted any role played by Aeneas, a Trojan, in the foundation of Rome if he thought doing so would be credible. Yet "the Trojan leader's role in Rome's beginnings was too well entrenched to be discarded or ignored"—an unpalatable situation for Dionysius, indeed.[40] According to Virgil's account, Dardanus, Aeneas's ancestor who gave rise to the Trojan people, was from Etruria (central Italy).[41] Dionysius turns this scenario upside down: he claims that Dardanus was in fact from the Peloponnesus (southern Greek peninsula) and only migrated to the Troad after his homeland was flooded (*Ant. rom.* 1.60–61).[42] The case of Dionysius demonstrates that, by the end of the first century BCE, the association of Aeneas with Rome had become culturally indisputable.[43]

Greek speakers in the provinces of the Roman Empire also attest to the ubiquity of Aeneas's association with Rome. Book 11 of the Jewish collection of Sibylline

---

[37] Bremmer and Horsfall, *Roman Myth*, 24.

[38] For a robust treatment of Dionysius of Halicarnassus, see Nicolas Wiater, *The Ideology of Classicism: Language, History, and Identity in Dionysius of Halicarnassus*, UALG 105 (Berlin: de Gruyter, 2011).

[39] See ibid., 165.

[40] Gruen, *Culture and National Identity*, 7.

[41] See *Aen.* 1.378–380; 3.94–96, 167–168; 7.206–207, 240; and Gruen, *Culture and National Identity*, 7.

[42] Varro concurs with Dionysius (see Servius, *Ad Aen.* 3.167). See Yasmin Syed, *Vergil's Aeneid and the Roman Self: Subject and Nation in Literary Discourse* (Ann Arbor: University of Michigan Press, 2005), 211–14.

[43] During this period, the Latin historian Sallust made the remarkable claim that Aeneas himself founded Rome (*Bell. Cat.* 6.1), despite a nearly four-hundred-year gap between the Trojan War and Rome's founding. Toward the end of the first century CE, in his *Trojan Oration*, Dio Chrysostom also identified Aeneas as the founder of Rome in his argument that the Trojans defeated the Greeks in the Trojan War (*Troj.* 138).

Oracles, possibly written sometime early in the first century CE, not only demonstrates an awareness of Aeneas's escape from Troy and the tradition that he established Rome but also praises the bard "by whose noble mind the whole world will be educated" (i.e., Virgil; see Sib. Or. 11:163–171).[44] After describing the fall of Troy at the hands of a "wooden deceit" (11:135) and the death of Agamemnon "at the hand of a deceitful woman" (11:143), the Sibyl describes Aeneas:

> A famous child of heroes from the race and blood
> of Assaracus will rule, a mighty and brave man.
> He will come from Troy when it has been destroyed by a great fire,
> fleeing from his fatherland on account of the turmoil of Ares.
> Carrying on his shoulders his elderly father,
> holding his only son by the hand, he will perform
> a pious deed, glancing around, he who split the onslaught
> of the fire of blazing Troy, and pressing on through the throng.
> In fear he will cross the land and frightful sea.
> He will have a name of three syllables; for the first letter
> is not insignificant but reveals the supreme man.
> Then he will set up the mighty city of the Latins.
> In the fifteenth year on the depths of brine
> perishing on the waters he will meet the end of death.
> But even when he dies the nations of men will not forget him.
> For the race of this man will later rule over all
> as far as the rivers Euphrates and Tigris, in the midst
> of the land of the Assyrians, where the Parthian tarried.
> It will come to pass in future generations when all these things happen.
> (Sib. Or. 11:144–162)

The Sibyl cryptically avoids Aeneas's name; nevertheless, there is no doubt that Aeneas is the subject of these hexameters. Most telling is the reference to carrying his elderly father on his shoulders as he leaves Troy—Aeneas's iconic pose in paintings, coinage, and sculptures. The Sibyl also tells a riddle about his name (11:153–154): "Aeneas" is three syllables long and shares the first letter of his name with Adam ("the supreme man").[45] This passage is significant for the present discussion of Luke-Acts in two ways: (1) the Sibyl not only associates Aeneas with Rome but explicitly claims that Aeneas himself founded Rome, "the mighty city of the Latins"

---

[44] For this proposed date of the Sibylline Oracles, see John J. Collins, "Sibylline Oracles (Second Century B.C.–Seventh Century A.D.), *OTP* 1:317–472, here 430–32. All translations of the Sibylline Oracles are from Collins (here 437–38).

[45] There are still other clues that Aeneas is the referent: the adjective "pious" (11:150) was Virgil's favorite epithet for Aeneas; in addition to Anchises, Aeneas also (importantly) delivered his son from Troy's destruction; finally, Aeneas, in traversing from Troy to Lavinium/Rome, had to cross land and sea (a Virgilian imitation of Odysseus's adventures from Troy to Ithaca in the *Odyssey*).

(11:155);[46] (2) though the oracle is written in Greek, the writer demonstrates an acquaintance with the *Aeneid* by describing Virgil immediately following the section on Aeneas and by relating Aeneas to the Roman emperors (11:158–162).[47]

The Sibyl's knowledge of Virgil's account also raises an important issue: the need to distinguish between knowledge of the Aeneas–Rome association and knowledge of Virgil's account of the connection. According to Johannes Irmscher, the Roman Empire was bilingual early on, and the most important works, whether originally composed in Latin or Greek, were made available for those in the upper class.[48] According to Seneca, Polybius, an imperial slave, was given the task (around the year 50 CE) of translating Homer into Latin and Virgil into Greek so that they might be disseminated among monolingual individuals (*Polyb.* 8.2; 11.5–6).[49] Other textual witnesses suggest that Virgil's *Aeneid* was more well known in the Greek East than scholars generally acknowledge: a papyrus found in the ruins of Masada (ca. 73–74 CE) contains a Latin quotation of *Aen.* 4.9, and among the papyri found in Oxyrhynchus, Egypt, the *Aeneid* is either cited or referred to nine times, including a Greek paraphrase of 4.661–705 and 5.1–6.[50] Of course, the general populace did not need access to either Latin or Greek versions of the *Aeneid* in order for the *content* of Virgil's epic to enter into the cultural consciousness of the Mediterranean world. Irmscher's contribution is important in that it explains *one* of the ways that the *Aeneid* was disseminated in the Greek-speaking parts of the Roman Empire. Arguably more important (and effective) were visual representations and performances. Ultimately, my argument here does not depend on whether the story of the *Aeneid* was known by those who could not understand Latin. Although Loveday Alexander does not address the issue of interpreting the Aeneas account in Acts 9, her statement is relevant here:

> The connection between Aeneas and Rome is nowhere made in Homer, but it was not Vergil's invention: Hellenistic and Roman traditions had completed the loop by the third century BCE, bringing Aeneas and the Trojan remnant to Italy and combining the post-Homeric story with Latin and Roman foundation myths. The story, the myth, in other words, could be known independently of the epic poem which became its most famous and successful carrier. To put it another way, the cultural hypotext may not be a text (in the obvious literary sense) at all.[51]

---

[46] Interestingly, cf. Ovid, *Ars* 3.337.

[47] Of course, knowledge of Julian descent from Aeneas need not be derived from Virgil.

[48] Johannes Irmscher, "Vergil in der griechischen Antike," *Klio* 67 (1985): 281–85, here 281–82.

[49] See Marianne Palmer Bonz, *The Past as Legacy: Luke-Acts and Ancient Epic* (Minneapolis: Fortress, 2000), 24–25.

[50] Jan M. Ziolkowski and Michael C. J. Putnam, eds., *The Virgilian Tradition: The First Fifteen Hundred Years* (New Haven: Yale University Press, 2008), 44.

[51] Loveday Alexander, *Acts in Its Ancient Literary Context: A Classicist Looks at the Acts of the Apostles*, LNTS 298 (New York: T&T Clark International, 2005), 170–71.

If anything certain can be drawn from this long review of Aeneas's association with Rome, it is that inhabitants of the ancient Mediterranean world did not need to know Virgil's *Aeneid* in order to be aware of Aeneas's association with Rome.

Roman claims of descent from Aeneas did not cease along with the Julian dynasty. For instance, Statius, a court poet for Domitian writing toward the end of the first century CE, attempted Virgil's strategy, portraying Domitian as a direct descendant of Aeneas and as the true heir of Aeneas's eternal empire (*Silv.* 4.3.128–133). Unlike earlier Flavian propagandists, Statius does not present Domitian as the fulfillment of Augustan ideals; Augustus goes unmentioned.[52] Hadrian similarly identified Trajan as "the descendant of Aeneas" (Anth. Pal. 6.332). In this literary and political context, I conclude that it would have been impossible for ancient readers to hear the name Aeneas and not think of Rome (similar to how Americans in the twenty-first century cannot hear the name Michael Jordan without thinking of basketball).

Accounting for the cultural freight carried by the name Aeneas and its strategic placement within Luke's narrative can influence how readers understand the macro-structure of Acts and its relation to the Gospel of Luke. The structural considerations that follow reveal how reading "Aeneas" as a literary signpost for Rome coheres with the macro-structure of Acts.[53] Luke's Gospel and the book of Acts share remarkably similar macro-structures.[54] After Luke's prologue to "Theophilus" (1:1–4), the birth narratives (1:5–2:52), an account of John the Baptist's ministry (3:1–20), and Jesus's baptism (3:21–22) and genealogy (3:23–38), there are three main sections in the gospel. The first section (4:1–9:50) focuses on Jesus's ministry in and around Galilee. Luke marks the transition to the gospel's second section, Jesus's journey to Jerusalem (9:51–19:27), in a conspicuous manner. In Luke 9:51, the narrator explains, "But when the days drew near for him to be taken up, he himself set his face to go to Jerusalem." He then reiterates his point: the Samaritans did not receive him "because his face was going to Jerusalem" (9:53b). Luke's identification of Jerusalem as the "city of destiny" is made all the more clear when Luke's account is compared to that of antecedent gospels: Jerusalem "is here explicitly mentioned (9:51), in contradistinction to Mark 10:1 or Matt 19:1."[55] This purposeful gesture sets the tone for all of Luke's second section: although he does

---

[52] See Bonz, *Past as Legacy*, 69–74.

[53] To be sure, the analysis that follows does not represent the only credible way to delineate the macro-structures of Luke or Acts.

[54] On the macro-structures of Luke and Acts, see Charles H. Talbert, *Literary Patterns, Theological Themes and the Genre of Luke-Acts*, SBLMS 20 (Missoula, MT: Scholars Press, 1974); Talbert, *Reading Acts: A Literary and Theological Commentary on the Acts of the Apostles*, Reading the New Testament (New York: Crossroad, 1997); Keener, *Acts*, 1:550–81; Pervo, *Acts*, 20–21. This article's contribution to this discussion is addressed below, namely, the structuring role played by Acts 9:32–43.

[55] Joseph A. Fitzmyer, *The Gospel according to Luke: Introduction, Translation, and Notes*, 2 vols., AB 28, 28A (Garden City, NY: Doubleday, 1981–1985), 1:824 (cf. 827).

not travel directly to Jerusalem, his circuitous meanderings never lose sight of this goal. The audience is reminded of it by the narrator twice (13:22; 17:11) and by Jesus's own speech once (18:31). The third section of Luke's Gospel (19:28–24:53) opens in this way: "And after saying these things, he went on ahead, going up into Jerusalem" (19:28). This final section narrates Jesus's Jerusalem activity, namely, his teachings in the temple, trial, passion, resurrection, and ascension.[56]

Commentators have well documented the progressively expansive nature of the plot of Acts.[57] The primary impetus for such a reading is the commission of the resurrected Jesus to his disciples in Acts 1:8, "You will be my witnesses in Jerusalem, in all Judea and Samaria, and to the end of the earth." The first three referents are straightforward enough; the final one is ambiguous. Concerning this final phrase, Pervo writes,

> As a geographical expression, the location of this limit depends on the extent of geographical knowledge and the orientation of the speaker or narrator. The latter contributes to the metaphorical sense of "far, far away." The range of geographical options is wide. The two locations most applicable to Acts are Ethiopia and Rome, the former because of the symbolism of 8:26–39, the latter because it is the geographical destination of the book. It is unlikely that Luke means the phrase in a particularly literal sense.[58]

Pervo argues that the phrase carries a sense of "missions" in Acts—in particular, the gentile mission—since the phrase was also used to describe the exploits of Heracles and Alexander the Great.[59] The final element of Jesus's commission, then, appears to have two primary meanings: first, it refers literally to the broad horizon of the known world and its inhabitants (e.g., as symbolized by Ethiopia); and, second, it refers to Rome, the center of the Mediterranean world and perhaps a symbol of the world's entirety.[60] Both meanings convey a sense of mission. The narrative that follows the proemium of Acts thus exhibits the following structure, related both to geography and to ethnic and religious identities. As in Luke's Gospel, the text can be divided into three sections. In the first section (Acts 1:15–9:31), the narrative is concerned primarily with the mission to Jews. Geographically, the narrative begins where Luke's Gospel left off: in Jerusalem (1:1–8:1a). The mission extends to Jews in the rest of Judea and in Samaria (8:1b–25), even to those *from* the ends of the earth (2:5–13; 8:26–39). Luke closes this first section in 9:31, "Meanwhile the church throughout Judea, Galilee, and Samaria had peace and was built

---

[56] Cf. François Bovon, *Luke: A Commentary on the Gospel of Luke*, 3 vols., Hermeneia (Minneapolis: Fortress, 2002–2013), 1:2–4; Bonz, *Past as Legacy*, 138.

[57] E.g., Barrett, *Acts of the Apostles*, 1:49; Fitzmyer, *Acts of the Apostles*, 119.

[58] Pervo, *Acts*, 44.

[59] Ibid.

[60] Bonz identifies Rome as the "proleptic symbol for the ends of the earth" (*Past as Legacy*, 173; cf. 138). See also Fitzmyer, *Acts of the Apostles*, 206–7; Pss. Sol. 8:15.

up. Living in the fear of the Lord and in the comfort of the Holy Spirit, it increased in numbers."

The second section (9:32–21:16) involves the opening and progressive expansion of the gentile mission as well as the realization of Rome as the "city of destiny" in Acts. On the one hand, the gentile mission explicitly begins with Luke's account of Peter and Cornelius (10:1–11:18); this episode is prefaced by a pair of miracle narratives (9:32–35 and 36–43). The subsequent progressive realization of the inclusion of gentiles is highlighted by the Jerusalem Council (15:1–35) and the evolving emphasis in Paul's mission, with his experience of opposition from some Jews and the redirection of his mission toward gentiles. In the assessment of Marianne Palmer Bonz, the mission to the Jews effectively ends as early as Acts 19.[61] On the other hand, the geographic *telos* of the book of Acts becomes explicit in this second section: Paul "must see Rome" (19:21).[62]

The third and final section of Acts (21:17–28:31), bearing some resemblance to the final section of Luke's Gospel, recounts Paul's trials in Jerusalem and Caesarea and his sea voyage to Rome, including a shipwreck at Malta. Although the narrative foregrounds these activities, the two trajectories that began with the Petrine narratives in Acts 9:32–11:18 continue. For instance, Paul concludes his *apologia* before a crowd in Jerusalem by relating the words spoken to him by the risen Jesus, "Go, for I will send you far away to the gentiles" (22:21).[63] Paul's speech to the Jews in Rome is a fitting capstone to Luke's foundation narrative: "Let it be known to you then that this salvation of God has been sent to the gentiles; they will listen" (28:28). Luke thus concludes the book of Acts with Paul in Rome having decided to take the gospel (exclusively?) to gentiles.[64]

Acts 9:32–43 thus occupies a critical place in the narrative of Acts, not to mention in the whole of Luke's *Doppelwerk*. It functions as the narrative's gateway to the gentile mission and to Rome itself. Many commentators, however, locate the significance of Acts 9:32–43 exclusively in its explanation of how Peter came to be

---

[61] Bonz, *Past as Legacy*, 166. Cf. Acts 19:9; 22:17–21.

[62] Even before Rome is explicitly mentioned, Bonz argues that Acts 16–19 "is clearly structured to illuminate this new direction as the ultimate intention of the divine plan. With the exception of chapter 17 ... Paul's missionary efforts are concentrated on three provincial cities: Philippi, Corinth, and Ephesus. In the narrative's time, as well as in Luke's own time, Corinth and Philippi each had the status of Roman colonies, and Ephesus was the seat of the Roman governor for the wealthy and important senatorial province of Asia" (*Past as Legacy*, 167).

[63] Note the twofold emphasis again: geographic ("far away") and religious/ethnic ("to the gentiles").

[64] For the argument that Paul's post-Acts mission is oriented exclusively toward gentiles, see Jacob Jervell, *Luke and the People of God: A New Look at Luke-Acts* (Minneapolis: Augsburg, 1972), 62–64; Jack T. Sanders, *The Jews in Luke-Acts* (Philadelphia: Fortress, 1987), 296–99; Pervo, *Acts*, 681. For the argument that Paul's post-Acts mission includes Jews, see Robert C. Tannehill, *The Shape of Luke's Story: Essays on Luke-Acts* (Eugene, OR: Cascade, 2005), 105–65; Tannehill, *Narrative Unity*, 2:344–57.

near Caesarea for his encounter with Cornelius. For example, Pervo writes, "The two acts of Peter in 9:32–43 bring him into proximity to Caesarea."⁶⁵ But if the purpose of Acts 9:32–43 was merely to situate Peter in proximity to Caesarea, Luke could have instead skipped these narratives and begun 10:1 the way he begins 9:32: "Now as Peter went here and there among all of them, he came down also to Caesarea. In Caesarea there was a man...." As it is, the narratives of Peter healing Aeneas in Lydda and raising Tabitha in Joppa bridge the gap between Luke's summary statement in Acts 9:31 and the Cornelius narrative in which a Roman soldier becomes the first gentile to gain inclusion in the kingdom of God in Luke-Acts. I propose that this bridge is constructed using two metonyms: "Aeneas" and "Joppa."

The first major section of the book of Acts concludes with the notice that "the church throughout Judea, Galilee, and Samaria had peace and was built up" (9:31). Of all the so-called success summaries in the book of Acts, 9:31 is remarkable for the way in which it evokes Jesus's commission in Acts 1:8: the disciples are to be Jesus's witnesses "in Jerusalem, in all Judea and Samaria, and to the end of the earth."⁶⁶ For the reader who recalls Jesus's commission, the summary of Acts 9:31 raises a question: what about "the end of the earth"? The audience resumes Luke's narrative and immediately encounters Peter healing an eight-year paralytic named Aeneas. The narrative thus answers the reader's question: in the book of Acts, as far as the movement of Jesus's followers is concerned, Rome will represent "the end of the earth."⁶⁷ That the narrative does in fact end in Rome confirms the credibility of reading Aeneas's name as a metonym for the imperial capital, all the more so considering its proximity to the summary in Acts 9:31. The inclusion of Cornelius, a Roman soldier from Italy, in Acts 10:1–11:18 reinforces the Aeneas–Rome trajectory. This forms a piece of the narrative arc extending from Acts 9:32–35 through Paul's travels to Roman cities (Philippi, Corinth, and Ephesus) all the way to his arrival in Rome.

---

⁶⁵ Pervo, *Acts*, 251–52. He adds, however, that these narratives "are dense with references to the stories of Elijah/Elisha (1 Kgs 17:17–24; 2 Kgs 4:32–37 [Acts 9:36–42]), Jesus (Luke 5:18–26; [7:11–17]; 8:40–56), and Paul (14:8–12; 20:7–13)" (252). See also Barrett, *Acts of the Apostles*, 1:478: "We know that the story of Cornelius was of great importance to [Luke]; he regarded it as the beginning of the Gentile mission (15.7). Here he is preparing for it"; Fitzmyer, *Acts of the Apostles*, 443: "Luke's account of Peter's tour of ministry in Lydda and Joppa is intended as a buildup to his coming missionary activity in the conversion of Cornelius and his household"; and Daniel Marguerat, *Les Actes des Apôtres*, 2 vols., CNT 5 (Geneva: Labor et Fides, 2007–2015), 1:348. Moreover, Pervo argues that 9:32–11:18 constitutes a single literary unit (*Acts*, 251–52); so also Josef Zmijewski, *Die Apostelgeschichte*, RNT (Regensburg: Pustet, 1994), 395–96. See also Wilfried Eckey, *Die Apostelgeschichte: Der Weg des Evangeliums von Jerusalem nach Rom*, 2 vols. (Neukirchen-Vluyn: Neukirchener Verlag, 2000), 1:226–27; Etienne Trocmé, *Le "Livre des Actes" et l'histoire* (Paris: Presses Universitaires de France, 1957), 169.

⁶⁶ Other "summaries of success" include Acts 6:7, 12:24, 16:5, 19:20, 28:31.

⁶⁷ This use of "Aeneas" can perhaps be read as a less explicit equivalent of Luke 9:51–53 for the book of Acts.

The narrative of Peter raising Tabitha from the dead (Acts 9:36–43) can be read as initiating a second literary trajectory, that of gentile inclusion, via the repeated mention of Joppa. It may also reinforce the earlier Aeneas–Rome trajectory. Luke repeats the name Joppa four times in Acts 9:36–43 (162 words) and six more times in the Cornelius account (10:1–11:18).[68] Even accounting for the need to reestablish the setting in a narrative that moves to and fro, "Joppa" is repeated with an uncommonly high frequency compared to other city names in Luke-Acts. More typically, Luke names a city when his protagonists arrive and leave. For example, although Aeneas's town, Lydda, is mentioned with a higher frequency in Acts 9:32–35 (62 words) than Joppa in 9:36–43, there are only two iterations: Peter comes down to Lydda (9:32), and, after Aeneas is healed, Luke notes that the residents of Lydda turned to the Lord (9:35). Similarly, after Paul arrives in Athens (17:15), Luke names Athens—obviously a name carrying cultural freight—only twice more: to indicate that Paul was waiting for Silas and Timothy to meet him there (17:16) and to indicate that Paul left (18:1).[69] So why does Luke call the readers' attention to Joppa with such uncharacteristic frequency? According to one rhetorical handbook, "reiteration of the same word makes a deep impression upon the hearer and inflicts a major wound upon the opposition—as if a weapon should repeatedly pierce the same part of the body" (Rhet. her. 4.28 [Caplan, LCL]). The "wound" inflicted by the narrative can be identified by attending to the cultural and literary freight carried by the name Joppa. I suggest that the repetition evokes the Jonah narrative, preparing the audience for Luke's characterization of Peter in Acts 10:1–11:18 and for the inclusion of gentiles more generally.[70]

Two themes of Jonah's mission are particularly relevant to Acts 9:36–11:18: Jonah's commission to preach to gentiles and his reluctance to actually do it. Joppa was the port city to which Jonah fled in order to avoid preaching to the Ninevites (Jonah 1:3). In Acts 9:36–43, Luke inflicts, so some rhetorical handbooks might say,

---

[68] Acts 9:36, 38, 42, 43; 10:5, 8, 23, 32; 11:5, 13.

[69] Luke also mentions Athenians in Acts 17:21, 22. There are 405 words in Acts 17:15–18:1.

[70] See Robert W. Wall, "Peter, 'Son' of Jonah: The Conversion of Cornelius in the Context of Canon," JSNT 29 (1987): 79–90, https://doi.org/10.1177/0142064x8700902904. According to Wall, some scholars have interpreted the Cornelius episode as an imitation—or, in Wall's terminology, "theo-logic" parallelism or "comparative midrash" (82)—of Jonah's gentile mission. Wall outlines six sequential parallels between the book of Jonah and Acts 10–11: (1) the location of Joppa (Jonah 1:3; Acts 9:43); (2) the symbolic use of three that ends the reluctance of the prophets (Jonah 2:1; Acts 10:16); (3) God's command to "arise and go" (Jonah 3:2; Acts 10:20); (4) the belief of the gentiles (Jonah 3:5; Acts 10:43); (5) the hostile response to gentile conversions (Jonah 4:1; Acts 11:2 [10:14]); and (6) God's rebuke of the hostile response (Jonah 4:2–11; Acts 11:17–18 [15:13–21]) (80). Distinctive elements among these parallels include the city of Joppa and verbal parallels.

Based on Matt 12:39–41 and Luke 11:29–32, we can infer that early Christians, including Luke's implied audience, were familiar with Jonah and associated him particularly with sitting in the belly of a fish for three days and with a reluctant ministry to gentiles.

a Joppa-shaped wound on his auditors, situating Peter in Joppa and evoking the thought world of Jonah. It is no surprise, then, that Peter is characterized as a *reluctant* missionary to gentiles in Acts 10. Peter is still in Joppa when Cornelius sends for him (10:8). Before the arrival of Cornelius's emissaries, Peter has a vision about clean and unclean animals in which he refuses to eat the unclean animals three times (10:10–16, 11:5–10), a metaphor for gentile inclusion (10:28, 34–35, 47; 11:18). The Lukan Peter is remarkably more obedient than Jonah, however. Whereas Jonah left Joppa on a ship to avoid preaching to gentiles, after his vision Peter abandons his reluctance in Joppa and initiates a gentile mission. The Tabitha narrative thus commences a second literary arc—that of gentile inclusion—which stretches all the way to the end of Acts.

By evoking the thought world of the Jonah narrative, Acts 9:36–43 can also be read as reinforcing the narrative arc established in the preceding passage: the destination of Rome. The entire Jonah story revolves around the so-called prophet's mission to preach to gentiles in the city of Nineveh (Jonah 1:2). Nineveh, of course, was the capital of the Assyrian Empire, during whose rule Jonah's story is set. In addition to the idea of ministry to gentiles, therefore, a reference to Jonah can evoke the narrative's imperial logic: movement to the capital of the empire to preach to gentiles. If Luke's characters play the role of Jonah, the reader can expect that the mission of the kingdom of God will take at least one of them to the capital of the current empire: Rome.

The final two chapters of Acts bring the narrative arcs initiated in Acts 9:32–43 to a close. Although some scholars have puzzled over the inclusion of Paul's perilous voyage and shipwreck in Acts 27, this chapter can be read as yet another instantiation of both literary arcs.[71] Scholars have long noted the parallels that Acts 27 shares with other ancient narratives, particularly the book of Jonah and Homer's *Odyssey*.[72] In Acts 9, the gratuitous repetition of Joppa evokes the thought world of Jonah; Peter soon thereafter plays the role of the eponymous prophet, resisting but then initiating a ministry to gentiles. In Acts 27, Paul plays the role of Jonah, getting caught in a dramatic storm while voyaging across the Mediterranean. Whereas Jonah embarked on a Mediterranean ship in order to avoid preaching to gentiles

---

[71] See Richard I. Pervo, *Profit with Delight: The Literary Genre of the Acts of the Apostles* (Philadelphia: Fortress, 1987), 51. Pervo suggests that, if Acts is a history or biography, the attention given to this account might have been better served elsewhere. Pervo, of course, reads the Acts narrative alongside ancient novels, where accounts of shipwrecks are a dime a dozen.

[72] For Acts 27:1–28:10 and the *Odyssey*, see Dennis R. MacDonald, "The Shipwrecks of Odysseus and Paul," *NTS* 45 (1999): 88–107, https://doi.org/10.1017/S0028688598000885; Susan Marie Praeder, "Acts 27:1–28:16: Sea Voyages in Ancient Literature and the Theology of Luke-Acts," *CBQ* 46 (1984): 683–706; Alexander, *Literary Context*, 175. For Acts 27:1–28:10 and Jonah, see Reinhard Kratz, *Rettungswunder: Motiv-, traditions-, und formkritische Aufarbeitung einer biblischen Gattung*, EHS 23.123 (Frankfurt am Main: Lang, 1979), 320–50; Pervo, *Acts*, 645, 652, 659, 666–67; Alexander, *Literary Context*, 84–85; James M. Beresford, "The Significance of the Fast in Acts 27:9," *NovT* 58 (2016): 155–66, https://doi.org/10.1163/15685365-12341519.

in the capital of the Assyrian Empire, Paul—in Roman custody—sails across the sea precisely in order to preach to gentiles in the capital of the Roman Empire (cf. Acts 23:11).

The parallels with the Jonah narrative notwithstanding, the presence of Homeric vocabulary is nigh undeniable.[73] According to Dennis R. MacDonald, the stories of Paul and Odysseus "share nautical images and vocabulary, the appearance of a goddess or angel assuring safety, the riding of planks, the arrival of the hero on an island among hospitable strangers, the mistaking of the hero as a god, and the sending of him on his way."[74] Nevertheless, Paul's sea voyages in Acts, beginning in Troas (16:11) and ending in Rome, recall another cultural figure: Aeneas.[75] Read in this way, Paul's journey to Rome becomes a fitting end to Luke's narrative, pregnant with potential for God's kingdom.[76] Aeneas traveled from Troy to Italy in order to establish the foundations of the Roman Empire; Paul travels from Troas to Rome with a mission to proclaim the kingdom of God as a witness to Jesus.

In Acts 28:14, Paul arrives in Rome. Although under house arrest, Paul is able to meet with the local Jewish leaders. After the Roman Jews offer a predictably mixed reception of Paul's message, Paul proclaims, "Let it be known to you then that this salvation of God has been sent to the gentiles; they will listen" (28:28).[77] Then the book of Acts ends with Paul in Rome welcoming "all who came to him" (28:30), underscoring the permanence of the inclusion of gentiles within his ministry. Thus conclude both literary arcs initiated in Acts 9:32–43.

Luke's tandem of healing miracles about Aeneas and Tabitha signals the

---

[73] Cf. F. F. Bruce, *Commentary on the Book of Acts* (Grand Rapids: Eerdmans, 1965), 498.

[74] MacDonald, "Shipwrecks of Odysseus and Paul," 88.

[75] Virgil's version of Aeneas's sea voyages and shipwreck imitates those of Odysseus in Homer's *Odyssey*. See Dennis R. MacDonald, *Luke and Vergil: Imitations of Classical Greek Literature*, New Testament and Greek Literature 2 (Lanham, MD: Rowman & Littlefield, 2015), 153–55. Of course, Virgil did not invent the story of Aeneas's movement from Troy to the Italian site of Rome. On the identification of Troas with Troy, see Suetonius, *Iul.* 1.79. See also Andrew Erskine, *Troy between Greece and Rome: Local Tradition and Imperial Power* (Oxford: Oxford University Press, 2001); Bart J. Koet, "Im Schatten des Aeneas: Paulus in Troas (Apg. 16,8–10)," in *Luke and His Readers: Festschrift A. Denaux*, ed. R. Bieringer, G. Van Belle, and J. Verheyden, BETL 187 (Leuven: Leuven University Press, 2005), 432–36; Koet, "It Started with a Dream: Paul's Dream (Acts 16,9–10) and Aeneas as a Biblical Example of Dreams as Intercultural Legitimation Strategy," *Dreaming* 18 (2008): 267–79, https://doi.org/10.1037/a0014084.

[76] On the ending of Acts, see Pervo, *Acts*, 688–90; Daniel Marguerat, *The First Christian Historian: Writing the 'Acts of the Apostles,'* SNTSMS 121 (Cambridge: Cambridge University Press, 2002), 205–30, https://doi.org/10.1017/CBO9780511488061.011; Hermann J. Hauser, *Strukturen der Abschlußerzählung der Apostelgeschichte (Apg 28,16–41)*, AnBib 86 (Rome: Pontifical Biblical Institute, 1979); Charles B. Puskas, *The Conclusion of Luke-Acts: The Significance of Acts 28:16–31* (Eugene, OR: Pickwick, 2009). Pervo judges the ending a disappointment, both from a literary perspective and as a work of history/biography (*Acts*, 688).

[77] See Joseph B. Tyson, *Images of Judaism in Luke-Acts* (Columbia: University of South Carolina Press, 1992), 174–78.

agenda for the remaining narrative in Acts. After providing a satisfying closure in Acts 9:31 to the Jewish mission in Judea and Samaria, Luke narrates the healing of a man named Aeneas and the resuscitation of a woman in Joppa. The story of Aeneas in Acts 9:32–35 suggests that the narrative will find its ultimate goal in the city of Rome; the story of Tabitha in 9:36–43, situated in Joppa, suggests that the mission will continue by expanding—even if the missionary is at first reluctant—to include gentiles, while also recalling the idea of ministry in the imperial capital.[78] These narrative threads reappear throughout the remainder of Acts: the mission to the gentiles is inaugurated with the extended narrative about Peter and (the Roman) Cornelius (Acts 10–11); Paul arrives in Rome in Acts 28 and proclaims that "this salvation of God has been sent to the gentiles" (28:28). Perhaps it is suggestive that a more coherent reading of Acts can be achieved by attending to the cultural freight carried by certain names, particularly in the case of Aeneas. Observing how a freighted Roman name is used to structure Luke's narrative opens a new line of inquiry into the dialectical relationship between Luke and the Roman Empire: exploring the ways that Luke constructed his narrative about the kingdom of God by reference to the language and imagery of Roman self-representation, in addition to the Septuagint. Such a literary strategy might even seem intuitive, communicating about the kingdom of God in a way that was readily comprehensible to a broad Mediterranean audience.

[78] To be sure, reading "Aeneas" and "Joppa" as structural metonyms does not preclude additional interpretations of these narratives. Intertextual and intratextual comparisons are particularly important in these passages. Cf. Pervo, *Acts*, 252.

New in Biblical Studies

WOMANIST MIDRASH

A REINTRODUCTION TO THE WOMEN OF THE TORAH AND THE THRONE

WILDA C. GAFNEY

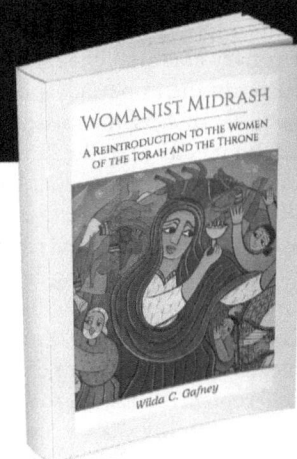

Paper • $35.00

"Gafney deftly deploys what she refers to uniquely as a womanist midrash (combining seriously impressive scholarship, a black womanist reading lens, and the inspiration of midrashic sages) to question and, best of all, fill in blanks to read women back into scripture as divine agents who resisted, persisted, subverted, disrupted and reconstituted the biblical (and the modern!) world order."

—Dr. Renita J. Weems, author of *Just a Sister Away: A Womanist Vision of Women's Relationships in the Bible*

Also Available

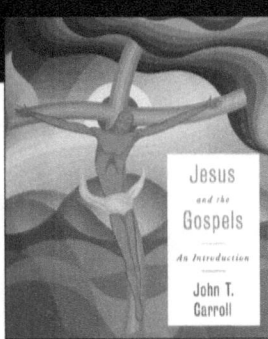

A Handbook to Old Testament Exegesis
William P. Brown
Paper • $35.00

Jesus and the Gospels An Introduction
John T. Carroll
Paper • $40.00

WJK WESTMINSTER JOHN KNOX PRESS
www.wjkbooks.com | 1.800.523.1631

Building Character on the Road to Emmaus: Lukan Characterization in Contemporary Literary Perspective

MICHAL BETH DINKLER
mb.dinkler@yale.edu
Yale University, New Haven, CT 06520

Despite the recent spate of scholarly publications related to characterization in New Testament narratives, no consensus has been reached. Scholars cannot agree on whether Luke's Jesus is characterized primarily as a teacher, as the Messiah, or as a rival to Caesar. Neither can scholars agree on whether Luke's disciples are flat paradigms of positive or negative behavior or on whether Luke liberates, oppresses, or sends "double messages" about women, the poor, and those who need healing. Some read Luke's religious and political authorities as uniformly negative "stock" characters, while others contend that they are more nuanced and complex. Contemporary theorists of characterization outside of biblical studies have focused on different questions from those typically asked by New Testament scholars. I contend that literary theorists' proposed solutions to their questions can profitably shift our considerations of characterization in New Testament narratives. This article proceeds in three movements. First, I sketch several trends in New Testament studies of characterization. Second, I describe three theoretical premises shared by many contemporary literary theorists regarding characterization. Finally, I consider how taking these literary-theoretical orientations as points of departure can shift the terms of our discussions of New Testament characterization. The illustrative text throughout is Luke 24:13–35, in which the risen Jesus meets the disciple Cleopas and his anonymous companion on the road to Emmaus.

The past several years have seen a spate of scholarly publications related to characterization in the canonical gospels, and the trend shows no signs of

My thanks go to Jerry Camery-Hoggatt, Stephen Moore, Scott Elliott, Elizabeth Struthers Malbon, Cornelis Bennema, and the anonymous *JBL* reviewer for their incisive engagements with this article. I also wish to thank those who offered helpful feedback on oral presentations of this work, including the members of the Columbia New Testament Seminar, the SBL Book of Acts and Gospel of Luke sections, and Yale University's Greco-Roman Lunch.

abating.¹ With respect to the Gospel of Luke, scholars agree that Luke's Jesus is defined in part by other characters' interactions with him. Critics cannot agree, however, on whether Luke's Jesus is primarily a teacher, a Messiah, or a rival to Caesar. Neither can scholars agree on whether Luke's disciples are flat paradigms of positive or negative behavior or on whether Luke liberates, oppresses, or sends "double messages" about women, the poor, and those who need healing.² Some read Luke's religious and political authorities as uniformly negative "stock" characters, while others contend that they are more nuanced and complex; οἱ Ἰουδαῖοι remain an especially contested character group.³ Such disagreements are compounded by the fact that scholars often do not share the same theoretical and methodological starting points, a situation exacerbated by geographical and institutional distance.⁴ Currently, scholarship on Lukan characterization is lively, but it can also be cacophonous.

Contemporary theorists of characterization in the field of literary studies have focused on different questions from those typically asked by New Testament scholars. I contend that literary theorists' proposed solutions to their questions can profitably shift our considerations of characterization in ancient narratives such as the gospels. This article proceeds in three movements. First, I will sketch several trends

---

¹ The following were published just in the past few years: Frank E. Dicken and Julia A. Snyder, eds., *Character and Characterization in Luke-Acts*, LNTS 548 (London: Bloomsbury T&T Clark, 2016); Christopher W. Skinner and Matthew Ryan Hauge, eds., *Character Studies and the Gospel of Mark*, LNTS 483 (London: Bloomsbury T&T Clark, 2015); Frank Dicken, *Herod as a Composite Character in Luke-Acts*, WUNT 2/375 (Tübingen: Mohr Siebeck, 2014); Cornelis Bennema, *Encountering Jesus: Character Studies in the Gospel of John*, 2nd ed. (Minneapolis: Augsburg, 2014); Bennema, *A Theory of Character in New Testament Narrative* (Minneapolis: Fortress, 2014); Steven A. Hunt, D. Francois Tolmie, and Ruben Zimmermann, eds., *Character Studies in the Fourth Gospel: Narrative Approaches to Seventy Figures in John*, WUNT 314 (Tübingen: Mohr Siebeck, 2013); D. Keith Campbell, *Of Heroes and Villains: The Influence of the Psalmic Lament on Synoptic Characterization* (Eugene, OR: Wipf & Stock, 2013); Christopher W. Skinner, ed., *Characters and Characterization in the Gospel of John*, LNTS 461 (London: Bloomsbury T&T Clark, 2013).

² See Turid Karlsen Seim, *The Double Message: Patterns of Gender in Luke-Acts*, SNTW (Edinburgh: T&T Clark, 1994). A more recent adjudication is F. Scott Spencer, *Salty Wives, Spirited Mothers, and Savvy Widows: Capable Women of Purpose and Persistence in Luke's Gospel* (Grand Rapids: Eerdmans, 2012).

³ Key works include David Gowler, *Host, Guest, Enemy, and Friend: Portraits of the Pharisees in Luke and Acts*, ESEC 2 (New York: Lang, 1991); Jack Dean Kingsbury, "The Pharisees in Luke-Acts," in *The Four Gospels, 1992: Festschrift Frans Neirynck*, ed. F. Van Segbroeck et al., 3 vols., BETL 100 (Leuven: Leuven University Press, 1992), 2:1497–1512; Joseph B. Tyson, *Luke, Judaism, and the Scholars: Critical Approaches to Luke-Acts* (Columbia: University of South Carolina Press, 1999).

⁴ See Christopher W. Skinner, "The Study of Character(s) in Gospel of Mark: A Survey of Research from Wrede to the Performance Critics (1901–2014)," in Skinner and Hauge, *Character Studies and the Gospel of Mark*, 3–34, here 30.

in studies of characterization in New Testament scholarship.[5] Second, I will describe three theoretical premises shared by many contemporary literary theorists regarding characterization. Finally, I will consider how taking these literary-theoretical orientations as points of departure can shift the terms of our discussions of characterization in the Gospel of Luke. The illustrative text will be Luke 24:13–35, in which the risen Jesus meets the disciple Cleopas and his anonymous companion (perhaps his wife) on the road to Emmaus.

The cacophony in discussions of Lukan characterization becomes a bit less harsh if we listen from within a wider disciplinary context. Unsurprisingly, many of the debates in Lukan scholarship stem from, echo, or respond to repeated refrains from the field of New Testament studies more broadly. Therefore, before turning specifically to Lukan characterization, I wish briefly to sketch a picture of the *status quaestionis* in New Testament scholarship.

I. Characterization Theories in New Testament Scholarship

In restricting my focus to scholarship on the gospels and Acts, I do not mean to imply that there is something distinctive about characterization in canonical texts. Neither do I mean to reify the categories used by the scholars to whom I refer (e.g., "New Testament characterization," "gospel characterization," or "biblical characterization"). As a literary phenomenon, characterization is instantiated and functions similarly across various ancient narratives (canonical or otherwise); many scholars, particularly classicists, are doing important comparative work that challenges New Testament scholars' tendency to privilege this one set of texts as exceptional literarily.[6]

---

[5] In the large body of secondary literature, foundational works include P. Létourneau and M. Talbot, eds., *Et vous, qui dites-vous que je suis? La gestion des personnages dans les récits bibliques* (Paris: Mediaspaul, 2006); David Rhoads and Kari Syreeni, eds., *Characterization in the Gospels: Reconceiving Narrative Criticism*, JSNTSup 184 (Sheffield: Sheffield Academic, 1999); John A. Darr, *On Character Building: The Reader and the Rhetoric of Characterization in Luke-Acts*, Literary Currents in Biblical Interpretation (Louisville: Westminster John Knox, 1992); Elizabeth Struthers Malbon and Adele Berlin, eds., *Characterization in Biblical Literature*, Semeia 63 (Atlanta: Scholars Press, 1993).

[6] I can only gesture toward such studies; engaging them directly would take us too far afield here. Some scholars consider specific genres or corpora, while others treat the same figure across multiple ancient texts. On the former, see, e.g., Koen De Temmerman, ed., *Crafting Characters: Heroes and Heroines in the Ancient Greek Novel* (Oxford: Oxford University Press, 2014); Luke Pitcher, "Characterization in Ancient Historiography," in *A Companion to Greek and Roman Historiography*, ed. John Marincola, Blackwell's Companions to the Ancient World (Oxford: Blackwell, 2007), 102–17; Richard Thompson, "Reading beyond the Text, Part II: Literary

It is ironic, given many New Testament scholars' reluctance to work with ancient narratives outside the canon, that comparisons with contemporary literature have been so seamlessly appropriated in discussions of "biblical characterization."[7] During the latter half of the twentieth century, treatments of characterization by scholars of the New Testament presupposed literary critic E. M. Forster's influential flat/round distinction (which is itself based on modern novels).[8] Scholars in the earliest camp of literary-minded biblical critics argued that, *unlike* round Hebrew Bible characters,[9] figures in the New Testament, following conventions of Hellenistic characterization, are generally flat.[10] Cornelis Bennema's 2014 summary of the *status quaestionis* points toward this dichotomy:

> Many scholars perceive character in the Hebrew Bible (where characters can develop) to be radically different from that in ancient Greek literature (where characters are supposedly consistent ethical types).... The majority of scholars regard most if not all [New Testament] characters as "flat" or "types."[11]

Bennema's account, however, is misleading. While it is true that in *early* treatments of characterization in the gospels and Acts, one finds with remarkable regularity

---

Creativity and Characterization in Narrative Religious Texts of the Greco-Roman World," *ARC: The Journal of the Faculty of Religious Studies, McGill University* 29 (2001): 81–122; Christopher Pelling, ed., *Characterization and Individuality in Greek Literature* (Oxford: Clarendon, 1990); on the latter, see Finn Damgaard, *Rewriting Peter as an Intertextual Character in the Canonical Gospels*, Copenhagen International Seminar (London: Routledge, 2016); Timothy Wiarda, *Peter in the Gospels: Pattern, Personality, and Relationship*, WUNT 2/127 (Tübingen: Mohr Siebeck, 2000); Helen K. Bond, *Pontius Pilate in History and Interpretation*, SNTSMS 100 (Cambridge: Cambridge University Press, 1998), https://doi.org/10.1017/CBO9780511585166.

[7] Stephen D. Moore explores the implications of this point in "Why There Are No Humans or Animals in the Gospel of Mark," in *Mark as Story: Retrospect and Prospect*, ed. Kelly R. Iverson and Christopher W. Skinner, RBS 65 (Atlanta: Society of Biblical Literature, 2011), 71–94.

[8] E. M. Forster famously distinguished between "flat," or predictable, simple characters and "round," or surprising, complex characters (*Aspects of the Novel* [London: Edward Arnold, 1927], 93–95).

[9] Influential voices addressing Hebrew Bible characterization include Robert Alter, *The Art of Biblical Narrative* (New York: Basic Books, 1981), 115–17; Shimon Bar-Efrat, *Narrative Art in the Bible*, BLS 17 (Sheffield: Sheffield Academic, 1989), 90–92; Adele Berlin, *Poetics and Interpretation of Biblical Narrative* (1983; repr., Winona Lake, IN: Eisenbrauns, 1994), 23–24, 37–38; Meir Sternberg, *The Poetics of Biblical Narrative: Ideological Literature and the Drama of Reading*, Indiana Literary Biblical Series (Bloomington: Indiana University Press, 1985), 326.

[10] E.g., Robert Scholes and Robert Kellogg, *The Nature of Narrative* (London: Oxford University Press, 1966), 169; R. Alan Culpepper, *Anatomy of the Fourth Gospel: A Study in Literary Design*, FF.NT (Philadelphia: Westminster, 1983), 103; David Rhoads and Donald Michie, *Mark as Story: An Introduction to the Narrative of a Gospel* (Philadelphia: Fortress, 1983), 100; D. Francois Tolmie, *Jesus' Farewell to the Disciples: John 13:1–17:26 in Narratological Perspective*, BibInt 12 (Leiden: Brill, 1995), 117–44.

[11] Here Bennema is discussing Johannine characterization but claims that his observations apply to New Testament scholarship generally (*Encountering Jesus*, 24).

the tendencies that Bennema identifies, the landscape of New Testament scholarship has long been more nuanced than his account portrays.[12]

Following the first wave of literary New Testament scholarship, the flat/round dichotomy was challenged as an oversimplification. This development in characterization studies occurred in part because the earlier polarization was predicated on a Hebrew/Hellenist generic distinction that does not fit ancient texts well. New Testament scholars also recognized that the same character can appear flat or round depending on the literary time and place and that audiences play an important role in "building" character as they read/hear a narrative sequentially in time.[13] These insights led to the now-common view in New Testament scholarship that characters ought to be located on a continuum, a sliding scale between flat and round based on "the *degree* of characterization."[14]

New Testament critics also have attended to *methods* of characterization, recognizing that authors achieve characterization through both explicit and implicit means (often described as "showing" and "telling" techniques). Characters can be portrayed via their actions.[15] Proper names communicate (consider Jesus's renaming of Simon in Mark 3:16),[16] as do professions (such as Zacchaeus's occupation as a tax collector in Luke 19:1–10),[17] or a character's clothing (Herod's clothing himself in kingly robes in Acts 12:21 is especially significant in light of Luke 23:11).[18]

---

[12] Bennema cites Marianne Meye Thompson ("'God's Voice You Have Never Heard, God's Form You Have Never Seen': The Characterization of God in the Gospel of John," in Malbon and Berlin, *Characterization in Biblical Literature*, 177–204, here 177) but does not recognize her assertion that by that point (over twenty years ago now), biblical scholars thought of characterization on a continuum.

[13] See John A. Darr's critique of those who ignore temporality in *Herod the Fox: Audience Criticism and Lukan Characterization*, JSNTSup 163 (Sheffield: Sheffield Academic, 1998), 175–77.

[14] Fred Burnett, "Characterization and Reader Construction of Characters in the Gospels," in Malbon and Berlin, *Characterization in Biblical Literature*, 3–28, here 15. Also see Berlin, *Poetics and Interpretation*, 32; Petri Merenlahti, "Characters in the Making: Individuality and Ideology in the Gospels," in Rhoads and Syreeni, *Characterization in the Gospels*, 49–72, here 55; Bennema, *Encountering Jesus*, 25.

[15] Burnett, "Characterization and Reader Construction," 11. Reading specific characters from this perspective are Claire Clivaz, "Douze noms pour une main: Nouveaux regards sur Judas à partir de Lc 22.21–22," NTS 48 (2002): 400–416; D. Francois Tolmie, "The Ἰουδαῖοι in the Fourth Gospel: A Narratological Perspective," in *Theology and Christology in the Fourth Gospel: Essays by Members of the SNTS Johannine Writings Seminar*, ed. Gilbert Van Belle, J. G. van der Watt, and P. Maritz, BETL 184 (Leuven: Leuven University Press, 2005), 377–98.

[16] Often God (re)assigns names; for example, Abram becomes Abraham (Gen 17:5), Sarai becomes Sarah (Gen 17:15), Jacob becomes Israel (Gen 35:10). God names Solomon (1 Chr 22:9), John the Baptist (Luke 1:13), and Jesus (Matt 1:23).

[17] On which, see Gary Yamasaki, *Watching a Biblical Narrative: Point of View in Biblical Exegesis* (London: T&T Clark, 2007), 189–205.

[18] Dicken, *Herod as a Composite Character*, 150; Christoph Gregor Müller, "Kleidung als

Characters are depicted through comparison with other characters (i.e., parallelism and literary foils), as well as through descriptions of their speech patterns, personality traits, inner thoughts, motives, and feelings. Increasingly, scholars are attending to the intersections of physical description, embodiment, affect, gender, and race in early Christian literature (though some ignore the narratological implications of such themes in practice).[19]

For many reasons (some obvious, some more complex),[20] considerations of characterization in New Testament scholarship tend to privilege Jesus.[21] Even without literary vocabulary, Jesus's characterization has long factored into debates over who Jesus is—debates that apparently date back to Jesus's own lifetime (Luke 9:18–20 and parallels)—but literary vocabulary has provided a new avenue for exploring the gospels' theological claims.[22] Nowhere is this more obvious than in the realm of "narrative Christology."[23] Literarily inflected work such as Elizabeth Struthers Malbon's studies of Mark have added helpful precision to such projects. Yet consensus about Jesus's characterization continues to elude Lukan scholars.[24]

Element der Charakterzeichnung im Neuen Testament und seiner Umwelt: Ein Streifzug durch das lukanische Erzählwerk," *SNTSU* 28 (2003): 187–214.

[19] James L. Resseguie omits physical appearance altogether (*Narrative Criticism of the New Testament: An Introduction* [Grand Rapids: Baker Academic, 2005], 121–22).

[20] Many New Testament scholars' concentration on Jesus is theologically motivated. Still, the continued overwhelming fixation on Jesus and on the New Testament canon in *literary* (or, in the least, *not* professedly theological) treatments like those cited in n. 1 merits closer attention. I have a larger project in progress addressing this and related issues in characterization studies.

[21] This is especially true in Johannine scholarship. See, e.g., Nicolas Farelly, *The Disciples in the Fourth Gospel: A Narrative Analysis of Their Faith and Understanding*, WUNT 2/290 (Tübingen: Mohr Siebeck, 2010); Susan E. Hylen, *Imperfect Believers: Ambiguous Characters in the Gospel of John* (Louisville: Westminster John Knox, 2009); Judith Hartenstein, *Charakterisierung im Dialog: Maria Magdalena, Petrus, Thomas und die Mutter Jesu im Johannesevangelium im Kontext frühchristlicher Darstellungen*, NTOA 64 (Göttingen: Vandenhoeck & Ruprecht, 2007); Colleen M. Conway, *Men and Women in the Fourth Gospel: Gender and Johannine Characterization*, SBLDS 167 (Atlanta: Society of Biblical Literature, 1999). One exception is Hunt, Tolmie, and Zimmermann, *Character Studies in the Fourth Gospel*, which does not include Jesus.

[22] This feature of characterization is not peculiar to narratives in the New Testament. Characterization is never neutral; characters always are valued and evaluated differently with respect to an implied author's ideological commitments.

[23] Robert C. Tannehill coined this phrase in "'The Gospel of Mark as Narrative Christology," in *Perspectives on Mark's Gospel*, ed. Norman R. Petersen, Semeia 16 (Atlanta: Scholars Press, 1979), 57–95, here 57. See also Burnett, "Characterization and Reader Construction," 3; Jacob Chacko Naluparayil, *The Identity of Jesus in Mark: An Essay on Narrative Christology*, SBFA 49 (Jerusalem: Franciscan Printing Press, 2000); Pheme Perkins, "Mark as Narrative Christology," in Reginald H. Fuller and Pheme Perkins, *Who Is This Christ? Gospel Christology and Contemporary Faith* (Philadelphia: Fortress, 1983).

[24] Elizabeth Struthers Malbon, "The Christology of Mark's Gospel: Narrative Christology and the Markan Jesus," in *Who Do You Say That I Am? Essays on Christology*, ed. Mark Allan Powell and David R. Bauer (Louisville: Westminster John Knox, 1999), 33–48, here 37. See also the

Some of these debates concern whether Luke's Jesus is "flat" or "round," "static" or "dynamic" (though often without using that vocabulary). For example, Hans Conzelmann saw in Luke a changing Jesus who begins as a powerful messiah in Galilee but ends as a suffering servant in Jerusalem; C. Kavin Rowe, in contrast, argued that Luke's Jesus is portrayed consistently as "lord" (κύριος) across the gospel narrative.[25] Or what are we to make of Daniel Marguerat's claim that Luke in particular "intègre l'affectif dans la caractérisation,"[26] as opposed to Joseph Fitzmyer's argument that Luke erases from Mark "anything that smacks of the violent, the passionate, or the emotional"?[27] Conclusions about Jesus's characterization in Luke often turn on the scholar's view of Lukan narration, and we find differences of opinion on that score as well.[28]

Given these disparate results, I contend that treatments of characterization in contemporary literary theory offer useful ways to shift our discussions in Lukan scholarship specifically, and in New Testament scholarship more generally. I make this claim despite a refrain so commonly asserted by New Testament scholars as to be nearly cliché, namely, that nonbiblical literary theory offers few resources on which to draw regarding literary characterization. At the end of the last century, D. Francois Tolmie declared that "contemporary literary criticism ha[d] not yet provided a systematic and comprehensive theory for the analysis of character."[29] More recently, Bennema wrote, "Literary criticism has not advanced beyond the well-known categories of 'flat' and 'round' coined by E. M. Forster in 1927 to classify characters."[30] Indeed, such sentiments appear often in New Testament scholarship.[31]

---

following articles by Struthers Malbon: "'Reflected Christology': An Aspect of Narrative Christology in the Gospel of Mark," *PRSt* 26 (1999): 127–45; "Narrative Christology and the Son of Man: What the Markan Jesus Says Instead," *BibInt* 11 (2003): 373–85; "Markan Narrative Christology and the Kingdom of God," in *Literary Encounters with the Reign of God*, ed. Sharon H. Ringe and H. C. Paul Kim (New York: T&T Clark International, 2004), 177–93.

[25] C. Kavin Rowe, *Early Narrative Christology: The Lord in the Gospel of Luke*, BZNW 139 (Berlin: de Gruyter, 2006).

[26] Daniel Marguerat, "Luc, metteur en scène des personnages," in *Analyse narrative et Bible: Deuxième Colloque international du PRENAB, Louvain-la-Neuve, avril 2004*, ed. Camille Focant and André Wénin, BETL 191 (Leuven: Leuven University Press, 2005), 281–95, here 283.

[27] Joseph A. Fitzmyer, *The Gospel according to Luke (X–XXIV): Introduction, Translation, and Notes*, AB 28A (Garden City, NY: Doubleday, 1986), 94.

[28] Compare James M. Dawsey, *The Lukan Voice: Confusion and Irony in the Gospel of Luke* (Macon, GA: Mercer University Press, 1986), to John Darr, "Narrator as Character: Mapping a Reader-Oriented Approach to Narration in Luke-Acts," in Malbon and Berlin, *Characterization in Biblical Literature*, 43–60, here 57.

[29] Tolmie, *Jesus' Farewell*, 118.

[30] Bennema, *Theory of Character*, 2.

[31] E.g., Kelly R. Iverson, *Gentiles in the Gospel of Mark: "Even the Dogs under the Table Eat the Children's Crumbs,"* LNTS 339 (London: T&T Clark, 2007), 1 n. 1; Matthew L. Skinner, *Locating Paul: Places of Custody as Narrative Settings in Acts 21–28*, AcBib 13 (Atlanta: Society of Biblical

Admittedly, this can be (and often is) supported by literary critics' dire assessments of their own field. Repeatedly one finds references to theorists like Seymour Chatman, who, surveying the literature on characterization from Aristotle to 1970s structuralist narratology, marveled at "how little has been said about the theory of character in literary history and criticism."[32] Nearly thirty years after Chatman, Willem Weststeijn lamented the "virtual disappearance of the concept of character from narrative theory."[33] Many such remonstrations, however, serve as the legitimating preface for the writers' own attempt(s) to redress the lacuna they lament. The reality is that characterization has hardly disappeared from the narratological scene; it is, on the contrary, a point of continued contention. Moreover, it is not as though warring theorists make no progress. Literary scholars' own disciplinary discontents notwithstanding, theories of characterization have in fact advanced over the past several decades.

II. Contemporary Characterization Theory

Contemporary characterization theories have been dominated not by literary figures' relative flatness or roundness or by methods of characterization but by an even more fundamental *existential* question: Where does a character exist? Is it only in the story world? Or is it in the minds and hearts of readers? Is a character a *textual* or an *extra*textual being? This question has given rise to a "seemingly implacable conflict."[34]

On one side of the theoretical divide stand proponents of a *referential* or *mimetic* position, which views literary characters as referring to, reflecting, and in some sense existing outside of the text. Here one might think of novelists' claim that characters "take on lives of their own," exceeding or eluding authorial control,[35]

Literature, 2003), 4 n. 6; Christoph Gregor Müller, *Mehr als ein Prophet: Die Charakterzeichnung Johannes des Täufers im lukanischen Erzählwerk*, HBS 31 (Freiburg im Breisgau: Herder, 2001), 23; Elizabeth Struthers Malbon, *In the Company of Jesus: Characters in Mark's Gospel* (Louisville: Westminster John Knox, 2000), 12; David Lee, *Luke's Stories of Jesus: Theological Reading of Gospel Narrative and the Legacy of Hans Frei*, JSNTSup 185 (Sheffield: Sheffield Academic, 1999), 185; Burnett, "Characterization and Reader Construction," 3.

[32] Seymour Chatman, *Story and Discourse: Narrative Structure in Fiction and Film* (Ithaca, NY: Cornell University Press, 1978), 107.

[33] Willem G. Weststeijn, "Towards a Cognitive Theory of Character," in *Analysieren als Deuten: Wolf Schmid zum 60. Geburtstag*, ed. Lazar Fleishman, Christine Gölz, and Aage A. Hansen-Löwe (Hamburg: Hamburg University Press, 2004), 53–65, here 55.

[34] Alex Woloch, *The One vs. the Many: Minor Characters and the Space of the Protagonist in the Novel* (Princeton: Princeton University Press, 2003), 15.

[35] For Forster, characters, always "full of the spirit of mutiny," often "get out of hand" (*Aspects of the Novel*, 46).

or the way that readers often naturally assume a "full congruity between the way we perceive people in literature and the way we perceive them in life."[36] The impressionistic view of literary characters dominated until the early twentieth century, with conjectures about characters' unnarrated lives producing psychologizing readings like Freud's famous analysis of Hamlet.[37]

On the other side stand literary scholars with a *formalist* or *nonmimetic* position. These scholars argue that, although anthropomorphic assumptions about literary figures might seem to make intuitive sense, characters *actually* exist only in the text. In Mieke Bal's oft-quoted formulation, characters are "fabricated creatures ... paper people, without flesh and blood."[38] Literary characters are semiotic representations, circumscribed by and only accessible in the narrative form through which they are encountered.[39] From this point of view, characters in written narratives should not be identified as actual persons; literary characters are necessarily partial and contingent because narrated discourse is inherently limited.

For strict antimimeticists, this is true even when a narrative refers to actual, flesh-and-blood historical persons. Extratextual historicity notwithstanding, literary characters exist within a constructed, *constricted* narrative story world; they are nonactual individuals insofar as they have been crafted by an author (or authors) in particular ways (which, importantly, could have been narrated otherwise). Analyses that describe the flatness or roundness of a character actually assume as much; a flat character by definition cannot represent the complexities and opacities of real-world humans, and even the roundest of literary characters is often more coherent than real people.

The nonreferential position, initiated by the Russian formalists, was picked up by the American New Critics and was theorized in different ways by French structuralists and poststructuralists alike. Structuralists typically analyzed characters as actants, or existents, based on their narratological functions.[40] Poststructuralists

---

[36] Baruch Hochman, *Character in Literature* (Ithaca, NY: Cornell University Press, 1985), 44.

[37] Sigmund Freud, *The Interpretation of Dreams* (1900; repr., New York: Modern Library, 1950). Fredric Jameson dubs such interpretations "ethical" because they consider the character's moral *ethos* (*The Political Unconscious: Narrative as a Socially Symbolic Act* [Ithaca, NY: Cornell University Press, 1981], 60).

[38] Mieke Bal, *Narratology: Introduction to the Theory of Narrative*, 2nd ed. (Toronto: University of Toronto Press, 1997), 115. In biblical studies, this is the presumption of, *inter alios*, Ruben Zimmermann, "'The Jews': Unreliable Figures or Unreliable Narration?," in Hunt, Tolmie, and Zimmermann, *Character Studies in the Fourth Gospel*, 71–109, here 79.

[39] See, e.g., L. C. Knights, *How Many Children Had Lady Macbeth? An Essay in the Theory and Practice of Shakespeare Criticism* (New York: Haskell House, 1933).

[40] Classic examples are V. Propp's seven basic character types (Hero, Villain, Donor, Helper, Princess/Father, Dispatcher, False Hero/Usurper) in *Morphology of the Folktale*, Bibliographical and Special Series of the American Folklore Society 9 (Bloomington: Research Center, Indiana

have focused less on the functional roles characters play and more on the play of the language through which they come into being. As Aleid Fokkema wrote in 1991, "Critics seem to agree that 'character' is outdated, that ... there are only fragile subject positions, that language is the only constituent 'self.'"[41]

Later mimeticists pushed back, however. Defenders of the connections readers make intuitively between literary characters and real people critique formalists for obscuring the singularly human dimensions that make characters (human or otherwise)[42] compelling in the first place.[43] John Frow, for example, asserts that strictly structuralist models do "little to explain the affective force of the imaginary unities of character."[44] Characters are actualized by and, in turn, engender responses in human readers. Authors create characters, *determining* the traits and properties they will (and will not) narrate, while readers actualize them, *discerning* which features are most relevant for the story and ascribing them to characters accordingly. At the same time, as the Derridean concept of *différance* reminds us, texts always contain the seeds of their own undoing; narratives constantly threaten to destabilize characters even as they establish them.[45] The precarious textuality of literary characters gives rise to their unique fragility.

In my view, the most successful adjudications between the mimetic and nonmimetic views share the following three features: distinctions between levels of narrative analysis; a processual approach that considers multiple levels to be simultaneously operative in character construction; and a paradoxical conception of characters as implied "paper people"—inscribed by, but always exceeding, textual parameters.

University, 1958) and A. J. Greimas's six actants (Sujet, Objet, Destinateur, Destinataire, Opposant, and Adjuvant) in *Sémantique structural: Recherche de méthode*, Langue et langage (Paris: Larousse, 1966); and Greimas, "Actants, Actors, and Figures," in Greimas, *On Meaning: Selected Writings in Semiotic Theory*, trans. Paul J. Perron and Frank H. Collins (Minneapolis: University of Minnesota Press, 1987).

[41] Aleid Fokkema, *Postmodern Characters: A Study of Characterization in British and American Postmodern Fiction* (Amsterdam: Rodopi, 1991), 13.

[42] This is indicative of a long-standing anthropomorphism that has come under scrutiny in recent decades. Animating the so-called posthuman turn in certain strands of literary theory (e.g., ecocriticism and animality studies) are efforts to decenter the human subject in critical discourse. See, e.g., Lee Spinks, "Thinking the Post-human: Literature, Affect, and the Politics of Style," *Textual Practice* 15 (2001): 23–46.

[43] E.g., Robert Alter, "Character and the Connection with Reality," in *The Pleasures of Reading in an Ideological Age* (New York: Simon & Schuster, 1989); Frank Palmer, *Literature and Moral Understanding: A Philosophical Essay on Ethics, Aesthetics, Education, and Culture* (Oxford: Clarendon, 1992), esp. 104.

[44] John Frow, *Character and Person* (Oxford: Oxford University Press, 2014), 15.

[45] Jacques Derrida, "Différance," in *Margins of Philosophy*, trans. Alan Bass (Chicago: University of Chicago Press, 1982), 1–27.

Analytical Distinctions

Literary theorists distinguish between different modes or "layers" of inquiry. As Frow wrote recently, "One way of moving beyond the tied dichotomy of structuralist reduction and humanist plenitude (of the actant and the fully human character)" is "to recast them as distinct *levels* of analysis."[46] A standard example is the well-known narratological distinction between story (what is told) and discourse (how it is told). Whereas techniques of characterization operate in the realm of the discourse, characters' behaviors, qualities, virtues, and vices belong to the domain of the story world. Other layers have been posited as well (such as Mieke Bal's *fabula*, *story*, and *text*).[47]

Questions about the existential or ontological status of characters (e.g., To what extent can literary characters be described as "human"?) belong to a different level analytically than questions related to authorial technique (e.g., What formal choices are made by the creator of this character, and why?). Discourse and story-related inquiries differ, in turn, from questions about readerly reception (e.g., How do different readers understand and relate to characters? Are readers' responses to characters similar to or different from their responses to real people?).

Distinguishing between levels of analysis allows for a further set of delineations on the level of the story, drawing on possible-worlds theories. A narrative establishes a possible universe (the fact domain of the story world), as well as alternative worlds (subdomains) projected by the characters' own (often imagined) accounts. The latter are embedded within the fact domain. Characters can inhabit any of these domains, and their characterization can be analyzed within or across multiple levels. Exploring relationships between analytical levels, literary theorists often employ a processual (as opposed to a solely descriptive) approach to characterization.

A Processual Approach

Multiple formal and contextual factors operate simultaneously in character construction (e.g., readerly dynamics, genre identification, plot and events, sequential development). I find Alex Woloch's reconfiguration of characterizational dynamics most useful for shifting attention from characterization's products to its constituent processes:

> Characterization has been such a divisive question in twentieth-century literary theory—and has created recurrent disputes between humanist and structural (or mimetic and formal) positions—because the literary character is itself divided, always emerging at the juncture between structure and reference. In other words,

---

[46] Frow, *Character and Person*, 17.
[47] Bal, *Narratology*, 18.

a literary *dialectic* that operates dynamically within the narrative text [has been] transformed into a theoretical *contradiction*, presenting students of literature with an unpalatable choice: language *or* reference, structure *or* individuality.[48]

Woloch "recasts theoretical conflict back into literary process" in order to "make the tension between structure and reference generative of, and integral to, narrative signification."[49] This productive processual tension resolves the "apparently implacable conflict" mentioned earlier between conceiving of characters as merely "paper people" and considering them to be, in essence, like actual human beings. They are, rather, both at once.

Literary Characters as Paradoxical Implied People

Rather than choose between the referential and formalist positions, critics ought to conceive of literary figures as created constructs that are words, but more than words—invented, but also independent. Characters are *implied people* (analogous to the more well-known categories of *implied author* and *implied reader*),[50] depicted referentially *and* emplotted structurally within narrative. Scott Elliott is right: characters are "not simply creatures of *a* discourse; they are discoursed creatures."[51] Characters are (part of) the narrat*ed* world (*erzählte Welt*, as opposed to *Erzählwelt*), located between the narrat*or* and the narrat*ee* but not unilaterally determined by either.

Two concepts drawn, again, from Woloch illuminate the nature of these "discoursed creatures": the *character-space* and the *character-system*. Woloch's description is worth quoting at length:

> The *character-space* marks the intersection of an implied human personality … with the definitively circumscribed form of a narrative…. The implied person behind any character is never directly reflected in the literary text but only partially inflected: each individual portrait has a radically contingent position within the story as a whole; our sense of the human figure (*as* implied person) is inseparable from the space that he or she occupies within the narrative totality.[52]

---

[48] Woloch, *One vs. the Many*, 17 (emphases original). Marta Figlerowicz develops a reversal of Woloch's theory in *Flat Protagonists: A Theory of Novel Character* (New York: Oxford University Press, 2016).

[49] Woloch, *One vs. the Many*, 17.

[50] With respect to the gospels, unlike the implied author and implied reader (who must be inferred from the text), characters often are explicitly described, requiring less inference. On the concept of the implied author, see Chatman, *Story and Discourse*, esp. 81; and Chatman, *Coming to Terms: The Rhetoric of Narrative in Fiction and Film* (Ithaca, NY: Cornell University Press, 1990), esp. chapter 5, "In Defense of the Implied Author." Chatman draws on Wayne C. Booth, *The Rhetoric of Fiction*, 2nd ed. (Chicago: University of Chicago Press, 1983), 70–76, 428–31.

[51] Scott S. Elliott, *Reconfiguring Mark's Jesus: Narrative Criticism after Poststructuralism*, Bible in the Modern World 41 (Sheffield: Sheffield Phoenix, 2011), 66.

[52] Woloch, *One vs. the Many*, 13.

Character-spaces then give rise to a *character-system*, or a "distributional matrix," by which "the discrete representation of any specific individual is intertwined with the narrative's continual apportioning of attention to different characters who jostle for limited space within the same fictive universe."[53]

To put these concepts into terms more familiar to New Testament scholars, critics involved in the social-scientific Context Group have long recognized the pervasive influence of agonism in the ancient world; this observation has advanced our understanding of how, on the level of the story, Jesus is characterized through conflict (ἀγών) with his adversaries.[54] Yet New Testament scholars rarely consider how characters compete for space and attention on the level of the discourse, as well—a point suggested by the etymology of the word *protagonist* itself (protoagonist). As protagonist, Jesus's character-space only arises relative to—and in asymmetric relationship with—the character-spaces of others (the deuteragonist and tritagonist et al.), all of whom interact within the character-system created by the narrative structure. As literary constructs, characters may not be best conceived as real, flesh-and-blood humans, but neither should they be read solely as words or narrative functions; these "paper people" play important roles in a narrative's rhetorical agenda.[55]

Underlying the term "implied" is, of course, the assumption that someone is receiving and making sense of the implications in the text. As a character's attributes accumulate over the course of a narrative, readers come to associate them with particular habitual behaviors and ultimately conclude that those traits—and the *lack* of other traits—define that character. It is important to note here that, as reader-response critics emphasize, readers' conclusions about characters' attributes will differ. Human selfhood and human behavior, like texts, always only acquire meaning within the socially constructed parameters of distinct social groups.

The following section suggests that the movements beyond the referential/formalist impasse outlined above offer scholars fresh ways of approaching characterization in the Lukan narrative.

III. Lukan Characterization in Contemporary Literary Perspective

Considerations of "who Jesus is" often depend on whether the critic reads Jesus through a *referential* or *nonmimetic* interpretive lens (without necessarily

---

[53] Ibid.

[54] See, e.g., Bruce J. Malina and Jerome H. Neyrey, "Honor and Shame in Luke-Acts: Pivotal Values of the Mediterranean World," in *The Social World of Luke-Acts: Models of Interpretation*, ed. Jerome H. Neyrey (Peabody, MA: Hendrickson, 1991), 25–65.

[55] For more on the rhetoricity of narrative, see Michal Beth Dinkler, "New Testament Rhetorical Narratology: An Invitation Toward Integration," *BibInt* 24 (2016): 203–28, https://doi.org/10.1163/15685152-00242p04.

using that vocabulary). Representative of the two extremes are historical critics who rely on a referential approach to the figure of Jesus[56] and poststructuralists who read Jesus through a nonmimeticist lens.[57] Many New Testament scholars who avow a narrative approach to the gospels would fit best on the referential end of the spectrum because their presumptive starting point is that the narratives in the New Testament are historical nonfiction. Petri Merenlahti and Raimo Hakola consider the gospels to be nonfiction because "the author vouches for the veracity of the narrative and assumes that the reader believes it."[58] Bennema also approaches gospel characters as "composites of historical people," appealing to the authors' claims to reliability and to the "many scholars" who "regard the narrative material of the New Testament as nonfictional in nature and as referring to real events and people in history."[59] Of course, there are significant problems with this position, not least that "nonfiction" is a misleading category when it comes to ancient narratives like the gospels, and postmodern historiography has blurred distinctions between "fact" and "fiction" in history writing more generally.[60]

Refocusing our attention instead on the interstitial space where diegesis and mimesis meet, where form and content collide, offers several helpful correctives to treatments of characterization in New Testament scholarship. First, it challenges those who imagine a singular, uniform reader (ancient or modern). Stephen D. Moore has rightly critiqued such approaches, arguing that too often New Testament critics advance unilateral interpretations that are overdetermined by the strictures of the text (strictures that are, in turn, governed by the author). Critiquing James Resseguie's 1984 article on reader-response criticism, Moore writes, "What we miss is any intimation that these detailed responses should be regarded as simply one response-set out of a wide spectrum of potential, no less

---

[56] William A. Beardslee, "What Is It About? Reference in New Testament Literary Criticism," in *The New Literary Criticism and the New Testament*, ed. Elizabeth Struthers Malbon and Edgar V. McKnight, JSOTSup 109 (Sheffield: Sheffield Academic, 1994), 367–86.

[57] E.g., Stephen D. Moore, *Mark and Luke in Poststructuralist Perspectives: Jesus Begins to Write* (New Haven: Yale University Press, 1992); Elliott, *Reconfiguring Mark's Jesus*; Laura E. Donaldson, "Cyborgs, Ciphers, and Sexuality: Re: Theorizing Literary and Biblical Character," in Malbon and Berlin, *Characterization in Biblical Literature*, 81–96.

[58] Petri Merenlahti and Raimo Hakola, "Reconceiving Narrative Criticism," in Rhoads and Syreeni, *Characterization in the Gospels*, 13–48, esp. 35–43.

[59] Bennema, *Theory of Character*, 64. This is somewhat odd, given the following recognition earlier in the same book: "While characters may resemble people, they only exist within the story world of the text (even when they represent real people in the real world)" (29).

[60] On the intersections of historical Jesus research, postmodern historiography, and narratology, see Michal Beth Dinkler, "Narratological Jesus Research: An Oxymoron?," in *Jesus, quo vadis? Entwicklungen und Perspektiven der aktuellen Jesusforschung; Conference Proceedings*, BThSt (Neukirchen-Vluyn: Neukirchener Verlag, forthcoming 2018).

valid response-sets."[61] Moore's assessment was appropriate in 1989, and it continues to apply to much of the work on characterization by New Testament scholars today. In contrast, a processual approach to characterization recognizes that narrative potentialities are instantiated differently based on readers' intertextual and extratextual repertoires, reading habits, and socially constructed interpretive frameworks; as such, it appropriately allows for multiple readerly perspectives.

Noticing Jesus's contingent centrality on the level of form also adds an important nuance to attempts to recuperate what Malbon has called the "major importance of minor characters" in the gospels.[62] Though New Testament scholars tend to privilege Jesus, Malbon and others have insisted that marginal characters play significant roles in the gospel narratives, embodying key themes, advancing the plot, and influencing readers. At times, for example, stock figures overturn generic expectations and thereby challenge readerly assumptions.[63] Literary figures (minor *and* major) also characterize one another. Characterization operates via a mutually illuminating dialectic, in what John Darr describes as "a web of interrelationships."[64] That is, characters are crafted by other characters within the story, taking shape vis-à-vis one another.

To anticipate the case study below, consider the Emmaus road scene in Luke: there, the narrator characterizes the three active agents with explicit description (e.g., Cleopas and the other disciple are "sad" [σκυθρωποί], 24:17) but also via characters' descriptions of one another. Cleopas characterizes Jesus as the "only stranger [μόνος παροικεῖς] in Jerusalem who does not know [οὐκ ἔγνως] what has happened" (24:18). To Cleopas, Jesus's ignorance of recent events is the defining trait that renders him a "stranger." Jesus, for his part, characterizes Cleopas and his companion as "foolish and slow of heart to believe [ἀνόητοι καὶ βραδεῖς τῇ καρδίᾳ τοῦ

---

[61] Stephen D. Moore, *Literary Criticism and the Gospels: The Theoretical Challenge* (New Haven: Yale University Press, 1989), 100.

[62] Elizabeth Struthers Malbon, "The Major Importance of the Minor Characters in Mark," in Malbon and McKnight, *New Literary Criticism*, 58–86; Malbon, *In the Company of Jesus*; see also James Howard, "The Significance of Minor Characters in the Gospel of John," *BSac* 163 (2006): 63–78; Martin Ebner, "Im Schatten der Großen: Kleine Erzählfiguren im Markusevangelium," *BZ* 44 (2000): 56–76; Joel F. Williams, *Other Followers of Jesus: Minor Characters as Major Figures in Mark's Gospel*, JSOTSup 102 (Sheffield: JSOT Press, 1994); and Resseguie, *Narrative Criticism of the New Testament*, 137–65.

[63] Uta Poplutz, for instance, argues that in Matthew, five *Randfiguren* are actually *Grenzgänger*, gaining significance by defying readerly expectations (*Erzählte Welt: Narratologische Studien zum Matthäusevangelium*, BThSt 100 [Neukirchen-Vluyn: Neukirchener Verlag, 2008], esp. 80–100).

[64] Darr, *On Character Building*, 41. More recently, see Sönke Finnern, *Narratologie und biblische Exegese: Eine integrative Methode der Erzählanalyse und ihr Ertrag am Beispiel von Matthäus 28*, WUNT 2/285 (Tübingen: Mohr Siebeck, 2010), esp. 162–64.

πιστεύειν]" the prophets (24:25). These details create a constellation of clues from which readers draw conclusions about characters.

These have been important advancements in New Testament scholars' understanding of characterization, but few have considered how the minor characters' "major importance" also lies precisely in their status as *minor*. As Woloch's emphasis on the asymmetry of attention reveals, Jesus's status as protagonist *depends on* other characters' marginality. What contemporary characterization theory adds to the insights above is the point that Darr's "web of interrelationships" is made up of threads of unequal lengths;[65] if all characters were apportioned the same amount of narrative space, there could not be one protagonist.

Moreover, insofar as the analysis of "major" versus "minor" characters—or Jesus vis-à-vis others—remains *only* on the story level, it can also serve simply as a different iteration of the same conventional descriptive model of characterization. A processual model prompts a (re)consideration of characters as defined not only discretely on separate story and discourse levels but also interdiscursively as story and discourse levels intersect and mutually constitute each other. Literary characterization functions not only within but also across and between narrative levels.[66] This will become more apparent in the case study below.

IV. Building Character on the Road to Emmaus

Returning to the end of the Gospel of Luke with these views of characterization in mind can deepen our understanding of the narrative dynamics at work in Luke 24:13–35. We see, for instance, that Jesus's crucifixion poses not only a theological or sociocommunal problem; it also poses a narratological problem. Jesus's death fractures the formal architecture of the narrative by depriving the plot of its main contiguous figure. The crucifixion therefore gives rise to a narrative exigency: Jesus's empty character-space creates a void in the character-system. Other figures fill that void, but only briefly and in complex relation to the (present-but-missing) protagonist.

Yet the void created by Jesus's bodily absence is not devoid of his voice: when the women visit the empty tomb, upon discovering Jesus's bodily absence they hear spoken witness to his physical presence elsewhere (24:5–7). Jesus's words are represented to the women through the mouths of two new characters, unnamed

---

[65] Darr, *On Character Building*, 41.

[66] In my own previous work on Lukan characterization, I have argued that several other binaries often assumed in treatments of characterization are problematic, namely, presence vs. absence, speech vs. silence, and introspective individualism vs. anti-introspective collectivism (*Silent Statements: Narrative Representations of Speech and Silence in the Gospel of Luke*, BZNW 191 [Berlin: de Gruyter, 2013]).

"men in dazzling clothes" (24:2): "Remember how he told you, while he was still in Galilee, that the Son of Man must be handed over to sinners, and be crucified, and on the third day rise again" (24:7). Thus, on the level of the story world, Jesus transitions "from a somatic to a linguistic presence";[67] the women then proceed to tell the tale to other disciples (24:9–10). Sjef van Tilborg and Patrick Chatelion Counet describe the narrative embeddedness of this series of scenes:

> The visit of the women to the tomb becomes the story of the women which contains the story of the two men which contains the story of Jesus.... The figure "the body of Jesus" dissolves completely into words ... the words of the women which imply the words of the two men which imply the words of Jesus [and result in Peter's] inner words about which nothing more is said.[68]

Jesus remains a "linguistic presence" at the start of the Emmaus road scene through the indirect dialogue of two more new characters,[69] Cleopas and his unnamed companion, whom the narrator explicitly describes as talking (ὁμιλέω, 24:14, 15) and discussing (συζητέω, 24:15) what had happened while they travel. Cleopas and his friend are a fine example of significant minor characters. Introduced only in the last chapter of Luke, they disappear as abruptly as they enter the narrative. Yet they speak with Jesus for a full six verses (24:19–24, 29), proportionally more than many of the characters who are present throughout the gospel story. They also serve the important role of reiterating the women's previously dismissed christological claims that Jesus is alive again (24:33–35). As François Bovon notes, "The two disciples are able to collect in a few sentences the origin, the ministry, and the passion of one who has occupied center stage for more than twenty chapters."[70]

At the same time, the significance of Cleopas and his friend to some degree depends on their role as "bit players." Their narrative identities revolve around Jesus's structural centrality as protagonist who has been on "center stage" but is now missing. In fact, there would be no narrative need for Cleopas and his fellow traveler at all without Jesus's absence, and it is only in light of Jesus's central role in the narrative that readers will be concerned about them in the first place. The asymmetric attention afforded these two disciples is simply a feature of Luke's narrative structure. As Wayne Booth observes:

---

[67] Sjef van Tilborg and Patrick Chatelion Counet, *Jesus' Appearances and Disappearances in Luke 24*, BibInt 45 (Leiden: Brill, 2000), 117.

[68] Ibid.

[69] Because Cleopas and his friend are entirely new characters, readers have no previous descriptions on which to base expectations about how they might behave.

[70] François Bovon, *Luke 3: A Commentary on the Gospel of Luke 19:28–24:53*, trans. James Crouch, Hermeneia (Minneapolis: Fortress, 2012), 368. Among others, Bovon draws on Jean-Noël Aletti, *L'art de raconter Jésus-Christ: L'écriture narrative de l'Évangile de Luc*, Parole de Dieu (Paris: Seuil, 1989).

Hamlet is not fair to Claudius.... But who cares? The novelist who chooses to tell this story cannot at the same time tell that story; in centering our interest, sympathy, or affection on one character, he inevitably excludes from our interest, sympathy, and affection some other character[s].[71]

Jesus reenters the narrative as a somatic being when he physically comes near to "go with" (συμπορεύομαι, 24:15) Cleopas and the other disciple, raising the possibility that the narrative dilemma created by the protagonist's death has been resolved. Yet when Jesus asks about the subject of their story—"What are you discussing [ἀντιβάλλετε]?" (24:17)—their failure to recognize him renders him effectively absent and thereby threatens the narrative destabilization of his character yet again.

Cleopas's story about "the things that happened" (τὰ γενόμενα, 24:18) creates a new existential subdomain.[72] He describes the protagonist of this subdomain explicitly as "Jesus of Nazareth, who was a prophet mighty in deed and word before God and all the people" (24:19). Secondarily embedded in Cleopas's narrative account is his reference to what he had hoped would happen: "But we were hoping that [ἡμεῖς δὲ ἠλπίζομεν ὅτι] he was the one to redeem Israel" (24:21). Three existential levels are therefore housed inside each other like Russian nesting dolls—the fact domain of the gospel's story world, the subdomain of Cleopas's narrative, and the version he had hoped would take place (but incorrectly believes has not).

The fact that the Emmaus road pericope is situated structurally near the end of the narrative means that attentive readers should know that in terms of the central character, these story worlds collapse into one another. That is, the Lukan narrator has already established that (1) the risen Jesus speaking with Cleopas and his companion, (2) the "Jesus of Nazareth" described by Cleopas, *and* (3) the redeemer for whom the disciples had hoped are all one and the same protagonist. They are one and the same protagonist, differently understood. As Bovon points out, Cleopas's characterization of Jesus as "of Nazareth" and "a prophet mighty in deed and word" (24:19) is factually accurate according to the narrative, but his incorrect subjective interpretation of that characterization "has a devastating effect."[73]

Many New Testament commentators have noted the dramatic irony of Cleopas's failure to see that he describes his dashed hopes to the one in whom those hopes have been fulfilled. Fewer have asked how that irony works rhetorically; it is in part due to characterizational dynamics. That Cleopas does not realize that the protagonist of the story he tells is the very person to whom he narrates characterizes Cleopas indirectly; judging by his own definitional understanding of a "stranger"

---

[71] Booth, *Rhetoric of Fiction*, 79.

[72] "Existential" in the sense that existents inhabit it. The use of γεγονός implies a change in a state of being, which makes this a story in the classically narratological sense developed by Tzvetan Todorov in *Grammaire du Décaméron* (The Hague: Mouton, 1969).

[73] Bovon, *Luke 3*, 373.

(παροικεῖς) as one who "does not know" (οὐκ ἔγνως, 24:18), Cleopas's failure to recognize Jesus ironically characterizes *Cleopas* as the stranger, as the one who is really living παρά the οἶκος ("outside the house"). The irony of the scene arises precisely in the disjuncture between the christological characterization of Jesus in the fact domain of the gospel and the mistaken interpretations of Jesus's character created in and through Cleopas's narrative accounts.

Jesus's corrections of the disciples' hermeneutical missteps (in 24:32 and 45) affirm and deepen his characterization as one who interprets and must himself be interpreted. Mark Coleridge notes that, as early as Luke 2:42–51, when the boy Jesus teaches in the temple and corrects his parents' (mis)understanding of who he is, Jesus "is born in the narrative as prime interpreter."[74] This depiction continues as Jesus begins his public ministry by interpreting the Hebrew Bible (Luke 4:16–30; cf. Mark 6:1–6; Matt 13:53–58), considers others' interpretations of the Scriptures (e.g., Luke 10:25–37), and interprets his own spoken narratives, the parables, for his disciples (e.g., Luke 8:11–15). By the end of the story, then, Jesus's "opening" (διανοίγω) of the Scriptures for the two Emmaus-bound disciples (24:32; cf. 24:45) confirms implicitly that, though he has risen, his character has not changed.

Jesus remains storyteller and interpreter, yet he is more. This scene indicates that, at least for the other characters in the story, the nature of his identity still requires translation (lit., in v. 27, διερμηνεύω). This verb, Bovon writes, "recognizes that there is a distance between the two realities that must be overcome (hence the prefix διά-, 'through'); a translation, transferring, explanation, interpretation is required."[75] Bovon refers here to a translation by one character in the fact domain of the gospel (Jesus) for the others (Cleopas and his friend). I suggest that a translation—that is, an "interpretation-through" (διά + ἑρμηνεύω)—occurs metatextually as well, inviting us to scrutinize Jesus's position as not only the Risen One, but the Written and Read One as well.

V. Concluding Thoughts

Sometimes changing the questions can offer the best solutions to old problems. I believe that the theoretical premises shared by many contemporary literary theorists as they stake claims in their disciplinary disputes about characterization can shift our discussions in the field of New Testament in fruitful new directions. Contemporary literary theorists invite us to consider characterization as a

---

[74] Mark Coleridge, *The Birth of the Lukan Narrative: Narrative as Christology in Luke 1–2*, JSOTSup 88 (Sheffield: JSOT Press, 1993), 222–23. See also Moore, *Mark and Luke in Poststructuralist Perspectives*, esp. 124.

[75] Bovon, *Luke 3*, 374.

multilayered process, which paradoxically gives rise to "implied people" who exist only within the narrated world but nevertheless exert extratextual effects.

Referring to Jesus's characterization in the Gospel of Luke to illustrate the benefits of such conceptual shifts, I have suggested that it is on the border of form and content that Luke's Jesus emerges as protagonist—namely, through the "asymmetric" attention allocated to him relative to other characters within the narrative's larger character-system. In sum, my view is this: Luke's characterization presents not a *flat Jesus* nor a *round Jesus*, not a *purely paper* nor even an extratextual *historical Jesus*. Rather, where mimeticism and referentiality meet, readerly attention is directed to an *implied Jesus*—a paradoxical protagonist Jesus who is constructed and circumscribed, defined and delimited, by the gospel's narrative form and by the wide range of readers (implied, real, ancient, or otherwise) who encounter it.[76]

---

[76] My thanks to Stephen Moore for his note about "real" readers in response to an earlier draft of this essay.

Paul the "god" in Acts 28: A Comparison with Philoctetes

M. DAVID LITWA
david.litwa@acu.edu.au
Institute for Religion and Critical Inquiry, Melbourne, Australia

This essay treats an instance of literary aemulatio. *Paul in Acts 28, like the famous hero Philoctetes, is bitten by a poisonous snake on a secluded island. The responses of these two figures to the bite, however, are fundamentally different. Philoctetes suffers extreme agony after his snakebite; Paul does not register any pain at all. Philoctetes issues horrible cries illustrating the depths of his suffering; Paul does not let out a whimper. Philoctetes begs to be burned with fire; Paul casually shakes off his viper into a fire. Philoctetes must be healed by doctors; Paul himself, after being bitten, becomes a healer. In this depiction, Paul transcends the values undergirding Greco-Roman conceptions of the manly hero. Paul is portrayed as a new kind of hero, one who is invulnerable and divine.*

Acts 28:1–10 is the culmination of the book's heroic portrait of Paul. Although several comparisons of Paul and Greek heroes have been made on the basis of this passage, the hero Philoctetes has not been treated at any length.[1] Like Paul, Philoctetes is bitten by a poisonous snake on a secluded island. Their responses to the bite, however, are fundamentally different. Philoctetes suffers extreme agony from his snakebite; Paul does not register any pain at all. Philoctetes issues horrible cries illustrating the depths of his suffering; Paul does not even whimper. Philoctetes begs to be burned with fire; Paul casually shakes off his viper into a fire. Philoctetes must be healed by doctors; Paul himself, after being bitten, becomes a healer. In

---

[1] Most commentators on Acts 28 ignore Philoctetes. Recently, Craig S. Keener's massive commentary offers Philoctetes a single line (*Acts: An Exegetical Commentary*, 4 vols. [Grand Rapids: Baker Academic, 2015], 4:3670). Other heroes are usually chosen for comparison. Dennis R. MacDonald compares Paul in Acts 28 with Odysseus in "The Shipwrecks of Odysseus and Paul," *NTS* 45 (1999): 88–107, esp. 102–3. Annette Weissenrieder proposes an assimilation of Paul to the deified Asclepius in "'He Is a God!' Acts 28:1–9 in Light of Iconographical and Textual Sources Related to Medicine," in *Picturing the New Testament: Studies in Ancient Visual Images*, ed. Annette Weissenrieder, Friederike Wendt, and Petra von Gemünden, WUNT 2/193 (Tübingen: Mohr Siebeck, 2005), 127–56.

this depiction, Paul transcends the values undergirding Greco-Roman conceptions of the manly hero. Paul is more than a hero; he is portrayed as nothing less than a god.

To engage in our comparison we must first ask about accessibility. Would the author of Acts have known the story of Philoctetes bitten by a snake on a secluded island? The fame of Philoctetes suggests yes. His story was mentioned by Homer and related at length in two poems of the Greek Epic Cycle (the *Cypria* and the *Little Iliad*).[2] In addition, all three of the great Athenian tragedians (Aeschylus, Sophocles, and Euripides) wrote an entire play on this character, although only the play of Sophocles fully survives. Later Hellenistic and Latin tragedians (Theodectes, Accius) wrote whole plays about Philoctetes, and the masterworks of major Roman poets (Virgil, Ovid) also mention him.[3] Depictions of Philoctetes in works of art were ubiquitous in antiquity. Seth L. Schein notes, "Vase painters represented Philoktetes frequently, and he appears on coins, gems, and mirrors and in other media from *c.* 460 BCE through to the third century CE."[4] In sum, it is likely that the author of Acts, evidently a writer of good literary education, knew about Philoctetes.[5] It is time, then, to bring this hero into the conversation about the composition and meaning of Acts 28:1–10.

---

[2] Martin West, ed., *Greek Epic Fragments from the Seventh to the Fifth Centuries BC*, LCL (Cambridge: Harvard University Press, 2003), 76–77 (*Cypria* argument 9), 120–21 (*Little Iliad* argument 2). See further Alan H. Sommerstein, "Tragedy and the Epic Cycle," in *The Greek Epic Cycle and Its Ancient Reception: A Companion*, ed. Marco Fantuzzi and Christos Tsagalis (Cambridge: Cambridge University Press, 2015), 461–86, esp. 467–68.

[3] According to the Latin poet Valerius Flaccus, Philoctetes was one of the Argonauts (*Argonautica* 1.391–393).

[4] Seth L. Schein, ed., *Sophocles; Philoctetes*, Cambridge Greek and Latin Classics (Cambridge: Cambridge University Press, 2013), 9. Maria Pipili comments, "The wounded Ph[iloctetes] ... was a popular subject throughout antiquity.... Ph[iloctetes] was a popular hero in Italy and is very often shown on Etruscan, Italic and Roman Republican gems" ("Philoctetes," in *Lexicon Iconographicum Mythologiae Classicae [LIMC]* [Zurich: Artemis, 1994], 7.1:376–85, here 384; 7.2:321–26). See also Erika Simon, "Philoktetes: Ein kranker Heros," in *Geschichte - Tradition - Reflexion: Festschrift für Martin Hengel zum 70. Geburtstag*, ed. Hubert Cancik, Hermann Lichtenberger, and Peter Schäfer, 3 vols. (Tübingen: Mohr Siebeck, 1996), 2:15–39; Simon, "Philoktetes," in *LIMC Supplementum 2009*, 2 vols. (Düsseldorf: Artemis, 2009), 1:426, with images in *LIMC Supplementum 2009*, 2:205; Carl Werner Müller, *Philoktet: Beiträge zur Wiedergewinnung einer Tragödie des Euripides aus der Geschichte ihrer Rezeption*, Beiträge zur Altertumskunde 100 (Stuttgart: Teubner, 1997), pls. 1–30; Oliver Taplin, *Pots and Plays: Interactions between Tragedy and Greek Vase-Painting of the Fourth Century B.C.* (Los Angeles: J. Paul Getty Museum, 2007), 98–100.

[5] From the text of Luke-Acts itself, Joseph A. Fitzmyer remarks that the author "is obviously a rather well-educated person, a writer of no little merit, acquainted with both OT literary traditions ... and Hellenistic literary techniques" (*The Gospel according to Luke: Introduction, Translation and Notes*, 2 vols., AB 28, 28A [Garden City, NY: Doubleday, 1981, 1985], 1:35). According to François Bovon, "The cultivated language [of Luke] indicates that the author's roots are in one of the higher strata of society, and that the author had a good education encompassing

Many of the details of Philoctetes's life will be treated in the comparison below; a brief synopsis of the hero's career will suffice here. Philoctetes, hailing from Thessaly, was the man who lit the pyre of Heracles, which made possible the latter's deification. As a reward, Heracles granted him his famous bow. Some years later, Philoctetes embarked with the Greek expedition to Troy. Before reaching Asia, however, disaster struck. On an Aegean island, Philoctetes was bitten by a poisonous snake. Unable to be healed, the hero was abandoned on the isle of Lemnos for ten years. As the result of a prophecy, however, he was conveyed to Troy, healed, and given victory over Paris (abductor of Helen). On his way back to Greece, however, he suffered shipwreck and was washed ashore in Italy. There he became the founder of several Italian cities and died in a war to protect his allies.[6]

Paul's story can perhaps most simply be told by offering a translation of Acts 28:1–10:[7]

> After being completely saved [from the shipwreck in Acts 27], we subsequently learned that the island [to which the crew swam ashore] was called Melite. The barbarians offered us extraordinary hospitality. After kindling a fire, they welcomed all of us on account of the onrushing rain and cold.
>
> When Paul was gathering a heap of wood and laying it on the fire, a viper was driven out by the heat and fastened onto his hand. As the barbarians observed the beast hanging from his hand, they conversed among each other: "Assuredly this man was a murderer. Though saved from the sea, Justice did not allow him to live." Paul, however, shook off the beast into the fire and suffered nothing harmful. They were expecting him to burn with fever and suddenly fall down dead. Maintaining this expectation for a long time, and observing that nothing unusual happened to him, they changed their minds and confessed that he was a god.
>
> In the surrounding region there were lands belonging to the first citizen of the island named Publius. He welcomed us and generously provided hospitality for three days. Publius's father was burning up, since he was afflicted with fever and dysentery. Paul visited him, prayed, laid his hands upon him, and healed him. When this occurred, the rest of the people on the island who had illnesses

---

Greek rhetoric as well as Jewish methods of exegesis" (*Luke 1: A Commentary on the Gospel of Luke 1:1–9:50*, trans. Christine M. Thomas, Hermeneia [Minneapolis: Fortress, 2002], 8).

[6] Standard encyclopedic works cover the varied aspects of Philoctetes's career. See, e.g., Jan Stenger, "Philoctetes," *BNP* A.11:66–67; Herbert Jennings Rose and Jenny Marsh, "Philoctetes," *OCD*, 1131–32. Fuller treatments can be found in Oscar Mandel, *Philoctetes and the Fall of Troy: Plays, Documents, Iconography, Interpretations* (Lincoln: University of Nebraska Press, 1981), 1–50; Timothy Gantz, *Early Greek Myth: A Guide to Literary and Artistic Sources* (Baltimore: Johns Hopkins University Press, 1993), 459–60, 589–90, 635–39, 649–50, 700–701; Hanna M. Roisman, *Sophocles, Philoctetes*, Duckworth Companions to Greek and Roman Tragedy (London: Duckworth, 2005), 24–40. Essential reading for the reception of Philoctetes in antiquity is Glen W. Bowersock, *Fiction as History: Nero to Julian*, Sather Classical Lectures 58 (Berkeley: University of California Press, 1994), 55–76.

[7] Unless otherwise noted, all translations of ancient works are my own.

came and were healed. They honored us with many honors and provided for our needs when we embarked.

As noted, this story immediately follows a scene of shipwreck. Paul and almost three hundred other people were forced to swim to an unknown shore as their boat was broken to pieces by the waves. The storm that blew them off course had whirled and lashed their vessel for over two weeks. The men had eaten little food and slept even less (Acts 27:13–44). One can imagine sailors and passengers crawling exhausted onto the sands of the island, somewhat like Odysseus after his shipwreck:

> His knees buckle
> and his stout arms fell limp; his heart was conquered by the sea
> All his flesh was swollen, and lots of sea water trickled
> From his mouth and nostrils. Then, breathless and speechless,
> He lay there enfeebled, as dire fatigue caught up with him. (Homer, *Od.* 5.453–457)[8]

Paul, surprisingly, seems rather unfazed by his whole experience. He is strong enough, at least, to stroll around the beach and haul pieces of firewood.[9]

From a stack of wood that Paul is carrying, a viper (ἔχιδνα) emerges and sinks its fangs into his hand. An ἔχιδνα, although a somewhat vague term, was widely recognized in the ancient world as a type of poisonous snake.[10] Obviously the natives assume this in the narrative. Logically, they deduce divine retribution. "This man must be a murderer," they remark. "Though saved from the sea, Justice [Δίκη] did not allow him to live!" (Acts 28:3–4).[11]

Horrible snakebites occur elsewhere in Greek and Roman mythology,[12] yet

---

[8] A more obscure text, Anth. pal. 7.290, is often cited because it combines the sailor exhausted from shipwreck with a snakebite.

[9] Note also the firewood or sticks for making fire (πυρεῖα) outside Philoctetes's cave (Sophocles, *Phil.* 36). For Philoctetes making a fire, see ibid., lines 295–297.

[10] See, e.g., Demosthenes, *Or.* 25.96.

[11] Justice is capitalized here because it refers to a female deity. Δίκη appears in Greek myth at least as early as the seventh century BCE in Hesiod's *Theogony* as the daughter of Zeus and Themis (line 902). She also appears in Hesiod's *Works and Days* weeping by the abodes of wicked people. When she is wronged, she sits beside her father Zeus and reports the evil deed (lines 220–224, 256–261). According to the poet Aratus, Δίκη lived with men of the Golden Age, put up with the Silver race, and finally left earth at the start of the Bronze Age (*Phaen.* 96–136; cf. Virgil, *Ecl.* 4.6; Ovid, *Metam.* 1.149–150; Ps.-Eratosthenes, *Cataster.* 9; Hyginus, *Astron.* 2.25). In her present state, she is often said to sit by Zeus, keeping a record of human wrongdoing (Sophocles, *Oed. col.* 1381–1382). Plutarch writes that the eye of Justice watches over all that happens at sea (*Symp. Sept.* 18 [*Mor.* 161e]). For Δίκη in Jewish mythology, cf. Wis 9:4; Philo, *Conf.* 118, *Ios.* 48; 4 Macc 18:22. See further Hugh Lloyd-Jones, *The Justice of Zeus*, Sather Classical Lectures 41 (Berkeley: University of California Press, 1971), 35–36, 86–87, 99–101; Lynn Allan Kauppi, *Foreign but Familiar Gods: Greco-Romans Read Religion in Acts*, LNTS 277 (London: T&T Clark, 2006), 110–12.

[12] Ps.-Apollodorus, *Bibl.* 1.3.2 (Eurydice); 3.6.4 (Opheltes); *Epit.* 5.18 (sons of Laocoön);

arguably the most famous case of a snakebite in this material was that of Philoctetes. Like Paul, he was bitten by a poisonous snake on a secluded island, which is variously named.[13] According to Pseudo-Apollodorus, it is Tenedos (*Epitome* 3.26–27); according to Pausanias it is the lost island of Chryse (*Descr.* 8.33.4). In the simplest version, reported by Hyginus, the island is Lemnos (*Fab.* 102), the same island where Philoctetes was later abandoned.

In Homer (*Il.* 2.723) and elsewhere the snake that bites Philoctetes is called a "water snake" (ὕδρα).[14] The mention of a hydra conforms Philoctetes to Heracles, who fought the famous Hydra of Lerna and was later slain by its poison (Sophocles, *Trach.* 572–574). Nevertheless, Philoctetes's snake (like Paul's) is also called a viper (ἐχίδνης) in Sophocles's play *Philoctetes* (line 267), in a summary of Euripides's homonymous play (Dio Chrysostom, *Or.* 59.3), and by the Roman playwright Accius (*viperino morsu*).[15]

According to Sophocles, Philoctetes was bitten on the foot—and this is the most common site of wounding in both poetry and art. According to the playwright Theodectes (fourth century BCE), however, the snake sunk its fangs into Philoctetes's hand (τὴν ἐμὴν χεῖρα)—where the viper also clung to Paul (τῆς χειρὸς αὐτοῦ, Acts 28:3).[16] For both Paul and Philoctetes, the viper bite was a manifestation of the divine will. In regard to Philoctetes, the bite prevented Troy from being captured before its time (Sophocles, *Phil.* 196–200). In Paul's case, the bite proved his innocence and—as we shall see—his divinity.

In the case of Philoctetes, the festering wound gave off such a stench that he was abandoned on Lemnos. At the time, Lemnos was occupied by so-called barbarians. Homer refers to the Sintian inhabitants of Lemnos as barbarous "speakers of a savage tongue" (ἀγριοφώνους, *Od.* 8.294). Herodotus (*Hist.* 6.138) reports that Pelasgians on Lemnos abducted Athenian women and made them their wives. Later they killed these women with their children (cf. Aeschylus, *Cho.* 631–638).

6.28 (Orestes); Ovid, *Metam.* 11.775–776 (Hesperie); Apollonius Rhodius, *Arg.* 4.1524–1527 (Mopsus). The Roman poet Lucan offers a spectacle of lethal snakebites in book 9 of his *Civil War*. Nicander (third or second century BCE) offers a virtual handbook of snakebites in his *Theriaca* 115–482 (note ἐχίδνης [line 129] and ἐχιδνήεσσαν [line 209]).

[13] The poison is emphasized by Ovid: "For nearly ten whole years the son of Poeas [Philoctetes] nursed the plague-bearing wound given by the puffed-up snake" (*pestiferum tumido vulnus ab angue datum*) (*Trist.* 5.2.13–14).

[14] *Cypria*, argument 9 in West, *Epic Fragments*, 76; cf. Pausanias, *Descr.* 10.33.4.

[15] Accius, *Philocteta* frag. XVII in Jacqueline Dangel, *Accius Oeuvres (fragments)*, CUFr Budé (Paris: Belles Lettres, 1995), 154–56. The line is quoted by Cicero in *Tusc.* 2.19. On types of snakes, see Christian Hühnemörder, "Snake," *BNP* A.13:554–58, here 554–55. On religious herpetology in general, see James H. Charlesworth, *The Good and Evil Serpent: How a Universal Symbol Became Christianized* (New Haven: Yale University Press, 2010), with Acts 28 discussed on 355–56.

[16] Bruno Snell, ed., *Tragicorum Graecorum Fragmenta*, 5 vols. (Göttingen: Vandenhoeck & Ruprecht, 1971), 1:233 (§72F 5b).

Thus "Lemnian deeds" (ἔργα Λήμνια) became proverbial for any wicked or barbarous act. Paul also encountered barbarians (βάρβαροι, Acts 28:2, 4) on the island of Melite (which most scholars identify with Malta). Surprisingly for him, the barbarians proved extraordinarily hospitable.[17]

Like Paul, Philoctetes was the subject of prophecy. The Trojan prince Helenus prophesied that, unless Philoctetes and his bow were brought to Troy, the city could not be taken.[18] Despite the hardships involved, Philoctetes was conveyed to Troy. In Acts, during a vision of the night, an angel informs Paul that he must stand trial before the emperor in Italy (Acts 27:24). In context, it seems more likely that Paul will be drowned in the raging sea—and yet the prophecy proves true. Paul suffers shipwreck, to be sure, but still ends up in Italy—and this is the very fate of Philoctetes.[19]

Both men, though they were shipwrecked and bitten by a poisonous snake, were innocent of wrongdoing. The goddess Justice was not punishing Paul. His preserved life was proof of his righteousness. Likewise, the chorus in Sophocles's

---

[17] It may be significant that, whereas Philoctetes is said to fight barbarians (μάχην συνάψασι πρὸς τοὺς ἐνοικοῦντας τῶν βαρβάρων ἐκείνην τὴν χώραν [Ps.-Aristotle, Mir. ausc. 107]), Paul is welcomed by them.

[18] Little Iliad argument 2 in West, Epic Fragments, 122; Sophocles, Phil. 610–613, 1334–1341. Calchas is the prophet in Ps.-Apollodorus, Epit. 5.8. See further A. E. Hinds, "The Prophecy of Helenus in Sophocles' Philoctetes," ClQ 17 (1967): 169–80, https://doi.org/10.1017/S0009838800010466. The prophecy is studied at length in Tamara Visser, Untersuchungen zum Sophokleischen Philoktet: Das auslösende Ereignis in der Stückgestaltung, BzA 110 (Stuttgart: Teubner, 1998).

[19] Philoctetes was driven off course and shipwrecked near Campania (Ps.-Apollodorus, Epit. 6.15b). The Hellenistic poet Euphorion (frag. 48 in B. A. van Groningen, Euphorion [Amsterdam: Hakkert, 1977], 113–16) speaks of a shipwreck off Euboea. (On this fragment, see further Enrico Livrea, "Il Philoctetes di Euforione," ZPE 139 [2002]: 35–39; Evina Sistakou, Reconstructing the Epic: Cross-Readings of the Trojan Myth in Hellenistic Poetry, Hellenistica Groningana 14 [Leuven: Peeters, 2008], 127–28). Euphorion fragment 49 (from Tzetzes in Eduard Scheer, Lycophronis Alexandra, 2 vols. [Berlin: Weidmann, 1881–1908], 2:293–94) says that Philoctetes made it to Campania and founded a temple to Apollo the Wanderer. See further Léon Lacroix, "La légende de Philoctète en Italie méridionale," RBPH 43 (1965): 5–21; Hatto H. Schmitt, "Philoktet in Unteritalien," in Bonner Festgabe Johannes Straub zum 65. Geburtstag am 18. Oktober 1977, Beihefte der Bonner Jahrbücher 39 (Bonn: Rheinland, 1977), 55–66; M. Giangiulio, "Filottete tra Sibari e Crotone: Osservazioni sulla tradizione letteraria," in Épéios et Philoctète en Italie: Données archéologiques et traditions légendaires; Actes du Colloque international du Centre de recherches archéologiques de la Université de Lille III, Lille, 23–24 novembre 1987, ed. J. de La Genière, Cahiers du Centre Jean Bérard 16 (Naples: Centre Jean Bérard, 1991); Christine Mauduit, "De Lemnos à Italie: Remarques sur le mythe de Philoctète," in Heros et voyageurs grecs dans l'Occident romain: Actes du colloque organisé au Centre des études et de recherches sur l'Occident romain de l'Université Jean Moulon-Lyon III, janvier 1996, ed. Alain Billaut, Collection du Centre d'études romaines et gallo-romaines NS 15 (Lyon: Centre d'Études et de Recherches sur l'Occident Romain, 1997), 9–32; Irad Malkin, "The Middle Ground: Philoctetes in Italy," Kernos 11 (1998): 131–41, esp. 135–37; Bowersock, Fiction as History, 60.

Philoctetes testifies, "There is none other among mortals whom I have heard of or have looked upon who has met with a more hateful destiny than this man [Philoctetes], who having done nothing to anyone, done no robbery, but being a just man among just men, was perishing thus undeservedly."[20] Δίκη was clearly not punishing Philoctetes either. The reason for his snakebite is usually unexplained, left to Fate, or to the will of the gods.[21]

In other versions, Philoctetes leads the Greek army to the altar of the nymph Chryse. The sacrifice is necessary for the safety and success of the Greeks at Troy. Yet by Chryse's altar, the hero is bitten. In his play *Philoctetes*, Euripides underscored the cruel irony of Philoctetes's fate. He made the hero declare, "For the salvation and victory of the community I fell into disaster, because I revealed Chryse's altar, where the Greeks must first sacrifice if they would conquer the foe; if not, our expedition was of no use" (Dio Chrysostom, *Or.* 59.9). Though he performed an act saving the whole expedition, Philoctetes is rewarded with unbearable chronic pain and desertion.[22] In the case of Paul, God guarantees the lives of all on board the ship because Paul himself is present (Acts 27:24). Then—despite the fact that every sailor, soldier, and passenger reaches the island alive—it is Paul who is bitten by the viper.

These densely packed similarities between Paul and Philoctetes (shipwreck, barbarian island, poisonous snakebite, prophecy, the hero's uprightness and salvific effect) make the differences between them all the more striking. Perhaps the most surprising fact is that, in response to his snakebite, Paul does not register any pain whatsoever. This fact should raise eyebrows given that his bite seems to be severe. The author of Acts says that the viper "fastened down" (καθῆψεν) on Paul's hand. The reader is led to imagine the snake sinking its fangs deep into Paul's flesh. The bite is so deep that the beast literally hangs from the wound. Evidently the viper has ample time to inject its full store of venom.[23] To remove the beast, Paul must strongly shake his hand (ἀποτινάξας, 28:5). In spite of the seriousness of the bite,

---

[20] Sophocles, *Phil.* 681–685: ἄλλον δ' οὔτιν' ἔγωγ' οἶδα κλύων οὐδ' ἐσιδὼν μοίρᾳ τοῦδ' ἐχθίονι συντυχόντα θνατῶν, ὅς οὔτε ῥέξας τιν', οὔτε νοσφίσας, ἀλλ' ἴσος ἐν <γ'> ἴσοις ἀνήρ, ὤλλυθ' ὧδ' ἀναξίως. Here I adopt the translation of Hugh Lloyd Jones in the LCL (1994), with slight modification. For a critical text with commentary, see Schein, *Sophocles*.

[21] Philoctetes suffers due to "divine fortune" (θεία τύχη, Sophocles, *Phil.* 1326). As Schein points out, Sophocles's Philoctetes "never refers to himself as impious or ethically wrong for transgressing the shrine of Chryse" ("Divine and Human in Sophocles' *Philoctetes*," in *The Soul of Tragedy: Essays on Athenian Drama*, ed. Victoria Pedrick and Steven M. Oberhelman [Chicago: University of Chicago Press, 2005], 27–48, here 40). Hyginus attributes the snakebite to the wrath of Hera, who was angry at Philoctetes for lighting Heracles's pyre (*Fab.* 102).

[22] See further Charles Segal, "Philoctetes and the Imperishable Piety," *Hermes* 105 (1977): 133–58, here 152.

[23] Dioscorides (a first-century CE physician) uses καθάπτομαι for poison entering the body. See this and other sources cited in William Kirk Hobart, *The Medical Language of St. Luke: A Proof from Internal Evidence* (London: Longmans, Green, 1882), 288–89. Cf. Epictetus, *Diatr.* 3.20.10.

the narrator explicitly remarks that Paul suffered or experienced nothing bad or painful (ἔπαθεν οὐδὲν κακόν).²⁴

Philoctetes was not so lucky. He responded to his snakebite with horrible paroxysms of pain. The agonies of Philoctetes are already emphasized by Homer. On sacred Lemnos, a supine Philoctetes "suffers mighty pains" (κεῖτο κρατέρ' ἄλγεα πάσχων, Il. 2.721). He is abandoned in anguish due to his festering wound (ἕλκεϊ μοχθίζοντα κακῷ, Il. 2.723). On the island, he lay in grief and dishonor (ἔνθ' ὅ γε κεῖτ' ἀχέων). Miles away, the Trojan War raged, and Philoctetes's men won glory (Il. 2.724–728). The fact that Philoctetes was deserted because of the horrible stench of his wound reveals how truly nauseating it was.²⁵

Paul, though punctured, does not make so much as a peep. But the pathetic cries of Philoctetes were notorious in Greek and Latin tragedy. In Sophocles's *Philoctetes*, Odysseus declares, "He [Philoctetes] filled the entire camp with savage and ill-omened cries, shouting and screaming." As Philoctetes himself comes on stage for the first time, the chorus sings, "A sound rang out, such as might haunt the lips of a man in agony.... I do not mistake from far off the grievous cry of a man in distress; the lament he utters rings out clearly!"²⁶ In the middle of the drama, Sophocles depicts pain as rushing uncontrollably upon the hero. Philoctetes tries to hide it, but the sting is so overwhelming that he involuntarily bursts into unintelligible ululations.²⁷ Thus he wails to his companion Neoptolemus:

> I am destroyed, child—I cannot conceal my suffering with you so close. ATTA-TAI. It shoots through me, shoots through me! How wretched I am—how pitiful! I am destroyed, child—I am shred in pieces! PAPAI. APAPPAPAI PAPA PAPA PAPA PAPAI. By the gods I beg you, if you have a dagger ready to hand, strike at my ankle—cut it off as quickly as you can! Do not spare my life! Do it, boy!²⁸

The impulse toward mutilation is striking here and illustrates the overwhelming nature of the pain. Driven mad by his agony, Sophocles's Philoctetes cries out, "O

---

²⁴ Edith Hall observes, "*Kaka* [the plural of κακόν] can mean 'evil', but it can also refer to illness, disease, pain, harm, suffering, misfortune, and even cowardice in the face of these afflictions" ("Ancient Greek Responses to Suffering: Thinking with Philoctetes," in *Perspectives on Human Suffering*, ed. Jeff Malpas and Norelle Lickiss [New York: Springer, 2012], 155–69, here 157).

²⁵ Note δυσοσμίαν in *Cypria* argument 9 (West, *Epic Fragments*, 76); δυσώδους γενομένου in Ps.-Apollodorus, *Epit.* 3.27.

²⁶ Sophocles, *Phil.* 10–11 (βοῶν, στενάζων), 202–204, 207–210 (βαρεῖα τηλόθεν αὐδὰ τρυσάνωρ. διάσημα θρηνεῖ). See further Emily Allen-Hornblower, "Sounds and Sufferings in Sophocles' *Philoctetes* and Gide's *Philoctète*," *SIFC* 11 (2013): 5–36, esp. 7–19.

²⁷ In contrast to Euripides, Sophocles intensifies the suffering of Philoctetes (Müller, *Philoktet*, 225). See also Sophocles, *Phil.* 215–218.

²⁸ Sophocles, *Phil.* 743–750 (ἀπόλωλα ... διέρχεται, δέρχεται δύστηνος ... βρύκομαι ... μὴ φείσῃ βίου). Cf. Heracles in Sophocles, *Trach.* 1023–1044, 1143–1149. These lines are also translated and cited by Cicero in *Tusc.* 2.20. Cf. Cicero's quotations of Accius in *Tusc.* 2.19; 2.33; *Fin.* 2.94–95, as well as Ovid, *Metam.* 13.48 (*saxa moves gemitu*).

Death, Death, why can you never come, though I do not cease to call you thus each day?"[29]

While experiencing the attack, Philoctetes begs Neoptolemus to burn him with fire (Sophocles, *Phil.* 799-804).[30] Possibly he means for the latter to hurl him, like the deified Empedocles, into a volcano.[31] (Lemnos was known for its volcanic activity.) But the desire to be burned also assimilates Philoctetes to the more famous hero deified by fire. According to Sophocles, Philoctetes himself recalls the moment when he lit the pyre of Heracles (Sophocles, *Phil.* 801-802). Shortly before this recollection, Heracles is said to have "joined the gods as a god, blazing with fire divine."[32] In a later Roman play, the fate of Heracles burning on his pyre is described from Philoctetes's own point of view:

> With trembling right hand I thrust in the blazing pine. The flames recoiled, the torches resisted and avoided his limbs, but Hercules pursued the fire when it held back.... No sound broke out from him, only the fire groaned. O heart of steel! Though set amidst the smoky wisps and menacing flames, he was unmoved, unshaken, not twisting his enflamed limbs to either side. Instead, he offered encouragement and counsel.... The whole crowd stood dumbfounded, and the flames barely seemed to perform their task. His brow was so calm! His majesty so great!... Then he thrust his face into the flames. His heavy beard lit up; but as the threatening fire now attacked his face and the flames licked his head, he did not close his eyes.[33]

Paul, for his part, has no wish to be burned. The wide-eyed natives expect him to be "burned with fever" (πίμπρημι).[34] Yet it is the snake, possibly symbolizing demonic forces (Luke 10:19), who is scorched. Paul rather casually shakes the beast into a fire. It seems more than just a coincidence that there is a fire so readily available. (The author of Acts mentions it three times in 28:2, 3, 5.)[35]

---

[29] Sophocles, *Phil.* 797-798: ὦ Θάνατα Θάνατε, πῶς ἀεὶ καλούμενος / οὕτω κατ' ἦμαρ οὐ δύνῃ μολεῖν ποτε; (cf. 1204-1209).

[30] For the suicidal impulse, see Cicero, *Tusc.* 2.19 (*mori cupiens*). See further Carl Werner Müller, *Euripides, Philoktet: Testimonien und Fragmente*, TK 21 (Berlin: de Gruyter, 2000), 44-45.

[31] On Empedocles and the volcano, see Peter Kingsley, *Ancient Philosophy, Mystery, and Magic: Empedocles and Pythagorean Tradition* (Oxford: Clarendon, 1995), 250-55. On volcanoes at Lemnos, see Charles Segal, *Tragedy and Civilization: An Interpretation of Sophocles*, Martin Classical Lectures 26 (Cambridge: Harvard University Press, 1981), 305-6.

[32] Sophocles, *Phil.* 726-727 (θεοῖς πλάθει θεὸς θείῳ πυρὶ παμφαής).

[33] Ps.-Seneca, *Herc. Oet.* 1727-1732, 1740-1743, 1745-1746, 1752-1755. The courageous endurance of Heracles in Sophocles, though not pronounced, shines through. Heracles exhorts himself, "Come, my hard soul, before this disease stirs again, put on a stone-studded bit of steel and cease your cry, accomplishing as something of joy a deed done by constraint" (*Trach.* 1259-1263).

[34] BDAG, 814, s.v. "πίμπρημι," definition 1.

[35] For the meaning of the fire, see further John Clabeaux, "The Story of the Maltese Viper and Luke's Apology for Paul," *CBQ* 67 (2005): 604-10, esp. 609. For heroes who oppose serpents

Philoctetes's ferocious pain ceases only when he is healed by a son of the deified doctor Asclepius.[36] This weakness and dependence on others for healing prove another contrast to Paul. Far from receiving healing, Paul immediately becomes a healer to others. He can cure dread diseases like fever and dysentery. His benefactions, moreover, are not limited to one man. All the sick people on the island receive healing at his hands (Acts 28:8–9).

To sum up so far, then, we see both striking similarities and differences between Philoctetes and Paul. As for the similarities:

1. Though both men are just, they experience shipwreck.
2. Both are bitten by a poisonous snake
3. On a secluded island
4. Inhabited by barbarians,
5. On which they are marooned for a period of time.
6. Finally, both are the subject of prophecies.

The differences are as follows:

1. Philoctetes suffers extreme pain after his snakebite; Paul does not register any pain at all.
2. Philoctetes issues horrible cries illustrating the depths of his agony; Paul does not even wince.
3. Philoctetes begs to be burned with fire; Paul casually shakes off his viper into a fire.
4. Philoctetes must be healed by doctors; Paul himself, after being bitten, becomes a healer of all who are sick.

One might conclude that these pointed similarities and differences are purposefully crafted. Dennis R. MacDonald, among others, has shown that the author of Luke-Acts is quite capable of literary mimesis.[37] There is no reason to think that, given the prominence of Philoctetes in literature and art, this hero was not an entry in the cultural encyclopedia of the author of Acts. In this case, however, one need not posit a direct genetic connection between texts. After all, there was no single canonical telling of the Philoctetes myth in antiquity. The author of Acts could have

---

with fire, see Daniel Ogden, *Drakōn: Dragon Myth and Serpent Cult in the Greek and Roman Worlds* (Oxford: Oxford University Press, 2013), 223–26, https://doi.org/10.1093/acprof:oso/9780199557325.001.0001.

[36] In *Little Iliad*, argument 2 (West, *Epic Fragments*, 122), the son is Machaon. In Ps.-Apollodorus, *Epit.* 5.8, it is Podaleirios.

[37] MacDonald's writings are extensive. See his own "auto-bibliography" in *Luke and Vergil: Imitations of Classical Greek Literature* (Lanham, MD: Rowman & Littlefield, 2015), 259. For criticism of MacDonald's method, see Margaret M. Mitchell, "Homer in the New Testament?," *JR* 83 (2003): 244–58; Karl Olav Sandnes, "*Imitatio Homeri*? An Appraisal of Dennis R. MacDonald's 'Mimesis Criticism,'" *JBL* 124 (2005): 715–32, https://doi.org/10.2307/30041066. In this study I attempt to avoid the pitfalls of MacDonald's method while employing its strengths.

depended on a diverse set of cultural media for his knowledge of the story of Philoctetes and adapted it for his own ends.

Mimesis, as MacDonald notes, means both imitation and emulation. In most cases, imitation and emulation work in tandem. The similarities shared by Paul and Philoctetes serve to highlight their differences. The thrust of Lukan emulation, as so often in Christian apologetics, seems to be a sophisticated game of one-upmanship. Paul, although he goes through experiences similar to those of Philoctetes, proves to be a far superior hero. His superiority is most poignantly highlighted by his calm demeanor after his snakebite.

But does calmness prove superiority? To answer this question, one must inquire into the cultural values that informed ancient conceptions of the hero. We have already met the Roman Hercules, lauded by Philoctetes himself: "O heart of steel!... His brow was so calm! His majesty so great!" ([Seneca], *Herc. Ot.* 1746). In this play, Hercules is depicted as a Stoic hero. As a general rule, Stoics did not believe that pain was an evil. They often claimed that perfect happiness was possible even for the person scorched and tortured on the rack.[38]

Seneca, a popular Stoic of the mid-first century, argues that the sage cannot succumb to pain. "He stands erect under any load. Nothing lays him low; nothing that must be endured displeases him. For he does not complain that what can afflict a human being afflicts him" (*Ep.* 71.26). Anyone can endure pain if one acts in accordance with Nature (*Ep.* 98.14). "Follow Nature" is a Stoic slogan wherein "Nature" is basically equivalent to God. As part of Nature, humans experience pain. As part of God (divine Reason), they endure it.

Nearer the time when Acts was written, the Stoic philosopher Musonius Rufus gained prominence in Rome. Musonius taught that a person should disdain pain (πόνου). Although people shun suffering by habit, Musonius declared that it was not an evil. In order to acquire virtue, he taught, one must be prepared to endure any hardship. Pain is necessary for virtue (ἀρετή), which is equivalent to complete happiness (εὐδαιμονίας ὅλης).[39] Musonius himself suffered exile and many hardships for his teachings. Yet he never admitted that extreme pain could exceed one's rational power calmly to endure it.

Although a century earlier, Cicero's comments about pain prove most relevant because they directly address Philoctetes. Cicero wrote, "We must consider it shameful, not to suffer pain (for this is sometimes necessary), but to pollute 'that Lemnian rock' with the screams of Philoctetes, '—a rock which, though mute, resounds with wails, plaints, groans, snorts and echoes tearful cries.' ... Let us rather

---

[38] Cicero, *Fin.* 3.42; 5.84–85; Plutarch, *Stoic abs.* 1 (*Mor.* 1057d).
[39] Musonius Rufus, treatise VII ("That One Should Disdain Pain") in Cora Lutz, "Musonius Rufus: the 'Roman Socrates,'" YCS 10 (New Haven: Yale University Press, 1947), 32–129, esp. 57–59.

say that it is a shame and unmanly to be weakened by pain, broken by it, subject to it" (*Fin.* 2.94–95).⁴⁰

A man, Cicero acknowledges, cannot avoid pain. All the same, he is expected to bear it manfully in order to show the virtues of bravery (*fortitudo*) and long-suffering (*patientia*). The brave man cannot succumb to mental sickness or distress (*aegritudo*) (*Tusc.* 3.15).⁴¹ Thus Philoctetes's loud cries and screams are seen as unnecessary, effeminate, and unseemly (*Tusc.* 2.55; *Fin.* 95).⁴² Cicero advises, "As long as you hold it disgraceful and unworthy of a man to groan, shriek, wail, break down, and be unnerved; so long as honor, so long as nobility, so long as worth remain, and so long as you restrain yourself by keeping your eyes upon them, assuredly pain will lead to virtue" (*Tusc.* 2.31).⁴³

Was, then, the author of Acts trying to make Paul better accord with Greco-Roman concepts of virtue? Naturally, Paul in Acts 28 is depicted as neither broken by nor subject to pain. Yet one readily inquires: can Paul actually be long-suffering and courageous *if he does not suffer pain at all*? Cicero writes, "I do not deny the reality of pain—why else should courage [*fortitudo*] be needed? Rather, I say that it is overcome by long-suffering [*patientia*]" (*Tusc.* 2.33; cf. 2.43). Paul lacks long-suffering because—by every indication—he lacks pain.

Paul in Acts 28:5–6 is not manly or a model of Roman courage. He is simply immune to the snakebite and, in this respect, invulnerable.⁴⁴ He does not faint due to the injected poison; he does not even wince.⁴⁵ At least in this episode, moreover, Paul's invulnerability seems intrinsic to himself. He does not need to pray or have faith to be healed. He is simply not harmed.⁴⁶

---

⁴⁰ Cf. Cicero, *Tusc.* 2.58. See further Müller, *Philoktet*, 8–308.

⁴¹ Courage (*fortitudo*) means "scorn of pain" (Cicero, *Tusc.* 2.43; cf. Seneca, *Ep.* 13.4).

⁴² Cf. Dio Chrysostom: "For he who cannot ... thrust pain aside [ἀπώσασθαι λύπην] ... must not such a man be incredibly weak, inferior to a woman, inferior to a eunuch?" (*Or.* 3.34). Martial (*Epigrams* 2.84) draws the link to Philoctetes: "The hero, son of Poeas [Philoctetes], was an effeminate who yielded easily to men" (trans. D. R. Shackleton Bailey, LCL).

⁴³ See further John T. Fitzgerald, *Cracks in an Earthen Vessel: An Examination of the Catalogues of Hardship in the Corinthian Correspondence*, SBLDS 99 (Atlanta: Scholars Press, 1988), 59–70; Felix Budelmann, "The Reception of Sophocles' Representation of Physical Pain," *AJP* 128 (2007): 443–67, esp. 446.

⁴⁴ On Luke's refashioning of manliness, see Brittany E. Wilson, *Unmanly Men: Refigurations of Masculinity in Luke-Acts* (Oxford: Oxford University Press, 2015), esp. 254–56.

⁴⁵ For the author of Luke de-emphasizing the frailty and pain of his central hero (Jesus), see Gregory E. Sterling, "*Mors philosophi*: The Death of Jesus in Luke," *HTR* 94 (2001): 383–402, esp. 393–400.

⁴⁶ To be sure, Paul's radical invulnerability has mythic precedents. When Pythagoras bit a poisonous snake, it was the snake, not Pythagoras, who perished! (Apollonius, *Hist. mir.* 6 in Janet Spittler, "Apollonios [BNJ 1672]," *FGH Continued*, Part IV 1, *Paradoxography*, ed. G. Schepens and Stefan Schorn. Brill Online). It was also said of Rabbi Hanina ben Dosa (first century CE) that, while praying, he was bitten by a poisonous snake (alternatively, a lizard). It was not the rabbi who expired in this story but the snake (y. Ber. 5:1, XIV.A, trans. Tzvee Zahavy, *The Talmud of the*

In short, there seems to be a different set of values at work here. Paul is not a model of manliness or virtue; he is something more than human. Aristotle observes that "a god does not have virtue.... Rather, a god has an excellence more precious than [human] virtue" (οὐδ' ἀρετή ... θεοῦ, ἀλλ' ἡ μὲν τιμιώτερον ἀρετῆς). In the same context, he quotes what was apparently a common saying: "gods arise from humans through superabundance of virtue" (ἐξ ἀνθρώπων γίνονται θεοὶ δι' ἀρετῆς ὑπερβολήν, *Eth. nic.* 7.1.2, 1145a20–27).[47] Aristotle applies this phrase to Homer's Hector, and it was later applied to other deified figures like Heracles, the Dioscuri, and Moses.[48] According to this theology, deification occurs not through virtue but through what *exceeds* virtue. Divinity is *above* the category of virtue. The "divine man" (θεῖον ἄνδρα—Aristotle's term) belongs to a higher order of being (*Eth. nic.* 7.1.2, 1145a28–29).

When the natives of Malta see that Paul is immune to the snakebite, they conclude that he is a god (Acts 28:6). The fact that the author of Acts does not attempt to revise this conclusion compels the reader to take it with utmost seriousness. He could have presented Paul as disputing the conclusion (as in Lycaonia in 14:15), but he refrains.[49] One cannot simply assume that a reader would apply Paul's response fourteen chapters earlier to the snakebite episode. Paul's immunity to the snakebite is the culminating miracle that reveals his true nature. The hero's ending is what the readers will remember, and the author of Acts crafted it well.

Immediately after the snakebite episode, the reader is escorted into a healing story (28:7–10). Paul's ability to heal proves all the more that divine power radiates in and through him. Though he prays for others, he does not need to pray for himself to be healed. Despite being bitten, he is not even wounded. Paul's extraordinary immunity and the wondrous benefits that he bestows make it logical, in ancient Mediterranean culture, to view him as a kind of deity.[50]

Here one must address possible misconceptions about deification in the ancient world. Although deity and humanity may be seen as mutually exclusive today, it was not so in ancient Mediterranean culture, where the deification of a human could involve an ontological transformation into an immortal being of untold energies. It could also consist of a sociopolitical status change through

---

Land of Israel: Preliminary Translation and Explanation, vol. 1 [Chicago: University of Chicago Press, 1989], 199–200). Cf. the different versions in t. Ber. 3.20; b. Ber. 33a.

[47] Cf. Aristotle, *Pol.* 3.1284a3–14; 1284b30–34.

[48] Diodorus, *Bibl. hist.* 4.8.5; 6.6.1; Josephus, *Ant.* 4.8.48 §326.

[49] Joshua W. Jipp, *Divine Visitations and Hospitality to Strangers in Luke-Acts: An Interpretation of the Malta Episode in Acts 28:1–10*, NovTSup 153 (Leiden: Brill, 2013), 45.

[50] Jipp rightly shows how the depiction of the Maltese as fickle and naïve is one-sided (ibid., 17–19). Still, Keener persists in the belief that the author of Acts is "making fun" of the barbarians (*Acts*, 4:3680). On the connection between benefaction and deity, see M. David Litwa, *Jesus Deus: The Early Christian Depiction of Jesus as a Mediterranean God* (Minneapolis: Fortress, 2014), 88–96.

receiving extreme honors.[51] These forms of deification are not mutually exclusive; often the former grounds the latter. The deified Heracles, for instance, became an immortal god on Mount Olympus with a new, super body. He also received sacrifice throughout the Mediterranean as a human hero and a god (Diodorus, *Bibl. hist.* 4.24.1–2; 4.39.1).

The logic of bestowing divine honors was already outlined by Aristotle:

> Honor is the approval given for benefaction [εὐεργετικῆς εὐδοξίας]. Those who have already bestowed benefactions [οἱ εὐεργετηκότες] are justly and above all honored.… The parts of honor are sacrifices [only given to gods and heroes], memorials in poetic meter or without it, privileges, precincts, the privilege of front seats, tombs, images, public maintenance, [and] barbarian things like prostrations and giving place. (*Rhet.* 1.5.9, 1361a27–37)[52]

Normally it is rulers and leading men who provide extreme benefaction;[53] yet Paul becomes a benefactor to the leading man on Malta. Ironically, Paul—who is supposed to be a prisoner—outcompetes the island's highest-ranking benefactor.

The greatest benefactor, according to Aristotle, is the founder of a city or civic community. Thus, the founder is the one most deserving of (divine and heroic) honors (*Pol.* 1.1.12, 1253a31–32).[54] Throughout the book of Acts, Paul is depicted as the founder of Christian communities (ἐκκλησίαι). It is often remarked how the term ἐκκλησία usually designates a civic body or "assembly." Although Paul founds no city (πόλις) built of brick and mortar, he is destined to found his final "assemblies" in Italy. For the author of Acts, Paul certainly is a founder figure. The book of Acts itself might be classified as a foundation myth.

When it comes to founding communities, Philoctetes once again proves helpful for comparison. According to tradition, Philoctetes founded the cities of Petelia, Crimissa, and Thurii in the instep of Italy.[55] After his death, Philoctetes was voted divine honors by the assemblies of these cities. According to the pseudo-Aristotelian tractate *On Marvelous Things Heard*, he was honored

---

[51] See further M. David Litwa, *Becoming Divine: An Introduction to Deification in Western Culture* (Eugene, OR: Cascade, 2013), 9–116.

[52] Cf. Aristotle, *Pol.* 3.8.1–2, 1284a3–14. Note also how in Homer honor is closely associated with being viewed as a god (*Il.* 12.310–312). See further Jon D. Mikalson, *Honor Thy Gods: Popular Religion in Greek Tragedy* (Chapel Hill: University of North Carolina Press, 1991), 133–202.

[53] Musonius Rufus treatise 8 in Lutz, "Musonius Rufus," 66; Augustus, Res gest. divi Aug. 15.1–35.1, in Robert K. Sherk, *The Roman Empire: Augustus to Hadrian*, Translated Documents of Greece and Rome 6 (Cambridge: Cambridge University Press, 1988), 45–50 ($26), https://doi.org/10.1017/CBO9780511552670; Philo, *Legat.* 148.

[54] Note the case of Brasidas in Thucydides, *Peloponnesian War* 5.11.1.

[55] Strabo, *Geogr.* 6.1.3 (Philoctetes founds Petelia on the coast of Bruttium and Crimissa in Calabria); Virgil, *Aen.* 3.401–402 (Petelia is the city of Philoctetes); Justin, *Epitome of the History of Pompeius Trogus*, 20.1.16 (Philoctetes founds Thurii). On these cities, see Giulio Giannelli, *Culti e miti della Magna Grecia: Contributo alla storia più antica delle colonie greche in occidente*, 2nd ed. (Florence: Sansoni, 1963), 161–69.

(τιμᾶσθαι)—that is, worshiped—by the Sybarites (or people of Sybaris) (Ps.-Aristotle, *Mir. ausc.* 107). Three lines (927–929) in Lycophron's *Alexandra* (third, or possibly second, century BCE) are more detailed:

> But in Makalla [a city of Bruttium in the foot of Italy] the inhabitants will build a great shrine [σηκὸν ... μέγαν]
> Above his [Philoctetes's] tomb, and will give him glory as an eternal god [αἰανῇ θεόν]
> With libations [λοιβαῖσι] and offerings of oxen [θύσθλοις βοῶν].[56]

We have here the widespread cultural pattern of profound benefaction: founding a civic community leads to deifying honors.[57]

The logic of Philoctetes's deification (unambiguously signified by the bestowal of animal sacrifice) is nevertheless different from that of Paul. Philoctetes is honored as a hero who suffered. In a sense, it is his suffering that made him sacred.[58] But his actual deification was made possible by—much like Heracles—*overcoming* his sufferings.[59] Only after patient endurance could he win glory as a fighter and founder of cities. At the end of Sophocles's *Philoctetes*, the deified Heracles himself declares to the suffering hero:

> First I will relate ...
> how many pains I suffered and overcame
> to obtain glorious immortality, such as you see.
> Now you ... must suffer as well
> and from your labors make your life glorious.[60]

Seneca (or an imitator) named Philoctetes the "heir of Hercules."[61] Charles Segal calls Philoctetes Heracles's "symbolic alter ego."[62] Christine Mauduit speaks of the "community of destiny" shared by the two heroes.[63] Cedric Whitman names Heracles, "the archetype of Philoctetes' greater self, the pattern of his glory."[64] What

---

[56] For commentary, see Simon Hornblower, *Lykophron Alexandra: Greek Text, Translation, Commentary, and Introduction* (Oxford: Oxford University Press, 2015), 343–49.

[57] The historian Appian (*Bell. civ.* 12.77) also mentions an altar to Philoctetes on the island of Chryse viewed by the Roman general Lucullus in 73 BCE.

[58] Philoctetes's sufferings are "divine" (θεία) and "the care of the gods" (θεῶν μέλετη) (Sophocles, *Phil.* 192, 196).

[59] It is no mistake that Sophocles elsewhere likens Heracles's death throe pains to a bite and the "blood-red poison of a hateful viper" (φοίνιος ἐχθρᾶς ἐχίδνης ἰός, *Trach.* 770–771).

[60] Sophocles, *Phil.* 1418–1422: καὶ πρῶτα μέν σοι τὰ ἐμὰς λέξω τύχας, / ὅσους πονήσας καὶ διεξελθὼν πόνους / ἀθάνατον ἀρετὴν ἔσχον, ὡς πάρεσθ' ὁρᾶν / καὶ σοί, σάφ' ἴσθι, τοῦτ' ὀφείλεται παθεῖν, / ἐκ τῶν πόνων τῶνδ' εὐκλεᾶ θέσθαι βίον.

[61] [Seneca], *Herc. Ot.* 1605 (*Herculis heres*)

[62] Segal, *Tragedy and Civilization*, 293.

[63] Mauduit, "De Lemnos," 27 (*communauté de destin*).

[64] Cedric H. Whitman, *Sophocles: A Study of Heroic Humanism* (Cambridge: Harvard

we can affirm is this: by participating in Herculean sufferings, Philoctetes shared in Herculean glory (apotheosis).[65]

In Acts, Paul preaches that the Christ must suffer (17:3, 26:23). Jesus himself says to Ananias in Acts 9: "I will show him [Paul] how much he must suffer for the sake of my name" (v. 16). There is a relation between the suffering of Paul and the suffering of Jesus. In both cases, suffering leads to glory. Yet in both cases their active and agonized suffering is not emphasized or valued for its own sake.

Paul's founding of Italian communities is still anticipated in Acts 28.[66] In verse 6, the missionary is deified by the natives because he is perceived to be invulnerable and unsuffering. In this respect, Paul trumps even Homeric gods, who can be wounded and suffer pain.[67] As an extraordinary benefactor through his ministry of healing, Paul also receives appropriate honors (28:10). The bestowal of great honors, Joshua W. Jipp observes, "is the appropriate response to deities."[68] It is the act, we can say, that constitutes Paul's literary deification.

This literary deification occurs on two levels. In the narrative itself, the natives call Paul a god and honor him accordingly. This is the deification "in" the text. But there is also a deification communicated in the very act of composing and publishing this text. The author's textual practice of writing a story featuring Paul's deification communicates something at another level. In brief, the author of Acts engages in a practice of "discursive deification," a literary form of deification in which a human being is intentionally depicted as a deity in a narrative.

There is another way in which one can approach Paul's discursive deification. Acts 28:1–10 operates, Jipp remarks, "according to the logic of a theoxeny."[69] (Theoxeny here designates the visit of a deity to the human world.) In theoxenies, gods typically come in disguised, humble—and almost always human—form to a foreign land or people. There is usually a recognition scene in which the divine nature of the god is revealed. Those who treated the deity poorly are punished, while those who treated the divinity hospitably are blessed. The author of Luke-Acts earlier presents Jesus as visiting the two disciples on the road to Emmaus using the tropes

---

University Press, 1951), 187. See further Charles M. Stang, *Our Divine Double* (Cambridge: Harvard University Press, 2016).

[65] See further S. J. Harrison, "Sophocles and the Cult of Philoctetes," *JHS* 109 (1989): 173–75, https://doi.org/10.2307/632045; Norman Austin, *Sophocles' Philoctetes and the Great Soul Robbery*, Wisconsin Studies in Classics (Madison: University of Wisconsin Press, 2011), 199–201.

[66] If it is assumed that Paul is also honored as the founder of a Christian community on Malta, then he may also have been honored as a founder already in Acts 28:10.

[67] Note Aphrodite in Homer, *Il.* 5.330–362.

[68] Jipp, *Divine Visitations*, 268. Jipp cites Euripides, *Bacch.* 192, 209–210, 321, 342; Aeschylus, *Cho.* 883–891; *Eum.* 846–868, 881–891; Ovid, *Metam.* 3.518–523.

[69] Jipp, *Divine Visitations*, 256.

of theoxeny (Luke 24:13–35).[70] Arguably Jesus's entire earthly ministry in the Gospel of Luke is presented as a kind of theoxeny.[71]

What is genuinely striking about Jipp's argument (and perhaps not enough emphasized by Jipp himself) is that in Acts 28 Paul plays the part of the disguised god. The Maltese welcome Paul as a stranger washed in by the sea. After an initially wrong assessment, they recognize the sign of his divinity (immunity, lack of suffering). They are subsequently rewarded by the newly recognized deity in a dramatic mass healing.

In this way, Paul brings salvation to Malta. For the Maltese, Paul himself was that salvation.[72] To the surprise of the commentators, the Maltese did not hear a word about Jesus from the lips of Paul. All they saw was the divine agent, the heroic missionary. As with Philoctetes and Heracles, Paul and Jesus share a community of destiny. But we can say more: by Acts 28, the identity of sender (Jesus) and that of the sent (Paul) have in some way merged. This logic appears already in Luke's Gospel during the mission of the seventy. Satan, the archenemy of Christ, is defeated in the ministry of the apostles. It is the apostles who have the same powers of exorcism as Jesus. It is in this context that Jesus gives the apostles authority to trample upon snakes and scorpions (Luke 10:17–20). In Acts 28, Paul manifests this very power with added flair.[73] No christological proclamation is given because none is required. Paul is the embodiment or manifestation of Jesus's power and divinity—and this is sufficient.[74]

---

[70] Ibid., 25, 234–35.

[71] See further A. Denaux, "The Theme of Divine Visits and Human (In)Hospitality in Luke-Acts," in *The Unity of Luke-Acts*, ed. Joseph Verheyden, BETL 142 (Leuven: Leuven University Press, 1999), 255–79, esp. 260–61, 266–68, 274–79.

[72] Cf. Richard I. Pervo: "Paul is not just a bearer of a saving message; he is also a saving figure" (*The Making of Paul: Constructions of the Apostle in Early Christianity* [Minneapolis: Fortress, 2010], 154–55); Paul is a "divine agent of salvation" (Jipp, *Divine Visitations*, 12).

[73] On power over snakes, see further James A. Kelhoffer, *Miracle and Mission: The Authentication of Missionaries and Their Message in the Longer Ending of Mark*, WUNT 2/112 (Tübingen: Mohr Siebeck, 2000), 340–416.

[74] One might even say that the same logic active in John's Gospel is incipiently present in Acts. Divine agent and sender are somehow one—although the exact nature of their unity is left open. See further Wayne A. Meeks, "The Divine Agent and His Counterfeit in Philo and the Fourth Gospel," in *Aspects of Religious Propaganda in Judaism and Early Christianity*, ed. Elisabeth Schüssler Fiorenza, SJCA 2 (Notre Dame, IN: University of Notre Dame Press, 1976), 43–67; Rudolf Schnackenburg, "'Der Vater, der mich gesandt hat': Zur johanneischen Christologie," in *Anfänge der Christologie: Festschrift für Ferdinand Hahn zum. 65. Geburtstag*, ed. Ciliers Breytenbach und Henning Paulsen (Göttingen: Vandenhoeck & Ruprecht, 1991), 275–92; Peder Borgen, "God's Agent in the Fourth Gospel," and "Observations on God's Agent and Agency in John's Gospel," in *The Gospel of John: More Light from Philo, Paul and Archaeology; The Scriptures, Tradition, Exposition, Settings, Meaning*, NovTSup 154 (Leiden: Brill, 2014), 167–78, 193–218, respectively.

But does the author of Acts really agree with the Maltese that Paul is a kind of god? Isn't the view of the natives still, as Jipp puts it, "theologically imprecise"?[75] It is true that the author of Acts himself was probably not prepared to call Paul θεός directly. One must keep in mind, however, that he does not directly call Jesus θεός either.[76] Nevertheless, the author was certainly aware that, in Mediterranean culture, offering extreme benefaction rightfully leads to honors—even divine ones. He uses the key term εὐεργετέω ("to bestow benefaction"), applying it to Jesus and his ministry of healing and exorcism (Acts 10:38; cf. Luke 22:25).[77] After his sacrificial death, Jesus is raised to the rank of "Lord and Messiah" (κύριον ... καὶ χριστόν, Acts 2:36). These are divine titles—fitting for a being of divine status.[78] In short, the author of Luke-Acts has no problem discursively deifying Jesus even as he avoids bald claims such as "Jesus is θεός."

A similar technique of discursive deification seems to be applied to Paul in Acts. In Acts 13–28, Paul imitates Jesus in his beneficent miracles. Just as Jesus heals Peter's mother-in-law from a fever, so Paul heals Publius by the imposition of his hands (Luke 4:38–39, Acts 28:8). And just as other sick people immediately come to Jesus for public healing, so Paul heals all the sick on Malta (Luke 4:40, Acts 28:9).[79] The parallels are precise and deliberate. They begin to make sense only when it is realized that the divine powers of the sender are operative in the deified missionary.

In some respects, Paul even surpasses Jesus in the power and drama of his marvels. Paul can blind an opponent on command (Acts 13:11). He can stay up all night preaching—only pausing to resurrect someone (20:7–11). He can walk away after being brutally stoned (14:20). He shows no signs of exhaustion after a

---

[75] Jipp, *Divine Visitations*, 263.

[76] Nina Henrichs-Tarasenkova, *Luke's Christology of Divine Identity*, LNTS 542 (London: Bloomsbury T&T Clark, 2016), 3–6. Henrichs-Tarasenkova herself argues that Luke "indirectly characterizes Jesus as God when he shows that Jesus shares YHWH's divine identity" (191).

[77] On the idea of benefaction, see F. Danker, "Graeco-Roman Cultural Accommodation in the Christology of Luke-Acts," in *SBL Seminar Papers 1983*, ed. Kent Harold Richards (Chico, CA: Scholars Press, 1983), 391–414; Jerome H. Neyrey, "God, Benefactor and Patron: The Major Cultural Model for Interpreting the Deity in Greco-Roman Antiquity," *JSNT* 27 (2005): 465–92, https://doi.org/10.1177/0142064x05055749. For a treatment of Jesus as benefactor in the gospels and Paul, see Luke Timothy Johnson, *Among the Gentiles: Greco-Roman Religion and Christianity* (New Haven: Yale University Press, 2009), 142–57.

[78] For general comments on these titles, see François Bovon, *Luke the Theologian: Thirty-Three Years of Research (1950–1983)*, trans. Ken McKinney (Allison Park, PA: Pickwick, 1987), 187–92. On the divine implications of κύριος, see H. Douglas Buckwalter, *The Character and Purpose of Luke's Christology*, SNTSMS 89 (Cambridge: Cambridge University Press, 1996), 184–96; C. Kavin Rowe, *Early Narrative Christology: The Lord in the Gospel of Luke* (Grand Rapids: Baker Academic, 2009), esp. 199–207. For some corrective comments, see Christopher M. Tuckett, "The Christology of Luke-Acts" in Verheyden, *Unity of Luke-Acts*, 133–64, esp. 149–57.

[79] See further Stefan Schreiber, *Paulus als Wundertäter: Redaktionsgeschichtliche Untersuchungen zur Apostelgeschichte und den authentischen Paulusbriefen*, BZNW 79 (Berlin: de Gruyter, 1996), 134–35; Jipp, *Divine Visitations*, 12–13, 48–49.

disastrous shipwreck (27:44–28:3).[80] His name has the same magical status as that of Jesus—the demons know and fear it (19:15). His power is so great and so tangible that it can even be conveyed through sweat rags and aprons that have merely touched his skin (19:12).[81] In Acts 28, finally, Paul easily survives a snakebite that would have been lethal to any normal human being. This triumph over the viper as a "demonic agent of death parallels Jesus's own vindication from death."[82]

The point here, of course, is not that Paul is depicted as *more* divine than Jesus or that Paul was actually venerated or worshiped in the earliest Christian communities. We can only speak of Paul's deification in terms of the narrative logic of Acts (that is, his discursive deification). Naturally, Paul is discursively deified only insofar as Jesus himself is. In other words, he is deified only by closely imitating Jesus in the narrative of Acts. Yet he is deified nonetheless—and according to the same cultural logic.

The discursive deification of Paul is represented as both ontological and political. Only as a being belonging to an ontologically higher register can Paul be immune to poison and radiate healing energy. The honors he receives—being called a god, receiving public maintenance and lavish hospitality—hint that he has been raised to a higher, divine status—at least one higher than Publius. This, then, is the realization necessary to interpret Acts 28:1–10: Paul *is* divine insofar as he shares the divine powers and honors of Jesus.

Jipp calls Paul in Acts 28:1–10 "the powerful agent of Jesus" and "the carrier of God's prophetic power."[83] I think it would be better to call Paul the embodied revelation of Jesus's power and deity. To be fair, Jipp closely agrees with this formulation when he says that Paul "embodies the powerful presence of Jesus."[84] One finds it odd, then, when Jipp concludes that "Paul is not a god, but the barbarians rightly perceive the divine presence at work in this powerful agent."[85] Surely in this case the perfected agent has become like his master (Luke 6:40). In our language, the agent narratively participates in the divinity of his sender and thus rightly receives the honors that accord with the sender's divine status. In Greco-Roman cultural mentality (shared by the author of Luke-Acts), one cannot separate, I think, *embodying divine presence* from *assuming a divine status*. Christ is Paul's true self—his divine double—just as Heracles is the second self of Philoctetes.

---

[80] God is not absent from the shipwreck scene but is present in Paul. God gives Jonah a command that is disobeyed and subsequently leads to a storm. Paul gives the sailors a command that, when disobeyed, introduces a similar storm (Acts 27:10–11, 21).

[81] Here readers of Luke-Acts might recall the woman healed by touching Jesus's garments (Luke 8:43–48). Cf. also Mark 6:56.

[82] Jipp, *Divine Visitations* 263.

[83] Ibid., 270, 272.

[84] Ibid., 261.

[85] Ibid., 263.

In this light, one can fully agree with Jipp when he says that "by virtue of his embodiment of Jesus' presence," Paul "is in some manner a divine figure."[86] Into which class of divinities Paul belongs is left open. Evidently Paul does not outrank the Lord and Messiah Jesus. Most definitely a deified Paul proves no threat to the Jewish high God. The author of Luke-Acts is evidently operating with a widespread cultural assumption—that there are many and multiple degrees of deity. Deities of lesser status and power do not threaten the high God, who ultimately dispenses power and receives due praise like the ebb and flow of Homer's Ocean.

In sum, the author of Luke-Acts walks a fine line. He portrays his heroes as undergoing personal and public catastrophes, but he does not depict them as actively suffering pain. In this way, he both avoids the disgraceful shrieks of Philoctetes and memorably underscores the divinity of his heroes (Jesus and Paul). Even though the author of Luke-Acts maintains the centrality of his primary divine hero, Jesus, other heroes who imitate him on the narrative level can also participate in his divine being and status. In sum, the Maltese are not chided for thinking Paul a god—and for good reason. Although not precise, perhaps, they are perfectly correct.

---

[86] Ibid., 261. Cf. Richard I. Pervo: "Paul is a kind of divine, indestructible being, delivered from the tomb of the sea" (*Acts: A Commentary*, Hermeneia [Minneapolis: Fortress, 2009], 673).

Gentile Gods at the Eschaton: A Reconsideration of Paul's "Principalities and Powers" in 1 Corinthians 15

EMMA WASSERMAN
wasserme@religion.rutgers.edu
Rutgers University, New Brunswick, NJ 08901

This article argues that Paul's "principalities and powers" in 1 Cor 15:23–24 are best understood as a subordinate host of gentile gods. Like texts such as Isa 24, the Book of the Watchers, the Animal Apocalypse of Enoch, and Dan 10, Paul treats gentile gods as belonging to the lower ranks of the divine order and envisions a time when they will be judged, punished, or destroyed. These traditions also shed light on the brief appearance of Christ's enemies in 15:23–24 and the heavy emphasis on Christ's submission in 15:24–28. Paul alludes to conflict in ways that suppress the possibility of rivalry, competition, and coup, in part by imagining a battle that takes place in the lower ranks where it is carried out by a warrior deputy, and in part by strategically telescoping to focus attention on the incomparable standing of the supreme God over all. These findings undermine a number of popular theories about evil forces and powers that are alleged to be central to Paul's apocalyptic thinking here and elsewhere in the letters.

In spite of great interest in the claim that Christ will defeat "every ruler, authority, and power" (πᾶσαν ἀρχὴν καὶ πᾶσαν ἐξουσίαν καὶ δύναμιν) in 1 Cor 15:24, scholars have struggled to identify illuminating historical contexts for understanding Paul's text. Much of the scholarship looks to Jewish traditions about lesser deities, instrumental opponents, and harassing spirits but construes this as evidence for Jewish apocalyptic views about so-called powers of evil. A careful and critical reading of texts such as Isa 24, Dan 7–10, the Enochic Book of the Watchers, the Animal Apocalypse of Enoch, the Astronomical Books of Enoch, and certain Qumran texts shows that their writers and editors do not envision unqualified evil forces and powers. Instead, they typically employ lower-ranking deities as foils for representing the Jewish God as an unmatched and invulnerable sovereign. This is the case whether they envision these deities as foolish insubordinates, doomed opponents, harassing earthly spirits, middle managers, or various classes of lesser deities mistakenly worshiped by gentiles. In place of vaguely defined battles and

727

threats posed by "evil powers," the texts develop myths about the divine political order that, in diverse and creative ways, work to suppress the possibility of divine competition. Understood in this way, such traditions shed much-needed light on Paul's text, especially Christ's briefly discussed conflict with lesser opponents, the heavy emphasis on the incomparable and irresistible power of the supreme deity in verses 24–28, and the repeated affirmations of Christ's noncompetition with this deity. Paul's "principalities and powers" will also reemerge as gentile gods.

I. Good versus Evil? Normative Constructions of the "Principalities and Powers"

Readers have shown great interest in the idea of an apocalyptic battle against "powers of evil" in Paul's thought.[1] Though the letters show relatively little interest in divine opponents, interpreters find a battle against such powers in 1 Cor 15:23–24, allusions to "malevolent forces" in the ἀρχαί, δυνάμεις, and ἄγγελοι of Rom 8:38, the "rulers of this age" (ἀρχόντων τοῦ αἰῶνος τούτου) in 1 Cor 2:6–8, and the "God of this age" in 2 Cor 4:4. Many interpreters also relate these so-called principalities and powers to discussions of *daimonia* (δαιμόνια) in 1 Cor 10:19–22, the *stoicheia* (στοιχεῖα) of Gal 4:3, 9, Satan (1 Cor 5:5, 2 Cor 2:11, 11:14, 12:7, 1 Thess 2:18, 3:5), Belial (2 Cor 6:15), and to similar language in Colossians and Ephesians.[2]

Oscar Cullmann and Ernst Käsemann did much to popularize the view that

---

[1] Oscar Cullmann, *The State in the New Testament* (New York: Scribner, 1956); Cullmann, *Christ and Time: The Primitive Christian Conception of Time and History*, trans. Floyd V. Filson (Philadelphia: Westminster, 1964); Ernst Käsemann, *Commentary on Romans*, trans. Geoffrey W. Bromiley (Grand Rapids: Eerdmans, 1980); Käsemann, "On the Subject of Primitive Christian Apocalyptic," in *New Testament Questions of Today*, trans. W. J. Montague (Philadelphia: Fortress, 1969), 108–37; Clinton Morrison, *The Powers That Be: Earthly Rulers and Demonic Powers in Romans 13, 1–7*, SBT 29 (Naperville, IL: Allenson, 1960); Heinrich Schlier, *Principalities and Powers in the New Testament*, QD 3 (New York: Herder & Herder, 1961); G. B. Caird, *Principalities and Powers: A Study in Pauline Theology*, The Chancellor's Lectures 1954 (Oxford: Clarendon, 1956); Johan Christiaan Beker, *The Triumph of God: The Essence of Paul's Thought*, trans. Loren T. Stuckenbruck (Minneapolis: Fortress, 1990); Walter Wink, *Naming the Powers: The Language of Power in the New Testament* (Philadelphia: Fortress, 1984); Clinton E. Arnold, *Powers of Darkness: Principalities and Powers in Paul's Letters* (Downers Grove, IL: InterVarsity Press, 1992); Beverly Roberts Gaventa, *Our Mother Saint Paul* (Louisville: Westminster John Knox, 2007). Cf. Christopher Forbes, "Paul's Principalities and Powers: Demythologizing Apocalyptic?," *JSNT* 82 (2001): 61–88.

[2] I argue elsewhere (*Apocalypse as Holy War: Divine Politics and Polemics in the World of Paul*, AYBRL [New Haven: Yale University Press, forthcoming]) that, like the "powers" of 1 Cor 15:23–28, the στοιχεῖα of Gal 4 and the δαιμόνια of 1 Cor 10 are best understood as gentile gods that have been reclassified as relatively powerless subordinates. For a similar view, see Paula Fredriksen, "Judaizing the Nations: The Ritual Demands of Paul's Gospel," *NTS* 56 (2010): 232–52.

early Christian apocalypticism centrally concerns a battle against powers of evil.[3] As influentially formulated by Käsemann and Cullmann, for instance, such powers explain Christ's victory at both the first and second comings. Though this battle appears imminent in texts such as 1 Cor 15:23–28 and 1 Thess 4:14–17, Cullmann infamously maintained that Christ's first coming marks the "D-Day" of Christian victory that has only to be completed at the "V-Day" of the parousia.[4] Similarly, Käsemann argued that Christ broke the rule of "cosmic powers" over the world, especially the supposed powers of sin and death that appear in Rom 6–8. To these interpreters, normative theological interests also happily coincide with the goals and methods of critical inquiry.[5] Thus, to Cullmann, Käsemann, and many after them, Paul's evil apocalyptic overlords explain the evils of the contemporary world, whether construed as disfavored political regimes or some aspect of pluralism, secularism, and modernity.[6]

Many interpreters have followed the lead of Cullmann and Käsemann in placing theories of principalities, cosmic powers, and evil potentates at the center of twentieth- and twenty-first-century theology. Like that of Cullmann and Käsemann, much of this work intermingles normative concepts and categories with second-order critical ones.[7] Among other problems, such interpretations tend to reappropriate evaluative claims that appear in some (but not all) of the literature and to impose a unifying ideological framework that obscures some of the most interesting patterns in the texts. In the 1950s, for instance G. H. C. Macgregor published an article that identified "astral religious beliefs" as the appropriate

[3] Supposed powers and opponent figures also feature prominently in earlier works. For instance, in the nineteenth century Johannes Weiss found the supposed defeat of Satan to be key for early Christian theology (*Jesus' Proclamation of the Kingdom of God*, ed. and trans. Richard Hyde Hiers and David Larrimore Holland [London: SCM, 1971]). Similarly, Otto Everling (*Die paulinische Angelologie und Dämonologie: Ein biblisch-theologischer Versuch* [Göttingen: Vandenhoeck & Ruprecht, 1888]) and Martin Dibelius (*Die Geisterwelt im Glauben des Paulus* [Göttingen: Vandenhoeck & Ruprecht, 1909]) also made "angels" and "demons" very central.

[4] See Cullmann, *Christ and Time*, 145; for more recent adaptations of this scheme, see Johan Christiaan Beker, *Paul the Apostle: The Triumph of God in Life and Thought* (Philadelphia: Fortress, 1980), 159–60.

[5] For an alternative view of sin and death in Rom 6–8 as literary personifications, see Stanley K. Stowers, *A Rereading of Romans: Justice, Jews, and Gentiles* (New Haven: Yale University Press, 1994), 179–89; Stowers, "Paul's Four Discourses about Sin," in *Celebrating Paul: Festschrift in Honor of Jerome Murphy O'Connor, O.P., and Joseph A. Fitzmyer, S. J.*, ed. Peter Spitaler, CBQMS 48 (Washington, DC: Catholic Biblical Association of America, 2011), 100–127.

[6] See, e.g., Wink (*Naming the Powers*) for a liberation theology reading of the principalities and powers and Arnold (*Powers of Darkness*) on the supposed evils of heavy metal music and New Age religion.

[7] See esp. Beker, *Triumph of God*; Gaventa, *Our Mother Saint Paul*; and Susan Eastman, *Recovering Paul's Mother Tongue: Language and Theology in Galatians* (Grand Rapids: Eerdmans, 2007).

context for making sense of Paul's thought about "powers of evil."⁸ In this article, Macgregor appeals to texts such as Deut 4:19, where gentiles worship the host, and Jub. 15:31, where they worship misleading "demons." The result is a picture of non-Jews as enslaved to the fate of the stars.⁹ On this approach, such ideas also reflect certain cultural and religious shifts in the Hellenistic period wherein the masses fell under the sway of a popular astrological fatalism influenced by Chaldean lore and Greek philosophy.¹⁰ Macgregor writes:

> The old rejected gods reappear as astral deities. The seven planets are enthroned as *kosmokratores* or "potentates of this world" and arbiters of human fate.... By a simple enough psychological process the stars which determined fate appeared to be hostile more often than kindly, so that the religious man becomes absorbed in nothing quite so much as devising means of escape from the prison-house of the stars.¹¹

The texts treated here are suggestive, but Macgregor's theory of astral determinism creatively repurposes an ideological polemic about legitimate and illegitimate forms of religion. In doing so, he relies on superficial amalgamations of the evidence and tendentious, ideologically charged categories of analysis. The end result is a vision of Christ victoriously freeing heathens from their alleged thralldom to a pseudo-science about the enslaving power of the stars. In spite of these problems, such theories have proved influential. The recent work of Clinton E. Arnold, for instance, argues that the στοιχεῖα of Gal 4 should be understood as "evil astral spirits."¹² Though he offers a more carefully argued historical case, Arnold labors over a single text (the Testament of Solomon), which probably dates to a later period.¹³ Even more problematic, however, is that Arnold never explains, qualifies, or defends the identification of στοιχεῖα as "evil" or "demonic," whether in the Testament of Solomon or in Gal 4.

An important article by Matthew Black also draws on and develops

---

⁸ G. H. C. Macgregor, "Principalities and Powers: The Cosmic Background of Paul's Thought," *NTS* 1 (1954) 17–28; reprinted in *New Testament Sidelights: Essays in Honor of Alexander Purdy*, ed. Harvey K. McArthur (Hartford, CT: Hartford Seminary Foundation, 1960), 88–104.

⁹ Macgregor also relies heavily on evidence drawn from the later Hermetic corpus and from the Testament of Solomon.

¹⁰ This theory draws on Gilbert Murray, *Five Stages of Greek Religion*, 3rd ed. (1955; repr., Mineola, NY: Dover, 2002), 144; see also Hans Lietzmann's argument about "astral forces" (*Sternenmächte*) in *An Die Korinther: I, II*, HNT 9 (Tübingen: Mohr Siebeck, 1949), 46.

¹¹ Macgregor, "Principalities and Powers," 92.

¹² Clinton E. Arnold, "Returning to the Domain of the Powers: 'stoicheia' as Evil Spirits in Galatians 4:3, 9," *NovT* 38 (1996): 57–60. Similarly, Martinus C. de Boer ("The Meaning of the Phrase *ta stoicheia tou kosmou* in Galatians," *NTS* 53 [2007]: 204–24) and J. Louis Martyn (*Galatians: A New Translation with Introduction and Commentary*, AB 33A [New York: Doubleday, 1997], 393–406) also appeal to normative language about evil powers, malevolent forces, and demons.

¹³ Arnold, "Returning to the Domain," 57–59.

Macgregor's work.[14] Black connects the principalities and powers in Pauline and post-Pauline literature with the appropriation of Ps 110:1 in Christian and Jewish traditions, especially Dan 7:27, which promises an eternal kingdom that "all the dominions will serve and obey."[15] According to Black, Dan 7 reinterprets Ps 110, "The Lord says to my lord, 'Sit at my right hand until I make your enemies your footstool,'" as do texts such as 1 Cor 15:24, Rom 8:38–39, 1 Pet 3:22, and many passages in Ephesians (esp. 1:20–21, 3:10, 6:12).[16] Black also relates these texts to the elaborate "angelologies" found in some Qumran literature and finds linguistic precedents for Paul's ἀρχαί and ἐξουσίαι in 1 En. 61:10, T. Levi 3:8, 2 Macc 3:24, 2 Enoch, and the Testament of Solomon.[17] On this basis, he concludes that the principalities and powers "are cosmic or celestial potentates whose empires are among the host of heaven, κοσμοκράτορας τοῦ σκότους τούτου, Eph 6:12, and most probably the astral deities of Hellenistic religions accommodated within Jewish-Hellenistic angelology."[18]

There are several problems with Black's theory. Not only are two of his key texts likely to be late and Christianized (1 En. 61 and T. Levi 3), but the literature he cites also envisions lower-ranking deities not as evil rebel powers but to exemplify the power of the supreme deity. For instance, in 1 En. 61:10, the host is called by God as "the Cherubim, the Seraphim, and Ophanim, and all the angels of power, and all the angels of principalities, and the Elect One, and the other powers on the earth"; 2 Macc 3:24 imagines Israel's God as "ruler of all spirits and of all powers [ὁ τῶν πνευμάτων καὶ πάσης ἐξουσία δυνάστης]"; and the writer of 1QH[a] IX, 11–12 depicts eternal spirits and stars as having dominion (ממשלת).[19] These texts imagine lower-ranking deities as obedient to their supreme divine commander and king, rather than to evil overlords. Like many before and after him, Black nevertheless

---

[14] Matthew Black, "πᾶσαι ἐχουσίαι αὐτῷ ὑποταγήσονται (All Powers Will Be Subject to Him)," in *Paul and Paulinism: Essays in Honour of C. K. Barrett*, ed. Morna D. Hooker and Stephen G. Wilson (London: SPCK, 1982), 74–82.

[15] Trans. John J. Collins, *Daniel: A Commentary on the Book of Daniel*, Hermeneia (Minneapolis: Fortress, 1993), 276.

[16] For a similar approach to Dan 7, see Chrys C. Caragounis, *The Ephesian Mysterion: Meaning and Content*, ConBNT 8 (Lund: Gleerup, 1977), 157–61; Caragounis, *The Son of Man: Vision and Interpretation*, WUNT 38 (Tübingen: Mohr Siebeck, 1986), 68–69. Caragounis is sharply criticized by Collins, *Daniel: A Commentary*, 322–23.

[17] Other studies have made 1 En. 61:10 central to the interpretation of the principalities and powers, e.g., Wilhelm Bousset, *Die Religion des Judentums im späthellenistischen Zeitalter*, 3rd ed., ed. Hugo Gressmann, HNT 21 (Tübingen: Mohr, 1966), 326; C. E. B. Cranfield, *A Critical and Exegetical Commentary on the Epistle to the Romans*, 2 vols., ICC (Edinburgh: T&T Clark, 1975–1979), 1:441–44.

[18] Black, "All Powers Will Be Subject," 76.

[19] Black's 1QH I, 11 (DJD XL: IX, 11–12). See also the "dominion of evil" in 1QM XVII, 5–6; of light and dark throughout the day in 1 QH[a] XX, 10; and language about *šeltanat* in 1 En. 72:1, 82:10; cf. 4QEnastr[b] 28.

characterizes this literature as evidence for "evil powers," "celestial 'potentates,'" and "tyrants," even though such evaluative language is often absent from the texts.

Many others scholars also presume the existence of robust traditions about evil powers and rebel overlords. Interpreters such as Walter Wink, Clinton Arnold, and Beverly Roberts Gaventa have worked to popularize theories about a victory against evil apocalyptic overlords. Many others also treat these theories as well-established foundations for historical-critical scholarship. For instance, Richard A. Horsley and Joseph A. Fitzmyer agree that Paul's language about δαιμόνια in 1 Cor 10 alludes to a battle against evil powers, even though they otherwise take very different approaches to the letter.[20] Horsley also characterizes the personification of death in 1 Cor 15 as "rooted in Paul's Jewish apocalyptic worldview in which superhuman forces are battling with God for control of society and history as well as individual lives (cf. Rom 5:12–21, Rev 6:8)."[21] Lacking critical perspective, rhetoric about a battle where God fights various "evil non-gods" comes to characterize a text that shows little interest in evil or opposition. Like Macgregor's "astral determinism" and Black's "evil potentates," Horsley's language about divine beings "controlling" persons and history is also misleading. Among other problems, such theories often mischaracterize the literature in question and mistakenly portray polemics about illegitimate gods as unique features of Jewish apocalyptic thought.

II. Gentile Gods at the Eschaton? Punishment, Subjection, and Conflict within the Divine Ranks

Scholars of ancient Judaism have successfully reframed discussion of so-called monotheism in biblical and Hellenistic Jewish literature.[22] Instead of a solitary

---

[20] Fitzmyer sidesteps the precise identification of the enemies in 1 Cor 15:24–25, but his work on δαιμόνια in 1 Cor 10 develops a version of the apocalyptic-demons theory (*First Corinthians: A New Translation with Introduction and Commentary*, AYB 32 [New Haven: Yale University Press, 2008], 330–52, 393–94). Similarly, see Horsley, *1 Corinthians*, ANTC (Nashville: Abingdon, 1998), 141. Likewise, Hans Conzelmann casually notes that "demonology is a standard part of the apocalyptic world picture. The designation of the demons are Jewish" (*1 Corinthians: A Commentary on the First Epistle to the Corinthians*, trans. James W. Leitch, Hermeneia [Philadelphia: Fortress, 1975], 271–72). See also Gordon D. Fee, *The First Epistle to the Corinthians*, NICNT (Grand Rapids: Eerdmans, 1987), 471–75, though without much emphasis (see n. 41); similarly, Dale B. Martin, *The Corinthian Body* (New Haven: Yale University Press, 1995), 132–33, drawing on Gerhard Kittel, "ἄγγελος," TDNT 1:74–87, here 86. To similar ends, see M. Gruber, "gillulim," DDD, 346–47.

[21] Horsley, *1 Corinthians*, 204.

[22] See Mark S. Smith, *The Origins of Biblical Monotheism: Israel's Polytheistic Background and the Ugaritic Texts* (Oxford: Oxford University Press, 2001), esp. 41–53; Smith, *The Early History of God: Yahweh and Other Deities in Ancient Israel*, 2nd ed. (Grand Rapids: Eerdmans, 2002); Patrick D. Miller, "Cosmology and World Order in the Old Testament: The Divine Council

divine ruler, they find a much more crowded cosmology, one that includes armies, stars, heavenly bodies, winds, rains, seasons, as well as anonymous assemblies, councils, and hosts.[23] The biblical literature typically characterizes these lesser deities as obedient to their supreme divine commander (among biblical texts, see, e.g., Gen 2:1, Isa 40:26, 45:12, Jer 33:22, Pss 33:6, 103:19–20, Neh 9:6). In a relatively small subset of the literature, however, we find allusions to moments of insubordination, disarray, and even conflict in the lower ranks. Within the biblical anthology, the most striking examples appear in Isa 24, 34, and Pss 58 and 82. These texts will offer helpful points of departure for reconsidering the roles of supposed evil agents in later Hellenistic works such Dan 7–12, Enochic traditions, and certain texts from Qumran.

The writer of Isa 24 imagines a time when the supreme God will castigate a lawless earth. As explained in verses 21–22, this punishment will also come to include at least some members of the heavenly ranks:

> On that day Yahweh will punish the host of heaven in heaven [צבא המרום במרום],[24] and on earth the kings of the earth. They will be gathered together like prisoners in a pit; they will be shut up in a prison, and after many days they will be punished. Then the moon will be abashed, and the sun ashamed; for Yahweh of hosts will reign on Mount Zion and in Jerusalem, and before his elders he will manifest his glory. (Isa 24:21–23; NRSV adapted)[25]

The looming punishment indicates some impropriety among the hosts, but the writer does not explore the nature of the implied misdeeds. Instead, the author focuses attention on images of inevitable judgment at the hands of Israel's deity, here construed as an omnipotent ruler who will descend to reign in the earthly sphere. The effect is to illustrate the consummate power of YHWH by evoking a future display of military/judicial reckoning. Similar images appear in Isa 34:3–4, which explores a coming, wrathful military judgment against the nations as well as

---

as Cosmo-Political Symbol," *HBT* 9 (1987): 53–78; E. Theodore Mullen Jr., *The Divine Council in Canaanite and Early Hebrew Literature*, HSM 24 (Chico, CA: Scholars Press, 1980), 114–20.

[23] See also 1 Kgs 22:19–28, Deut 17:3, Isa 6:1–8, Dan 8:10–11; Heinrich Niehr, "Host of Heaven," *DDD*, 428–30. On the anonymity of the host, see Patrick D. Miller Jr., *The Divine Warrior in Early Israel*, HSM 5 (Cambridge: Harvard University Press, 1973), 152–55.

[24] The LXX reads, "God will bring his hand against the ornament of heaven [ἐπὶ τὸν κόσμον τοῦ οὐρανοῦ]."

[25] On the pattern of the victorious warrior deity subduing enemies and then taking the throne, see Debra Scoggins Ballentine, *The Conflict Myth and the Biblical Tradition* (New York: Oxford University Press, 2015), 129–30. Compare also the sea dragon in Isa 27:1, Ps 74:13–14, *KTU* 1.3 III 41–42. In some contrast, Joseph Blenkinsopp relates Isa 24 to other literature (e.g., Deut 4:19; the Enuma Elish; 1 En. 90:22–25; Dan 10; and Rev 9:2, 11) but construes the opponents as malevolent, controlling astrological beings (*Isaiah 1–39: A New Translation with Introduction and Commentary*, AB 19 [New York: Doubleday, 2000], 326–34); similarly Hans Wildberger, *Isaiah: A Continental Commentary*, 3 vols. (Minneapolis: Fortress, 1991–2002), 2:506–10.

against "their hosts," which YHWH has "destined for slaughter" (Isa 34:2).[26] Like Isa 24, the subsequent verses in chapter 34 explore an upheaval among the heavenly ranks and among the nations on earth:

> All the host of heaven shall rot away ["fall" or "dissolve," נמקו], and the skies roll up like a scroll. All their host shall wither like a leaf withering on a vine, or fruit withering on a fig tree. When my sword has drunk its fill in the heavens, behold, it will descend upon Edom, upon the people I have doomed to judgment. (34:4–5; cf. Isa 13:10, 13)[27]

Here we find images of a destructive collapse and punishment but nothing to explain the heavenly misconduct to which this punishment alludes. Taking these verses as alluding to gentile gods—here construed as lesser deities—makes good sense of the wrongdoing implicitly ascribed to them (cf. Isa 26:13–14). More basically, however, the writers/editors work to suppress the possibility of rivalry and threat by envisioning an irresistible sovereign and military power that visits punishment on the lesser ranks.

Psalms 58 and 82 also celebrate YHWH's punishing justice against wayward gods. Psalm 58 impugns unjust gods and calls on YHWH to inflict vengeful justice so that all will know that "there is a God that judges the earth [אלהים שפטים בארץ]" (Ps 58:11). Similarly, Ps 82 imagines a high God seated in the divine council and pronouncing a decree: "'You are gods, children of the most high [אלהים אתם ובני עליון], all of you; nevertheless, you shall die like mortals [כאדם] and fall like any prince [השרים].' Rise up, O God [אלהים], judge the earth; for all the nations belong to you!" (82:6–8).[28] These texts employ quite different language and imagery but are similar insofar as they imagine wayward deities as lesser powers that wreak havoc on earth. Predictably, the lesser status and punishment of these deities accentuate the superior rank and status of Israel's God.

The texts considered so far do not explicitly identify gentile gods with the punished hosts, though this could be implied. A wide range of other texts address gentile gods more directly, understanding them as servants and subordinates of Israel's deity. To give only a few examples drawn from biblical and Hellenistic literature, Deut 17:3 polemicizes against the nations that serve other gods: "whether the sun or the moon or any of the host of heaven [צבא השמים], which I have forbidden" and the writers of 2 Kings, Jeremiah, and Zephaniah develop similar rhetoric that connects the host with gentile practices deemed illegitimate or "idolatrous"

---

[26] The NRSV translates צבאם as "armies," but "host (of divine beings)" makes better sense in context.

[27] Wildberger avoids the premise of conflict by insisting that the nations are summoned only to act as witnesses (*Isaiah*, 3:318–19).

[28] On this interpretation, see Robert P. Gordon, "The Gods Must Die: A Theme in Isaiah and Beyond," in *Isaiah in Context: Studies in Honour of Arie van der Kooij on the Occasion of His Sixty-Fifth Birthday*, ed. Michael N. van der Meer, VTSup 138 (Leiden: Brill, 2010), 45–61. See also the prince of Tyre in Ezek 28 and the Legend of King Keret C i–ii: 10, 20.

(2 Kgs 17:16, 21:3–5, 23:4–5, Jer 19:13, Zeph 1:4–5). The idea that gentile idolatry arises from foolish delusion—specifically, from category mistakes about the ranks and relationships of power among divinities—also proves central to writers such as Philo of Alexandria, Josephus, and the unknown author of the Wisdom of Solomon, among many others. So Josephus portrays Abraham as uniquely realizing that the cycles of change observed on the earth and in the heavens all come about "through the might of their commanding sovereign" (*Ant.* 1.7.1 §§154–157; cf. Philo, *Abr.* 15; Apoc. Abr. 7) rather than through their own volition or independent power. Similarly, Philo derides gentiles for ignoring the father of all and the "one cause above all, that provided for the world and all that is in it" (*Virt.* 216).[29]

Idolatry polemics typically construe gentile gods as obedient functionaries or powerless nongods. As noted above, texts such as Isa 24, 34, and Pss 58 and 82 suggest that the lesser ranks will be liable to punishment at the hands of their heavenly king. Similar patterns appear in Hellenistic texts such as the Enochic Book of the Watchers, the Animal Apocalypse of Enoch, Dan 7–10, and Jubilees. Though scholars often take this literature as evidence for evil opponents or apocalyptic overlords, the texts more characteristically explore moments of insubordination, conflict, and military defeat in the lower tiers of the divine order. Moreover, members of the lower ranks typically appear as bit players in myths that celebrate the supreme and providential rule of Israel's God, whether the political drama involves the prince of the host in Dan 7–8, the watchers in Enochic traditions, or the battle between Michael and the prince of darkness in certain Qumran texts. Thus, I contend that these texts are best understood as traditions of mythmaking that, in diverse and creative ways, represent the divine cosmo-political order as subservient to Israel's God. The varying roles that gentile deities play in this literature makes sense in light of this rather basic political project.

The much-discussed Book of the Watchers (1 En. 1–36) tells of a group of heavenly beings that, provoked by the beauty of women, steal away to earth to sate their desires. Catastrophe and punishment ensue, all in ways that illustrate the power and justice of the supreme sovereign. Rather than plot mutiny or a coup, for instance, the writer/editor imagines heavenly fools that turn their gaze downward; spatially removed from heaven, they cause destruction on earth in the short term and ongoing troubles in the long term. All of this comes about by accident, not design; their terror and remorse are total, their punishment unequivocal. The writer/editor of the Book of the Watchers frequently uses this myth of divine disobedience as an occasion for celebrating the order, power, and justice of heaven, whether in the lengthy descriptions of an exalted heavenly court (9:1–11:2, 14:8–16:4) or in the celebrations of the divine political order that feature prominently in Enoch's cosmic tour (chs. 17–36; cf. 2:1–5:4).

---

[29] See also Philo, *Spec.* 32–35 and Wis 13:1–19, among many other examples. Translations of Philo are from the LCL.

As the Book of the Watchers unfolds, the heavenly sovereign punishes the impudent watchers and destroys the giants, their monstrous offspring. Harmful spirits then emerge from the bodies of the giants, and these become sources of ongoing trouble. So 1 En. 15 explores a range of problems caused by these spirits and labors over their eventual punishment:

> The spirits [*manfas*; τὰ πνεύματα] of the giants <lead astray>,[30] do violence, make desolate, and attack and wrestle and hurl upon the earth and <cause illnesses>.[31] They eat nothing, but abstain from food and are thirsty and smite. These spirits (will) rise up against the sons of men and against the women, for they have come forth from them. From the day of the slaughter and destruction and death of the giants, from the soul of whose flesh the spirits are proceeding, they are making desolate without (incurring) judgment. Thus they will make desolate until the day of the consummation of the great judgment, when the great age will be consummated. It will be consummated all at once. (15:11–16:1)[32]

The language about evil and harm may fruitfully be compared to the charges of criminal injustice in Ps 82 (and perhaps also Isa 24 and 34). In this case, however, lesser deities emerge as divine leftovers that menace the earthly sphere. Two generations removed from the reckless watchers and of much diminished power and influence, these spirits wreak vengeance on humankind, at least for a set time. The writer/editor again emphasizes their lesser status in chapter 19, where they are identified with the gods of the nations. Here Enoch's divine guide points to a place of punishment deep in the earth, explaining, "There stand the angels [*malāʾekt*; ἄγγελοι] who mingled with the women. And their spirits [*wa-manāfestihomu*; πνεύματα]—having assumed many forms—bring destruction on men and lead them astray to sacrifice to demons [*ʾamālekt*; δαιμονίοις] as to Gods until the day of the great judgment, in which they will be judged with finality" (19:1).[33] Whereas 1 En. 15 pictures lower-ranking spirits that threaten humans on earth, 19:1–2 makes them objects of gentile worship. Thus, "demons" emerge here not as

---

[30] R. H. Charles (*The Book of Enoch or 1 Enoch* [Oxford: Clarendon, 1912], 36–37) takes Syncellus's νεμόμενα as "afflict," while George W. E. Nickelsburg (*1 Enoch 1: A Commentary on the Book of 1 Enoch, Chapters 1–36; 81–108*, Hermeneia [Minneapolis: Fortress, 2001], 268) takes this as "pasturing," a translation of the Aramaic רעין which he takes as corrupt for תעין ("lead astray") or רעעין ("shatter").

[31] The text here is very difficult. Both Greek manuscripts agree on δρόμους ποιοῦντα ("making flights/races"). Charles suggests that δρόμους may be corrupt for τρόμους, to be translated "but nevertheless hunger" (*Book of Enoch*, 37). Nickelsburg suggests that δρόμους translates מרוצה, which could plausibly be taken as "running/oppression" or may be corrupt for Aramaic מרועא ("illness") (*1 Enoch 1*, 268). Cf. Jub. 10:5–11; Matt 8:29.

[32] Translation from James W. E. Nickelsburg and James C. VanderKam, *1 Enoch: The Hermeneia Translation* (Minneapolis: Fortress, 2012). See T. F. Glasson, *Greek Influence in Jewish Eschatology, with Special Reference to the Apocalypses and Pseudepigraphs*, BMSPCK (London: SPCK, 1961), 57–61, on the possible influence of Hesiod's *Works and Days*.

[33] See Loren T. Stuckenbruck, *1 Enoch 91–108*, CEJL (Berlin: de Gruyter, 2007), 401–3.

unqualified forces of evil but rather as bit players in a larger religious and political drama about favored and disfavored peoples, legitimate and illegitimate religious beliefs, and more- versus less-powerful deities.

In contrast to the myths developed in 1 En. 15 and 19, the Animal Apocalypse of Enoch (1 En. 85–90) presents a remarkable story that recasts gentile gods as divine managers and functionaries of Israel's deity. Playing on the division of the nations in Deut 32, the writer of the Animal Apocalypse develops a very elaborate image of divine bureaucracy and explores one particular tier of this bureaucracy to explain the rule of foreign empires over Israel. As developed here, the supreme God acted to hand over Israel to the rule of divine managers (the gods of the Assyrian, Persian, and Greek Empires) as a form of just punishment. So 1 En. 89 depicts the high God commissioning divine shepherd managers (*nolâweyân*) to rule over the disobedient "sheep" of Israel: "Every one of you from now on shall pasture the sheep, and everything that I command you, do. I am handing them over to you duly numbered, and I will tell you which of them are to be destroyed. Destroy them" (89:60). In an elaborately wrought conceit, the writer reclassifies the gods of foreign empires as divine functionaries. Further, though the writer construes this as a justly deserved punishment, it is also predicted that the managers will become overzealous in carrying out this mandate against Israel. Thus, the divine kingdom appears here as a multilevel bureaucracy, and it comes to include a heavenly manager charged with recording the excesses of the shepherds (89:61–64, 65–72a, 89:74–90:1). Though they commit acts of overreach and excess, not full-scale rebellion, their crimes will be subject to punishment.[34] Though the shepherds operate as instruments of heavenly rule, in chapter 90 they are to perish (90:20) along with the seven stars/watchers and the "blinded sheep" of Israel. In this way, the writer/editor allows for some degree of imperfection, misunderstanding, and excess but carefully delimits and confines this to certain operatives in the lower ranks of the divine order.

In the Animal Apocalypse, the gods of the conquering nations reemerge as lower-level functionaries that serve as instruments of heavenly rule and punishment. By imagining gentile gods as overzealous managers, the text moves even further away from the kind of myth familiar from the Book of the Watchers, though the punishment of the stars in 1 En. 90 seems to allude to it. Similar patterns inform the Astronomical Book of Enoch. In its current form, the Astronomical Book labors to portray the heavenly bodies as an organized, multitiered hierarchy of beings that obey Uriel, a mid-level manager. The writer/editor generally depicts the luminaries as flawlessly obedient but in chapter 80 predicts a time of great upheaval. Here some of the stars will disobey or mishear their commands and provoke a cascading series of evils:

---

[34] In 1 En. 90:2–5, the writer allegorizes the success of the Maccabean uprising as a result of the accounting deity's intercession with God; see Patrick A. Tiller, *A Commentary on the Animal Apocalypse of 1 Enoch*, EJL 4 (Atlanta: Scholars Press, 1993), 7–8.

Many heads [ʾarʾest] of the stars will stray from the command[35] and will change their ways and actions and will not appear at the times prescribed for them. The entire law of the stars will be closed to the sinners and the thoughts of those on the earth will err regarding them. They will turn back from all their ways, will err, and will take them to be gods. Evil will multiply against them and punishment will come upon them to destroy all. (80:6–8)

In some contrast to the Book of the Watchers and the Animal Apocalypse, this text imagines a moment of confusion among the stars that leads some people to mistake them for gods. Here a mistake or straying among the luminaries gives rise to inappropriate worship so that illegitimate peoples come to revere lesser deities instead of their true ruler and ultimate king. Fittingly, the text goes on to associate true astronomical knowledge with an elect that will survive this time of upheaval and confusion because they understand the true order of power and privilege within the heavenly ranks.

The writer of Jubilees shows no interest in the punishment of gentile gods but works consistently to cast them as lesser powers, obedient functionaries, and instruments of the supreme deity. Lower-level spirits and princes play a variety of roles in the text and are frequently associated with the gods of the nations. In Jub. 1, for instance, the writer/editor develops a series of *ex eventu* prophecies about Israel's crimes and pays particular attention to the worship of other gods: "When they eat and are full [having gained the land of milk and honey] they will turn to foreign gods—to ones which will not save them from any of their afflictions" (1:8). The subsequent verses add, "they will sacrifice their children to demons [ʾagānent] and to every product (conceived by) their erring minds" (1:11).[36] The "demons" do not appear to be heavenly rebels or to compete with other gods for power and priority. Rather, they seem to be implicated in a category mistake in which the principal actors are human beings. Likewise, when harmful spirits appear in chapters 7, 10, 11, and 15, they are consistently associated with delusion, failures of mind, and idolatry. Chapter 10, for instance, presents a version of the watchers myth in which the leader of the harmful spirits (Mastema) successfully negotiates with the supreme deity to retain a portion of them so that he can punish the

---

[35] Some manuscripts read "stars of the command." So Michael Knibb translates as "heads of stars in command" (ʾarʾestihomu lakawākebta teʾzâz) in *The Ethiopic Book of Enoch: A New Edition in Light of the Aramaic Dead Sea Fragments* (New York: Oxford University Press, 1979). Less plausibly, Matthew Black reconstructs this as "stray from the commandments (of God)," in *The Book of Enoch or 1 Enoch: A New English Edition with Commentary and Textual Notes*, SVTP 7 (Leiden, Brill, 1985), 253.

[36] Trans. James C. VanderKam, *Book of Jubilees*, CSCO 510–511 (Leuven: Peeters, 1989). See also VanderKam, "The Demons in the Book of Jubilees," in *Die Dämonen: Die Dämonologie der israelitisch-jüdischen und frühchristlichen Literatur im Kontext ihrer Umwelt/Demons: The Demonology of Israelite-Jewish and Early Christian Literature in Context of Their Environment*, ed. Armin Lange, Hermann Lichtenberger, and K. F. Diethard Römheld (Tübingen: Mohr Siebeck, 2003), 339–64, here 340–41.

rampant evils of humankind. By reclassifying these spirits as a host of subordinates—indeed, a punishing host managed and ruled by their own prince—this text develops a myth about a misleading, harassing host that serves the divine plan for punishment and reward.[37] Similar relationships of power emerge in Jub. 15, though with no mention of Mastema or his punishing host:

> For there are many nations and many peoples and all belong to him. He made spirits rule over all in order to lead them astray from following him [*wa-diba kwellu ʾaslaṭa manāfesta kama yāsḥetomu ʾem-dexrēhu*]. But over Israel he made no angel or spirit [*malʾaka wa-manfasa*] rule because he alone is their ruler. He will guard them and require them for himself from his angels, his spirits, and everyone, and all his powers so that he may guard them and bless them and so that they may be his and he theirs from now and forever. (15:31–32; cf. 19:28)

Adapting Deut 32, Israel's God hands over other nations to be governed by lesser divinities. These deities, however, are to lead the nations astray by design. Far from the reckless watchers, harassing spirits, and excessive bureaucrats familiar from Enochic traditions, and further still from myths of competition and coup, the writer of Jubilees confines ambiguity and wickedness to the human sphere, whether it involves the deluded hearts and minds of wayward Israel or of the gentile nations writ large.

The writer of Dan 7 presents a dramatic scene of heaven where a majestic court sits in judgment on the earth's political affairs. This heavenly council punishes the "Median," Persian, Assyrian, and Greek Empires and promises Israel an eternal, matchless kingdom to which all others will submit (7:28). Set within the larger context of Dan 7–12, this scene sets the stage for a series of myths about moments of conflict and political intrigue within the lower ranks. In chapter 7 a terrible fourth kingdom appears (7:23–27) with a ruler (Antiochus IV Epiphanes) who commits outrage against the temple. In chapter 8 (vv. 10–14 and 25), the writer/editor replays this political-religious drama as a confrontation between a human king and the host of heaven (or the prince of the host in v. 25). Though this text allows for a temporary defeat of some members of the host, this unfolds as a highly asymmetrical conflict in which an arrogant earthly ruler undertakes a mad campaign against a portion of the host. Elsewhere, the text labors to construe this as punishment for Israel's misdeeds (see 8:12; 9:7–19, 24–27; 11:31–39) so that conflict, weakness, and even military defeat come to exemplify the impartial justice of heaven. In ways that are similar and different, Dan 10 briefly entertains a battle between Michael and Gabriel and the princes of Persia and Greece. So Gabriel explains that he has just left the midst of a battle with the prince (שר) of Persia:

---

[37] Fittingly, when Ur begins to make idols (Jub. 11), the writer blames "the spirits of the savage ones" (11:4) that work for "Prince Mastema." In other contexts, however, Belial proves more prominent, as in Jub. 15:33: "all the people of Belial will leave their sons uncircumcised."

> Do you know why I have come to you? And now I will return to fight with the prince of Persia, and behold, when I go out the prince of Greece will come. But I will tell you what is written in the book of truth. There is no one who supports me against these except Michael your prince. (Dan 10:20–21; cf. 1 En. 20:5)

This text seems to allude to a divine battle against the princes of the Persian and Greek Empires. Remarkably, it also implies that their political dominance results from the weakness and even defeat of Michael and Gabriel. Nevertheless, by staging this as a conflict between lower-ranking princes, and by implying that Michael and Gabriel survive it, the writer also works to suppress the possibility of usurpation and coup against the ultimate ruler of heaven. Such a conflict stands in some tension with images of a mad king battling the host, stars, and prince of the host in Dan 7–8, but it employs the lower ranks of the divine order to similar ideological ends.

A number of Qumran-related texts explore battles between lower-ranking deities. Though the specifics often vary, figures such as Michael, Melchizedek, and the Prince of Light are in many cases conceived of as opponents of Belial or the prince of darkness and each also presides, leads, or rules over groups such as the "lot of light" or "lot of darkness" (e.g., 4Q177, 4Q286). This literature shows little explicit concern with gentile gods but boldly impugns groups within Israel that are construed as misled, inauthentic, or illegitimate. Whereas traditions such as the Animal Apocalypse and Jubilees polemicize against both disobedient Israel and the gentile nations, the Qumran texts focus instead on the categories of true versus false Israel. So the writer/editor of the Damascus Document (CD) imagines a time when "Belial will be sent against Israel" (CD IV, 13); discusses Israel's errors in terms of the three "nets of Belial" (CD IV, 15); and in CD V, 18–19 notes, "For in ancient times there arose Moses and Aaron, by the hand of the Prince of Lights and Belial, with his cunning, raised up Jannes and his brother during the first deliverance of Israel."[38] Here Belial harasses, misleads, and conspires against the true or legitimate people of God. In the more intimate present, however, the spirit of Belial dominates sinners (CD VIII, 2 and XII, 2), and in XIX, 14 covenant violators are to be handed over to Belial for destruction.

In another very distinctive myth about the lower ranks of divinity, the War Scroll (1QM) imagines a great battle between favored and disfavored agents and lots of beings.[39] For instance, column I depicts opponents as "the lot of the sons of

---

[38] Jean Duhaime argues that this is a secondary addition ("Dualistic Reworking of the Scrolls from Qumran," *CBQ* 49 [1987]: 32–56, esp. 51–55). For a different view, see Devorah Dimant, "Qumran Sectarian Literature," in *Jewish Writings of the Second Temple Period: Apocrypha, Pseudepigrapha, Qumran Sectarian Writings, Philo, Josephus*, ed. Michael E. Stone, CRINT (Philadelphia: Fortress, 1984), 493.

[39] Most scholars agree that columns I and XV–XIX were originally distinct from II–IX; on further problems associated with the fragments from Cave 4, see Jean Duhaime, "War Scroll (1QM, 1Q33)," in *The Dead Sea Scrolls: Hebrew, Aramaic, and Greek Texts with English Translations*,

darkness, the army of Belial [בגורל בני חושך בחיל בליעל]" (line 1) and predicts a time in the future when the lot of Belial will be destroyed completely (lines 6–7). By contrast, the "[sons of jus]tice shall shine to all the edges of the earth, they shall go on shining, up to the end of all the periods of darkness; and in the time of God, his exalted greatness will shine for all the et[ernal] times, for peace and blessing, glory and joy, and length of days for all the sons of light" (lines 8–9). These examples show a marked interest in conflicts between favored and disfavored divine beings, but they consistently construe these beings as lower-level operatives whose conflicts in some way serve the providential plan for history.

The patterns observed in CD and 1QM are also consistent with the Community Rule (1QS III–IV), one of the most remarkable and much-discussed texts found at Qumran. Here a writer/editor envisions two spirits (רוחות) placed inside human beings at the beginning of creation:

> He created man to rule the world and placed within him two spirits so that he would walk with them until the moment of his visitation: they are the spirits of truth and deceit [והואה ברא אנוש לממשלת תבל וישם לו שתי רוחות להתהלב בם עד מועד פקודתו הנה רוחות האמת והעול]. From the spring of light stem the generations of truth, and from the source of darkness the generations of deceit. And in the hand of the Prince of Lights is dominion over all the sons of justice [ביד שר אורים ממשלת כול בני צדק]; they walk on paths of light. And in the hand of the Angel of Darkness is total dominion over the sons of deceit [וביד מלאך חושך כול ממשלת בני עול]; they walk on paths of darkness. (III, 17–21)

Here the supreme God intentionally—and providentially—creates twin types or lots of human beings, each overseen by divine patrons. The writer/editor also shows an intense preoccupation with moralizing rhetoric about truth and goodness and about opposition, conflict, and struggle. Understood in context, this distinctive creation story sets the stage for myths about past, present, and future conflicts between true and false Israel. Such competing lots or types appear throughout the Community Rule, as in column II, where the writer explores a testing within the community "during the dominion of Belial" (I, 18; see also II, 19, 23–24). This suggests that the writer/editor of the text—at least in this form—envisioned the spirits of Belial or the Prince of Darkness as harassing, hindering, and harming the sons of light, especially the weak at the margins. As in other Qumran literature, the writers also labor to represent these conflicts, battles, princes, and dominions as instruments of a supreme God who fixes their roles in history in accord with "his glorious design" (see, e.g., 1QS III, 13–17). In this way, the much-discussed determinism that characterizes 1QS III–IV, the War Scroll, and much other Qumran literature functions to suppress the possibility of disobedience, conflict, and rebellion within the divine ranks.

---

ed. James H. Charlesworth, PTSDSSP 2 (Tübingen: Mohr Siebeck; Louisville: Westminster John Knox, 1995), 180–203.

III. Gentile Gods as Enemies in 1 Corinthians 15

The traditions explored above shed light on the sudden appearance and disappearance of Christ's enemies in 1 Cor 15:23–28 (see also 1 Thess 5; 2 Thess 1–2). A battle is explored briefly in verses 23–28 in the context of a series of arguments about the privileges of election that span verses 20–57. As in other discussions of conflicts within the lower ranks, Paul imagines a struggle that unfolds at a distance from the supreme God. So he writes:

> But each in their own order: Christ is the first fruits, then those who are of Christ at his parousia, then comes the end, when he hands over the kingdom to God the father, when he has destroyed every rule and every authority and every power [ὅταν καταργήσῃ πᾶσαν ἀρχὴν καὶ πᾶσαν ἐξουσίαν καὶ δύναμιν]. For it is necessary that he rule until he has put all his enemies under his feet.[40] The last enemy to be defeated is death, "For God has put all things under his feet." But when it says, "all things have been subjected," it is clear that it excepts the one to whom all things are subjected. When all things are subjected to him, then the son himself will be subjected to the one who subjected all things to himself, in order that God may be all to all [ὅταν δὲ ὑποταγῇ αὐτῷ τὰ πάντα, τότε καὶ αὐτὸς ὁ υἱὸς ὑποταγήσεται τῷ ὑποτάξαντι αὐτῷ τὰ πάντα ἵνα ᾖ ὁ θεὸς τὰ πάντα ἐν πᾶσιν]. (1 Cor 15:24–28; cf. Phil 3:20–21)[41]

This text heavily emphasizes Christ's power, obedience, and submission but does not linger over Christ's enemies, whether to explain how they might come to oppose Christ or what their defeat may entail.

Without positing genetic relationships or simplistic parallels to the kinds of texts explored above, we can understand Paul's text as working with familiar assumptions about the divine political order. More like Isa 24 than the 1QM or 1QS III, Paul represents Christ as having enemies that require "subjection" of some kind, but he provides virtually no mythmaking about the nature of this conflict. Instead of lingering over images of battle, Paul shifts attention to the upper tiers of the divine hierarchy. The effect is to portray the upper ranks as stable and Christ's victory as inevitable. In this regard, Ps 110 serves as a convenient pretext for turning the spotlight onto the supreme deity. Likewise, Paul's almost obsessive concern with Christ's relationship to this supreme God in verses 27–28 serves both to distract from any intimations of intrigue and struggle in the lower ranks and to emphasize

---

[40] On the humiliating representation of enemies as under the foot of the conquering warrior, see, e.g., 1QM XII, 11; Sennacherib Prism, 13–15; 38–60; 44; A. L. Oppenheim, "Neo-Assyrian and Neo-Babylonian Empires," in *The Symbolic Instrument in Early Times*, ed. Harold D. Lasswell, Daniel Lerner, and Hans Speier, Propaganda and Communication in World History 1 (Honolulu: University Press of Hawaii, 1979), 111–44.

[41] On the use of Ps 110, see David M. Hay, *Glory at the Right Hand: Psalm 110 in Early Christianity*, SBLMS 18 (Nashville: Abingdon, 1973), 59–62.

Christ's submissive posture. There may be war on the horizon, then, but there will be no threat of usurpation, matched battle, or competition with the high God, least of all from Christ. Like other mythmakers and ideologues, Paul accomplishes this sleight of hand by assimilating all other deities to the lower ranks and by telescoping to focus on images of the irresistible power of a supreme deity.

The brief appearance of Christ's enemies in verses 23–24 also fits with other Jewish traditions about the future destruction or punishment of gentile gods. As in texts such as Isa 24 and 1 En. 19, a number of biblical and Hellenistic texts imagine the eventual punishment of these gods, whether they are conceived of as intermediary beings or as mere cult statues.[42] So Zech 13 imagines a time when Israel's God will "cut off the names of the idols from the land, so they shall not be mentioned again" (13:2); Jer 10 ridicules the delusional worship of mere statuary but adds, "at the time of their punishment they will perish" (10:15; similarly Isa 2:18, 20; 17:7–8; Mic 5:13); and the Epistle of Enoch imagines an elaborate scenario in which "the idols of the nations will be given up, and the tower(s) will be burned with fire" (91:8) prior to an ingathering and transformation of all peoples. As discussed above, the Animal Apocalypse also depicts gentile gods as punishing operatives of the Jewish God (e.g., 89:59–90:1) that must nevertheless be destroyed prior to an ingathering and transformation of the gentiles (90:18; cf. 1 QM XVII, 7–8; Dan 7:27–28; Jub. 1:22–25). Though the texts prove distinctive, their writers and editors envision the destruction or punishment of gentile gods as a prelude to the full submission of all peoples to Israel's God, that is, to the true, though largely unacknowledged, master of the universe. Though Paul's language in verse 28 (ὁ θεὸς τὰ πάντα ἐν πᾶσιν) is ambiguous, it probably alludes to the idea that the nations will come to worship Israel's deity after their own so-called gods have been destroyed, punished, or reined in (cf. Phil 2:5–11; 3:21).[43] Taking Christ's enemies as gentile gods—albeit as members of the lesser ranks—offers a way to contextualize a number of difficult features of the text. In particular, this allows for a more precise identification of the

---

[42] Other scholars draw similar connections between this body of literature and Paul's eschatological scenario; see Terence L. Donaldson, *Paul and the Gentiles: Remapping the Apostle's Convictional World* (Minneapolis: Fortress, 1997), 69–74, 224–30; Paula Fredriksen, "Judaism, the Circumcision of Gentiles, and Apocalyptic Hope," *JTS* 42 (1991): 532–64; E. P. Sanders, *Paul, the Law, and the Jewish People* (Philadelphia: Fortress, 1985), 171–79; Stanley K. Stowers, *A Rereading of Romans: Justice, Jews, and Gentiles* (New Haven: Yale University Press, 1994), esp. 95–97.

[43] A wealth of literature also attests to the idea of a gentile ingathering, from Ps 22, which predicts a time when all the peoples of the earth will simply "remember" the true ruler (22:27–29), to Isa 45, where the nations bring their wealth in tribute and submit to and worship Israel's God (45:14–16; cf. Isa 60). Similarly, Jubilees imagines a time when "the Lord will appear to the eyes of all, and all will know that I am the God of Israel" (1:27–28; cf. 23:29–30). See esp. Zech 8:20–23; Mic (esp. 4:1–2; 7:17); Tob 13–14; Sib. Or. 3:703–720; cf. 1 En. 10:21–22; Isa 60; Pss. Sol. 17 and 18; Wis 3:5–8; Dan 7:27; cf. Apoc. Abr. 31:4–9.

much-discussed "principalities and powers" and explains Paul's telescoping focus on the upper tiers of the divine order.

Taking the enemies of 1 Cor 15:23–24 as divine intermediaries also fits with Paul's language about ἀρχαί, δυνάμεις, στοιχεῖα, and δαιμονία elsewhere in the letters. So in Rom 8, Paul imagines Christ in heaven alongside the supreme deity and affirms, "neither death, nor life, nor angels, nor rulers, nor things present, nor things to come, nor powers, nor height, nor depth, nor anything else in all creation, will be able to separate us from the love of God in Christ Jesus our lord" (8:38–39). Here ἄγγελοι, ἀρχαί, and δυνάμεις appear as potential obstacles that might stand in the way of the Christ elect. Understood as intermediary deities, these also bear some resemblance to the στοιχεῖα of Gal 4, which emerge as relatively powerless lesser beings that the gentile Christ-followers formerly (and mistakenly) worshiped. Likewise, Paul identifies idols as powerless nongods in 1 Cor 8:4–8 and as δαιμονία in chapter 10, the worship of which threatens to insult the supreme God (10:6–22). Myths that depict gentile gods as foolish or ignorant functionaries also shed light on Paul's comments about the "rulers of this age" (ἀρχόντων τοῦ αἰῶνος τούτου) in 1 Cor 2:6–8. These rulers are discussed briefly but in ways that emphasize their ignorance.

Paul's terms ἄρχων, ἐξουσία, and δύναμις in 1 Cor 15 never appear together again in the letters. His use of them here is best understood in light of the confluence of their semantic ranges and certain assumptions about the political structure of the divine world. As often noted, ἄρχων, ἐξουσία, and δύναμις are relatively standard Greek words for rulers, magistrates, or high officials.[44] In the Hellenistic period, for instance, the term ἄρχων has a broad range of meanings that include various types of officials and magistrates. To cite only a few examples, the Septuagint uses ἄρχων to translate thirty-six different words for leaders in the priestly and military ranks, including ראש (e.g., Deut 33:5; Job 29:25; Ezek 38:2, 3) and נשיא. More in line with 1 Cor 15:23–24, Philo applies the term to heavenly beings that govern the sublunary sphere (*Spec.* 1.13–14; *Gig.* 6; cf. Eph 2:2; John 12:31); the Greek fragments of the Book of the Watchers use it for Shemihaza and many of his subordinates (1 En. 6); and the Septuagint of Dan 10 translates שר with ἄρχων, though in Dan 12:2 στρατηγός is preferred. These linguistic patterns suggest a shared sensibility about the divine world, namely, that it involves a plurality of divine beings that function together on analogy with human political institutions.

Finally, it is important to stress that Paul's brief discussion of an eschatological

---

[44] So David Aune, "Archon," *DDD*, 82–85; e.g., Thucydides, *Hist.* 1.126; Aristotle, *Ath. Pol.* 13.10–12; cf. Josephus, *Ant.* 14.10.2 §190; 16.6.7 §172. A number of philosophical texts also use ἄρχων for substances and heavenly bodies, e.g., Plato, *Laws* 10.903b–d; Plutarch, *Mor.* 601A; Apuleius, *Metam.* 11.5.2; Cicero, *Somn. Sc.* 6.17. For polemics that charge other philosophers with allegorizing the elements and heavenly bodies as gods, see Plutarch, *Mor.* 377B–378A; cf. *Mor.* 20A; David Winston, *The Wisdom of Solomon: A New Translation with Introduction and Commentary*, AB 43 (New York: Doubleday, 1979), 248–51.

battle implicitly includes human kings, rulers, and armies. The fact that so many ancient writers imagine relations of reciprocity between human and divine rulers (and their respective subjects) makes it virtually certain that Paul envisions the defeat of gentile gods as entailing the political-military subjection of their rulers and peoples. Indeed, images of the nations streaming to Israel in order to pay tribute, to worship, and to serve Israel's God are images of political subordination or, at the very least, of political unity conceived of as a form of religious integration and subjection. Some scholars have even argued that Christ's enemies in 1 Cor 15 are merely human rulers and kings, not divine beings at all.[45] Of course, a great deal of literature prefers to ignore or omit gentile gods from the world of divinity. In many such cases, however, writers labor to strip kings and rulers of their divine patrons, whether by reclassifying them as mere statuary (e.g., Isa 36–37) or by simply portraying conflicts between heavenly forces and mere earthly rulers, as in Dan 7–8. In some contrast, Paul's arguments in 1 Corinthians (esp. chs. 2, 8–10, and 15) and in Gal 4 employ a subordinating strategy that accommodates gentile gods to the ranks of divinity, somewhat like the mythmaking found in Dan 10, in various traditions drawn from 1 Enoch, Jubilees, and probably in Isa 24 and Ps 82 as well. Likewise, though Paul's language about "every knee" bowing to Christ in heaven, on earth, and under the earth (Phil 2:10–11) stands in some tension with the images of Christ defeating or subjecting the lower ranks in 1 Cor 15:23–28, it reflects similar notions of an ideal political order. As in 1 Cor 15, Christ's role in Phil 2:4–5 and 3:21 is to "subject all things to himself," to bring about a more perfect system of rule wherein all lower-ranked beings duly submit to their rightful commander, invincible ruler, and heavenly king.

IV. Conclusion

I have argued against popular theories that figures such as the Enochic watchers, shepherd managers, and even the Prince of Darkness belong to a single morass of unqualified evil, rebellion, and threat. I contend that the relevant literature does not provide evidence of "powers of evil" conceived of as an unqualified class of evil beings. Rather, it suggests a much more ambiguous collection of characters, the diverse and idiosyncratic characterizations of which serve the interests of particular writers, editors, and mythmakers. To the extent that common patterns do appear in the literature, these lesser beings generally serve as foils for representing a divine political order that is favorable to Israel's deity, whether they are foolish watchers that steal away to earth, spirits that pursue vengeance against humans,

---

[45] See Gene Miller, "*Archontōn tou aiōnos toutou*: A New Look at 1 Corinthians 2:6–8," *JBL* 91 (1972): 522–28; Wesley Carr, *Angels and Principalities: The Background, Meaning, and Development of the Pauline Phrase hai archai kai exousiai*, SNTSMS 42 (Cambridge: Cambridge University Press, 1981).

heavenly princes and middle managers, or harassing hosts like the army of Belial or spirits of Mastema. Consistent with this general picture, writers typically labor to portray conflicts as confined to or managed within the lower tiers, whether by the Prince of Lights in the War Scroll or by Michael and Gabriel in Dan 10 (see also the Prince of the host in Dan 7–8 and Michael in Rev 12). Understood in this way, these texts illuminate the emergence of Christ in 1 Cor 15:23–28 as a deputy warrior who subdues lesser powers and then dutifully hands the kingdom back to the father. Like a range of other mythmakers, Paul shows a marked concern to suppress the possibility of divine rebellion and coup, as proves especially clear in his affirmations about Christ's noncompetition and lack of rivalry in verses 26–28.

A range of surviving traditions present much more developed myths about conflict, opposition, and insurrection in the world of divinity. I maintain, however, that the dramatic confrontations and extended myths of intrigue and battle in the Enuma Elish, the Epic of Anzu, and the Theogony, among others, are less relevant for understanding 1 Cor 15:23–28. As I have argued here, Paul's claims about enemies and opponents make more sense in light of biblical and Hellenistic Jewish traditions about harassing hosts and foolish insubordinates. As in 1 Cor 15, these wayward lesser gods often play supporting roles in myths that represent Israel's God as unique, irresistible, and invulnerable. The lesser ranks of divinity thus provide a useful site for assimilating and subordinating gentile gods so that they pose little military-political threat. Like the wayward host of Isaiah, the overzealous shepherds that will be judged for their crimes, harassing spirits to be thrown into prison, or even the "idols" that will be destroyed at a time of reckoning, Paul's principalities and powers emerge as nonthreating threats, instrumental opponents, and lesser powers that will be subjected to punishing justice from above. Where writers allow that gentile gods exist in some form, they take pains to represent them as lesser powers that pose no threat as rebels, usurpers, or military opponents. Even if they are stupid, ignorant, or vengeful, they will inevitably be punished, subdued, corrected, or killed when the supreme God gets around to perfecting the divine political order.

COMING THIS FALL!

Nogalski's introduction to the prophets invites modern readers to hear these scrolls through the processes that shaped them, to recognize the thematic threads that traverse them, and to react to the words that confront religious and ethical complacency, that speak truth to power, and that offer hope to the oppressed.

James D. Nogalski is Professor and Director of Graduate Studies in Religion at Baylor University. His primary area of research is the Book of the Twelve (Minor Prophets), but he has also published articles on aspects of Psalms and translated books on methodology, form criticism, prophetic theology, and the editing of the Pentateuch.

AbingdonAcademic.com   Abingdon ACADEMIC

*THE CULMINATING WORK OF A
LEADING ARCHAEOLOGIST OF THE BIBLICAL WORLD*

BEYOND THE TEXTS
An Archaeological Portrait of Ancient Israel and Judah
William G. Dever

William G. Dever offers a welcome perspective on ancient Israel and Judah that prioritizes the archaeological remains to render history as it was—not as the biblical writers argue it should have been. Drawing from the most recent archaeological data as interpreted from a nontheological point of view and supplementing that data with biblical material only when it converges with the archaeological record, Dever analyzes all the evidence at hand to provide a new history of ancient Israel and Judah that is accessible to all interested readers.

**FROM SBL PRESS
OCTOBER 2017**

More than 80 maps and illustrations
Hardcover ISBN 978-0-88414-218-8
E-book ISBN 978-0-88414-217-1
Hardcover or E-book $49.95

Order online at
https://tinyurl.com/SBLPressDeverBeyond

Phone: 877-725-3334 (toll-free) or 802-864-6185
Fax: 802-864-7626

*Conference Discount at Annual Meetings 2017 Booth 2104
November 18–21, 2017 • Boston*

SBL PRESS

SUSTAINABLE FORESTRY INITIATIVE
Certified Sourcing
www.sfiprogram.org
SFI-00453

www.ingramcontent.com/pod-product-compliance
Lightning Source LLC
Chambersburg PA
CBHW021353300426
44114CB00012B/1205